# Theme and VARIATION IN THE SHORT STORY

*Edited by*

JOHN DE LANCEY FERGUSON

HAROLD A. BLAINE

WILSON R. DUMBLE

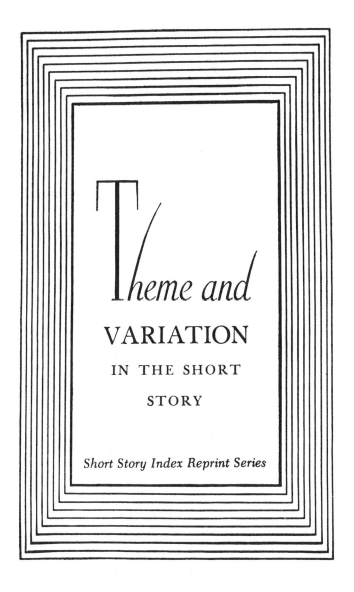

# Theme and
## VARIATION
### IN THE SHORT
### STORY

*Short Story Index Reprint Series*

**BOOKS FOR LIBRARIES PRESS**
FREEPORT, NEW YORK

First Published 1938
Reprinted 1972

INTERNATIONAL STANDARD BOOK NUMBER:
0-8369-4100-4


LIBRARY OF CONGRESS CATALOG CARD NUMBER:
74-37541


PRINTED IN THE UNITED STATES OF AMERICA
BY
NEW WORLD BOOK MANUFACTURING CO., INC.
HALLANDALE, FLORIDA 33009

# PREFACE

SO MANY short story collections have been published that the editors of a new one are put on the defensive. What excuse have they for adding to the congestion on the shelves?

We reply that most anthologies on the market have no more plan than a child's nosegay. Their editors bring together a group of stories—usually excellent stories—and let it go at that. The anthology with any pattern more analytical than listing the stories alphabetically by authors, or chronologically by date of publication, is a rarity. Our defense is that we have built our whole collection on a critical plan which we believe is intelligible and hope is interesting.

The plan is this: We have chosen our stories to illustrate the changes in narrative technique which the short story has undergone during the past century. To this end we select themes which recur, and give three stories employing each theme. Our first idea was that the three stories in each section should illustrate the three major techniques summarized in the Introduction. In practice we found that so mathematically neat an arrangement was impossible for all the ten groups, but nevertheless no two stories in any group display the same method or point of view.

We hasten to add that we know our choice of groups is arbitrary. Several other collections could be made on this same plan without exhausting the supply of recurrent themes in the short story; even the present list has been narrowed down from an original nearly twice its length. We also realize that our classification is often arbitrary, too. Stories which we have grouped as History, or War, could equally well have been called Adventure. But this, we hope, may help the teacher by enabling him, if he wishes, to extend his discussion of a theme beyond the specimens given under its own heading.

Of course no single book can even pretend to cover all the phases of any large and varied literary form. All we claim for the present volume is that the student who completes it ought to understand more clearly a few aspects of the materials and technique of the short story.

If he does, he ought to understand also that behind the book and its editors are the authors and publishers of copyright material without whose permission to reprint we could have done nothing. We have made specific acknowledgment in the notes to each story; we here offer our general thanks.

# TABLE OF CONTENTS

I. ADVENTURE 16
Herman Melville: *The Town-Ho's Story* 19
Rudyard Kipling: *The Man Who Would Be King* 42
John Russell: *The Price of the Head* 81

II. PSYCHOLOGY 96
Edgar Allan Poe: *The Black Cat* 99
Charlotte Perkins Gilman: *The Yellow Wallpaper* 111
Helen R. Hull: *Clay-Shuttered Doors* 130

III. HISTORY 154
John Buchan: *The Company of the Marjolaine* 157
Robert Louis Stevenson: *A Lodging for the Night* 184
Walter D. Edmonds: *Adam Helmer's Run* 207

IV. HUMOR 228
Mark Twain: *Jim Baker's Blue-Jay Yarn* 231
Don Marquis: *A Keeper of Tradition* 237
Dorothy Parker: *You Were Perfectly Fine* 249

V. DETECTION 256
Edgar Allan Poe: *The Purloined Letter* 259
Sir Arthur Conan Doyle: *The Red-Headed League* 278
Dorothy Sayers: *The Article in Question* 305

VI. COUNTRY 320
David Grayson: *The Country Doctor* 323
Meridel LeSueur: *The Trap* 335
Ring Lardner: *The Maysville Minstrel* 352

VII. CITY                                                      366

    O. Henry: *The Furnished Room*                     369
    Ben Hecht: *The Pig*                                       377
    William Faulkner: *Pennsylvania Station*          382

VIII. WAR                                                       400

    Rudyard Kipling: *The Drums of the Fore and Aft*   403
    Ambrose Bierce: *The Affair at Coulter's Notch*    438
    Jo Sinclair: *Children at Play*                     449

IX. SOCIAL CONSCIOUSNESS                                 458

    Rebecca Harding Davis: *Life in the Iron Mills*    461
    Michael Gold: *Blood Money*                          502
    Albert Maltz: *Man on a Road*                       515

X. REPORTAGE                                                   526

    Catherine Carswell: *At the Café Royal*             529
    John Reed: *Revolution*                              535
    John Dos Passos: *Doves in the Bullring*            540

NOTES ON CONTRIBUTORS                                      544

# INTRODUCTION

IN ITS century and more of existence as a clearly defined literary form, the short story has undergone three major shifts in technique. As with all changes in literary fashions, the time boundaries are vague. Poe and Stevenson wrote some "modern" stories; some of our contemporaries produce tales essentially Victorian in form. Nevertheless we can distinguish three periods, each dominated by a single method of writing. Up to about 1890, the prevalent short story form in America and England was the simple tale of the Hawthorne-Poe-Bret Harte type. For the twenty years after 1890 the terse, tightly plotted narrative of the Maupassant-Kipling-O. Henry school almost monopolized the field. Since O. Henry's death in 1910 the emphasis has been increasingly on the psychological or slice-of-life story of the Chekov-Katherine Mansfield-Hemingway sort.

Edgar Allan Poe first formulated critical rules for the short story, but he was neither the first to write artistic stories nor the most typical author of his generation. With their constant emphasis on emotional atmosphere and logical structure his stories were at once ahead of their time and too highly individual to be characteristic of it. The typical nineteenth century tale is leisurely in construction and its authors are much inclined to moralize and sentimentalize. Bret Harte was far more popular than Poe, and his model was much less Poe than Dickens. He indeed avowed freely his admiration of and his indebtedness to the novelist from whom he derived the formula which marks most of his stories and which continues to be a sure-fire device with Damon Runyon and other modern contributors to the popular magazines.

This formula is a skillful blending of surface realism with sentiment. In the typical Harte situation a rough, coarse, or lawless character reveals in a crisis a heart of gold. John Oakhurst, Jack Hamlin, Colonel Starbottle, Yuba Bill, Kentuck and the rest of the gallery are all the sort of people Dickens would have created had he written of California instead of London; they exist in a world which despite its local color is nearer to Cloudcuckooland than to the actual mining camps of the Sierras. The blend of humor with sentiment accurately follows the successful Dickens prescription; the pathos of uncomplaining devotion and of child life—not to mention child death—is aimed to wring tears from the most hardened reader.

Into this late Victorian world of sentiment and melodrama the bleak objectivity of Guy de Maupassant cut like a northwest wind. Most of the alert younger writers of the 1880s read Maupassant's French, but when they began to imitate him they fell into the common error of disciples of great artists. They copied his tricks and mannerisms, as a whole generation of sculptors copied the rough-finished backgrounds of Rodin, instead of reproducing his point of view. In 1893, for instance, Henry Cuyler Bunner published a volume called *Made in France*, which he described as French tales retold with a United States twist. The tales are adaptations from Maupassant; the twist generally consists in giving the French story tighter plot structure and increased humor. Devices like the surprise ending of "The Necklace," which Maupassant used only rarely, were widely copied by many writers besides Bunner. By the close of the century Maupassant was everywhere in the British and American short story, but the type specimen was a hybrid and not a copy.

The early stories of Rudyard Kipling (1865-1936), which held the same place in public favor in the 1890s that Harte's had held in the 1870s, are most successful examples of hybridization. Technically, *Plain Tales from the Hills* and *Soldiers Three* are Maupassant; spiritually they are Bret Harte. The formula of the rough character with a heart of gold is used over and over again; children are unconsciously tragic or heroic; the local color of British India replaces the local color of the Sierras. But Kipling's ideal technique is the terse objectivity of Maupassant; he avoids overt sentimentalizing and moralizing except when he regards it as the essential theme of his story. This telling of old stories in a new way was what the large reading public wanted. When Kipling moved on to the richer, more poetic, and more personal technique of such later work as "They," "An Habitation Enforced," and the stories from history he left much of his public behind him.

His place in the popular esteem of the Anglo-American world was taken by O. Henry (William Sydney Porter, 1862-1910). For the first decade of the present century the latter's brief, witty, slangy stories, or imitations of them complete with surprise endings, almost monopolized the magazines; even today their influence has not wholly faded. Beneath the snappy technique, analysis reveals the familiar Dickens-Harte themes. Parted lovers romantically seek and find each other in the city; virtue, heroism, and self-sacrifice blossom in unexpected places. O. Henry's intellect went no deeper than an occasional wise-crack; he wrote as he lived, in gusts of easy emotion. His contribution to the short story was to carry the tightly constructed plot as far as it could go. After him the story had either to find a fresh technique or perish.

The new model was furnished by the Russian stories of Anton Chekov (1860-1904), translations of which began to reach English readers as early as 1905. Chekov, like Maupassant, used a new technique in masterly fashion. The old notions of plot he did not so much discard as ignore. "Chekov," says Frances Newman, "always began at the beginning—and not at a beginning ingeniously near the end. He wrote down the name of the man he was going to describe and his exact social condition and his precise situation at that moment. . . . He walked in and out of his hero's thoughts, in and out of his life, and in and out of the lives of the men and women who affected his life. He wrote stories that have no rhetoric of phrase or of emotion, that are alive with the Comic Spirit but that have no phrases which leap away from the other phrases—

stories that have no interest in Reversals and Recognitions and no unity except the unity of their hero's character. He did not judge his fellow mortals as harshly as their creator is commonly supposed to judge them, he did not judge the President of the Immortals harshly, he did not expect his hero's end to astonish a rational leader and he did not hurry it into one sentence as if the curtain might come down in another minute and leave it untold forever."

That indeed is the core of the Chekov method: unity of character takes precedence over the old unities of time, place, and action. A story like "The Darling" disregards all three and yet achieves a higher unity from the continuity of a negative personality. It compresses twenty years of Olenka's life into less than that number of pages, and she emerges as both a completely known individual and an eternal feminine type. Yet when he chose, Chekov employed all the unities as strictly as a classical dramatist. Tales like "Little Vanka" and "The Cockroach" reveal a person's whole life and character in a single glimpse of action covering only a few hours. Of the four greatest masters of the short story—Poe, Maupassant, Kipling, and Chekov—the Russian is today the one whose influence, direct or indirect, is strongest.

One of his earliest and most devoted English disciples was Katherine Mansfield (1890-1923), who earned a reputation and for some years exerted an influence disproportionate to the mass of her achievement. After her death her husband, John Middleton Murry, did his best to obscure her work by rushing into print her journals and all the unfinished or rejected stories he found among her papers. Viewed today, her stories seem not so remarkable as they did in the early 1920s; the best ones, such as "The Fly," are the most obviously Chekovian. She owed her reputation more to the fact that she was the first successful practitioner of the Chekov technique in English than to any great depth or range of creative talent.

During the 1920s stories employing Chekov's methods became

increasingly frequent, first in the experimental magazines, then in the "quality" group, and finally invading the popular field. As the method spread, the material underwent the same changes that Maupassant's had at the hands of Bunner, Kipling, and O. Henry. Ring Lardner and Dorothy Parker masked with humor their bitter satires on human weakness and stupidity; Ernest Hemingway covered with a hard-boiled manner themes and episodes which at heart resemble Dickens more than Maupassant. Almost every writer, from Lardner to Katherine Brush, George Milburn, and William Saroyan, who has come into prominence in recent years, has done so with some modification or other of the Chekov method. The last of the significant followers of the O. Henry technique was Wilbur Daniel Steele, whose stories are frequent in the anthologies published before 1930. Today, his compactly contrived plots seem almost as old-fashioned as crinolines.

Since Chekov's influence has restored emphasis to character instead of plot, the short story is probably in a far healthier state than it was a quarter century ago. The purpose of the present collection is to show how basic themes carry on through all changes in technique and point of view. There is no such thing as a new story; there are only new ways of telling old ones. But the possible new ways are limited only by the number of writers who view the old world through new eyes.

# I. ADVENTURE

# I. ADVENTURE

WHATEVER inroads the stream of consciousness and other psychological indirections of structure may make in the general field of the short story, one type at least remains essentially unchanged. It is impossible to write a story of adventure without action, as it is impossible to write a detective story without a problem. The action may involve as much fine character portrayal and analysis of motive as the author is capable of, but these must not impede the movement. Broadly speaking, indeed, the author can choose only between the technique of the simple tale, which makes his story like a single episode from a picaresque romance, and the tightly plotted structure which reserves a surprise for the denouement.

Of course modifications of both techniques are used. One of the commonest is the frame situation. A stock device of the older writers was to assemble a group of men before the fire. Something said or done would remind one of the group of an experience; this character would then begin to tell the real story. Sometimes his auditors were kept in the reader's consciousness by having them put questions or make comments, but often the group, after serving to introduce the tale, was almost ignored. In such a case, to be sure, they had no real business there at all; their presence simply showed in the author the same diffidence or incompetence which makes an undergraduate waste the first pages of his story in explaining how he happened to write it. On the other hand, a frame situation fully integrated with the main narrative may greatly enrich it.

"The Man Who Would Be King" is a masterly example of effective framing. The narrator plays an integral, though minor, part in the story, and the "before" and "after" halves of the main narrative gain vividness and coherence by being both set against the commonplace background of the Indian newspaper office in hot weather. Herman Melville in "The *Town-Ho's* Story" exhibits a more primitive use of the frame. (The opening paragraphs may be disregarded; they are merely the clumsy device by which Melville lugged a previously written short story into the vast fabric of *Moby Dick.*) Here the whole tale is related at second hand, but the auditors are kept before the reader throughout, and a contrast is always suggested between the savage actions and emotions of the tale itself and the civilized setting in which it is told.

Both tales, furthermore, exhibit variations of the "straight" technique of narration. Melville employs no indirection; the chronological sequence of events is as straightforward as a chapter of Genesis. Kipling, on the other hand, has a much more eventful story to tell. Told fully, in straight chronology, it might easily fill a volume. By giving the main events at second hand, through the broken mind of Peachey Carnehan, he achieves the compression requisite for fitting the tale into the space of a short story, and at the same time avoids the need for detailed explanations in spots where such explanations might overtax the reader's credulity. As it is, he has the air of leaving the reader free to believe as much or as little as he chooses, to dismiss it all as a fever dream if he will.

In contrast with the Melville and Kipling stories, "The Price of the Head" is a brilliant example of tight plot structure applied to the adventure story. John Russell has discarded all traces of a frame situation. Though the events go forward in a chronological order as direct as Melville's, their full meaning is not revealed until the end, when we learn the motive for Karaki's devoted interest in Christopher Alexander Pellett. The ending, like that of Maupassant's "The Necklace," is a first-rate example of legitimate surprise. When a writer withholds, as O. Henry sometimes does in his weaker moments, an essential piece of information which is known to his characters but is concealed from the reader, the surprise is illegitimate. It becomes merely a trick played on the reader. But Russell's ending is legitimate because it is as much of a surprise to Pellett as it is to us. It is logical, according to the logic of the head-hunting Melanesians, and, like Pellett, we feel when it is too late that we should have foreseen it. Moreover, by ending the story not on the revelation but on Pellett's reaction to it, Russell achieves a second and deeper surprise in the flash of insight into the man's character.

These three stories, then, represent almost the entire range of technical effects possible in the tale of adventure. It depends for its perennial appeal not on fresh subtleties of construction but on the infinite variety and interest of human action and character revealed under stress.

*Herman Melville*

# THE TOWN-HO'S STORY

THE Cape of Good Hope, and all the watery region round about there, is much like some noted four corners of a great highway, where you meet more travellers than in any other part.

It was not very long after speaking the Goney that another homeward-bound whaleman, the Town-Ho,[1] was encountered. She was manned almost wholly by Polynesians. In the short gam that ensued she gave us strong news of Moby Dick. To some the general interest in the White Whale was now wildly heightened by a circumstance of the Town-Ho's story, which seemed obscurely to involve with the whale a certain wondrous, inverted visitation of one of those so called judgments of God which at times are said to overtake some men. This latter circumstance, with its own particular accompaniments, forming what may be called the secret part of the tragedy about to be narrated, never reached the ears of Captain Ahab or his mates. For that secret part of the story was unknown to the captain of the Town-Ho himself. It was the private property of three confederate white seamen of that ship, one of whom, it seems, communicated it to Tashtego with Romish injunctions of secrecy, but the following night Tashtego rambled

---

[1] The ancient whale-cry upon first sighting a whale from the mast-head, still used by whalemen in hunting the famous Gallipagos terrapin. [Melville's note.]

in his sleep, and revealed so much of it in that way, that when he was wakened he could not well withhold the rest. Nevertheless, so potent an influence did this thing have on those seamen in the Pequod who came to the full knowledge of it, and by such a strange delicacy, to call it so, were they governed in this matter, that they kept the secret among themselves so that it never transpired abaft the Pequod's main-mast. Interweaving in its proper place this darker thread with the story as publicly narrated on the ship, the whole of this strange affair I now proceed to put on lasting record.

For my humor's sake, I shall preserve the style in which I once narrated it at Lima, to a lounging circle of my Spanish friends, one saint's eve, smoking upon the thick-gilt tiled piazza of the Golden Inn. Of those fine cavaliers, the young Dons, Pedro and Sebastian, were on the closer terms with me; and hence the interluding questions they occasionally put, and which are duly answered at the time.

"Some two years prior to my first learning the events which I am about rehearsing to you, gentlemen, the Town-Ho, Sperm Whaler of Nantucket, was cruising in your Pacific here, not very many days' sail eastward from the eaves of this good Golden Inn. She was somewhere to the northward of the Line. One morning upon handling the pumps, according to daily usage, it was observed that she made more water in her hold than common. They supposed a sword-fish had stabbed her, gentlemen. But the captain, having some unusual reason for believing that rare good luck awaited him in those latitudes; and therefore being very averse to quit them, and the leak not being then considered at all dangerous, though, indeed, they could not find it after searching the hold as low down as was possible in rather heavy weather, the ship still continued her cruisings, the mariners working at the pumps at wide and easy intervals; but no good luck came; more days went by, and not only was the leak yet undiscovered, but it sensibly increased. So much so, that now taking some alarm, the captain,

making all sail, stood away for the nearest harbor among the
islands, there to have his hull hove out and repaired.

"Though no small passage was before her, yet, if the commonest
chance favored, he did not at all fear that his ship would founder
by the way, because his pumps were of the best, and being period-
ically relieved at them, those six-and-thirty men of his could easily
keep the ship free; never mind if the leak should double on her.
In truth, well nigh the whole of this passage being attended by
very prosperous breezes, the Town-Ho had all but certainly arrived
in perfect safety at her port without the occurrence of the least
fatality, had it not been for the brutal overbearing of Radney, the
mate, a Vineyarder, and the bitterly provoked vengeance of Steelkilt, a Lakeman and desperado from Buffalo.

" 'Lakeman!—Buffalo! Pray, what is a Lakeman, and where is
Buffalo?' said Don Sebastian, rising in his swinging mat of grass.

"On the eastern shore of our Lake Erie, Don; but—I crave your
courtesy—may be, you shall soon hear further of all that. Now,
gentlemen, in square-sail brigs and three-masted ships, well nigh
as large and stout as any that ever sailed out of your old Callao to
far Manilla; this Lakeman, in the land-locked heart of our America,
had yet been nurtured by all those agrarian freebooting impressions popularly connected with the open ocean. For in their inter-
flowing aggregate, those grand fresh-water seas of ours,—Erie, and
Ontario, and Huron, and Superior, and Michigan,—possess an
ocean-like expansiveness, with many of the ocean's noblest traits;
with many of its rimmed varieties of races and of climes. They
contain round archipelagoes of romantic isles, even as the Poly-
nesian waters do; in large part, are shored by two great contrasting
nations, as the Atlantic is; they furnish long maritime approaches
to our numerous territorial colonies from the East, dotted all
round their banks; here and there are frowned upon by batteries,
and by the goat-like craggy guns of lofty Mackinaw; they have
heard the fleet thunderings of naval victories; at intervals, they
yield their beaches to wild barbarians, whose red painted faces

flash from out their peltry wigwams; for leagues and leagues are
flanked by ancient and unentered forests, where the gaunt pines
stand like serried lines of kings in Gothic genealogies; those same
woods harboring wild Afric beasts of prey, and silken creatures
whose exported furs give robes to Tartar Emperors; they mirror
the paved capitals of Buffalo and Cleveland, as well as Winnebago
villages; they float alike the full-rigged merchant ship, the armed
cruiser of the State, the steamer, and the birch canoe; they are
swept by Borean and dismasting blasts as direful as any that lash
the salted wave; they know what shipwrecks are, for out of sight
of land, however inland, they have drowned full many a midnight
ship with all its shrieking crew. Thus, gentlemen, though an in-
lander, Steelkilt was wild-ocean born, and wild-ocean nurtured;
as much of an audacious mariner as any. And for Radney, though
in his infancy he may have laid him down on the lone Nantucket
beach, to nurse at his maternal sea; though in after life he had
long followed our austere Atlantic and your contemplative Pacific;
yet was he quite as vengeful and full of social quarrel as the back-
woods seaman, fresh from the latitudes of buckhorn-handled Bowie-
knives. Yet was this Nantucketer a man with some good-hearted
traits; and this Lakeman, a mariner, who though a sort of devil
indeed, might yet by inflexible firmness, only tempered by that
common decency of human recognition which is the meanest
slave's right; thus treated, this Steelkilt had long been retained
harmless and docile. At all events, he had proved so thus far; but
Radney was doomed and made mad, and Steelkilt—but, gentlemen, you shall hear.

"It was not more than a day or two at the furthest after pointing her prow for her island haven, that the Town-Ho's leak
seemed again increasing, but only so as to require an hour or more
at the pumps every day. You must know that in a settled and
civilized ocean like our Atlantic, for example, some skippers think
little of pumping their whole way across it; though of a still, sleepy
night, should the officer of the deck happen to forget his duty in

that respect, the probability would be that he and his shipmates would never again remember it, on account of all hands gently subsiding to the bottom. Nor in the solitary and savage seas far from you to the westward, gentlemen, is it altogether unusual for ships to keep clanging at their pump-handles in full chorus even for a voyage of considerable length! that is, if it lie along a tolerably accessible coast, or if any other reasonable retreat is afforded them. It is only when a leaky vessel is in some very out of the way part of those waters, some really landless latitude, that her captain begins to feel a little anxious.

"Much this way had it been with the Town-Ho; so when her leak was found gaining once more, there was in truth some small concern manifested by several of her company; especially by Radney the mate. He commanded the upper sails to be well hoisted, sheeted home anew, and every way expanded to the breeze. Now this Radney, I suppose, was as little of a coward, and as little inclined to any sort of nervous apprehensiveness touching his own person as any fearless, unthinking creature on land or on sea that you can conveniently imagine, gentlemen. Therefore when he betrayed this solicitude about the safety of the ship, some of the seamen declared that it was only on account of his being a part owner in her. So when they were working that evening at the pumps, there was on this head no small gamesomeness slily going on among them, as they stood with their feet continually overflowed by the rippling clear water; clear as any mountain spring, gentlemen—that bubbling from the pumps ran across the deck, and poured itself out in steady spouts at the lee scupper-holes.

"Now, as you well know, it is not seldom the case in this conventional world of ours—watery or otherwise; that when a person placed in command over his fellow-men finds one of them to be very significantly his superior in general pride of manhood, straightway against that man he conceives an unconquerable dislike and bitterness; and if he have a chance he will pull down and pulverize that subaltern's tower, and make a little heap of dust of it. Be this conceit of mine as it may, gentlemen, at all events Steelkilt was a tall and noble animal with a head like a Roman, and a flowing golden beard like the tasseled housings of your last viceroy's snorting charger; and a brain, and a heart, and a soul in him, gentlemen, which had made Steelkilt Charlemagne, had he been born son to Charlemagne's father. But Radney, the mate, was ugly as a mule; yet as hardy, as stubborn, as malicious. He did not love Steelkilt, and Steelkilt knew it.

"Espying the mate drawing near as he was toiling at the pump with the rest, the Lakeman affected not to notice him, but unawed, went on with his gay banterings.

" 'Aye, aye, my merry lads, it's a lively leak this; hold a cannikin, one of ye, and let's have a taste. By the Lord, it's worth bottling! I tell ye what, men, old Rad's investment must go for it! he had best cut away his part of the hull and tow it home. The fact is, boys, that sword-fish only began the job; he's come back again with a gang of ship-carpenters, saw-fish, and file-fish, and what not; and the whole posse of 'em are now hard at work cutting and slashing at the bottom; making improvements, I suppose. If old Rad were here now, I'd tell him to jump overboard and scatter 'em. They're playing the devil with his estate, I can tell him. But he's a simple old soul,—Rad, and a beauty too. Boys, they say the rest of his property is invested in looking-glasses. I wonder if he'd give a poor devil like me the model of his nose.'

" 'Damn your eyes! what's that pump stopping for?' roared Radney, pretending not to have heard the sailors' talk. 'Thunder away at it!'

" 'Aye, aye, sir,' said Steelkilt, merry as a cricket. 'Lively, boys, lively, now!' And with that the pump clanged like fifty fire-engines; the men tossed their hats off to it, and ere long that peculiar gasping of the lungs was heard which denotes the fullest tension of life's utmost energies.

"Quitting the pump at last, with the rest of his band, the Lakeman went forward all panting, and sat himself down on the windlass; his face fiery red, his eyes bloodshot, and wiping the profuse sweat from his brow. Now what cozening fiend it was, gentlemen, that possessed Radney to meddle with such a man in that corporeally exasperated state, I know not; but so it happened. Intolerably striding along the deck, the mate commanded him to get a broom and sweep down the planks, and also a shovel, and remove some offensive matters consequent upon allowing a pig to run at large.

"Now, gentlemen, sweeping a ship's deck at sea is a piece of household work which in all times but raging gales is regularly attended to every evening; it has been known to be done in the case of ships actually foundering at the time. Such, gentlemen, is the inflexibility of sea-usages and the instinctive love of neatness in seamen; some of whom would not willingly drown without first washing their faces. But in all vessels this broom business is the prescriptive province of the boys, if boys there be aboard. Besides, it was the stronger men in the Town-Ho that had been divided into gangs, taking turns at the pumps; and being the most athletic seaman of them all, Steelkilt had been regularly assigned captain of one of the gangs; consequently he should have been freed from any trivial business not connected with truly nautical duties, such being the case with his comrades. I mention all these particulars so that you may understand exactly how this affair stood between the two men.

"But there was more than this: the order about the shovel was almost as plainly meant to sting and insult Steelkilt, as though Radney had spat in his face. Any man who has gone sailor in a whale-ship will understand this; and all this and doubtless much more, the Lakeman fully comprehended when the mate uttered his command. But as he sat still for a moment, and as he steadfastly looked into the mate's malignant eye and perceived the stacks of powder-casks heaped up in him and the slow-match silently burning along towards them; as he instinctively saw all this, that strange forbearance and unwillingness to stir up the deeper passionateness in any already ireful being—a repugnance most felt, when felt at all, by really valiant men even when aggrieved—this nameless phantom feeling, gentlemen, stole over Steelkilt.

"Therefore, in his ordinary tone, only a little broken by the bodily exhaustion he was temporarily in, he answered him saying that sweeping the deck was not his business, and he would not do it. And then, without at all alluding to the shovel, he pointed to three lads as the customary sweepers; who, not being billeted at the pumps, had done little or nothing all day. To this, Radney replied with an oath, in a most domineering and outrageous manner unconditionally reiterating his command; meanwhile advancing upon the still seated Lakeman, with an uplifted cooper's club hammer which he had snatched from a cask near by.

"Heated and irritated as he was by his spasmodic toil at the pumps, for all his first nameless feeling of forbearance the sweating Steelkilt could but ill brook this bearing in the mate; but somehow still smothering the conflagration within him, without speaking he remained doggedly rooted to his seat, till at last the incensed Radney shook the hammer within a few inches of his face, furiously commanding him to do his bidding.

"Steelkilt rose, and slowly retreating round the windlass, steadily followed by the mate with his menacing hammer, deliberately repeated his intention not to obey. Seeing, however, that his forbearance had not the slightest effect, by an awful and unspeakable intimation with his twisted hand he warned off the foolish and infatuated man; but it was to no purpose. And in this way the two went once slowly round the windlass; when, resolved at last no longer to retreat, bethinking him that he had now forborne as much as comported with his humor, the Lakeman paused on the hatches and thus spoke to the officer:

"'Mr. Radney, I will not obey you. Take that hammer away, or look to yourself.' But the predestinated mate coming still closer to him, where the Lakeman stood fixed, now shook the heavy hammer within an inch of his teeth; meanwhile repeating a string of insufferable maledictions. Retreating not the thousandth part of an inch; stabbing him in the eye with the unflinching poniard of his glance, Steelkilt, clenching his right hand behind him and creepingly drawing it back, told his persecutor that if the hammer but grazed his cheek he (Steelkilt) would murder him. But, gentlemen, the fool had been branded for the slaughter by the gods. Immediately the hammer touched the cheek; the next instant the lower jaw of the mate was stove in his head; he fell on the hatch spouting blood like a whale.

"Ere the cry could go aft Steelkilt was shaking one of the backstays leading far aloft to where two of his comrades were standing their mast-heads. They were both Canallers.

"'Canallers!' cried Don Pedro. 'We have seen many whaleships in our harbors, but never heard of your Canallers. Pardon: who and what are they?'

"'Canallers, Don, are the boatmen belonging to our grand Erie Canal. You must have heard of it.'

"'Nay, Señor; hereabouts in this dull, warm, most lazy, and hereditary land, we know but little of your vigorous North.'

"'Aye? Well then, Don, refill my cup. Your chicha's very fine; and ere proceeding further I will tell ye what our Canallers are; for such information may throw side-light upon my story.'

"For three hundred and sixty miles, gentlemen, through the entire breadth of the state of New York; through numerous populous cities and most thriving villages; through long, dismal, uninhabited swamps, and affluent, cultivated fields, unrivalled for fertility; by billiard-room and barroom; through the holy-of-holies of great forests; on Roman arches over Indian rivers; through sun and shade; by happy hearts or broken; through all the wide contrasting scenery of those noble Mohawk counties; and especially, by rows of snow-white chapels, whose spires stand almost like milestones, flows one continual stream of Venetianly corrupt and often lawless life. There's your true Ashantee, gentlemen; there howl your pagans; where you ever find them, next door to you; under the long-flung shadow, and the snug patronizing lee of churches. For by some curious fatality, as it is often noted of your metropolitan freebooters that they ever encamp around the halls of justice, so sinners, gentlemen, most abound in holiest vicinities.

"'Is that a friar passing?' said Don Pedro, looking downwards into the crowded plaza, with humorous concern.

"'Well for our northern friend, Dame Isabella's Inquisition wanes in Lima,' laughed Don Sebastian. 'Proceed, Señor.'

"'A moment! Pardon!' cried another of the company. 'In the name of all us Limeese, I but desire to express to you, sir sailor, that we have by no means overlooked your delicacy in not substituting present Lima for distant Venice in your corrupt comparison. Oh! do not bow and look surprised: you know the proverb all along this coast—"Corrupt as Lima." It but bears out your saying, too; churches more plentiful than billiard-tables, and for ever open—and "Corrupt as Lima." So, too, Venice; I have been there; the holy city of the blessed evangelist, St. Mark!—St. Dominic, purge it! Your cup! Thanks: here I refill; now, you pour out again.'

"Freely depicted in his own vocation, gentlemen, the Canaller would make a fine dramatic hero, so abundantly and picturesquely wicked he is. Like Mark Antony, for days and days along his green-turfed, flowery Nile, he indolently floats, openly toying with his red-cheeked Cleopatra, ripening his apricot thigh upon the sunny deck. But ashore, all this effeminacy is dashed. The brigandish guise which the Canaller so proudly sports; his slouched and gaily-ribboned hat betoken his grand features. A terror to the smiling innocence of the villages through which he floats; his swart visage and bold swagger are not unshunned in cities. Once a vagabond on his own canal, I have received good turns from one of these Canallers; I thank him heartily; would fain be not ungrateful; but it is often one of the prime redeeming qualities of your man of violence, that at times he has as stiff an arm to back a poor stranger in a strait, as to plunder a wealthy one. In sum, gentlemen, what the wildness of this canal life is, is emphatically evinced by this; that our wild whale-fishery contains so many of its most finished graduates, and that scarce any race of mankind, except Sydney men, are so much distrusted by our whaling captains. Nor does it at all diminish the curiousness of this matter, that to many thousands of our rural boys and young men born along its line, the probationary life of the Grand Canal furnishes the sole transition between quietly reaping in a Christian corn-field, and recklessly ploughing the waters of the most barbaric seas.

" 'I see! I see!' impetuously exclaimed Don Pedro, spilling his chicha upon his silvery ruffles. 'No need to travel! The world's one Lima. I had thought, now, that at your temperate North the generations were cold and holy as the hills.—But the story.'

"I left off, gentlemen, where the Lakeman shook the back-stay. Hardly had he done so, when he was surrounded by the three junior mates and the four harpooneers, who all crowded him to the deck. But sliding down the ropes like baleful comets, the two Canallers rushed into the uproar, and sought to drag their man out of it towards the forecastle. Others of the sailors joined with them in this attempt, and a twisted turmoil ensued; while standing out of harm's way, the valiant captain danced up and down with a whale-pike, calling upon his officers to manhandle that atrocious scoundrel, and smoke him along to the quarter-deck. At intervals, he ran close up to the revolving border of the confusion, and prying into the heart of it with his pike, sought to prick out the object of his resentment. But Steelkilt and his desperadoes were too much for them all; they succeeded in gaining the forecastle deck, where, hastily slewing about three or four large casks in a line with the windlass, these sea-Parisians entrenched themselves behind the barricade.

" 'Come out of that, ye pirates!' roared the captain, now menacing them with a pistol in each hand, just brought to him by the steward. 'Come out of that, ye cut-throats!'

"Steelkilt leaped on the barricade, and striding up and down there, defied the worst the pistols could do; but gave the captain to understand distinctly, that his (Steelkilt's) death would be the signal for a murderous mutiny on the part of all hands. Fearing in his heart lest this might prove but too true, the Captain a little desisted, but still commanded the insurgents instantly to return to their duty.

"'Will you promise not to touch us, if we do?' demanded their ringleader.

"'Turn to! turn to!—I make no promise;—to your duty! Do you want to sink the ship, by knocking off at a time like this? Turn to!' and he once more raised a pistol.

"'Sink the ship?' cried Steelkilt. 'Aye, let her sink. Not a man of us turns to, unless you swear not to raise a rope-yarn against us. What say ye, men?' turning to his comrades. A fierce cheer was their response.

"The Lakeman now patrolled the barricade, all the while keeping his eye on the Captain, and jerking out such sentences as these:—'It's not our fault; we didn't want it; I told him to take his hammer away; it was boy's business; he might have known me before this; I told him not to prick the buffalo; I believe I have broken a finger here against his cursed jaw; ain't those mincing knives down in the forecastle there, men? look to those handspikes, my hearties. Captain, by God, look to yourself; say the word; don't be a fool; forget it all; we are ready to turn to; treat us decently, and we're your men; but we won't be flogged.'

"'Turn to! I make no promises, turn to, I say!'

"'Look ye, now,' cried the Lakeman, flinging out his arm towards him, 'there are a few of us here (and I am one of them) who have shipped for the cruise, d'ye see; now as you well know, sir, we can claim our discharge as soon as the anchor is down; so we don't want a row; it's not our interest; we want to be peaceable; we are ready to work, but we won't be flogged.'

"'Turn to!' roared the Captain.

"Steelkilt glanced round him a moment, and then said:—'I tell you what it is now, Captain, rather than kill ye, and be hung for such a shabby rascal, we won't lift a hand against ye unless ye attack us; but till you say the word about not flogging us, we don't do a hand's turn.'

" 'Down into the forecastle then, down with ye, I'll keep ye there till ye're sick of it. Down ye go.'

" 'Shall we?' cried the ringleader to his men. Most of them were against it; but at length, in obedience to Steelkilt, they preceded him down into their dark den, growlingly disappearing, like bears into a cave.

"As the Lakeman's bare head was just level with the planks, the Captain and his posse leaped the barricade, and rapidly drawing over the slide of the scuttle, planted their group of hands upon it, and loudly called for the steward to bring the heavy brass padlock belonging to the companionway. Then opening the slide a little, the Captain whispered something down the crack, closed it, and turned the key upon them—ten in number—leaving on deck some twenty or more, who thus far had remained neutral.

"All night a wide-awake watch was kept by all the officers, forward and aft, especially about the forecastle scuttle and fore hatchway; at which last place it was feared the insurgents might emerge, after breaking through the bulkhead below. But the hours of darkness passed in peace; the men who still remained at their duty toiling hard at the pumps, whose clinking and clanking at intervals through the dreary night dismally resounded through the ship.

"At sunrise the Captain went forward, and knocking on the deck, summoned the prisoners to work; but with a yell they refused. Water was then lowered down to them, and a couple of handfuls of biscuit were tossed after it; when again turning the key upon them and pocketing it, the Captain returned to the quarter-deck. Twice every day for three days this was repeated; but on the fourth morning a confused wrangling, and then a scuffling was heard, as the customary summons was delivered; and suddenly four men burst up from the forecastle, saying they were ready to turn to. The fetid closeness of the air, and a famishing diet, united perhaps to some fears of ultimate retribution, had constrained them to surrender at discretion. Emboldened by this, the Captain reiterated his demand to the rest, but Steelkilt shouted up to him a terrific hint to stop his babbling and betake himself where he belonged. On the fifth morning three others of the mutineers bolted up into the air from the desperate arms below that sought to restrain them. Only three were left.

" 'Better turn to, now?" said the Captain with a heartless jeer.

" 'Shut us up again, will ye!' cried Steelkilt.

" 'Oh, certainly,' said the Captain, and the key clicked.

"It was at this point, gentlemen, that enraged by the defection of seven of his former associates, and stung by the mocking voice that had last hailed him, and maddened by his long entombment in a place as black as the bowels of despair; it was then that Steelkilt proposed to the two Canallers, thus far apparently of one mind with him, to burst out of their hole at the next summoning of the garrison; and armed with their keen mincing knives (long, crescentic, heavy implements with a handle at each end) run amuck from the bowsprit to the taffrail; and if by any devilishness of desperation possible, seize the ship. For himself, he would do this, he said, whether they joined him or not. That was the last night he should spend in that den. But the scheme met with no opposition on the part of the other two; they swore they were ready for that, or for any other mad thing, for anything in short but a surrender. And what was more, they each insisted upon being the first man on deck, when the time to make the rush should come. But to this their leader as fiercely objected, reserving that priority for himself; particularly as his two comrades would not yield, the one to the other, in the matter; and both of them could not be first, for the ladder would but admit one man at a time. And here, gentlemen, the foul play of these miscreants must come out.

"Upon hearing the frantic project of their leader, each in his own separate soul had suddenly lighted, it would seem, upon the same piece of treachery, namely: to be the foremost in breaking out, in order to be the first of the three, though the last of the ten, to surrender; and thereby secure whatever small chance of pardon such conduct might merit. But when Steelkilt made known his determination still to lead them to the last, they in some way, by some subtle chemistry of villainy, mixed their before secret treacheries together; and when their leader fell into a doze, verbally opened their souls to each other in three sentences; and bound the sleeper with cords, and gagged him with cords; and shrieked out for the Captain at midnight.

"Thinking murder at hand, and smelling in the dark for the blood, he and all his armed mates and harpooneers rushed for the forecastle. In a few minutes the scuttle was opened, and, bound hand and foot, the still struggling ringleader was shoved up into the air by his perfidious allies, who at once claimed the honor of securing a man who had been fully ripe for murder. But all these were collared, and dragged along the deck like dead cattle; and, side by side, were seized up into the mizen rigging, like three quarters of meat, and there they hung till morning. 'Damn ye,' cried the Captain, pacing to and fro before them, 'the vultures would not touch ye, ye villains!'

"At sunrise he summoned all hands; and separating those who had rebelled from those who had taken no part in the mutiny, he told the former that he had a good mind to flog them all round—thought, upon the while, he would do so—he ought to—justice demanded it; but for the present, considering their timely surrender, he would let them go with a reprimand, which he accordingly administered in the vernacular.

" 'But as for you, ye carrion rogues,' turning to the three men in the rigging—'for you, I mean to mince ye up for the try-pots;' and, seizing a rope, he applied it with all his might to the backs of the two traitors, till they yelled no more, but lifelessly hung their heads sideways, as the two crucified thieves are drawn.

" 'My wrist is sprained with ye!' he cried, at last; 'but there is still rope enough left for you, my fine bantam, that wouldn't give up. Take that gag from his mouth, and let us hear what he can say for himself.'

"For a moment the exhausted mutineer made a tremulous motion of his cramped jaws, and then painfully twisting round his head, said in a sort of hiss, 'What I say is this—and mind it well—if you flog me, I murder you!'

" 'Say ye so? then see how ye frighten me'—and the Captain drew off with the rope to strike.

" 'Best not,' hissed the Lakeman.

" 'But I must,'—and the rope was once more drawn back for the stroke.

"Steelkilt here hissed out something, inaudible to all but the Captain; who, to the amazement of all hands, started back, paced the deck rapidly two or three times, and then suddenly throwing down his rope, said, 'I won't do it—let him go—cut him down: d'ye hear?'

"But as the junior mates were hurrying to execute the order, a pale man, with a bandaged head, arrested them—Radney the chief mate. Ever since the blow, he had lain in his berth; but that morning, hearing the tumult on the deck, he had crept out, and thus far had watched the whole scene. Such was the state of his mouth, that he could hardly speak; but mumbling something about *his* being willing and able to do what the Captain dared not attempt, he snatched the rope and advanced to his pinioned foe.

" 'You are a coward!' hissed the Lakeman.

" 'So I am, but take that.' The mate was in the very act of striking, when another hiss stayed his uplifted arm. He paused: and then pausing no more, made good his word, spite of Steelkilt's threat, whatever that might have been. The three men were then cut down, all hands were turned to, and, sullenly worked by the moody seamen, the iron pumps clanged as before.

"Just after dark that day, when one watch had retired below, a clamor was heard in the forecastle; and the two trembling traitors running up, besieged the cabin door, saying they durst not consort with the crew. Entreaties, cuffs, and kicks could not drive them back, so at their own instance they were put down in the ship's run for salvation. Still, no sign of mutiny reappeared among the rest. On the contrary, it seemed, that mainly at Steelkilt's instigation, they had resolved to maintain the strictest peacefulness, obey all orders to the last, and, when the ship reached port, desert her in a body. But in order to insure the speediest end to the voyage, they all agreed to another thing—namely, not to sing out for whales, in case any should be discovered. For, in spite of her leak, and spite of all her other perils, the Town-Ho still maintained her mast-heads, and her captain was just as willing to lower for a fish that moment, as on the day his craft first struck the cruising ground; and Radney the mate was quite as ready to change his berth for a boat, and with his bandaged mouth seek to gag in death the vital jaw of the whale.

"But though the Lakeman had induced the seamen to adopt this sort of passiveness in their conduct, he kept his own counsel (at least till all was over) concerning his own proper and private revenge upon the man who had stung him in the ventricles of his heart. He was in Radney the chief mate's watch; and as if the infatuated man sought to run more than half way to meet his doom, after the scene at the rigging, he insisted, against the express counsel of the Captain, upon resuming the head of his watch at night. Upon this, and one or two other circumstances, Steelkilt systematically built the plan of his revenge.

"During the night, Radney had an unseaman-like way of sitting on the bulwarks of the quarter-deck, and leaning his arm upon the gunwale of the boat which was hoisted up there, a little above the ship's side. In this attitude, it was well known, he sometimes dozed. There was a considerable vacancy between the boat and the ship, and down between this was the sea. Steelkilt calculated his time, and found that his next trick at the helm would come round at two o'clock, in the morning of the third day from that in which he had been betrayed. At his leisure, he employed the interval in braiding something very carefully in his watches below.

"'What are you making there?' said a shipmate.

"'What do you think? what does it look like?'

"'Like a lanyard for your bag; but it's an odd one, seems to me.'

"'Yes, rather oddish,' said the Lakeman, holding it at arm's length before him; 'but I think it will answer. Shipmate, I haven't enough twine,—have you any?'

"But there was none in the forecastle.

"'Then I must get some from old Rad;' and he rose to go aft.

"'You don't mean to go a begging to *him!*' said a sailor.

"'Why not? Do you think he won't do me a turn, when it's to help himself in the end, shipmate?' and going to the mate, he looked at him quietly, and asked him for some twine to mend his hammock. It was given him—neither twine nor lanyard were seen again; but the next night an iron ball, closely netted, partly rolled from the pocket of the Lakeman's monkey jacket, as he was tucking the coat into his hammock for a pillow. Twenty-four hours after, his trick at the silent helm—nigh to the man who was apt to doze over the grave always ready dug to the seaman's hand— that fatal hour was then to come; and in the foreordaining soul of Steelkilt, the mate was already stark and stretched as a corpse, with his forehead crushed in.

"But, gentlemen, a fool saved the would-be murderer from the bloody deed he had planned. Yet complete revenge he had, and without being the avenger. For by a mysterious fatality, Heaven itself seemed to step in to take out of his hands into its own the damning thing he would have done.

"It was just between daybreak and sunrise of the morning of the second day, when they were washing down the decks, that a stupid Teneriffe man, drawing water in the main-chains, all at once shouted out, 'There she rolls! there she rolls! Jesu, what a whale!' It was Moby Dick.

" 'Moby Dick!' cried Don Sebastian; 'St. Dominic! Sir sailor, but do whales have christenings? Whom call you Moby Dick?'

" 'A very white, and famous, and most deadly immortal monster, Don;—but that would be too long a story.'

" 'How? how?' cried all the young Spaniards, crowding.

" 'Nay, Dons, Dons—nay, nay! I cannot rehearse that now. Let me get more into the air, sirs.'

" 'The chicha! the chicha!' cried Don Pedro; 'our vigorous friend looks faint;—fill up his empty glass!'

"No need, gentlemen; one moment, and I proceed.—Now, gentlemen, so suddenly perceiving the snowy whale within fifty yards of the ship—forgetful of the compact among the crew—in the excitement of the moment, the Teneriffe man had instinctively and involuntarily lifted his voice for the monster, though for some little time past it had been plainly beheld from the three sullen mast-heads. All was now a phrensy. 'The White Whale—the White Whale!' was the cry from Captain, mates, and harpooners, who, undeterred by fearful rumors, were all anxious to capture so famous and precious a fish; while the dogged crew eyed askance, and with curses, the appalling beauty of the vast milky mass, that lit up by a horizontal spangling sun, shifted and glistened like a living opal in the blue morning sea. Gentlemen, a strange fatality pervades the whole career of these events, as if verily mapped out before the world itself was charted. The mutineer was the bowsman of the mate, and when fast to a fish, it was his duty to sit next him, while Radney stood up with his lance in the prow, and haul in or slacken the line, at the word of command. Moreover, when the four boats were lowered, the mate's got the start; and none howled more fiercely with delight than did Steelkilt, as he strained at his oar. After a stiff pull, their harpooneer got fast, and, spear in hand, Radney sprang to the bow. He was always a furious man, it seems, in a boat. And now his bandaged cry was, to beach him on the whale's topmost back. Nothing loath, his bowsman hauled him up and up, through a blinding foam that blent two whitenesses together; till of a sudden the boat struck as against a sunken ledge, and keeling over, spilled out the standing mate. That instant, as he fell on the whale's slippery back, the boat righted, and was dashed aside by the swell, while Radney was tossed over into the sea, on the other flank of the whale. He struck out through the spray, and, for an instant, was dimly seen through that veil, wildly seeking to remove himself from the eye of Moby Dick. But the whale rushed round in a sudden maelstrom; seized the swimmer between his jaws; and rearing high up with him, plunged headlong again, and went down.

"Meantime, at the first tap of the boat's bottom, the Lakeman had slackened the line, so as to drop astern from the whirlpool; calmly looking on, he thought his own thoughts. But a sudden, terrific, downward jerking of the boat, quickly brought his knife to the line. He cut it; and the whale was free. But, at some distance, Moby Dick rose again, with some tatters of Radney's red woollen shirt, caught in the teeth that had destroyed him. All four boats gave chase again; but the whale eluded them, and finally wholly disappeared.

"In good time, the Town-Ho reached her port—a savage, solitary place—where no civilized creature resided. There, headed by the Lakeman, all but five or six of the foremastmen deliberately deserted among the palms; eventually, as it turned out, seizing a large double war-canoe of the savages, and setting sail for some other harbor.

"The ship's company being reduced to but a handful, the Captain called upon the islanders to assist him in the laborious business of heaving down the ship to stop the leak. But to such unresting vigilance over their dangerous allies was this small band of whites necessitated, both by night and by day, and so extreme was the hard work they underwent, that upon the vessel being ready again for sea, they were in such a weakened condition that the Captain durst not put off with them in so heavy a vessel. After taking counsel with his officers, he anchored the ship as far off shore as possible; loaded and ran out his two cannon from the bows; stacked his muskets on the poop; and warning the islanders not to approach the ship at their peril, took one man with him, and setting the sail of his best whaleboat, steered straight before the wind for Tahiti, five hundred miles distant, to procure a reinforcement to his crew.

"On the fourth day of the sail, a large canoe was descried, which seemed to have touched at a low isle of corals. He steered away from it; but the savage craft bore down on him; and soon the voice of Steelkilt hailed him to heave to, or he would run him under water. The Captain presented a pistol. With one foot on each prow of the yoked war-canoes, the Lakeman laughed him to scorn; assuring him that if the pistol so much as clicked in the lock, he would bury him in bubbles and foam.

" 'What do you want of me?' cried the Captain.

" 'Where are you bound? and for what are you bound?' demanded Steelkilt; 'no lies.'

" 'I am bound to Tahiti for more men.'

" 'Very good. Let me board you a moment—I come in peace.' With that he leaped from the canoe, swam to the boat; and climbing the gunwale, stood face to face with the Captain.

" 'Cross your arms, sir; throw back your head. Now, repeat after me. As soon as Steelkilt leaves me, I swear to beach this boat on yonder island, and remain there six days. If I do not, may lightnings strike me!'

" 'A pretty scholar,' laughed the Lakeman. 'Adios, Señor!' and leaping into the sea, he swam back to his comrades.

"Watching the boat till it was fairly beached, and drawn up to the roots of the cocoa-nut trees, Steelkilt made sail again, and in due time arrived at Tahiti, his own place of destination. There, luck befriended him; two ships were about to sail for France, and were providentially in want of precisely that number of men which the sailor headed. They embarked, and so for ever got the start of their former captain, had he been at all minded to work them legal retribution.

"Some ten days after the French ships sailed, the whaleboat arrived, and the Captain was forced to enlist some of the more civilized Tahitians, who had been somewhat used to the sea. Chartering a small native schooner, he returned with them to his vessel; and finding all right there, again resumed his cruisings.

"Where Steelkilt now is, gentlemen, none know; but upon the island of Nantucket, the widow of Radney still turns to the sea which refuses to give up its dead; still in dreams sees the awful white whale that destroyed him. . . .

" 'Are you through?' said Don Sebastian, quietly.

" 'I am, Don.'

" 'Then I entreat you, tell me if to the best of your own convictions, this your story is in substance really true? It is so passing wonderful! Did you get it from an unquestionable source? Bear with me if I seem to press.'

" 'Also bear with all of us, sir sailor; for we all join in Don Sebastian's suit,' cried the company, with exceeding interest.

" 'Is there a copy of the Holy Evangelists in the Golden Inn, gentlemen?'

" 'Nay,' said Don Sebastian; 'but I know a worthy priest near by, who will quickly procure one for me. I go for it; but are you well advised? this may grow too serious.'

" 'Will you be so good as to bring the priest also, Don?'

" 'Though there are no Auto-da-Fés in Lima now,' said one of the company to another: 'I fear our sailor friend runs risks of the archiepiscopacy. Let us withdraw more out of the moonlight. I see no need of this.'

" 'Excuse me for running after you, Don Sebastian; but may I also beg that you will be particular in procuring the largest-sized Evangelists you can?'

.    .    .    .    .    .    .    .    .

" 'This is the priest, he brings you the Evangelists,' said Don Sebastian, gravely, returning with a tall and solemn figure.

" 'Let me remove my hat. Now, venerable priest, further into the light, and hold the Holy Book before me that I may touch it.

" 'So help me Heaven, and on my honor, the story I have told ye, gentlemen, is in substance and its great items, true. I know it to be true; it happened on this ball; I trod the ship; I knew the crew; I have seen and talked with Steelkilt since the death of Radney.' "

1. Does the story gain anything by its supposed Lima setting?
2. Do you feel that Melville's humor and digressions add to or detract from the story?
3. What do you fancy Steelkilt said to the Captain that urged the latter to have him cut down?
4. The call of the lookout on the whaler was commonly "There she blows!" What is the meaning of the cry "There she rolls!"—a phrase which also signified that a whale had been sighted.
5. Melville was one of the greatest of all writers of sea tales. List the accouterments of the sea which appear in the story.

*Rudyard Kipling*

# THE MAN WHO
# WOULD BE KING

"Brother to a Prince and fellow to a beggar if he be found worthy."

THE law, as quoted, lays down a fair conduct of life, and one not easy to follow. I have been fellow to a beggar again and again under circumstances which prevented either of us finding out whether the other was worthy. I have still to be brother to a Prince, though I once came near to kinship with what might have been a veritable King and was promised the reversion of a Kingdom—army, law-courts, revenue and policy all complete. But, to-day, I greatly fear that my King is dead, and if I want a crown I must go and hunt it for myself.

The beginning of everything was in a railway train upon the road to Mhow from Ajmir. There had been a Deficit in the Budget, which necessitated travelling, not Second-class, which is only half as dear as First-class, but by Intermediate, which is very awful indeed. There are no cushions in the Intermediate class, and the population are either Intermediate, which is Eurasian, or native, which for a long night journey is nasty, or Loafer, which is amusing though intoxicated. Intermediates do not patronize refreshment-rooms. They carry their food in bundles and pots.

and buy sweets from the native sweetmeat sellers, and drink the roadside water. That is why in the hot weather Intermediates are taken out of the carriages dead, and in all weathers are most properly looked down upon.

My particular Intermediate happened to be empty till I reached Nasirabad, when a huge gentleman in shirt-sleeves entered, and, following the custom of Intermediates, passed the time of day. He was a wanderer and a vagabond like myself, but with an educated taste for whisky. He told tales of things he had seen and done, of out-of-the-way corners of the Empire into which he had penetrated, and of adventures in which he risked his life for a few days' food. "If India was filled with men like you and me, not knowing more than the crows where they'd get their next day's rations, it isn't seventy millions of revenue the land would be paying—it's seven hundred millions," said he; and as I looked at his mouth and chin I was disposed to agree with him. We talked politics—the politics of Loaferdom that sees things from the underside where the lath and plaster is not smoothed off— and we talked postal arrangements because my friend wanted to send a telegram back from the next station to Ajmir, which is the turning-off place from the Bombay to the Mhow line as you travel westward. My friend had no money beyond eight annas which he wanted for dinner, and I had no money at all, owing to the hitch in the Budget before mentioned. Further, I was going into a wilderness where, though I should resume touch with the Treasury, there were no telegraph offices. I was, therefore, unable to help him in any way.

"We might threaten a Station-master, and make him send a wire on tick," said my friend, "but that'd mean inquiries for you and for me, and I've got my hands full these days. Did you say you were travelling back along this line within any days?"

"Within ten," I said.

"Can't you make it eight?" said he. "Mine is rather urgent business."

"I can send your telegram within ten days if that will serve you," I said.

"I couldn't trust the wire to fetch him, now I think of it. It's this way. He leaves Delhi on the 23rd for Bombay. That means he'll be running through Ajmir about the night of the 23rd."

"But I'm going into the Indian Desert," I explained.

"Well and good," said he. "You'll be changing at Marwar Junction to get into Jodhpore territory—you must do that—and he'll be coming through Marwar Junction in the early morning of the 24th by the Bombay Mail. Can you be at Marwar Junction on that time? 'Twon't be inconveniencing you, because I know that there's precious few pickings to be got out of those Central India States—even though you pretend to be correspondent of the *Backwoodsman*."

"Have you ever tried that trick?" I asked.

"Again and again, but the Residents find you out, and then you get escorted to the Border before you've time to get your knife into them. But about my friend here. I must give him word o' mouth to tell him what's come to me or else he won't know where to go. I would take it more than kind of you if you was to come out of Central India in time to catch him at Marwar Junction, and say to him: 'He has gone South for the week.' He'll know what that means. He's a big man with a red beard, and a great swell he is. You'll find him sleeping like a gentleman with all his luggage round him in a Second-class compartment. But don't you be afraid. Slip down the window and say: 'He has gone South for the week,' and he'll tumble. It's only cutting your time of stay in those parts by two days. I ask you as a stranger—going to the West," he said with emphasis.

"Where have you come from?" said I.

"From the East," said he, "and I am hoping that you will give him the message on the square—for the sake of my Mother as well as your own."

Englishmen are not usually softened by appeals to the memory of their mothers, but for certain reasons, which will be fully apparent, I saw fit to agree.

"It's more than a little matter," said he, "and that's why I ask you to do it—and now I know that I can depend on you doing it. A Second-class carriage at Marwar Junction, and a red-haired man asleep in it. You'll be sure to remember. I get out at the next station, and I must hold on there till he comes or sends me what I want."

"I'll give the message if I catch him," I said, "and for the sake of your Mother as well as mine I'll give you a word of advice. Don't try to run the Central India States just now as the correspondent of the *Backwoodsman*. There's a real one knocking about here, and it might lead to trouble."

"Thank you," said he simply, "and when will the swine be gone? I can't starve because he's ruining my work. I wanted to get hold of the Degumber Rajah down here about his father's widow, and give him a jump."

"What did he do to his father's widow, then?"

"Filled her up with red pepper and slippered her to death as she hung from a beam. I found that out myself and I'm the only man that would dare going into the State to get hush-money for it. They'll try to poison me, same as they did in Chortumna when I went on the loot there. But you'll give the man at Marwar Junction my message?"

He got out at a little roadside station, and I reflected. I had heard, more than once, of men personating correspondents of newspapers and bleeding small Native States with threats of exposure, but I had never met any of the caste before. They lead a hard life, and generally die with great suddenness. The Native States have a wholesome horror of English newspapers, which may throw light on their peculiar methods of government, and do their best to choke correspondents with champagne, or drive them out of their mind with four-in-hand barouches. They do not understand that nobody cares a straw for the internal administration of Native States so long as oppression and crime are kept within decent limits, and the ruler is not drugged, drunk or diseased from one end of the year to the other. Native States were created by Providence in order to supply picturesque scenery, tigers and tall writing. They are the dark places of the earth, full of unimaginable cruelty, touching the Railway and the Telegraph on one side, and on the other the days of Harun-al-Raschid. When I left the train I did business with divers Kings, and in eight days passed through many changes of life. Sometimes I wore dress clothes and consorted with Princes and Politicals, drinking from crystal and eating from silver. Sometimes I lay out upon the ground and devoured what I could get from a plate made of a flapjack, and drank the running water, and slept under the same rug as my servant. It was all in the day's work.

Then I headed for the Great Indian Desert upon the proper date, as I had promised, and the night Mail set me down at Marwar Junction, where a funny little happy-go-lucky, native-managed railway runs to Jodhpore. The Bombay Mail from Delhi makes a short halt at Marwar. She arrived as I got in, and I had just time to hurry to her platform and go down the carriages. There was only one Second-class on the train. I slipped the window and looked down upon a flaming red beard, half-covered by a railway rug. That was my man, fast asleep, and I dug him gently in the ribs. He woke with a grunt and I saw his face in the light of the lamps. It was a great and shining face.

"Tickets again?" said he.

"No," said I. "I am to tell you that he is gone South for the week. He is gone South for the week!"

The train had begun to move out. The red man rubbed his eyes. "He has gone South for the week," he repeated. "Now that's just like his impidence. Did he say that I was to give you anything? 'Cause I won't."

"He didn't," I said and dropped away, and watched the red lights die out in the dark. It was horribly cold because the wind was blowing off the sands. I climbed into my own train—not an Intermediate Carriage this time—and went to sleep.

If the man with the beard had given me a rupee I should have kept it as a memento of a rather curious affair. But the consciousness of having done my duty was my only reward.

Later on I reflected that two gentlemen like my friends could not do any good if they foregathered and personated correspondents of newspapers, and might, if they "stuck up" one of the little rat-trap States of Central India or Southern Rajputana, get themselves into serious difficulties. I therefore took some trouble to describe them as accurately as I could remember to people who would be interested in deporting them: and succeeded, so I was later informed, in having them headed back from the Degumber borders.

Then I became respectable, and returned to an Office where there were no Kings and no incidents except the daily manufacture of a newspaper. A newspaper office seems to attract every conceivable sort of person to the prejudice of discipline. Zenana-mission ladies arrive, and beg that the Editor will instantly abandon all his duties to describe a Christian prize-giving in a back slum of a perfectly inaccessible village; Colonels who have been overpassed for commands sit down and sketch the outline of a series of ten, twelve or twenty-four leading articles on Seniority versus Selection; missionaries wish to know why they have not been permitted to escape from their regular vehicles of abuse and swear at a brother missionary under special patronage of the editorial We; stranded theatrical companies troop up to explain that they cannot pay for their advertisements, but on their return from New Zealand or Tahiti will do so with interest; inventors of patent punkah-pulling machines, carriage couplings and unbreakable swords and axletrees call with specifications in their pockets and hours at their disposal; tea companies enter and elaborate their prospectuses with the office pens; secretaries of ball committees clamor to have the glories of their last dance more fully ex-

pounded; strange ladies rustle in and say: "I want a hundred lady's
cards printed at once, please," which is manifestly part of an editor's duty; and every dissolute ruffian that ever tramped the Grand
Trunk Road makes it his business to ask for employment as a
proof-reader. And, all the time, the telephone bell is ringing
madly, and Kings are being killed on the Continent, and Empires
are saying: "You're another," and Mister Gladstone is calling
down brimstone upon the British Dominions, and the little black
copy boys are whining "kaa-pi chay-ha-yeh" (copy wanted) like
tired bees, and most of the paper is as blank as Modred's shield.

But that is the amusing part of the year. There are other six
months wherein none ever come to call, and the thermometer
walks inch by inch up to the top of the glass, and the office is
darkened to just above reading light, and the press machines are
red-hot of touch, and nobody writes anything but accounts of
amusements in the Hill-stations, or obituary notices. Then the
telephone becomes a tinkling terror, because it tells you of the
sudden deaths of men and women that you knew intimately, and
the prickly heat covers you as with a garment, and you sit down
and write: "A slight increase of sickness is reported from the
Khuda Janta Khan District. The outbreak is purely sporadic in
its nature, and thanks to the energetic efforts of the District authorities, is now almost at an end. It is, however, with deep regret
we record the death, etc."

Then the sickness really breaks out, and the less recording and
reporting the better for the peace of the subscribers. But the
Empires and Kings continue to divert themselves as selfishly as
before, and the Foreman thinks that a daily paper really ought
to come out once in twenty-four hours, and all the people at the
Hill-stations in the middle of their amusements say: "Good gracious! Why can't the paper be sparkling? I'm sure there's plenty
going on up here."

That is the dark half of the moon, and as the advertisements
say, "must be experienced to be appreciated."

It was in that season, and a remarkably evil season, that the paper began running the last issue of the week on Saturday night, which is to say Sunday morning, after the custom of a London paper. This was a great convenience, for immediately after the paper was put to bed the dawn would lower the thermometer from 96° to almost 84° for half an hour, and in that chill—you have no idea how cold is 84° on the grass until you begin to pray for it—a very tired man could get off to sleep ere the heat roused him.

One Saturday night it was my pleasant duty to put the paper to bed alone. A King or courtier or a courtesan or a community was going to die or get a new constitution, or do something that was important on the other side of the world, and the paper was to be held open till the latest possible minute in order to catch the telegram. It was a pitchy black night, as stifling as a June night can be, and the *loo*, the red-hot wind from the westward, was booming among the tinder-dry trees and pretending that the rain was on its heels. Now and again a spot of almost boiling water would fall on the dust with the flop of a frog, but all our weary world knew that was only pretence. It was a shade cooler in the press-room than the office, so I sat there while the type clicked and clicked, and the night-jars hooted at the windows, and the all but naked compositors wiped the sweat from their foreheads and called for water. The thing that was keeping us back, whatever it was, would not come off, though the *loo* dropped and the last type was set, and the whole round earth stood still in the choking heat, with its finger on its lip, to wait the event. I drowsed, and wondered whether the telegraph was a blessing, and whether this dying man or struggling people was aware of the inconvenience the delay was causing. There was no special reason beyond the heat and worry to make tension, but as the clock hands crept up to three o'clock and the machines spun their flywheels two and three times to see that all was in order, before I said the word that would set them off, I could have shrieked aloud.

Then the roar and rattle of the wheels shivered the quiet into little bits. I rose to go away, but two men in white clothes stood in front of me. The first one said: "It's him!" The second said: "So it is!" And they both laughed almost as loudly as the machinery roared, and mopped their foreheads. "We see there was a light burning across the road and we were sleeping in that ditch there for coolness, and I said to my friend here: 'The office is open. Let's come along and speak to him as turned us back from the Degumber State,'" said the smaller of the two. He was the man I had met in the Mhow train, and his fellow was the red-bearded man of Marwar Junction. There was no mistaking the eyebrows of the one or the beard of the other.

I was not pleased, because I wished to go to sleep, not to squabble with loafers. "What do you want?" I asked.

"Half an hour's talk with you cool and comfortable, in the office," said the red-bearded man. "We'd *like* some drink—the Contrack doesn't begin yet, Peachey, so you needn't look—but what we really want is advice. We don't want money. We ask you as a favor, because you did us a bad turn about Degumber."

I led from the press-room to the stifling office with the maps on the walls, and the red-haired man rubbed his hands. "That's something like," said he. "This was the proper shop to come to. Now, sir, let me introduce to you Brother Peachey Carnehan, that's him, and Brother Daniel Dravot, that is me, and the less said about our professions the better, for we have been most things in our time. Soldier, sailor, compositor, photographer, proofreader, street preacher, and correspondents of the *Backwoodsman* when we thought the paper wanted one. Carnehan is sober, and so am I. Look at us first and see that's sure. It will save you cutting into my talk. We'll take one of your cigars apiece, and you shall see us light it."

I watched the test. The men were absolutely sober, so I gave them each a tepid peg.

"Well *and* good," said Carnehan of the eyebrows, wiping the froth from his mustache. "Let me talk now, Dan. We have been all over India, mostly on foot. We have been boiler-fitters, engine-drivers, petty contractors, and all that, and we have decided that India isn't big enough for such as us."

They certainly were too big for the office. Dravot's beard seemed to fill half the room and Carnehan's shoulders the other half, as they sat on the big table. Carnehan continued: "The country isn't half worked out because they that governs it won't let you touch it. They spend all their blessed time in governing it, and you can't lift a spade, nor chip a rock, nor look for oil, nor anything like that without all the Government saying: 'Leave it alone and let us govern.' Therefore, such as it is, we will let it alone, and go away to some other place where a man isn't crowded and can come to his own. We are not little men, and there is nothing that we are afraid of except Drink, and we have signed a Contrack on that. Therefore, we are going away to be Kings."

"Kings in our own right," muttered Dravot.

"Yes, of course," I said. "You've been tramping in the sun, and it's a very warm night, and hadn't you better sleep over the notion? Come to-morrow."

"Neither drunk nor sunstruck," said Dravot. "We have slept over the notion half a year, and require to see Books and Atlases, and we have decided that there is only one place now in the world that two strong men can Sar-a-whack. They call it Kafiristan. By my reckoning it's the top right-hand corner of Afghanistan, not more than three hundred miles from Peshawar. They have two-and-thirty heathen idols there, and we'll be the thirty-third and fourth. It's a mountaineous country, and the women of those parts are very beautiful."

"But that is provided against in the Contrack," said Carnehan. "Neither Woman nor Liqu-or, Daniel."

"And that's all we know, except that no one has gone there, and they fight, and in any place where they fight a man who knows how to drill men can always be a King. We shall go to those parts and say to any King we find: 'D'you want to vanquish your foes?' and we will show him how to drill men; for that we know better than anything else. Then we will subvert that King and seize his Throne and establish a Dy-nasty."

"You'll be cut to pieces before you're fifty miles across the Border," I said. "You have to travel through Afghanistan to get to that country. It's one mass of mountains and peaks and glaciers, and no Englishman has been through it. The people are utter brutes, and even if you reached them you couldn't do anything."

"That's more like," said Carnehan. "If you could think us a little more mad we would be more pleased. We have come to you to know about this country, to read a book about it, and to be shown maps. We want you to tell us that we are fools and to show us your books."

He turned to the bookcases.

"Are you at all in earnest?" I said.

"A little," said Dravot sweetly. "As big a map as you have got, even if it's all blank where Kafiristan is, and any books you've got. We can read, though we aren't very educated."

I uncased the big thirty-two-miles-to-the-inch map of India, and two smaller Frontier maps, hauled down volume INF-KAN of the *Encyclopædia Britannica*, and the men consulted them.

"See here!" said Dravot, his thumb on the map. "Up to Jagdallak, Peachey and me know the road. We was there with Roberts's Army. We'll have to turn off to the right at Jagdallak through Laghmann territory. Then we get among the hills—fourteen thousand feet—fifteen thousand—it will be cold work there, but it don't look very far on the map."

I handed him Wood on the *Sources of the Oxus*. Carnehan was deep in the *Encyclopædia*.

"They're a mixed lot," said Dravot reflectively; "and it won't help us to know the names of their tribes. The more tribes the more they'll fight, and the better for us. From Jagdallak to Ashang. H'mm!"

"But all the information about the country is as sketchy and inaccurate as can be," I protested. "No one knows anything about it really. Here's the file of the *United Services' Institute*. Read what Bellew says."

"Blow Bellew!" said Carnehan. "Dan, they're an all-fired lot of heathens, but this book here says they think they're related to us English."

I smoked while the men pored over Raverty, Wood, the maps and the *Encyclopædia*.

"There is no use your waiting," said Dravot politely. "It's about four o'clock now. We'll go before six o'clock if you want to sleep, and we won't steal any of the papers. Don't you sit up. We're two harmless lunatics, and if you come to-morrow evening down to the Serai we'll say good-bye to you."

"You are two fools," I answered. "You'll be turned back at the Frontier or cut up the minute you set foot in Afghanistan. Do you want any money or a recommendation down-country? I can help you to the chance of work next week."

"Next week we shall be hard at work ourselves, thank you," said Dravot. "It isn't so easy being a King as it looks. When we've got our Kingdom in going order we'll let you know, and you can come up and help us to govern it."

"Would two lunatics make a Contrack like that?" said Carnehan, with subdued pride, showing me a greasy half-sheet of notepaper on which was written the following. I copied it, then and there, as a curiosity:

This Contract between me and you persuing witnesseth in the name of God—Amen and so forth.
(One)      That me and you will settle this matter together: i.e., to be Kings of Kafiristan.
(Two)      That you and me will not, while this matter is being settled, look at any Liquor, nor any Woman black, white or brown, so as to get mixed up with one or the other harmful.

(Three)    That we conduct ourselves with dignity and discretion, and if one of us gets into trouble the
other will stay by him.

Signed by you and me this day.

Peachey Taliaferro Carnehan.

Daniel Dravot.

Both Gentlemen at Large.

"There was no need for the last article," said Carnehan, blush-ing modestly; "but it looks regular. Now you know the sort of men that loafers are—we are loafers, Dan, until we get out of India—and do you think that we would sign a Contrack like that unless we was in earnest? We have kept away from the two things that make life worth having."

"You won't enjoy your lives much longer if you are going to try this idiotic adventure. Don't set the office on fire," I said, "and go away before nine o'clock."

I left them still poring over the maps and making notes on the back of the "Contrack." "Be sure to come down to the Serai to-morrow," were their parting words.

The Kumharsen Serai is the great four-square sink of humanity where the strings of camels and horses from the North load and unload. All the nationalities of Central Asia may be found there, and most of the folk of India proper. Balkh and Bokhara there meet Bengal and Bombay, and try to draw eye-teeth. You can buy ponies, turquoises, Persian pussy-cats, saddle-bags, fat-tailed sheep and musk in the Kumharsen Serai, and get many strange things for nothing. In the afternoon I went down there to see whether my friends intended to keep their word or were lying about drunk.

A priest attired in fragments of ribbons and rags stalked up to me, gravely twisting a child's paper whirligig. Behind him was his servant bending under the load of a crate of mud toys. The two were loading up two camels, and the inhabitants of the Serai watched them with shrieks of laughter.

"The priest is mad," said a horse-dealer to me. "He is going up to Kabul to sell toys to the Amir. He will either be raised to honor or have his head cut off. He came in here this morning and has been behaving madly ever since."

"The witless are under the protection of God," stammered a flat-cheeked Usbeg in broken Hindi. "They foretell future events."

"Would they could have foretold that my caravan would have been cut up by the Shinwaris almost within shadow of the Pass!" grunted the Eusufzai agent of a Rajputana trading-house whose goods had been feloniously diverted into the hands of other robbers just across the Border, and whose misfortunes were the laughing-stock of the bazar. "Ohé, priest, whence come you and whither do you go?"

"From Roum have I come," shouted the priest, waving his whirligig; "from Roum, blown by the breath of a hundred devils across the sea! O thieves, robbers, liars, the blessing of Pir Khan on pigs, dogs and perjurers! Who will take the Protected of God to the North to sell charms that are never still to the Amir? The camels shall not gall, the sons shall not fall sick, and the wives shall remain faithful while they are away, of the men who give me place in their caravan. Who will assist me to slipper the King of the Roos with a golden slipper with a silver heel? The protection of Pir Khan be upon his labors!" He spread out the skirts of his gaberdine and pirouetted between the lines of tethered horses.

"There starts a caravan from Peshawar to Kabul in twenty days, *Huzrut,*" said the Eusufzai trader. "My camels go therewith. Do thou also go and bring us good-luck."

"I will go even now!" shouted the priest. "I will depart upon my winged camels, and be at Peshawar in a day! Ho! Hazar Mir Khan," he yelled to his servant, "drive out the camels, but let me first mount my own."

He leaped on the back of his beast as it knelt, and, turning round to me, cried: "Come thou also, Sahib, a little along the road, and I will sell thee a charm—an amulet that shall make thee King of Kafiristan."

Then the light broke upon me, and I followed the two camels out of the Serai till we reached open road and the priest halted.

"What d'you think o' that?" said he in English. "Carnehan can't talk their patter, so I've made him my servant. He makes a handsome servant. 'Tisn't for nothing that I've been knocking about the country for fourteen years. Didn't I do that talk neat? We'll hitch on to a caravan at Peshawar till we get to Jagdallak, and then we'll see if we can get donkeys for our camels, and strike into Kafiristan. Whirligigs for the Amir, O Lor! Put your hand under the camel-bags and tell me what you feel."

I felt the butt of a Martini, and another and another.

"Twenty of 'em," said Dravot placidly. "Twenty of 'em, and ammunition to correspond, under the whirligigs and the mud dolls."

"Heaven help you if you are caught with those things!" I said. "A Martini is worth her weight in silver among the Pathans."

"Fifteen hundred rupees of capital—every rupee we could beg, borrow, or steal—are invested on these two camels," said Dravot. "We won't get caught. We're going through the Khaiber with a regular caravan. Who'd touch a poor mad priest?"

"Have you got everything you want?" I asked, overcome with astonishment.

"Not yet, but we shall soon. Give us a memento of your kindness, *Brother*. You did me a service yesterday, and that time in Marwar. Half my Kingdom shall you have, as the saying is." I slipped a small charm compass from my watch-chain and handed it up to the priest.

"Good-bye," said Dravot, giving me his hand cautiously. "It's the last time we'll shake hands with an Englishman these many days. Shake hands with him, Carnehan," he cried, as the second camel passed me.

Carnehan leaned down and shook hands. Then the camels

passed away along the dusty road, and I was left alone to wonder. My eye could detect no failure in the disguises. The scene in the Serai attested that they were complete to the native mind. There was just the chance, therefore, that Carnehan and Dravot would be able to wander through Afghanistan without detection. But, beyond, they would find death, certain and awful death.

Ten days later a native friend of mine, giving me the news of the day from Peshawar, wound up his letter with: "There has been much laughter here on account of a certain mad priest who is going in his estimation to sell petty gauds and insignificant trinkets which he ascribes as great charms to H. H. the Amir of Bokhara. He passed through Peshawar and associated himself to the Second Summer caravan that goes to Kabul. The merchants are pleased because through superstition they imagine that such mad fellows bring good fortune."

The two, then, were beyond the Border. I would have prayed for them, but that night a real King died in Europe, and demanded an obituary notice.

.    .    .    .    .    .    .

The wheel of the world swings through the same phases again and again. Summer passed and winter thereafter, and came and passed again. The daily paper continued and I with it, and upon the third summer there fell a hot night, a night-issue, and a strained waiting for something to be telegraphed from the other side of the world, exactly as had happened before. A few great men had died in the past two years, the machines worked with more clatter, and some of the trees in the Office garden were a few feet taller. But that was all the difference.

I passed over to the press-room, and went through just such a scene as I have already described. The nervous tension was stronger than it had been two years before, and I felt the heat more acutely. At three o'clock I cried "Print off," and turned to go, when there crept to my chair what was left of a man. He was bent into a circle, his head was sunk between his shoulders, and he moved his feet one over the other like a bear. I could hardly see whether he walked or crawled—this rag-wrapped, whining cripple who addressed me by name, crying that he was come back. "Can you give me a drink?" he whimpered. "For the Lord's sake, give me a drink!"

I went back to the office, the man following with groans of pain, and I turned up the lamp.

"Don't you know me?" he gasped, dropping into a chair, and he turned his drawn face, surmounted by a shock of gray hair, to the light.

I looked at him intently. Once before had I seen eyebrows that met over the nose in an inch-broad black band, but for the life of me I could not tell where.

"I don't know you," I said, handing him the whisky. "What can I do for you?"

He took a gulp of the spirit raw, and shivered in spite of the suffocating heat.

"I've come back," he repeated; "and I was the King of Kafiristan—me and Dravot—crowned Kings we was! In this office we settled it—you setting there and giving us the books. I am Peachey—Peachey Taliaferro Carnehan, and you've been setting here ever since—O Lord!"

I was more than a little astonished and expressed my feelings accordingly.

"It's true," said Carnehan, with a dry cackle, nursing his feet, which were wrapped in rags. "True as gospel. Kings we were, with crowns upon our heads—me and Dravot—poor Dan—oh, poor, poor Dan, that would never take advice, not though I begged of him!"

"Take the whisky," I said, "and take your own time. Tell me all you can recollect of everything from beginning to end. You got across the Border on your camels, Dravot dressed as a mad priest, and you his servant. Do you remember that?"

"I ain't mad—yet, but I shall be that way soon. Of course I

remember. Keep looking at me, or maybe my words will go all to pieces. Keep looking at me in my eyes and don't say anything."

I leaned forward and looked into his face as steadily as I could. He dropped one hand upon the table and I grasped it by the wrist. It was twisted like a bird's claw, and upon the back was a ragged, red, diamond-shaped scar.

"No, don't look there. Look at me," said Carnehan. "That comes afterwards, but for the Lord's sake don't distrack me. We left with that caravan, me and Dravot playing all sorts of antics to amuse the people we were with. Dravot used to make us laugh in the evening when all the people was cooking their dinners— cooking their dinners, and . . . what did they do then? They lit little fires with sparks that went into Dravot's beard, and we all laughed—fit to die. Little red fires they was, going into Dravot's big red beard—so funny." His eyes left mine and he smiled foolishly.

"You went as far as Jagdallak with that caravan," I said at a venture, "after you had lit those fires. To Jagdallak, where you turned off to try to get into Kafiristan."

"No, we didn't neither. What are you talking about? We turned off before Jagdallak, because we heard the roads was good. But they wasn't good enough for our two camels—mine and Dravot's. When we left the caravan Dravot took off all his clothes and mine too, and said we would be heathen, because the Kafirs didn't allow Mohammedans to talk to them. So we dressed betwixt and between, and such a sight as Daniel Dravot I never saw yet nor expect to see again. He burned half his beard, and slung a sheepskin over his shoulder, and shaved his head into patterns. He shaved mine, too, and made me wear outrageous things to look like a heathen. That was in a most mountaineous country, and our camels couldn't go along any more because of the mountains. They were tall and black, and coming home I saw them fight like wild goats—there are lots of goats in Kafiristan. And these mountains, they never keep still, no more than the goats. Always fighting they are, and don't let you sleep at night."

"Take some more whisky," I said very slowly. "What did you and Daniel Dravot do when the camels could go no further because of the rough roads that led into Kafiristan?"

"What did which do? There was a party called Peachey Taliaferro Carnehan that was with Dravot. Shall I tell you about him? He died out there in the cold. Slap from the bridge fell old Peachey, turning and twisting in the air like a penny whirligig that you can sell to the Amir.—No; they was two for three ha'-pence, those whirligigs, or I am much mistaken and woful sore. And then these camels were no use, and Peachey said to Dravot: 'For the Lord's sake, let's get out of this before our heads are chopped off,' and with that they killed the camels all among the mountains, not having anything in particular to eat, but first they took off the boxes with the guns and the ammunition, till two men came along driving four mules. Dravot up and dances in front of them, singing: 'Sell me four mules.' Says the first man: 'If you are rich enough to buy you are rich enough to rob'; but before ever he could put his hand to his knife Dravot breaks his neck over his knee, and the other party runs away. So Carnehan loaded the mules with the rifles that was taken off the camels, and together we starts forward into those bitter cold mountaineous parts, and never a road broader than the back of your hand."

He paused for a moment, while I asked him if he could remember the nature of the country through which he had journeyed.

"I am telling you as straight as I can, but my head isn't as good as it might be. They drove nails through it to make me hear better how Dravot died. The country was mountaineous and the mules were most contrary, and the inhabitants was dispersed and solitary. They went up and up, and down and down, and that other party, Carnehan, was imploring of Dravot not to sing and whistle so loud, for fear of bringing down the tremenjus avalanches. But Dravot says that if a King couldn't sing it wasn't worth being King, and whacked the mules over the rump, and never took no heed for ten cold days. We came to a big level valley all among the mountains, and the mules were near dead, so we killed them, not having anything in special for them or us to eat. We sat upon the boxes, and played odd and even with the cartridges that was jolted out.

"Then ten men with bows and arrows ran down that valley chasing twenty men with bows and arrows, and the row was tremenjus. They was fair men—fairer than you or me—with yellow hair and remarkable well built. Says Dravot, unpacking the guns: 'This is the beginning of the business. We'll fight for the ten men,' and with that he fires two rifles at the twenty men, and drops one of them at two hundred yards from the rock where we was sitting. The other men began to run, but Carnehan and Dravot sits on the boxes picking them off at all ranges, up and down the valley. Then we goes up to the ten men that had run across the snow, too, and they fires a footy little arrow at us. Dravot he shoots above their heads and they all falls down flat. Then he walks over them and kicks them, and then he lifts them up and shakes hands all round to make them friendly like. He calls them and gives them the boxes to carry, and waves his hand for all the world as though he was King already. They take the boxes and him across the valley and up the hill into a pine wood on the top, where there was half a dozen big stone idols. Dravot he goes to the biggest—a fellow they call Imbra—and lays a rifle and a cartridge at his feet, rubbing his nose respectful with his own nose, patting him on the head, and saluting in front of it. He turns round to the men and nods his head, and says, 'That's all right. I'm in the know, too, and all these old jim-jams are my friends.' Then he opens his mouth and points down it, and when the first man brings him food, he says—'No'; and when the second man brings him food, he says—'No'; but when one of the old priests and the boss of the village brings him food, he says—'Yes,' very haughty, and eats it slow. That was how we came to our first village, without any trouble, just as though we had tumbled from the skies. But we tumbled from one of those damned rope-bridges, you see, and you couldn't expect a man to laugh much after that."

"Take some more whisky and go on," I said. "That was the first village you came into. How did you get to be King?"

"I wasn't King," said Carnehan. "Dravot he was the King, and a handsome man he looked with the gold crown on his head and all. Him and the other party stayed in that village, and every morning Dravot sat by the side of old Imbra, and the people came and worshipped. That was Dravot's order. Then a lot of men came into the valley, and Carnehan and Dravot picks them off with the rifles before they knew where they was, and runs down into the valley and up again the other side, and finds another village, same as the first one, and the people all falls down flat on their faces, and Dravot says, 'Now what is the trouble between you two villages?' and the people points to a woman, as fair as you or me, that was carried off, and Dravot takes her back to the first village and counts up the dead—eight there was. For each dead man Dravot pours a little milk on the ground and waves his arms like a whirligig and 'That's all right,' says he. Then he and Carnehan takes the big boss of each village by the arm and walks them down into the valley, and shows them how to scratch a line with a spear right down the valley, and gives each a sod of turf from both sides o' the line. Then all the people comes down and shouts like the Devil and all, and Dravot says, 'Go and dig the land, and be fruitful and multiply,' which they did, though they didn't understand. Then we asks the names of things in their lingo—bread and water and fire and idols and such, and Dravot leads the priest of each village up to the idol, and says he must sit there and judge the people, and if anything goes wrong he is to be shot.

"Next week they was all turning up the land in the valley as quiet as bees and much prettier, and the priests heard all the complaints and told Dravot in dumb show what it was about.

'That's just the beginning,' says Dravot. 'They think we're Gods.'
He and Carnehan picks out twenty good men and shows them
how to click off a rifle and form fours, and advance in line, and
they was very pleased to do so, and clever to see the hang of it.
Then he takes out his pipe and his baccy-pouch and leaves one
at one village and one at the other, and off we two goes to see
what was to be done in the next valley. That was all rock, and
there was a little village there, and Carnehan says,—'Send 'em
to the old valley to plant,' and takes 'em there and gives 'em
some land that wasn't took before. They were a poor lot, and we
blooded 'em with a kid before letting 'em into the new Kingdom.
That was to impress the people, and then they settled down
quiet, and Carnehan went back to Dravot, who had got into
another valley all snow and ice and most mountaineous. There
was no people there and the Army got afraid, so Dravot shoots
one of them, and goes on till he finds some people in a village,
and the Army explains that unless the people wants to be killed
they had better not shoot their little matchlocks; for they had
matchlocks. We makes friends with the priest and I stays there
alone with two of the Army, teaching the men how to drill, and
a thundering big Chief comes across the snow with kettle-drums
and horns twanging, because he heard there was a new God kicking about. Carnehan sights for the brown of the men half a mile
across the snow and wings one of them. Then he sends a message
to the Chief that, unless he wished to be killed, he must come
and shake hands with me and leave his arms behind. The Chief
comes alone first, and Carnehan shakes hands with him and whirls
his arms about same as Dravot used, and very much surprised
that Chief was, and strokes my eyebrows. Then Carnehan goes
alone to the Chief and asks him in dumb show if he had an
enemy he hated. 'I have,' says the Chief. So Carnehan weeds out
the pick of his men, and sets the two of the Army to show them
drill and at the end of two weeks the men can manœuvre about
as well as Volunteers. So he marches with the Chief to a great

big plain on the top of a mountain, and the Chief's men rushes into a village and takes it; we three Martinis firing into the brown of the enemy. So we took that village too, and I gives the Chief a rag from my coat, and says, 'Occupy till I come,' which was scriptural. By way of a reminder, when me and the Army was eighteen hundred yards away, I drops a bullet near him standing on the snow, and all the people falls flat on their faces. Then I sends a letter to Dravot, wherever he be by land or by sea."

At the risk of throwing the creature out of train I interrupted, "How could you write a letter up yonder?"

"The letter? Oh! The letter! Keep looking at me between the eyes, please. It was a string-talk letter, that we'd learned the way of it from a blind beggar in the Punjab."

I remembered that there had once come to the office a blind man with a knotted twig and a piece of string which he wound round the twig according to some cipher of his own. He could, after the lapse of days or hours, repeat the sentence which he had reeled up. He had reduced the alphabet to eleven primitive sounds; and tried to teach me his method, but failed.

"I sent that letter to Dravot," said Carnehan; "and told him to come back because this Kingdom was growing too big for me to handle, and then I struck for the first valley, to see how the priests were working. They called the village we took along with the Chief, Bashkai, and the first village we took Er-Heb. The priests at Er-Heb was doing all right, but they had a lot of pending cases about land to show me, and some men from another village had been firing arrows at night. I went out and looked for that village and fired four rounds at it from a thousand yards. That used all the cartridges I cared to spend, and I waited for Dravot, who had been away two or three months, and I kept my people quiet.

"One morning I heard the devil's own noise of drums and horns, and Dan Dravot marches down the hill with his Army and a tail of hundreds of men, and, which was the most amazing—a great gold crown on his head. 'My Gord, Carnehan,' says Daniel, 'this is a tremenjus business, and we've got the whole country as far as it's worth having. I am the son of Alexander by Queen Semiramis, and you're my younger brother and a God too! It's the biggest thing we've ever seen. I've been marching and fighting for six weeks with the Army, and every footy little village for fifty miles has come in rejoiceful; and more than that, I've got the key of the whole show, as you'll see, and I've got a crown for you! I told 'em to make two of 'em at a place called Shu, where the gold lies in the rock like suet in mutton. Gold I've seen, and turquoise I've kicked out of the cliffs, and there's garnets in the sands of the river, and here's a chunk of amber that a man brought me. Call up all the priests and, here, take your crown.'

"One of the men opens a black hair bag and I slips the crown on. It was too small and too heavy, but I wore it for the glory. Hammered gold it was—five-pound weight, like a hoop of a barrel.

" 'Peachey,' says Dravot, 'we don't want to fight no more. The Craft's the trick, so help me!' and he brings forward that same Chief that I left at Bashkai—Billy Fish we called him afterwards, because he was so like Billy Fish that drove the big tank-engine at Mach on the Bolan in the old days. 'Shake hands with him,' says Dravot, and I shook hands and nearly dropped, for Billy Fish gave me the Grip. I said nothing, but tried him with the Fellow Craft Grip. He answers all right, and I tried the Master's Grip, but that was a slip. 'A Fellow Craft he is!' I says to Dan. 'Does he know the word?' 'He does,' says Dan, 'and all the priests know. It's a miracle! The Chiefs and the priests can work a Fellow Craft Lodge in a way that's very like ours, and they've cut the marks on the rocks, but they don't know the Third Degree, and they've come to find out. It's Gord's Truth. I've known these long years that the Afghans knew up to the Fellow Craft Degree, but this is a miracle. A God and a Grand-Master of the Craft am I, and a Lodge in the Third Degree I will open, and we'll raise the head priests and the Chiefs of the villages.'

" 'It's against all the law,' I says, 'holding a Lodge without warrant from any one; and we never held office in any Lodge.'

" 'It's a master-stroke of policy,' says Dravot. 'It means running the country as easy as a four-wheeled bogy on a down grade. We can't stop to inquire now, or they'll turn against us. I've forty Chiefs at my heel, and passed and raised according to their merit they shall be. Billet these men on the villages, and see that we run up a Lodge of some kind. The temple of Imbra will do for the Lodge room. The women must make aprons as you show them. I'll hold a levee of Chiefs to-night and Lodge to-morrow.'

"I was fair run off my legs, but I wasn't such a fool as not to see what a pull this Craft business gave us. I showed the priests' families how to make aprons of the degrees, but for Dravot's apron the blue border and marks was made of turquoise lumps on white hide, not cloth. We took a great square stone in the temple for the Master's chair, and little stones for the officers' chairs, and painted the black pavement with white squares, and did what we could to make things regular.

"At the levee which was held that night on the hillside with big bonfires, Dravot gives out that him and me were Gods and sons of Alexander, and Past Grand-Masters in the Craft, and was come to make Kafiristan a country where every man should eat in peace and drink in quiet, and specially obey us. Then the Chiefs come round to shake hands, and they was so hairy and white and fair it was just shaking hands with old friends. We gave them names according as they were like men we had known in India— Billy Fish, Holly Dilworth, Pikky Kergan that was Bazar-master when I was at Mhow, and so on and so on.

"The most amazing miracle was at Lodge next night. One of the old priests was watching us continuous, and I felt uneasy, for I knew we'd have to fudge the Ritual, and I didn't know what the men knew. The old priest was a stranger come in from beyond the village of Bashkai. The minute Dravot puts on the Master's apron that the girls had made for him, the priest fetches a whoop

and a howl, and tries to overturn the stone that Dravot was sitting on. 'It's all up now,' I says. 'That comes of meddling with
the Craft without warrant!' Dravot never winked an eye, not when
ten priests took and tilted over the Grand-Master's chair—which
was to say the stone of Imbra. The priest begins rubbing the
bottom of it to clear away the black dirt, and presently he shows
all the other priests the Master's Mark, same as was on Dravot's
apron, cut into the stone. Not even the priests of the temple of
Imbra knew it was there. The old chap falls flat on his face at
Dravot's feet and kisses 'em. 'Luck again,' says Dravot, across the
Lodge to me, 'they say it's the missing Mark that no one could
understand the why of. We're more than safe now.' Then he bangs
the butt of his gun for a gavel and says: 'By virtue of the authority vested in me by my own right hand and the help of Peachey,
I declare myself Grand-Master of all Freemasonry in Kafiristan in
this the Mother Lodge o' the country, and King of Kafiristan
equally with Peachey!' At that he puts on his crown and I puts
on mine—I was doing Senior Warden—and we opens the Lodge
in most ample form. It was an amazing miracle! The priests moved
in Lodge through the first two degrees almost without telling, as
if the memory was coming back to them. After that Peachey and
Dravot raised such as was worthy—high priests and Chiefs of far-
off villages. Billy Fish was the first, and I can tell you we scared
the soul out of him. It was not in any way according to Ritual,
but it served our turn. We didn't raise more than ten of the biggest men because we didn't want to make the Degree common.
And they was clamoring to be raised.

" 'In another six months,' says Dravot, 'we'll hold another Communication and see how you are working.' Then he asks them
about their villages, and learns that they was fighting one against
the other and were fair sick and tired of it. And when they wasn't
doing that they was fighting with the Mohammedans. 'You can
fight those when they come into our country,' says Dravot. 'Tell
off every tenth man of your tribes for a Frontier guard, and send

two hundred at a time to this valley to be drilled. Nobody is going to be shot or speared any more so long as he does well, and I know that you won't cheat me because you're white people— sons of Alexander—and not like common, black Mohammedans. You are *my* people, and by God,' says he, running off into English at the end—'I'll make a damned fine Nation of you, or I'll die in the making!'

"I can't tell all we did for the next six months, because Dravot did a lot I couldn't see the hang of, and he learned their lingo in a way I never could. My work was to help the people plough, and now and again go out with some of the Army and see what the other villages were doing, and make 'em throw rope bridges across the ravines which cut up the country horrid. Dravot was very kind to me, but when he walked up and down in the pine wood pulling that bloody red beard of his with both fists I knew he was thinking plans I could not advise him about and I just waited for orders.

"But Dravot never showed me disrespect before the people. They were afraid of me and the Army, but they loved Dan. He was the best of friends with the priests and the Chiefs; but any one could come across the hills with a complaint and Dravot would hear him out fair, and call four priests together and say what was to be done. He used to call in Billy Fish from Bashkai and Pikky Kergan from Shu, and an old Chief we called Kafuze-lum—it was like enough to his real name—and held councils with 'em when there was any fighting to be done in small villages. That was his Council of War, and the four priests of Bashkai, Shu, Khawak and Madora was his Privy Council. Between the lot of 'em they sent me, with forty men and twenty rifles, and sixty men carrying turquoises, into the Ghorband country to buy those hand-made Martini rifles that come out of the Amir's workshops at Kabul, from one of the Amir's Herati regiments that would have sold the very teeth out of their mouths for turquoises.

"I stayed in Ghorband a month, and gave the Governor there

the pick of my baskets for hush-money, and bribed the Colonel of the regiment some more, and between the two and the tribes-people, we got more than a hundred hand-made Martinis, a hundred good Kohat Jezails that'll throw to six hundred yards, and forty man-loads of very bad ammunition for the rifles. I came back with what I had, and distributed 'em among the men that the Chiefs sent in to me to drill. Dravot was too busy to attend to those things, but the old Army that we first made helped me, and we turned out five hundred men that could drill, and two hundred that knew how to hold arms pretty straight. Even those cork-screwed, hand-made guns was a miracle to them. Dravot talked big about powder-shops and factories, walking up and down in the pine wood when the winter was coming on.

" 'I won't make a Nation,' says he. 'I'll make an Empire! These men aren't niggers; they're English! Look at their eyes—look at their mouths. Look at the way they stand up. They sit on chairs in their own houses. They're the Lost Tribes, or something like it, and they've grown to be English. I'll take a census in the spring if the priests don't get frightened. There must be fair two million of 'em in these hills. The villages are full o' little children. Two million people—two hundred and fifty thousand fighting men—and all English! They only want the rifles and a little drilling. Two hundred and fifty thousand men, ready to cut in on Russia's right flank when she tries for India! Peachey, man,' he says, chewing his beard in great hunks, 'we shall be Emperors—Emperors of the Earth! Rajah Brooke will be a suckling to us. I'll treat with the Viceroy on equal terms. I'll ask him to send me twelve picked English—twelve that I know of—to help us govern a bit. There's Mackray, Sergeant-pensioner at Segowli—many's the good dinner he's given me, and his wife a pair of trousers. There's Donkin, the Warder of Tounghoo Jail; there's hundreds that I could lay my hands on if I was in India. The Viceroy shall do it for me. I'll send a man through in the spring for those men, and I'll write for a dispensation from the Grand Lodge for what I've done as

Grand-Master. That—and all the Sniders that'll be thrown out when the native troops in India take up the Martini. They'll be worn smooth, but they'll do for fighting in these hills. Twelve English, a hundred thousand Sniders run through the Amir's country in driblets—I'd be content with twenty thousand in one year—and we'd be an Empire. When everything was shipshape, I'd hand over the crown—this crown I'm wearing now—to Queen Victoria on my knees, and she'd say: "Rise up, Sir Daniel Dravot." Oh, it's big! It's big, I tell you! But there's so much to be done in every place—Bashkai, Khawak, Shu, and everywhere else.'

" 'What is it?' I says. 'There are no more men coming in to be drilled this autumn. Look at those fat, black clouds. They're bringing the snow.'

" 'It isn't that,' says Daniel, putting his hand very hard on my shoulder; 'and I don't wish to say anything that's against you, for no other living man would have followed me and made me what I am as you have done. You're a first-class Commander-in-Chief, and the people know you; but—it's a big country, and somehow you can't help me, Peachey, in the way I want to be helped.'

" 'Go to your blasted priests, then!' I said, and I was sorry when I made that remark, but it did hurt me sore to find Daniel talking so superior when I'd drilled all the men, and done all he told me.

" 'Don't let's quarrel, Peachey,' says Daniel without cursing. 'You're a King too, and the half of this Kingdom is yours; but can't you see, Peachey, we want cleverer men than us now—three or four of 'em, that we can scatter about for our Deputies. It's a huge great State, and I can't always tell the right thing to do, and I haven't time for all I want to do, and here's the winter coming on and all.' He put half his beard into his mouth, and it was as red as the gold of his crown.

" 'I'm sorry, Daniel,' says I. 'I've done all I could. I've drilled the men and shown the people how to stack their oats better; and I've brought in those tinware rifles from Ghorband—but I know what you're driving at. I take it Kings always feel oppressed that way.'

" 'There's another thing, too,' says Dravot, walking up and down. 'The winter's coming and these people won't be giving much trouble, and if they do we can't move about. I want a wife.'

" 'For Gord's sake leave the women alone!' I says. 'We've both got all the work we can, though I am a fool. Remember the Contrack and keep clear o' women.'

" 'The Contrack only lasted till such time as we was Kings; and Kings we have been these months past,' says Dravot, weighing his crown in his hand. 'You go get a wife too, Peachey, a nice, strappin', plump girl that'll keep you warm in the winter. They're prettier than English girls, and we can take the pick of 'em. Boil 'em once or twice in hot water, and they'll come as fair as chicken and ham.'

" 'Don't tempt me!' I says. 'I will not have any dealings with a woman, not till we are a dam' sight more settled than we are now. I've been doing the work o' two men, and you've been doing the work o' three. Let's lie off a bit, and see if we can get some better tobacco from Afghan country and run in some good liquor; but no women.'

" 'Who's talking o' women?' says Dravot. 'I said wife—a Queen to breed a King's son for the King. A Queen out of the strongest tribe, that'll make them your blood-brothers, and that'll lie by your side and tell you all the people thinks about you and their own affairs. That's what I want.'

" 'Do you remember that Bengali woman I kept at Mogul Serai when I was a plate layer?' says I. 'A fat lot o' good she was to me. She taught me the lingo and one or two other things; but what happened? She ran away with the Station Master's servant and half my month's pay. Then she turned up at Dadur Junction in tow of a half-caste, and had the impidence to say I was her husband— all among the drivers in the running-shed!'

" 'We've done with that,' says Dravot. 'These women are whiter than you or me, and a Queen I will have for the winter months.'

" 'For the last time o' asking, Dan, do *not*,' I says. 'It'll only bring us harm. The Bible says that Kings ain't to waste their strength on women, 'specially when they've got a new raw Kingdom to work over.'

" 'For the last time of answering I will,' says Dravot, and he went away through the pine-trees looking like a big red devil. The low sun hit his crown and beard on one side, and the two blazed like hot coals.

"But getting a wife was not as easy as Dan thought. He put it before the Council, and there was no answer till Billy Fish said that he'd better ask the girls. Dravot damned them all round. 'What's wrong with me?' he shouts, standing by the idol Imbra. 'Am I a dog or am I not enough of a man for your wenches? Haven't I put the shadow of my hand over this country? Who stopped the last Afghan raid?' It was me really, but Dravot was too angry to remember. 'Who bought your guns? Who repaired the bridges? Who's the Grand-Master of the sign cut in the stone?' and he thumped his hand on the block that he used to sit on in Lodge, and at Council, which opened like Lodge always. Billy Fish said nothing and no more did the others. 'Keep your hair on, Dan,' said I, 'and ask the girls. That's how it's done at Home, and these people are quite English.'

" 'The marriage of the King is a matter of State,' says Dan, in a white-hot rage, for he could feel, I hope, that he was going against his better mind. He walked out of the Council room, and the others sat still, looking at the ground.

" 'Billy Fish,' says I to the Chief of the Bashkai, 'what's the difficulty here? A straight answer to a true friend.' 'You know,' says Billy Fish. 'How should a man tell you, who knows everything? How can daughters of men marry Gods or Devils? It's not proper.'

"I remembered something like that in the Bible; but if, after seeing us as long as they had, they still believed we were Gods, it wasn't for me to undeceive them.

" 'A God can do anything,' says I. 'If the King is fond of a girl he'll not let her die.' 'She'll have to,' said Billy Fish. 'There are all sorts of Gods and Devils in these mountains, and now and again a girl marries one of them and isn't seen any more. Besides, you two know the Mark cut in the stone. Only the Gods know that. We thought you were men till you showed the sign of the Master.'

"I wished then that we had explained about the loss of the genuine secrets of a Master-Mason at the first go-off; but I said nothing. All that night there was a blowing of horns in a little dark temple half-way down the hill, and I heard a girl crying fit to die. One of the priests told us that she was being prepared to marry the King.

" 'I'll have no nonsense of that kind,' says Dan. 'I don't want to interfere with your customs, but I'll take my own wife.' 'The girl's a little bit afraid,' says the priest. 'She thinks she's going to die, and they are a-heartening her up down in the temple.'

" 'Hearten her very tender, then,' says Dravot, 'or I'll hearten you with the butt of a gun so that you'll never want to be heartened again.' He licked his lips, did Dan, and stayed up walking about more than half the night, thinking of the wife that he was going to get in the morning. I wasn't any means comfortable, for I knew that dealings with a woman in foreign parts, though you was a crowned King twenty times over, could not but be risky. I got up very early in the morning while Dravot was asleep, and I saw the priests talking together in whispers, and the Chiefs talking together, too, and they looked at me out of the corners of their eyes.

" 'What is up, Fish?' I says to the Bashkai man, who was wrapped up in his furs and looking splendid to behold.

" 'I can't rightly say,' says he; 'but if you can induce the King to drop all this nonsense about marriage you'll be doing him and me and yourself a great service.'

" 'That I do believe,' says I. 'But sure, you know, Billy, as well as me, having fought against and for us, that the King and me are nothing more than two of the finest men that God Almighty ever made. Nothing more, I do assure you.'

" 'That may be,' says Billy Fish, 'and yet I should be sorry if it was.' He sinks his head upon his great fur coat for a minute and thinks. 'King,' says he, 'be you man or God or Devil, I'll stick by you to-day. I have twenty of my men with me, and they will follow me. We'll go to Bashkai until the storm blows over.'

"A little snow had fallen in the night, and everything was white except the greasy fat clouds that blew down and down from the north. Dravot came out with his crown on his head, swinging his arms and stamping his feet, and looking more pleased than Punch.

" 'For the last time drop it, Dan,' says I in a whisper. 'Billy Fish here says that there will be a row.'

" 'A row among my people!' says Dravot. 'Not much. Peachey, you're a fool not to get a wife too. Where's the girl?' says he with a voice as loud as the braying of a jackass. 'Call up all the Chiefs and priests, and let the Emperor see if his wife suits him.'

"There was no need to call any one. They were all there leaning on their guns and spears round the clearing in the centre of the pine wood. A deputation of priests went down to the little temple to bring up the girl, and the horns blew fit to wake the dead. Billy Fish saunters round and gets as close to Daniel as he could, and behind him stood his twenty men with matchlocks. Not a man of them under six feet. I was next to Dravot, and behind me was twenty men of the regular Army. Up comes the girl, and a strapping wench she was, covered with silver and turquoises, but white as death, and looking back every minute at the priests.

" 'She'll do,' said Dan, looking her over. 'What's to be afraid of, lass? Come and kiss me.' He puts his arm round her. She shuts her eyes, gives a bit of a squeak, and down goes her face in the side of Dan's flaming red beard.

" 'The slut's bitten me!' says he, clapping his hand to his neck;

and sure enough his hand was red with blood. Billy Fish and two of his matchlock-men catches hold of Dan by the shoulders and drags him into the Bashkai lot, while the priests howls in their lingo, 'Neither God nor Devil but a man!' I was all taken aback, for a priest cut at me in front, and the Army began firing into the Bashkai men.

"'God A-mighty!' says Dan. 'What is the meaning o' this?'

"'Come back! Come away!' says Billy Fish. 'Ruin and Mutiny is the matter. We'll break for Bashkai if we can.

"I tried to give some sort of orders to my men—the men o' the regular Army—but it was no use, so I fired into the brown of 'em with an English Martini and drilled three beggars in a line. The valley was full of shouting, howling creatures, and every soul was shrieking, 'Not a God nor a Devil but only a man!' The Bashkai troops stuck to Billy Fish all they were worth, but their match-locks wasn't half as good as the Kabul breech-loaders and four of them dropped. Dan was bellowing like a bull, for he was very wrathy; and Billy Fish had a hard job to prevent him running out at the crowd.

"'We can't stand,' says Billy Fish. 'Make a run for it down the valley! The whole place is against us.' The matchlock-men ran, and we went down the valley in spite of Dravot's protestations. He was swearing horribly and crying out that he was a King. The priests rolled great stones on us, and the regular Army fired hard, and there wasn't more than six men, not counting Dan, Billy Fish and Me, that came down to the bottom of the valley alive.

"Then they stopped firing and the horns in the temple blew again. 'Come away—for Gord's sake come away!' says Billy Fish. 'They'll send runners out to all the villages before ever we get to Bashkai. I can protect you there, but I can't do anything now.'

"My own notion is that Dan began to go mad in his head from that hour. He stared up and down like a stuck pig. Then he was all for walking back alone and killing the priests with his bare hands, which he could have done. 'An Emperor am I,' says Daniel, 'and next year I shall be a Knight of the Queen.'

" 'All right, Dan,' says I; 'but come along now while there's time.'

" 'It's your fault,' says he, 'for not looking after your Army better. There was mutiny in the midst, and you didn't know—you damned engine-driving, plate-laying, missionaries'-pass-hunting hound!' He sat upon a rock and called me every foul name he could lay tongue to. I was too heartsick to care, though it was all his foolishness that brought the smash.

" 'I'm sorry, Dan,' says I, 'but there's no accounting for natives. This business is our Fifty-Seven. Maybe we'll make something out of it yet, when we've got back to Bashkai.'

" 'Let's get to Bashkai, then,' says Dan, 'and by God, when I come back here again I'll sweep the valley so there isn't a bug in a blanket left!'

"We walked all that day, and all that night Dan was stumping up and down on the snow, chewing his beard and muttering to himself.

" 'There's no hope o' getting clear,' says Billy Fish. 'The priests will have sent runners to the villages to say that you are only men. Why didn't you stick on as Gods till things was more settled? I'm a dead man,' says Billy Fish, and he throws himself down on the snow and begins to pray to his Gods.

"Next morning we was in a cruel bad country—all up and down, no level ground at all, and no food either. The six Bashkai men looked at Billy Fish hungry-wise as if they wanted to ask something, but they said never a word. At noon we came to the top of a flat mountain all covered with snow, and when we climbed up into it, behold, there was an Army in position waiting in the middle!

" 'The runners have been very quick,' says Billy Fish, with a little bit of a laugh. 'They are waiting for us.'

"Three or four men began to fire from the enemy's side, and a chance shot took Daniel in the calf of the leg. That brought him to his senses. He looks across the snow at the Army, and sees the rifles that we had brought into the country.

" 'We're done for,' says he. 'They are Englishmen, these people—and it's my blasted nonsense that has brought you to this. Get back, Billy Fish, and take your men away; you've done what you could, and not cut for it. Carnehan,' says he, 'shake hands with me and go along with Billy. Maybe they won't kill you. I'll go and meet 'em alone. It's me that did it. Me, the King!'

" 'Go!' says I. 'Go to Hell, Dan. I'm with you here. Billy Fish, you clear out and we two will meet those folk.'

" 'I'm a Chief,' says Billy Fish quite quiet. 'I stay with you. My men can go.'

"The Bashkai fellows didn't wait for a second word but ran off, and Dan and Me and Billy Fish walked across to where the drums were drumming and the horns were horning. It was cold—awful cold. I've got that cold in the back of my head now. There's a lump of it there."

The punkah-coolies had gone to sleep. Two kerosene lamps were blazing in the office, and the perspiration poured down my face and splashed on the blotter as I leaned forward. Carnehan was shivering, and I feared that his mind might go. I wiped my face, took a fresh grip of the piteously mangled hands and said:— "What happened after that?"

The momentary shift of my eyes had broken the clear current.

"What was you pleased to say?" whined Carnehan. "They took them without any sound. Not a little whisper all along the snow, not though the King knocked down the first man that set hand on him—not though old Peachey fired his last cartridge into the brown of 'em. Not a single solitary sound did those swines make. They just closed up tight, and I tell you their furs stunk. There was a man called Billy Fish, a good friend of us all, and they cut his throat, Sir, then and there, like a pig; and the King kicks up the bloody snow and says:—'We've had a dashed fine run for our money. What's coming next?' But Peachey, Peachey Taliaferro, I tell you, Sir, in confidence as betwixt two friends, he lost his head, Sir. No, he didn't either. The King lost his head, so he did, all along o' one of those cunning rope-bridges. Kindly let me have the paper-cutter, Sir. It tilted this way. They marched him a mile across that snow to a rope-bridge over a ravine with a river at the bottom. You may have seen such. They prodded him behind like an ox. 'Damn your eyes!' says the King. 'D'you suppose I can't die like a gentleman?' He turns to Peachey—Peachey that was crying like a child. 'I've brought you to this, Peachey,' says he. 'Brought you out of your happy life to be killed in Kafiristan, where you was late Commander-in-Chief of the Emperor's forces. Say you forgive me, Peachey.' 'I do,' says Peachey. 'Fully and freely do I forgive you, Dan.' 'Shake hands, Peachey,' says he. 'I'm going now.' Out he goes, looking neither right nor left, and when he was plumb in the middle of those dizzy dancing ropes, 'Cut, you beggars,' he shouts; and they cut, and old Dan fell, turning round and round and round, twenty thousand miles, for he took half an hour to fall till he struck the water, and I could see his body caught on a rock with the gold crown close beside.

"But do you know what they did to Peachey between two pine-trees? They crucified him, Sir, as Peachey's hands will show. They used wooden pegs for his hands and his feet; and he didn't die. He hung there and screamed; and they took him down next day and said it was a miracle that he wasn't dead. They took him down —poor old Peachey that hadn't done them any harm—that hadn't done them any . . ."

He rocked to and fro and wept bitterly, wiping his eyes with the back of his scarred hands and moaning like a child for some ten minutes.

"They was cruel enough to feed him up in the temple, because they said he was more of a God than old Daniel that was a man. Then they turned him out on the snow, and told him to go home; and Peachey came home in about a year, begging along the roads quite safe; for Daniel Dravot he walked before and said: 'Come along, Peachey. It's a big thing we're doing.' The mountains they danced at night, and the mountains they tried to fall on Peachey's head, but Dan he held up his hand and Peachey came along bent double. He never let go of Dan's hand, and he never let go of Dan's head. They gave it to him as a present in the temple, to remind him not to come again, and though the crown was pure gold, and Peachey was starving, never would Peachey sell the same. You knew Dravot, Sir! You knew Right Worshipful Brother Dravot! Look at him now!"

He fumbled in the mass of rags round his bent waist; brought out a black horsehair bag embroidered with silver thread; and shook therefrom onto my table—the dried, withered head of Daniel Dravot! The morning sun that had long been paling the lamps struck the red beard and blind, sunken eyes; struck, too, a heavy circlet of gold studded with raw turquoises, that Carnehan placed tenderly on the battered temples.

"You behold now," said Carnehan, "the Emperor in his habit as he lived—the King of Kafiristan with his crown upon his head. Poor old Daniel that was a monarch once!"

I shuddered, for, in spite of defacements manifold, I recognized the head of the man of Marwar Junction. Carnehan rose to go. I attempted to stop him. He was not fit to walk abroad. "Let me take away the whisky and give me a little money," he gasped. "I was a King once. I'll go to the Deputy Commissioner and ask to set in the Poorhouse till I get my health. No, thank you, I can't wait till you get a carriage for me. I've urgent private affairs—in the south—at Marwar."

He shambled out of the office and departed in the direction of the Deputy Commissioner's house. That day at noon I had occasion to go down the blinding hot Mall, and I saw a crooked man crawling along the white dust of the roadside, his hat in his hand, quavering dolorously after the fashion of street-singers at Home. There was not a soul in sight, and he was out of all possible earshot of the houses. And he sang through his nose, turning his head from right to left:

> "The Son of Man goes forth to war,
>   A golden crown to gain:
> His blood-red banner streams afar—
>   Who follows in his train?"

I waited to hear no more, but put the poor wretch into my carriage and drove him off to the nearest missionary for eventual transfer to the Asylum. He repeated the hymn twice while he was with me, whom he did not in the least recognize, and I left him singing it to the missionary.

Two days later I inquired after his welfare of the Superintendent of the Asylum.

"He was admitted suffering from sunstroke. He died early yesterday morning," said the Superintendent. "Is it true that he was half an hour bareheaded in the sun at midday?"

"Yes," said I; "but do you happen to know if he had anything upon him by any chance when he died?"

"Not to my knowledge," said the Superintendent.

And there the matter rests.

1. Why is the story teller a newspaper man?
2. Rudyard Kipling gave the Western world its most vivid pictures of India; what does the reader learn of India from this story?
3. Is Kipling's purpose the portrayal of Oriental color or the telling of a melodramatic story?
4. Do you believe that two such blasphemous rascals as Carnehan and Dravot could have perpetrated such a hoax in Kafiristan?
5. What are the implications of the Superintendent's query as to Carnehan's being bareheaded in the sun for half an hour?

## John Russell

# THE PRICE OF THE HEAD

THE possessions of Christopher Alexander Pellett were these: his name, which he was always careful to retain intact; a suit of ducks, no longer intact, in which he lived and slept; a continuous thirst for liquor, and a set of red whiskers. Also he had a friend. Now, no man can gain friendship, even among the gentle islands of Polynesia, except by virtue of some quality attaching to him. Strength, humor, villainy: he must show some trait by which the friend can catch and hold. How, then, explain the loving devotion lavished upon Christopher Alexander Pellett by Karaki, the company boat boy? This was the mystery at Fufuti.

There was no harm in Pellett. He never quarreled. He never raised his fist. Apparently he had never learned that a white man's foot, though it wabble ever so much, is given him wherewith to kick natives out of the road. He never even cursed any one except himself and the Chinese half-caste who sold him brandy: which was certainly allowable because the brandy was very bad.

On the other hand, there was no perceptible good in him. He had long lost the will to toil, and latterly even the skill to beg. He did not smile, nor dance, nor exhibit any of the amiable eccentricities that sometimes recommend the drunken to a certain toleration. In any other part of the world he must have passed without a struggle. But some chance had drifted him to the beaches where life is as easy as a song and his particular fate had given him a friend. And so he persisted. That was all. He persisted, a sodden lump of flesh preserved in alcohol. . . .

Karaki, his friend, was a heathen from Bougainville, where some people are smoked and others eaten. Being a black, a Melanesian, he was as much an alien in brown Fufuti as any white. He was a serious, efficient little man with deeply sunken eyes, a great mop of kinky hair, and a complete absence of expression. His tastes were simple. He wore a red cotton kerchief belted around his waist and a brass curtain ring suspended from his nose.

Some powerful chief in his home island had sold Karaki into the service of the trading company for three years, annexing his salary of tobacco and beads in advance. When the time should be accomplished, Karaki would be shipped back to Bougainville, a matter of some eight hundred miles, where he would land no richer than before except in experience. This was the custom. Karaki may have had plans of his own.

It is seldom that one of the black races of the Pacific shows any of the virtues for which subject populations are admired. Fidelity and humility can be exacted from other colors between tan and chocolate. But the black remains the inscrutable savage. His secret heart is his own. Hence the astonishment of Fufuti, which knew the ways of black recruits, when Karaki took the worthless beachcomber to his bosom.

"Hy, you, Johnny," called Moy Jack, the Chinese half-caste. "Better you come catch this fella mahster b'long you. He fella plenty too much drunk, galow."

Karaki left the shade of the copra shed where he had been waiting an hour or more and came forward to receive the sagging bulk that was thrust out of doors. He took it scientifically by wrist and armpit and swung toward the beach. Moy Jack stood on his threshold watching with cynic interest.

"Hy, you," he said; "what name you make so much bobeley 'long that fella mahster? S'pose you bling me all them fella pearl; me pay you one dam fella good trade—my word!"

It annoyed Moy Jack that he had to provide the white man with a daily drunk in exchange for the little seed pearls with which Pellett was always flush. He knew where those pearls came from. Karaki did forbidden diving in the lagoon to get them. Moy Jack made a good thing of the traffic, but he could have made a much better thing by trading directly with Karaki for a few sticks of tobacco.

"What name you give that fella mahster all them fella pearl?" demanded Moy Jack offensively. "He plenty too much no good, galow. Close up he die altogether."

Karaki did not reply. He looked at Moy Jack once, and the half-caste trailed off into mutterings. For an instant there showed a strange light in Karaki's dull eyes, like the flat, green flicker of a turning shark glimpsed ten fathoms down. . . .

Karaki bore his charge down the beach to the little thatched shelter of pandanus leaves that was all his home. Tenderly he eased Pellett to a mat, pillowed his head, bathed him with cool water, brushed the filth from his hair and whiskers. Pellett's whiskers were true whiskers, the kind that sprout like the barbels of a catfish, and they were a glorious coppery, sun-gilt red. Karaki combed them out with a sandalwood comb. Later he sat by with a fan and kept the flies from the bloated face of the drunkard.

It was a little past midday when something brought him scurrying into the open. For weeks he had been studying every weather sign. He knew that the change was due when the southeast trade begins to harden through this flawed belt of calms and cross winds. And now, as he watched, the sharp shadows began to blur along the sands and a film crept over the face of the sun.

All Fufuti was asleep. The house boys snored in the back veranda. Under his netting the agent dreamed happily of big copra shipments and bonuses. Moy Jack dozed among his bottles.

Nobody would have been mad enough to stir abroad in the noon hour of repose: nobody but Karaki, the untamed black, who cared nothing for custom nor yet for dreams. The light pad of his steps was lost in the surf drone on the barrier reefs. He flitted to and fro like a wraith. And while Fufuti slept he applied himself to a job for which he had never been hired. . . .

Karaki had long ago ascertained two vital facts: where the key to the trade room was kept and where the rifles and ammunition were hidden. He opened the trade room and selected three bolts of turkey red cloth, a few knives, two cases of tobacco, and a fine small ax. There was much else he might have taken as well. But Karaki was a man of simple tastes, and efficient.

With the ax he next forced the rifle chest and removed therefrom one Winchester and a big box of cartridges. With the ax again he broke into the boat sheds. Finally with the ax he smashed the bottoms out of the whaleboat and the two cutters so they would be of no use to any one for many days to come. It was really a very handy little ax, a true tomahawk, ground to a shaving edge. Karaki took a workman's pleasure in its keen, deep strokes. It was almost his chief prize.

On the beach lay a big proa, a stout outrigger canoe of the kind Karaki's own people used at Bougainville, so high of prow and stern as to be nearly crescent-shaped. The northwest monsoon of last season had washed it ashore at Fufuti, and Karaki had repaired it, by the agent's own order. This proa he now launched in the lagoon, and aboard of it he stored his loot.

Of supplies he had to make a hasty selection. He took a bag of rice and another of sweet potatoes. He took as many coconuts as he could carry in a net in three trips. He took a cask of water and a box of biscuit.

And here happened an odd thing.

In his search for the biscuit he came upon the agent's private store of liquor, a dozen bottles of rare Irish whisky. He glanced at them and passed them by. He knew what the stuff was, and he was a savage, a black man. But he passed it by. When Moy Jack heard of that later he remembered what he had seen in Karaki's eyes and ventured the surprising prediction that Karaki would never be taken alive.

When all was ready Karaki went back to his thatch and aroused Christopher Alexander Pellett.

"Hy, mahster, you come 'long me."

Mr. Pellett sat up and looked at him. That is to say, he looked. Whether he saw anything or not belongs among the obscurer questions of psychopathy.

"Too late," said Mr. Pellett profoundly. "This shop is closed. Copy boy! Give all those damned loafers good night. I'm—I'm goin'—bed!"

Whereupon he fell flat on his back.

"Wake up, mahster," insisted Karaki, shaking him. "You too much strong fella sleep. Hy-ah, mahster! Rum! You like'm rum? You catch'm rum any amount—my word! Plenty rum, mahster!"

But even this magic call, which never failed to rouse Pellett from his couch in the mornings, fell now on deaf ears. Pellett had had his skinful, and the fitness of things decreed that he should soak the clock around.

Karaki knelt beside him, pried him up until he could get a shoulder under his middle, and lifted him like a loose bag of meal. Pellett weighed one hundred and fifty pounds; Karaki not much more than a hundred. Yet in some deft coolie fashion of his own the little black man packed his burden, with the feet dragging behind, clear down to the beach. Moreover, he managed to get it aboard the proa. Pellett was half drowned and the proa half swamped. But Karaki managed.

No man saw their departure. Fufuti still dreamed on. Long before the agent awoke to wrath and ruin their queer crescent craft had slipped from the lagoon and faded away on the wings of the trade.

That first day Karaki had all he could do to keep the proa running straight before the wind. Big smoky seas came piling up out of the southeast and would have piled aboard if he had given them the least chance. He was only a heathen who did not know a compass from a degree of latitude. But his forefathers used to people these waters on cockleshell voyages that make the venture of Columbus look like a ride in a ferry-boat. Karaki bailed with a tin pan and sailed with a mat and steered with a paddle: but he proceeded.

Along about sunrise Mr. Pellett stirred in the bilge and raised a peagreen face. He took one bewildered glance overside at the seething waste and collapsed with a groan. After a decent interval he tried again, but this was an illusion that would not pass, and he twisted around to Karaki sitting crouched and all aglisten with spray in the stern.

"Rum!" he demanded.

Karaki shook his head, and a haunted look crept into Pellett's eyes.

"Take—take away all that stuff," he begged pathetically, pointing at the ocean. . . .

Thereafter for two days he was very, very sick, and he learned how a small boat in any kind of a sea can move forty-seven different ways within one and the same minute. This is no trifling bit of knowledge, as those who have acquired it can tell. It was nearly fatal to Pellett.

On the third day he awoke with a mouth and a stomach of fumed leather and a great weakness, but otherwise in command of his few faculties. The gale had fallen and Karaki was quietly preparing fresh coconuts. Pellett quaffed two before he thought to miss the brandy with which his breakfast draft was always laced. But when he remembered the milk choked in his throat.

"Me like'm rum."

"No got'm rum."

Pellett looked forward and aft, to windward and to lee. There was a great deal of horizon in sight, but nothing else. For the first time he was aware of a strangeness in events.

"What name you come so far?" he asked.

"We catch'm one big fella wind," explained Karaki.

Pellett was in no condition to question his statement nor to observe from the careful stocking of the proa that they had not been blown to sea on a casual fishing trip. Pellett had other things to think of. Some of the things were pink and others purple and others were striped like the rainbow in most surprising designs, and all were highly novel and interesting. They came thronging out of the vasty deep to entertain Christopher Alexander Pellett. Which they did.

You cannot cut off alcohol from a man who has been continuously pickled for two years without results more or less picturesque. These were days when the proa went shouting across the empty southern seas to madrigal and choric song. Tied hand and foot and lashed under a thwart, Pellett raved in the numbers of his innocent youth. It would have been singular hearing had there been any to hear, but there was only Karaki, who did not care for the lesser Cavalier poets and on whom whole pages of "Atalanta in Calydon" were quite wasted. Now and then he threw a dipperful of sea water over the white man, or spread a mat to keep the sun from him, or fed him coconut milk by force. Karaki was a poor audience, but an excellent nurse. Also, he combed Pellett's whiskers twice every day.

They ran into calms. But the trade picked them up again more gently, so that Karaki ventured to make westing, and they fled under skies as bright as polished brass.

> My heart is within me
>    As an ash in the fire;
> Whosoever hath seen me
>    Without lute, without lyre,
> Shall sing of me grievous things,
>    even things that were ill
>    to desire—

Thus chanted Christopher Alexander Pellett, whose face began to show a little more like flesh and a little less like rotten kelp. . . .

Whenever a fair chance offered Karaki landed on the lee of some one of the tiny islets with which the Santa Cruz region is peppered and would make shift to cook rice and potatoes in the tin dipper. This was risky, for one day the islet proved to be inhabited. Two white men in a cutter came out to stop them. Karaki could not hide his resemblance to a runaway nigger, and he did not try to. But when the cutter approached within fifty yards he suddenly announced himself as a runaway nigger with a gun. He left the cutter sinking and one of the men dead.

"There's a bullet hole alongside me here," said Pellett from under the thwart. "You'd better plug it."

Karaki plugged it and released his passenger, who sat up and began stretching himself with a certain naive curiosity of his own body.

"So you're real," observed Pellett, staring hard at Karaki. "By George, you are, and that's comfort."

He was right. Karaki was very real.

"What side you take'm this fella canoe?"

"Balbi," said Karaki, using the native word for Bougainville.

Pellett whistled. An eight-hundred-mile evasion in an open boat was considerable undertaking. It enlisted his respect. Moreover, he had just had emphatic proof of the efficiency of this little black man.

"Balbi all some home b'long you?"

"Yes."

"All right, commodore," said Pellett. "Lead on. I don't know why you shipped me for supercargo, but I'll see you through."

Strangely—or perhaps not so strangely—the whole Fufuti interval of his history had been fading from his brain while the poison was ebbing from his tissues. The Christopher Alexander Pellett that emerged was one from earlier years: pretty much of a wreck, it was true, and a feckless, indolent, paltry creature at best, but ordinarily human and rather more than ordinarily intelligent.

He was very feeble at first, but Karaki's diet of coconuts and sweet potatoes did wonders for him, and the time came when he could rejoice in the good salt taste of the spray on his lips and forget for hours together the crazy craving for stimulant. They made a strange crew, this pair—simple savage and convalescent drunkard—but there was never any question as to which was in command. That was well seen in the third week when their food began to fail and Pellett noticed that Karaki ate nothing for a whole day.

"See here, this won't do," he cried. "You've given me the last coconut and kept none for yourself."

"Me no like'm eat," said Karaki shortly.

Christopher Alexander Pellett pondered many matters in long, idle hours while the rush of foam under the proa and the creak and fling of her outriggers were the only sounds between sea and sky. Sometimes his brow was knotted with pain. It is not always pleasant to be wrenched back into level contact with one's memories. Thoughts are no sweeter company for having long been drowned. He had met the horrors of delirium. He had now to face the livelier devils of his past. He had fled them before.

·But here was no escape of any kind. So he turned and grappled with them and laid them one by one.

When they had been at sea twenty-nine days they had nothing left of their provisions but a little water. Karaki doled it out by moistening a shred of coconut husk and giving Pellett the shred to suck. In spite of Pellett's petulant protest, he would take none himself. Again the heathen nursed the derelict, this time through the last stages of thirst, scraping the staves of the cask and feeding him the ultimate drop of moisture on the point of a knife.

On the thirty-sixth day from Fufuti they sighted Choiseul, a great green wall that built up slowly across the west.

Once fairly under its headlands, Karaki might have indulged a certain triumph. He had taken as his target the whole length of the Solomons, some six hundred miles. But to have fetched the broadside of them anywhere in such a craft as the proa through storm and current, without instrument or chart, was distinctly a feat of navigation. Karaki, however, did no celebrating. Instead, he stared long and anxiously over his shoulder into the east.

The wind had been fitful since morning. By noon it was dead calm on a restless, oily sea. A barometer would have told evil tales, but Karaki must have guessed them anyway, for he staggered forward and unstepped the little mast. Then he bound all his cargo securely under the thwarts and put all his remaining strength into the paddle, heading for a small outpost island where a line of white showed beach. They had been very lucky thus far, but they were still two miles off-shore when the first rush of the hurricane caught them.

Karaki himself was reduced to a rattle of bones in a dried skin, and Pellett could scarce lift a hand. But Karaki fought for Pellett among the waves that leaped up like sheets of fire on the reef. Why or how they got through neither could have said. Perhaps because it was written that after drink, illness, madness, and starvation the white man should be saved by the black man again and a last time from ravening waters. When they came ashore on the islet they were both nearly flayed, but they were alive, and Karaki still gripped Pellett's shirt. . . .

For a week they stayed while Pellett fattened on unlimited coconut and Karaki tinkered the proa. It had landed in a water-logged tangle, but Karaki's treasures were safe. He got his bearings from a passing native fisherman, and then he knew that *all* his treasures were safe. His home island lay across Bougainville Strait, the stretch of water just beyond. . . .

"Balbi over there?" asked Pellett.

"Yes," said Karaki.

"And a mighty good thing too," cried Pellett heartily. "This is the limit of British authority, old boy. Big fella mahster b'long Beretani stop'm here, no can go that side."

Karaki was quite aware of it. If he feared one thing in the world, he feared the Fiji High Court and its Resident Commissioner for the Southern Solomons, who did sure justice upon all who transgressed in its jurisdiction. Once beyond the Strait he might still be liable for the stolen goods and the broken contract. But never— this was the point—never could he be punished for anything he might choose to do over there in Bougainville.

So Karaki was content.

And so was Christopher Alexander Pellett. His body had been wrung and swept and scoured, and he had downed his devils. Sweet air and sunshine were on his lips and in his heart. His bones were sweet in him. As his vigor returned he swam the lagoon or helped Karaki at the proa. He would spend hours hugging the warm sand or rejoicing in the delicate tracery of some tiny sea shell, singing softly to himself while the ground swell hushed along the beach, savoring life as he never had done.

"Oh, this is good—good!" he said.

Karaki puzzled him. Not that he vexed himself, for a smiling wonder at everything, almost childlike, filled him these days. But he thought of this taciturn savage, how he had capped thankless service with rarest sacrifice.

And now that he could consider soberly, the why of it eluded him. Why? Affection? Friendship? It must be so, and he warmed toward the silent little man with the sunken eyes and the expressionless face from which he could never raise a wink.

"Hy, you, Karaki, what name you no laugh all same me? What? You too much fright 'long that fella stuff you steal? Forget it, you old black scamp. If they ever trouble you, I'll square them somehow. By George, I'll say I stole it myself!"

Karaki only grunted and sat down to clean his Winchester with a bit of rag and some drops of oil he had crushed from a dried coconut.

"No, that don't reach him either," murmured Pellett, baffled. "I'd like to know what's going on under that topknot of yours, old chap. You're like Kipling's cat, that walks by himself. God knows I'm not ungrateful. I wish I could show you—"

He sprang up.

"Karaki! Me one big fella friend 'long you: savee? You one big fella friend 'long me: savee? We two dam big fella friend, my word! . . . What?"

"Yes," said Karaki. No other response. He looked at Pellett and he looked away toward Bougainville. "Yes," he said, "my word," and went on cleaning his gun—the black islander, inscrutable, incomprehensible, an enigma always, and to the end.

The end came two days later at Bougainville.

Under a gorgeous dawn they came into a bay that opened before their prow as with jeweled arms of welcome. The land lay lapped in bright garments like a sleeper half awakened, all flushed and smiling, sensuous, intimate, thrilling with life, breathing warm scents—

These were some of the foolish phrases Pellett babbled to himself as he leaped ashore and ran up on a rocky point to see and to feel and to draw all the charm of the place to himself.

Meanwhile Karaki, that simple and efficient little man, was proceeding methodically about his own affairs. He landed his bolts of cloth, his tobacco, his knives, and the other loot. He landed his box of cartridges and his rifle and his fine tomahawk. The goods were somewhat damaged by sea water, but the weapons had been carefully cleaned and polished. . . .

Pellett was declaiming poetry aloud to the alluring solitude when he was aware of a gentle footfall and turned, surprised to find Karaki standing just behind him with the rifle at his hip and the ax in his hand.

"Well," said Pellett cheerfully, "what d'you want, old chappie?"

"Me like," said Karaki, while there gleamed in his eyes the strange light that Moy Jack had glimpsed there, like the flicker of a turning shark; "me like'm too much one fella head b'long you!"

"What? Head! Whose—my head?"

"Yes," said Karaki simply.

That was the way of it. That was all the mystery. The savage had fallen enamored of the head of the beachcomber, and Christopher Alexander Pellett had been betrayed by his fatal red whiskers. In Karaki's country a white man's head, well smoked, is a thing to be desired above wealth, above lands and chief-ships, fame, and the love of women. In all Karaki's country was no head like the head of Pellett. Therefore Karaki had served to win it with the patience and single faith of a Jacob. For this he had schemed and waited, committed theft and murder, expended sweat and cunning, starved and denied himself, nursed, watched, tended, fed, and saved his man that he might bring the head alive and on the hoof—so to speak—to the spot where he could remove it at leisure and enjoy the fruits of his labor in safety.

Pellett saw all this at a flash, understood it so far as any white could understand: the whole elemental and stupendous simplicity of it. And standing there in his new strength and sanity under the fair promise of the morning, he gave a laugh that pealed across the waters and started the sea birds from their cliffs, the deep-throated laugh of a man who fathoms and accepts the last great jest. . . .

For finally, by corrected list, the possessions of Christopher Alexander Pellett were these: his name, still intact; the ruins of some rusty ducks; his precious red whiskers—and a soul which had been neatly recovered, renewed, refurbished, reanimated, and restored to him by his good friend Karaki.

Thou shouldst die as he dies
For whom none sheddeth tears;
Filling thine eyes
And fulfilling thine ears
With the brillance . . . the bloom
and the beauty . . .

Thus chanted Christopher Alexander Pellett over the waters of the bay, and then whirled, throwing wide his arms:
"Shoot, damn you! It's cheap at the price!"

From *Color of the East*, W. W. Norton & Company, Inc., by permission of the publisher.

1. What definite foreshadowing of Karaki's purpose does Russell give the reader?
2. What is copra, the pandanus, a proa, the monsoon, and pidgin English?
3. Do you believe such events as are chronicled in the story might actually have transpired?
    a. Would Karaki have been able to steal the trade goods, the rifle, and the white man?
    b. Would Karaki be capable of such premeditation and effort to obtain his objective?
    c. Could the two men, equipped as they were, have traveled so great a distance?
4. What is meant by the phrase that Pellett saw "the whole elemental and stupendous stupidity of it"?
5. After the disclosure of Karaki's design, does Pellett still hold the savage to be his friend?

# II. PSYCHOLOGY

# II. PSYCHOLOGY

THE tale of terror, of "ghaisties and ghoulies, and long-leggity beasties, and things that go bump in the night," strikes at our most primitive emotion, fear, which lies far beneath the level of rational thought. As a literary form it therefore reaches back to the earliest folk-tales. But not until well into the nineteenth century was any clear distinction drawn between the ghost story, or the tale of the supernatural, and the psychological story proper. In the tale of the supernatural, both the terror and its explanation depend on extra-human agencies; in the true psychological story they depend on abnormal or pathological phases of human nature.

The Gothic romances of the eighteenth and early nineteenth centuries mingled these two elements indiscriminately. Some writers, like Ann Radcliffe, attempted at the end a rational explanation of the terrors, but the explanations were often perfunctory and unconvincing because they involved superhuman credulity on the part of their victims and motiveless perversion on the part of their perpetrators. Others, like Walpole in *The Castle of Otranto* and Lewis in *The Monk*, let the events stand as the work of extra-human forces. In either case, the narrative too often suggests a Grimm fairy tale. It is more likely to evoke giggles than shudders from the modern reader. Nevertheless, the closing years of the eighteenth century saw the development of the formula which has ever since governed successful stories of the supernatural or the occult.

Briefly put, the formula is this: everything in the story should finally be capable of rational explanation, *except one detail.* The first masterpiece exemplifying this formula is Burns's *Tam o' Shanter* (1791). In that story the whole adventure might be Tam's drunken dream—if his mare hadn't lost her tail. In "Wandering Willie's Tale" Sir Walter Scott repeated Burns's formula, and Burns's success. In each instance the author seems to say to the skeptical reader, All right, you may claim that Tam, or Steenie, dreamed all this, but if so, how do you explain Maggie's tail, or Steenie's receipt? And from Burns and Scott down to Kipling and Edith Wharton, the formula has always brought results. It avoids too much strain on the reader's credulity, and at the same time leaves in his mind a teasing doubt that perhaps after all this world contains things not easily explained in a rational or material way.

Poe was a direct descendant of the Gothic romancers, with additional elements derived from the German romantics. In tales like "Ligeia" he employed the true supernatural; in "The Fall of the House of Usher" he rationally explained the terrors, as Mrs. Radcliffe used to explain them. His fresh contribution to this type of literature, apart from his vastly more artistic and convincing technique, was his development of the genuinely psychological story in such dramatizations of madness or conscience as "The Tell-Tale Heart" and "The Black Cat." It sounds paradoxical to say that he put the tale of terror on a rational basis, yet that is in effect what he did. Though he lived when scientific study of abnormal mental states had scarcely begun, Poe worked out his portrayals of madness with an attention to detail found in none of his predecessors and not surpassed until authors, almost in our own day, began to make fictional use of the discoveries of the psychopathologists.

As late as the end of the nineteenth century the horror stories of Kipling and Ambrose Bierce employ substantially the same technique that Poe had used fifty years before. The former's "The Mark of the Beast" and "The Strange Ride of Morrowbie Jukes" are almost straight Poe in an Indian setting; the latter's "The Man and the Snake" merely substitutes extreme fear for the madness of "The Tell-Tale Heart." But Charlotte Perkins Gilman's "The Yellow Wallpaper" (1899) struck a new note of terror. Horace

Scudder, refusing it admission to *The Atlantic Monthly*, said it was so terribly good that it ought never to be printed. Emotionally, William Dean Howells agreed, but intellectually he so admired its artistry that he persuaded the editor of *The New England Magazine* to publish it. Founded in part on its author's own recollections of mental illness, it has been called one of the best accounts ever written of the progressive breakdown of a mind afflicted with dementia praecox. Similar use of case histories of specific types of mental derangement appears in stories like Willa Cather's "Paul's Case," Kipling's late "The Tender Achilles," and many of William Faulkner's.

In *The Turn of the Screw* Henry James achieved a combination of the psychological story with the traditional theme of the supernatural. He builds up his situation so artfully that at the end he leaves the reader wondering whether it was really an encounter with disembodied powers of evil, or merely a record of the progressive mental derangement of the governess who narrates it. And James's disciple, Edith Wharton, ran the whole gamut, from a story like "The Eyes," which is a dramatization of conscience, to "Kerfol" and "Bewitched," which involve the old device of the single inexplicable detail. Helen Hull's story, here printed, is one of the most successful modern examples of the traditional manner, blending something of the eeriness of Poe with the sharp characterization of James and Mrs. Wharton. And though ghost stories of the older sort are increasingly difficult to make convincing to modern readers, the terror story based on mental pathology is probably still in its infancy. So long as we continue to fear the unknown, the type will survive in some form or other.

*Edgar Allan Poe*

# THE BLACK CAT

FOR the most wild, yet most homely narrative which I am about to pen, I neither expect nor solicit belief. Mad indeed would I be to expect it, in a case where my very senses reject their own evidence. Yet, mad am I not—and very surely do I not dream. But to-morrow I die, and to-day I would unburthen my soul. My immediate purpose is to place before the world, plainly, succinctly, and without comment, a series of mere household events. In their consequences, these events have terrified—have tortured—have destroyed me. Yet I will not attempt to expound them. To me, they have presented little but Horror—to many they will seem less terrible than *baroques*. Hereafter, perhaps, some intellect may be found which will reduce my phantasm to the common-place—some intellect more calm, more logical, and far less excitable than my own, which will perceive, in the circumstances I detail with awe, nothing more than an ordinary succession of very natural causes and effects.

From my infancy I was noted for the docility and humanity of my disposition. My tenderness of heart was even so conspicuous as to make me the jest of my companions. I was especially fond of animals, and was indulged by my parents with a great variety of pets. With these I spent most of my time, and never was so happy as when feeding and caressing them. This peculiarity of character grew with my growth, and, in my manhood, I derived from it one of my principal sources of pleasure. To those who have cherished an affection for a faithful and sagacious dog, I need hardly be at the trouble of explaining the nature or the intensity of the gratification thus derivable. There is something in the unselfish and self-sacrificing love of a brute, which goes directly to the heart of him who has had frequent occasion to test the paltry friendship and gossamer fidelity of mere Man.

I married early, and was happy to find in my wife a disposition not uncongenial with my own. Observing my partiality for domestic pets, she lost no opportunity of procuring those of the most agreeable kind. We had birds, gold fish, a fine dog, rabbits, a small monkey, and a *cat.*

This latter was a remarkably large and beautiful animal, entirely black, and sagacious to an astonishing degree. In speaking of his intelligence, my wife, who at heart was not a little tinctured with superstition, made frequent allusion to the ancient popular notion, which regarded all black cats as witches in disguise. Not that she was ever *serious* upon this point—and I mention the matter at all for no better reason than that it happens, just now, to be remembered.

Pluto—this was the cat's name—was my favorite pet and playmate. I alone fed him, and he attended me wherever I went about the house. It was even with difficulty that I could prevent him from following me through the streets.

Our friendship lasted, in this manner, for several years, during which my general temperament and character—through the instrumentality of the Fiend Intemperance—had (I blush to confess it) experienced a radical alteration for the worse. I grew, day by day, more moody, more irritable, more regardless of the feelings of others. I suffered myself to use intemperate language to my wife. At length, I even offered her personal violence. My pets, of course, were made to feel the change in my disposition. I not only neglected, but ill-used them. For Pluto, however, I still retained sufficient regard to restrain me from maltreating him, as I made no scruple of maltreating the rabbits, the monkey, or even the dog, when by accident, or through affection, they came in my way. But my disease grew upon me—for what disease is like Alcohol!—and at length even Pluto, who was now becoming old, and consequently somewhat peevish—even Pluto began to experience the effects of my ill temper.

One night, returning home, much intoxicated, from one of my haunts about town, I fancied that the cat avoided my presence. I seized him; when, in his fright at my violence, he inflicted a slight wound upon my hand with his teeth. The fury of a demon instantly possessed me. I knew myself no longer. My original soul seemed, at once, to take its flight from my body; and a more than fiendish malevolence, gin-nurtured, thrilled every fibre of my frame. I took from my waistcoat-pocket a pen-knife, opened it, grasped the poor beast by the throat, and deliberately cut one of its eyes from the socket! I blush, I burn, I shudder, while I pen the damnable atrocity.

When reason returned with the morning—when I had slept off the fumes of the night's debauch—I experienced a sentiment half of horror, half of remorse, for the crime of which I had been guilty; but it was, at best, a feeble and equivocal feeling, and the soul remained untouched. I again plunged into excess, and soon drowned in wine all memory of the deed.

In the mean time the cat slowly recovered. The socket of the lost eye presented, it is true, a frightful appearance, but he no longer appeared to suffer any pain. He went about the house as usual, but, as might be expected, fled in extreme terror at my approach. I had so much of my old heart left, as to be at first grieved by this evident dislike on the part of a creature which had once so loved me. But this feeling soon gave place to irritation. And then came, as if to my final and irrevocable overthrow, the spirit of PERVERSENESS. Of this spirit philosophy takes no account. Yet I am not more sure that my soul lives, than I am that perverseness is one of the primitive impulses of the human heart—one of the indivisible primary faculties, or sentiments, which give direction to the character of Man. Who has not, a hundred times, found himself committing a vile or a silly action, for no other reason than because he knows he should *not*? Have we not a perpetual inclination, in the teeth of our best judgment, to violate that which is *Law*, merely because we understand it to be such? This spirit of perverseness, I say, came to my final overthrow. It was this unfathomable longing of the soul *to vex itself*—to offer violence to its own nature—to do wrong for the wrong's sake only—that urged me to continue and finally to consummate the injury I had inflicted upon the unoffending brute. One morning, in cool blood, I slipped a noose about its neck and hung it to the limb of a tree;—hung it with the tears streaming from my eyes, and with the bitterest remorse at my heart;—hung it *because* I knew that it had loved me, and *because* I felt it had given me no reason of offence;—hung it *because* I knew that in so doing I was committing a sin—a deadly sin that would so jeopardize my immortal soul as to place it—if such a thing were possible—even beyond the reach of the infinite mercy of the Most Merciful and Most Terrible God.

On the night of the day on which this cruel deed was done, I was aroused from sleep by the cry of fire. The curtains of my bed were in flames. The whole house was blazing. It was with great difficulty that my wife, a servant, and myself, made our escape from the conflagration. The destruction was complete. My entire worldly wealth was swallowed up, and I resigned myself thenceforward to despair.

I am above the weakness of seeking to establish a sequence of cause and effect, between the disaster and the atrocity. But I am detailing a chain of facts—and wish not to leave even a possible link imperfect. On the day succeeding the fire, I visited the ruins. The walls, with one exception, had fallen in. This exception was found in a compartment wall, not very thick, which stood about the middle of the house, and against which had rested the head of my bed. The plastering had here, in great measure, resisted the action of the fire—a fact which I attributed to its having been recently spread. About this wall a dense crowd were collected, and many persons seemed to be examining a particular portion of it with very minute and eager attention. The words "strange!" "singular!" and other similar expressions, excited my curiosity. I approached and saw, as if graven in *bas relief* upon the white surface, the figure of a gigantic cat. The impression was given with an accuracy truly marvellous. There was a rope about the animal's neck.

When I first beheld this apparition—for I could scarcely regard it as less—my wonder and my terror were extreme. But at length reflection came to my aid. The cat, I remembered, had been hung in a garden adjacent to the house. Upon the alarm of fire, this garden had been immediately filled by the crowd—by some one of whom the animal must have been cut from the tree and thrown, through an open window, into my chamber. This had probably been done with the view of arousing me from sleep. The falling of other walls had compressed the victim of my cruelty into the substance of the freshly-spread plaster; the lime of which, with the flames, and the ammonia from the carcass, had then accomplished the portraiture as I saw it.

Although I thus readily accounted to my reason, if not altogether to my conscience, for the startling fact just detailed, it did not the less fail to make a deep impression upon my fancy. For months I could not rid myself of the phantasm of the cat; and, during this period, there came back into my spirit a half-sentiment that seemed, but was not, remorse. I went so far as to regret the loss of the animal, and to look about me, among the vile haunts which I now habitually frequented, for another pet of the same species, and of somewhat similar appearance, with which to supply its place.

One night as I sat, half stupefied, in a den of more than infamy, my attention was suddenly drawn to some black object, reposing upon the head of one of the immense hogsheads of Gin, or of Rum, which constituted the chief furniture of the apartment. I had been looking steadily at the top of this hogshead for some minutes, and what now caused me surprise was the fact that I had not sooner perceived the object thereupon. I approached it, and touched it with my hand. It was a black cat—a very large one—fully as large as Pluto, and closely resembling him in every respect but one. Pluto had not a white hair upon any portion of his body; but this cat had a large, although indefinite splotch of white, covering nearly the whole region of the breast.

Upon my touching him, he immediately arose, purred loudly, rubbed against my hand, and appeared delighted with my notice. This, then, was the very creature of which I was in search. I at once offered to purchase it of the landlord; but this person made no claim to it—knew nothing of it—had never seen it before.

I continued my caresses, and, when I prepared to go home, the animal evinced a disposition to accompany me. I permitted it to do so; occasionally stooping and patting it as I proceeded. When it reached the house it domesticated itself at once, and became immediately a great favorite with my wife.

For my own part, I soon found a dislike to it arising within me. This was just the reverse of what I had anticipated; but I know not how or why it was—its evident fondness for myself rather disgusted and annoyed. By slow degrees, these feelings of disgust and annoyance rose into the bitterness of hatred. I avoided the creature; a certain sense of shame, and the remembrance of my former deed of cruelty, preventing me from physically abusing it. I did not, for some weeks, strike, or otherwise violently ill use it; but gradually—very gradually—I came to look upon it with unutterable loathing, and to flee silently from its odious presence, as from the breath of a pestilence.

What added, no doubt, to my hatred of the beast, was the discovery, on the morning after I brought it home, that, like Pluto, it also had been deprived of one of its eyes. This circumstance, however, only endeared it to my wife, who, as I have already said, possessed, in a high degree, that humanity of feeling which had once been my distinguishing trait, and the source of many of my simplest and purest pleasures.

With my aversion to this cat, however, its partiality for myself seemed to increase. It followed my footsteps with a pertinacity which it would be difficult to make the reader comprehend. Whenever I sat, it would crouch beneath my chair, or spring upon my knees, covering me with its loathsome caresses. If I arose to walk it would get between my feet and thus nearly throw me down, or, fastening its long and sharp claws in my dress, clamber, in this manner, to my breast. At such times, although I longed to destroy it with a blow, I was yet withheld from so doing, partly by a memory of my former crime, but chiefly—let me confess it at once—by absolute dread of the beast.

This dread was not exactly a dread of physical evil—and yet I should be at a loss how otherwise to define it. I am almost ashamed to own—yes, even in this felon's cell, I am almost ashamed to own—that the terror and horror with which the animal inspired me, had been heightened by one of the merest chimeras it would be possible to conceive. My wife had called my attention, more than once, to the character of the mark of white hair, of which I have spoken, and which constituted the sole visible difference between the strange beast and the one I had destroyed. The reader will remember that this mark, although large, had been originally very indefinite; but, by slow degrees—degrees nearly imperceptible, and which for a long time my Reason struggled to reject as fanciful—it had, at length, assumed a rigorous distinctness of outline. It was now the representation of an object that I shudder to name—and for this, above all, I loathed, and dreaded, and would have rid myself of the monster *had I dared*—it was now, I say, the image of a hideous—of a ghastly thing—of the GALLOWS!

—oh, mournful and terrible engine of Horror and of Crime—of Agony and of Death!

And now was I indeed wretched beyond the wretchedness of mere Humanity. And a *brute beast*—whose fellow I had contemptuously destroyed—a *brute beast* to work out for *me*—for me a man, fashioned in the image of the High God—so much of insufferable woe! Alas! neither by day nor by night knew I the blessing of Rest any more! During the former the creature left me no moment alone; and, in the latter, I started, hourly, from dreams of unutterable fear, to find the hot breath of *the thing* upon my face, and its vast weight—an incarnate Night-Mare that I had no power to shake off—incumbent eternally upon my *heart!*

Beneath the pressure of torments such as these, the feeble remnant of the good within me succumbed. Evil thoughts became my sole intimates—the darkest and most evil of thoughts. The moodiness of my usual temper increased to hatred of all things and of all mankind; while, from the sudden, frequent, and ungovernable outbursts of a fury to which I now blindly abandoned myself, my uncomplaining wife, alas! was the most usual and the most patient of sufferers.

One day she accompanied me, upon some household errand, into the cellar of the old building which our poverty compelled us to inhabit. The cat followed me down the steep stairs, and, nearly throwing me headlong, exasperated me to madness. Uplifting an axe, and forgetting, in my wrath, the childish dread which had hitherto stayed my hand, I aimed a blow at the animal which, of course, would have proved instantly fatal had it descended as I wished. But this blow was arrested by the hand of my wife. Goaded, by the interference, into a rage more than demoniacal, I withdrew my arm from her grasp and buried the axe in her brain. She fell dead upon the spot, without a groan.

This hideous murder accomplished, I set myself forthwith, and with entire deliberation, to the task of concealing the body. I knew that I could not remove it from the house, either by day or by night, without the risk of being observed by the neighbors. Many projects entered my mind. At one period I thought of cutting the corpse into minute fragments, and destroying them by fire. At another, I resolved to dig a grave for it in the floor of the cellar. Again, I deliberated about casting it in the well in the yard—about packing it in a box, as if merchandise, with the usual arrangements, and so getting a porter to take it from the house. Finally I hit upon what I considered a far better expedient than either of these. I determined to wall it up in the cellar—as the monks of the middle ages are recorded to have walled up their victims.

For a purpose such as this the cellar was well adapted. Its walls were loosely constructed, and had lately been plastered throughout with a rough plaster, which the dampness of the atmosphere had prevented from hardening. Moreover, in one of the walls was a projection, caused by a false chimney, or fireplace, that had been filled up, and made to resemble the rest of the cellar. I made no doubt that I could readily displace the bricks at this point, insert the corpse, and wall the whole up as before, so that no eye could detect any thing suspicious.

And in this calculation I was not deceived. By means of a crowbar I easily dislodged the bricks, and, having carefully deposited the body against the inner wall, I propped it in that position, while, with little trouble, I re-laid the whole structure as it originally stood. Having procured mortar, sand, and hair, with every possible precaution, I prepared a plaster which could not be distinguished from the old, and with this I very carefully went over the new brick-work. When I had finished, I felt satisfied that all was right. The wall did not present the slightest appearance of having been disturbed. The rubbish on the floor was picked up with the minutest care. I looked around triumphantly, and said to myself—"Here at least, then, my labor has not been in vain."

My next step was to look for the beast which had been the cause of so much wretchedness; for I had, at length, firmly resolved to put it to death. Had I been able to meet with it, at the moment, there could have been no doubt of its fate; but it appeared that the crafty animal had been alarmed at the violence of my previous anger, and forbore to present itself in my present mood. It is impossible to describe, or to imagine, the deep, the blissful sense of relief which the absence of the detested creature occasioned in my bosom. It did not make its appearance during the night—and thus for one night at least, since its introduction into the house, I soundly and tranquilly slept; aye, *slept* even with the burden of murder upon my soul!

The second and the third day passed, and still my tormentor came not. Once again I breathed as a free-man. The monster, in terror, had fled the premises forever! I should behold it no more! My happiness was supreme! The guilt of my dark deed disturbed me but little. Some few inquiries had been made, but these had been readily answered. Even a search had been instituted—but of course nothing was to be discovered. I looked upon my future felicity as secured.

Upon the fourth day of the assassination, a party of the police came, very unexpectedly, into the house, and proceeded again to make rigorous investigation of the premises. Secure, however, in the inscrutability of my place of concealment, I felt no embarrassment whatever. The officers bade me accompany them in their search. They left no nook or corner unexplored. At length, for the third or fourth time, they descended into the cellar. I quivered not in a muscle. My heart beat calmly as that of one who slumbers in innocence. I walked the cellar from end to end. I folded my arms upon my bosom, and roamed easily to and fro. The police were thoroughly satisfied and prepared to depart. The glee at my heart was too strong to be restrained. I burned to say if but one word, by way of triumph, and to render doubly sure their assurance of my guiltlessness.

"Gentlemen," I said at last, as the party ascended the steps, "I delight to have allayed your suspicions. I wish you all health, and a little more courtesy. By the bye, gentlemen, this—this is a very well-constructed house." (In the rabid desire to say something easily, I scarcely knew what I uttered at all.)—"I may say an *excellently* well-constructed house. These walls—are you going, gentlemen?—these walls are solidly put together": and here, through the mere phrenzy of bravado, I rapped heavily, with a cane which I held in my hand, upon that very portion of the brick-work behind which stood the corpse of the wife of my bosom.

But may God shield and deliver me from the fangs of the Arch-Fiend! No sooner had the reverberation of my blows sunk into silence, than I was answered by a voice from within the tomb!—by a cry, at first muffled and broken, like the sobbing of a child, and then quickly swelling into one long, loud, and continuous scream, utterly anomalous and inhuman—a howl—a wailing shriek, half of horror and half of triumph, such as might have arisen only out of hell, conjointly from the throats of the damned in their agony and of the demons that exult in the damnation.

Of my own thoughts it is folly to speak. Swooning, I staggered to the opposite wall. For one instant the party upon the stairs remained motionless, through extremity of terror and of awe. In the next, a dozen stout arms were toiling at the wall. It fell bodily. The corpse, already greatly decayed and clotted with gore, stood erect before the eyes of the spectators. Upon its head, with red extended mouth and solitary eye of fire, sat the hideous beast whose craft had seduced me into murder, and whose informing voice had consigned me to the hangman. I had walled the monster up within the tomb!

1. Why does the narrator express a disbelief in his own story?
2. Do you believe that the change in the author's nature from one of "docility" and "tenderness of heart" was brought about solely by intemperance?
3. If there is symbolism in the burning house after the hanging of the Black Cat, what do you think it is?

4. What incident in this story resembles (in a measure) one in Poe's "A Case of Amontillado"? Is this repetition of incident, and similar scenes elsewhere in his works, indicative of any special fear on the part of Poe?
5. Why does the narrator protest so much?

*Charlotte Perkins Gilman*

# THE YELLOW WALLPAPER

IT IS very seldom that mere ordinary people like John and my-self secure ancestral halls for the summer.

A colonial mansion, a hereditary estate, I would say a haunted house, and reach the height of romantic felicity—but that would be asking too much of fate!

Still I will proudly declare that there is something queer about it.

Else, why should it be let so cheaply? And why have stood so long untenanted?

John laughs at me, of course, but one expects that.

John is practical in the extreme. He has no patience with faith, an intense horror of superstition, and he scoffs openly at any talk of things not to be felt and seen and put down in figures.

John is a physician, and perhaps—(I would not say it to a living soul, of course, but this is dead paper and a great relief to my mind)—perhaps that is one reason I do not get well faster.

You see he does not believe I am sick! And what can one do?

If a physician of high standing, and one's own husband, assures friends and relatives that there is really nothing the matter with one but temporary nervous depression—a slight hysterical tendency —what is one to do?

My brother is also a physician, and also of high standing, and he says the same thing.

So I take phosphates or phosphites—whichever it is—and tonics, and air and exercise, and journeys, and am absolutely forbidden to "work" until I am well again.

Personally, I disagree with their ideas.

Personally, I believe that congenial work, with excitement and change, would do me good.

But what is one to do?

I did write for a while in spite of them; but it *does* exhaust me a good deal—having to be so sly about it, or else meet with heavy opposition.

I sometimes fancy that in my condition if I had less opposition and more society and stimulus—but John says the very worst thing I can do is to think about my condition, and I confess it always makes me feel bad.

So I will let it alone and talk about the house.

The most beautiful place! It is quite alone, standing well back from the road, quite three miles from the village. It makes me think of English places that you read about, for there are hedges and walls and gates that lock, and lots of separate little houses for the gardeners and people.

There is a *delicious* garden! I never saw such a garden—large and shady, full of box-bordered paths, and lined with long grape-covered arbors with seats under them.

There were greenhouses, but they are all broken now.

There was some legal trouble, I believe, something about the heirs and co-heirs; anyhow the place has been empty for years.

That spoils my ghostliness, I am afraid, but I don't care—there is something strange about the house—I can feel it.

I even said so to John one moonlight evening, but he said what I felt was a draught, and shut the window.

I get unreasonably angry with John sometimes. I'm sure I never used to be so sensitive. I think it is due to this nervous condition.

But John says if I feel so I shall neglect proper self-control; so I take pains to control myself—before him, at least, and that makes me very tired.

I don't like our room a bit. I wanted one downstairs that opened on the piazza and had roses all over the window, and such pretty old-fashioned chintz hangings! But John would not hear of it.

He said there was only one window and not room for two beds, and no near room for him if he took another.

He is very careful and loving, and hardly lets me stir without special direction.

I have a schedule prescription for each hour in the day; he takes all care from me, and so I feel basely ungrateful not to value it more.

He said he came here solely on my account, that I was to have perfect rest and all the air I could get. "Your exercise depends on your strength, my dear," said he, "and your food somewhat on your appetite; but air you can absorb all the time." So we took the nursery at the top of the house.

It is a big, airy room, the whole floor nearly, with windows that look all ways, and air and sunshine galore. It was nursery first, and then playroom and gymnasium, I should judge; for the windows are barred for little children, and there are rings and things in the walls.

The paint and paper look as if a boys' school had used it. It is stripped off—the paper—in great patches all around the head of my bed, about as far as I can reach, and in a great place on the other side of the room low down. I never saw a worse paper in my life.

One of those sprawling, flamboyant patterns committing every artistic sin.

It is dull enough to confuse the eye in following, pronounced enough constantly to irritate and provoke study, and when you follow the lame uncertain curves for a little distance they suddenly

commit suicide—plunge off at outrageous angles, destroy themselves in unheard-of contradictions.

The color is repellent, almost revolting; a smouldering unclean
yellow, strangely faded by the slow-turning sunlight.

It is a dull yet lurid orange in some places, a sickly sulphur tint
in others.

No wonder the children hated it! I should hate it myself if I
had to live in this room long.

There comes John, and I must put this away—he hates to have
me write a word.

We have been here two weeks, and I haven't felt like writing
before, since that first day.

I am sitting by the window now, up in this atrocious nursery,
and there is nothing to hinder my writing as much as I please,
save lack of strength.

John is away all day, and even some nights when his cases are
serious.

I am glad my case is not serious!

But these nervous troubles are dreadfully depressing.

John does not know how much I really suffer. He knows there
is no *reason* to suffer, and that satisfies him.

Of course it is only nervousness. It does weigh on me so not to
do my duty in any way!

I meant to be such a help to John, such a real rest and comfort,
and here I am a comparative burden already!

Nobody would believe what an effort it is to do what little I
am able—to dress and entertain, and order things.

It is fortunate Mary is so good with the baby. Such a dear baby!

And yet I *cannot* be with him, it makes me so nervous.

I suppose John never was nervous in his life. He laughs at me
so about this wallpaper!

At first he meant to repaper the room, but afterward he said that I was letting it get the better of me, and that nothing was worse for a nervous patient than to give way to such fancies.

He said that after the wallpaper was changed it would be the heavy bedstead, and then the barred windows, and then that gate at the head of the stairs, and so on.

"You know the place is doing you good," he said, "and really, dear, I don't care to renovate the house just for a three months' rental."

"Then do let us go downstairs," I said, "there are such pretty rooms there."

Then he took me in his arms and called me a blessed little goose, and said he would go down cellar, if I wished, and have it whitewashed into the bargain.

But he is right enough about the beds and windows and things.

It is an airy and comfortable room as any one need wish, and, of course, I would not be so silly as to make him uncomfortable just for a whim.

I'm really getting quite fond of the big room, all but that horrid paper.

Out of one window I can see the garden, those mysterious deep-shaded arbors, the riotous old-fashioned flowers, and bushes and gnarly trees.

Out of another I get a lovely view of the bay and a little private wharf belonging to the estate. There is a beautiful shaded lane that runs down there from the house. I always fancy I see people walking in these numerous paths and arbors, but John has cautioned me not to give way to fancy in the least. He says that with my imaginative power and habit of story-making, a nervous weakness like mine is sure to lead to all manner of excited fancies, and that I ought to use my will and good sense to check the tendency. So I try.

I think sometimes that if I were only well enough to write a little, it would relieve the press of ideas and rest me.

But I find I get pretty tired when I try.

It is so discouraging not to have any advice and companionship about my work. When I get really well, John says we will ask Cousin Henry and Julia down for a long visit; but he says he would as soon put fireworks in my pillow-case as to let me have those stimulating people about now.

I wish I could get well faster.

But I must not think about that. This paper looks to me as if it *knew* what a vicious influence it had!

There is a recurrent spot where the pattern lolls like a broken neck and two bulbous eyes stare at you upside down.

I get positively angry with the impertinence of it and the everlastingness. Up and down and sideways they crawl and those absurd, unblinking eyes are everywhere. There is one place where two breadths didn't match, and the eyes go all up and down the line, one a little higher than the other.

I never saw so much expression in an inanimate thing before, and we all know how much expression they have! I used to lie awake as a child and get more entertainment and terror out of black walls and plain furniture than most children could find in a toy-store.

I remember what a kindly wink the knobs of our big, old bureau used to have, and there was one chair that always seemed like a strong friend.

I used to feel that if any of the other things looked too fierce I could always hop into that chair and be safe.

The furniture in this room is no worse than inharmonious, however, for we had to bring it all from downstairs. I suppose when this was used as a playroom they had to take the nursery things out, and no wonder! I never saw such ravages as the children have made here.

The wallpaper, as I said before, is torn off in spots, and it sticketh closer than a brother—they must have had perseverance as well as hatred.

Then the floor is scratched and gouged and splintered, the plaster itself is dug out here and there, and this great heavy bed which is all we found in the room, looks as if it had been through the wars.

But I don't mind it a bit—only the paper.

There comes John's sister. Such a dear girl as she is, and so careful of me! I must not let her find me writing.

She is a perfect and enthusiastic housekeeper, and hopes for no better profession. I verily believe she thinks it is the writing which made me sick!

But I can write when she is out, and see her a long way off from these windows.

There is one that commands the road, a lovely shaded winding road, and one that just looks off over the country. A lovely country, too, full of great elms and velvet meadows.

This wallpaper has a kind of sub-pattern in a different shade, a particularly irritating one, for you can only see it in certain lights, and not clearly then.

But in the places where it isn't faded and where the sun is just so—I can see a strange, provoking, formless sort of figure, that seems to skulk about behind that silly and conspicuous front design.

There's sister on the stairs!

Well, the Fourth of July is over! The people are all gone and I am tired out. John thought it might do me good to see a little company, so we just had mother and Nellie and the children down for a week.

Of course I didn't do a thing. Jennie sees to everything now.

But it tired me all the same.

John says if I don't pick up faster he shall send me to Weir Mitchell in the fall.

But I don't want to go there at all. I had a friend who was in his hands once, and she says he is just like John and my brother, only more so!

Besides, it is such an undertaking to go so far.

I don't feel as if it was worth while to turn my hand over for anything, and I'm getting dreadfully fretful and querulous.

I cry at nothing, and cry most of the time.

Of course I don't when John is here, or anybody else, but when I am alone.

And I am alone a good deal just now. John is kept in town very often by serious cases, and Jennie is good and lets me alone when I want her to.

So I walk a little in the garden or down that lovely lane, sit on the porch under the roses, and lie down up here a good deal.

I'm getting really fond of the room in spite of the wallpaper. Perhaps *because* of the wallpaper.

It dwells in my mind so!

I lie here on this great immovable bed—it is nailed down, I believe—and follow that pattern about by the hour. It is as good as gymnastics, I assure you. I start, we'll say, at the bottom, down in the corner over there where it has not been touched, and I determine for the thousandth time that I *will* follow that pointless pattern to some sort of a conclusion.

I know a little of the principle of design, and I know this thing was not arranged on any laws of radiation, or alternation, or repetition, or symmetry, or anything else that I ever heard of.

It is repeated, of course, by the breadths, but not otherwise.

Looked at in one way each breadth stands alone, the bloated curves and flourishes—a kind of "debased Romanesque" with delirium tremens—go waddling up and down in isolated columns of fatuity.

But, on the other hand, they connect diagonally, and the sprawling outlines run off in great slanting waves of optic horror, like a lot of wallowing sea-weeds in full chase.

The whole thing goes horizontally, too, at least it seems so, and I exhaust myself trying to distinguish the order of its going in that direction.

They have used a horizontal breadth for a frieze, and that adds wonderfully to the confusion.

There is one end of the room where it is almost intact, and there, when the crosslights fade and the low sun shines directly upon it, I can almost fancy radiation after all—the interminable grotesque seems to form around a common centre and rush off in headlong plunges of equal distraction.

It makes me tired to follow it. I will take a nap, I guess.

I don't know why I should write this.

I don't want to.

I don't feel able.

And I know John would think it absurd. But I must say what I feel and think in some way—it is such a relief!

But the effort is getting to be greater than the relief.

Half the time now I am awfully lazy, and lie down ever so much. John says I mustn't lose my strength, and has me take cod liver oil and lots of tonics and things, to say nothing of ale and wine and rare meat.

Dear John! He loves me very dearly, and hates to have me sick. I tried to have a real earnest, reasonable talk with him the other day, and tell him how I wish he would let me go and make a visit to Cousin Henry and Julia.

But he said I wasn't able to go, nor able to stand it after I got there; and I did not make out a very good case for myself, for I was crying before I had finished.

It is getting to be a great effort for me to think straight. Just this nervous weakness, I suppose.

And dear John gathered me up in his arms, and just carried me upstairs and laid me on the bed, and sat by me and read to me till it tired my head.

He said I was his darling and his comfort and all he had, and that I must take care of myself for his sake, and keep well.

He says no one but myself can help me out of it, that I must use my will and self-control and not let any silly fancies run away with me.

There's one comfort, the baby is well and happy, and does not have to occupy this nursery with the horrid wallpaper.

If we had not used it, that blessed child would have! What a fortunate escape! Why, I wouldn't have a child of mine, an impressionable little thing, live in such a room for worlds.

I never thought of it before, but it is lucky that John kept me here after all. I can stand it so much easier than a baby, you see.

Of course I never mention it to them any more—I am too wise—but I keep watch for it all the same.

There are things in that wallpaper that nobody knows about but me, or ever will.

Behind that outside pattern the dim shapes get clearer every day.

It is always the same shape, only very numerous.

And it is like a woman stooping down and creeping about behind that pattern. I don't like it a bit. I wonder—I begin to think—I wish John would take me away from here!

It is so hard to talk with John about my case, because he is so wise, and because he loves me so.

But I tried it last night.

It was moonlight. The moon shines in all around just as the sun does.

I hate to see it sometimes, it creeps so slowly, and always comes in by one window or another.

John was asleep and I hated to waken him, so I kept still and watched the moonlight on that undulating wallpaper till I felt creepy.

The faint figure behind seemed to shake the pattern, just as if she wanted to get out.

I got up softly and went to feel and see if the paper *did* move, and when I came back John was awake.

"What is it, little girl?" he said. "Don't go walking about like that—you'll get cold."

I thought it was a good time to talk so I told him that I really was not gaining here, and that I wished he would take me away.

"Why, darling!" said he, "our lease will be up in three weeks, and I can't see how to leave before.

"The repairs are not done at home, and I cannot possibly leave town just now. Of course if you were in any danger, I could and would, but you really are better, dear, whether you can see it or not. I am a doctor, dear, and I know. You are gaining flesh and color, your appetite is better, I feel really much easier about you."

"I don't weigh a bit more," said I, "nor as much; and my appetite may be better in the evening when you are here, but it is worse in the morning when you are away!"

"Bless her little heart!" said he with a big hug, "she shall be as sick as she pleases! But now let's improve the shining hours by going to sleep and talk about it in the morning!"

"And you won't go away?" I asked gloomily.

"Why, how can I, dear? It is only three weeks more, and then we will take a nice little trip of a few days while Jennie is getting the house ready. Really, dear, you are better!"

"Better in body perhaps—" I began, and stopped short, for he sat up straight and looked at me with such a stern, reproachful look that I could not say another word.

"My darling," said he, "I beg of you, for my sake and for our child's sake, as well as for your own, that you will never for one instant let that idea enter your mind! There is nothing so dangerous, so fascinating, to a temperament like yours. It is a false and foolish fancy. Can you not trust me as a physician when I tell you so?"

So of course I said no more on that score, and we went to sleep before long. He thought I was asleep first, but I wasn't, and lay there for hours trying to decide whether that front pattern and the back pattern really did move together or separately.

On a pattern like this, by daylight, there is a lack of sequence, a defiance of law, that is a constant irritant to a normal mind.

The color is hideous enough, and unreliable enough, and infuriating enough, but the pattern is torturing.

You think you have mastered it, but just as you get well under way in following, it turns a back-somersault and there you are. It slaps you in the face, knocks you down, and tramples upon you. It is like a bad dream.

The outside pattern is a florid arabesque, reminding one of a fungus. If you can imagine a toadstool in joints, an interminable string of toadstools, budding and sprouting in endless convolutions—why, that is something like it.

That is, sometimes!

There is one marked peculiarity about this paper, a thing nobody seems to notice but myself, and that is that it changes as the light changes.

When the sun shoots in through the east window—I always watch for that first, long, straight ray—it changes so quickly that I never can quite believe it.

That is why I watch it always.

By moonlight—the moon shines in all night when there is a moon—I wouldn't know it was the same paper.

At night in any kind of light, in twilight, candlelight, lamplight, and worst of all by moonlight, it becomes bars! The outside pattern I mean, and the woman behind it is as plain as can be.

I didn't realize for a long time what the thing was that showed behind, that dim sub-pattern, but now I am quite sure it is a woman.

By daylight she is subdued, quiet. I fancy it is the pattern that keeps her so still. It is so puzzling. It keeps me quiet by the hour.

I lie down ever so much now. John says it is good for me, and to sleep all I can.

Indeed he started the habit by making me lie down for an hour after each meal.

It is a very bad habit, I am convinced, for you see I don't sleep.

And that cultivates deceit, for I don't tell them I'm awake— oh, no!

The fact is I am getting a little afraid of John.

He seems very queer sometimes, and even Jennie has an inexplicable look.

It strikes me occasionally, just as a scientific hypothesis, that perhaps it is the paper!

I have watched John when he did not know I was looking, and come into the room suddenly on the most innocent excuses, and I've caught him several times *looking at the paper!* And Jennie too. I caught Jennie with her hand on it once.

She didn't know I was in the room, and when I asked her in a quiet, a very quiet voice, with the most restrained manner possible, what she was doing with the paper—she turned around as if she had been caught stealing, and looked quite angry—asked me why I should frighten her so!

Then she said that the paper stained everything it touched, that she had found yellow smooches on all my clothes and John's, and she wished we would be more careful!

Did not that sound innocent? But I know she was studying that pattern, and I am determined that nobody shall find it out but myself!

Life is very much more exciting now than it used to be. You see I have something more to expect, to look forward to, to watch. I really do eat better, and am more quiet than I was.

John is so pleased to see me improve! He laughed a little the other day, and said I seemed to be flourishing in spite of my wallpaper.

I turned it off with a laugh. I had no intention of telling him it was *because* of the wallpaper—he would make fun of me. He might even want to take me away.

I don't want to leave now until I have found it out. There is a week more, and I think that will be enough.

I'm feeling so much better!

I don't sleep much at night, for it is so interesting to watch developments; but I sleep a good deal during the daytime.

In the daytime it is tiresome and perplexing.

There are always new shoots on the fungus, and new shades of yellow all over it. I cannot keep count of them, though I have tried conscientiously.

It is the strangest yellow, that wallpaper! It makes me think of all the yellow things I ever saw—not beautiful ones like buttercups, but old foul, bad yellow things.

But there is something else about that paper—the smell! I noticed it the moment we came into the room, but with so much air and sun it was not bad. Now we have had a week of fog and rain and whether the windows are open or not, the smell is here.

It creeps all over the house.

I find it hovering in the dining-room, skulking in the parlor, hiding in the hall, lying in wait for me on the stairs.

It gets into my hair.

Even when I go to ride, if I turn my head suddenly and surprise it—there is that smell!

Such a peculiar odor, too! I have spent hours in trying to analyze it, to find what it smelled like.

It is not bad—at first, and very gentle, but quite the subtlest, most enduring odor I ever met.

In this damp weather it is awful. I wake up in the night and find it hanging over me.

It used to disturb me at first. I thought seriously of burning the house—to reach the smell.

But now I am used to it. The only thing I can think of that it is like is the color of the paper! A yellow smell.

There is a very funny mark on this wall, low down, near the mop-board. A streak that runs round the room. It goes behind every piece of furniture, except the bed, a long, straight, even smooch, as if it had been rubbed over and over.

I wonder how it was done and who did it, and what they did it for. Round and round and round—round and round and round —it makes me dizzy!

I really have discovered something at last.

Through watching so much at night, when it changes so, I have finally found out.

The front pattern *does* move—and no wonder! The woman behind shakes it!

Sometimes I think there are a great many women behind, and sometimes only one, and she crawls around fast, and her crawling shakes it all over.

Then in the very bright spots she keeps still, and in the very shady spots she just takes hold of the bars and shakes them hard.

And she is all the time trying to climb through. But nobody could climb through that pattern—it strangles so; I think that is why it has so many heads.

They get through, and then the pattern strangles them off and turns them upside down, and makes their eyes white!

If those heads were covered or taken off it would not be half so bad.

I think that woman gets out in the daytime!

And I'll tell you why—privately—I've seen her!

I can see her out of every one of my windows!

It is the same woman, I know, for she is always creeping, and most women do not creep by daylight.

I see her in that long shaded lane, creeping up and down. I see her in those dark grape arbors, creeping all around the garden.

I see her on that long road under the trees, creeping along, and when a carriage comes she hides under the blackberry vines.

I don't blame her a bit. It must be very humiliating to be caught creeping by daylight!

I always lock the door when I creep by daylight. I can't do it at night, for I know John would suspect something at once.

And John is so queer now, that I don't want to irritate him. I wish he would take another room! Besides, I don't want anybody to get that woman out at night but myself.

I often wonder if I could see her out of all the windows at once.

But, turn as fast as I can, I can only see out of one at one time.

And though I always see her, she may be able to creep faster than I can turn! I have watched her sometimes away off in the open country, creeping as fast as a cloud shadow in a wind.

If only that top pattern could be gotten off from the under one! I mean to try it, little by little.

I have found out another funny thing, but I shan't tell it this time! It does not do to trust people too much.

There are only two more days to get this paper off, and I believe John is beginning to notice. I don't like the look in his eyes.

And I heard him ask Jennie a lot of professional questions about me. She had a very good report to give.

She said I slept a good deal in the daytime.

John knows I don't sleep very well at night, for all I'm so quiet!

He asked me all sorts of questions, too, and pretended to be very loving and kind.

As if I couldn't see through him!

Still, I don't wonder he acts so, sleeping under this paper for three months.

It only interests me, but I feel sure John and Jennie are affected by it.

Hurrah! This is the last day, but it is enough. John is to stay in town over night, and won't be out until this evening.

Jennie wanted to sleep with me—the sly thing; but I told her I should undoubtedly rest better for a night all alone.

That was clever, for really I wasn't alone a bit! As soon as it was moonlight and that poor thing began to crawl and shake the pattern, I got up and ran to help her.

I pulled and she shook, I shook and she pulled, and before morning we had peeled off yards of that paper.

A strip about as high as my head and half around the room.

And then when the sun came and that awful pattern began to laugh at me, I declared I would finish it today!

We go away tomorrow, and they are moving all my furniture down again to leave things as they were before.

Jennie looked at the wall in amazement, but I told her merrily that I did it out of pure spite at the vicious thing.

She laughed and said she wouldn't mind doing it herself, but I must not get tired.

How she betrayed herself that time!

But I am here, and no person touches this paper but Me—not alive!

She tried to get me out of the room—it was too patent! But I said it was so quiet and empty and clean now that I believed I would lie down again and sleep all I could; and not to wake me even for dinner—I would call when I woke.

So now she is gone, and the servants are gone, and the things are gone, and there is nothing left but that great bedstead nailed down, with the canvas mattress we found on it.

We shall sleep downstairs tonight, and take the boat home tomorrow.

I quite enjoy the room, now it is bare again.

How those children did tear about here!

This bedstead is fairly gnawed!

But I must get to work.

I have locked the door and thrown the key down into the front path.

I don't want to go out, and I don't want to have anybody come in, till John comes.

I want to astonish him.

I've got a rope up here that even Jennie did not find. If that woman does get out, and tries to get away, I can tie her!

But I forgot I could not reach far without anything to stand on! This bed will *not* move!

I tried to lift and push it until I was lame, and then I got so angry I bit off a little piece at one corner—but it hurt my teeth.

Then I peeled off all the paper I could reach standing on the floor. It sticks horribly and the pattern just enjoys it! All those strangled heads and bulbous eyes and waddling fungus growths just shriek with derision!

I am getting angry enough to do something desperate. To jump out of the window would be admirable exercise, but the bars are too strong even to try.

Besides I wouldn't do it. Of course not. I know well enough that a step like that is improper and might be misconstrued.

I don't like to *look* out of the windows even—there are so many of those creeping women, and they creep so fast.

I wonder if they all come out of that wallpaper as I did?

But I am securely fastened now by my well-hidden rope—you don't get *me* out in the road there!

I suppose I shall have to get back behind the pattern when it comes night, and that is hard!

It is so pleasant to be out in this great room and creep around as I please!

I don't want to go outside. I won't, even if Jennie asks me to.

For outside you have to creep on the ground, and everything is green instead of yellow.

But here I can creep smoothly on the floor, and my shoulder just fits in that long smooch around the wall, so I cannot lose my way.

Why there's John at the door!

It is no use, young man, you can't open it!

How he does call and pound!

Now he's crying to Jennie for an axe.

It would be a shame to break down that beautiful door!

"John, dear!" said I in the gentlest voice, "the key is down by the front steps, under a plantain leaf!"

That silenced him for a few moments.

Then he said, very quietly indeed, "Open the door, my darling!"

"I can't," said I. "The key is down by the front door under a plantain leaf!" And then I said it again, several times, very gently and slowly, and said it so often that he had to go and see, and he got it of course, and came in. He stopped short by the door.

"What is the matter?" he cried. "For God's sake, what are you doing!"

I kept on creeping just the same, but I looked at him over my shoulder.

"I've got out at last," said I, "in spite of you and Jane. And I've pulled off most of the paper, so you can't put me back!"

Now, why should that man have fainted? But he did, and right across my path by the wall, so that I had to creep over him every time!

Reprinted by permission of Katharine Beecher Stetson Chamberlin, executrix.

1. What is the terrible significance of the nursery with its "air and sunshine galore"?
2. The woman speaks of "the pointless pattern" of the wallpaper; how is this related to the story?
3. Why does the woman think that her husband "seems very queer sometimes, and even Jennie has an inexplicable look"?
4. With what attributes does the woman invest the wallpaper?
5. Do you think that the woman was driven to hopeless madness by the wallpaper alone?

*Helen R. Hull*

# CLAY-SHUTTERED DOORS

**F**OR months I have tried not to think about Thalia Corson.
Anything may invoke her, with her languorous fragility,
thin wrists and throat, her elusive face with its long eyelids. I can't quite remember her mouth. When I try to
visualize her sharply I get soft pale hair, the lovely curve from
her temple to chin, and eyes blue and intense. Her boy, Fletcher,
has eyes like hers.

Today I came back to New York, and my taxi to an uptown
hotel was held for a few minutes in Broadway traffic where the
afternoon sunlight fused into a dazzle a great expanse of plateglass
and elaborate show motor cars. The "Regal Eight"—Winchester
Corson's establishment. I huddled as the taxi jerked ahead, in
spite of knowledge that Winchester would scarcely peer out of
that elegant setting into taxicabs. I didn't wish to see him, nor
would he care to see me. But the glimpse had started the whole
affair churning again, and I went through it deliberately, hoping
that it might have smoothed out into some rational explanation.
Sometimes things do, if you leave them alone, like logs submerged
in water that float up later, encrusted thickly. This affair won't
add to itself. It stays unique and smooth, sliding through the rest
of life without annexing a scrap of seaweed.

I suppose, for an outsider, it all begins with the moment on

Brooklyn Bridge; behind that are the years of my friendship with Thalia. Our families had summer cottages on the Cape. She was just enough older, however, so that not until I had finished college did I catch up to any intimacy with her. She had married Winchester Corson, who at that time fitted snugly into the phrase "a rising young man." During those first years, while his yeast sent up preliminary bubbles, Thalia continued to spend her summers near Boston, with Winchester coming for occasional week-ends. Fletcher was, unintentionally, born there; he began his difficult existence by arriving as a seven-months baby. Two years later Thalia had a second baby to bring down with her. Those were the summers which gave my friendship for Thalia its sturdy roots. They made me wonder, too, why she had chosen Winchester Corson. He was personable enough; tall, with prominent dark eyes and full mouth under a neat mustache, restless hands, and an uncertain disposition. He could be a charming companion, sailing the catboat with dash, managing lobster parties on the shore; or he would, unaccountably, settle into a foggy grouch, when everyone—children and females particularly—was supposed to approach only on tiptoe, bearing burnt offerings. The last time he spent a fortnight there, before he moved the family to the new Long Island estate, I had my own difficulties with him. There had always been an undertone of sex in his attitude toward me, but I had thought "that's just his male conceit." That summer he was a nuisance, coming upon me with his insistent, messy kisses, usually with Thalia in the next room. They were the insulting kind of kisses that aren't at all personal, and I could have ended them fast enough if there hadn't been the complication of Thalia and my love for her. If I made Winchester angry he'd put an end to Thalia's relation to me. I didn't, anyway, want her to know what a fool he was. Of course she did know, but I thought then that I could protect her.

There are, I have decided, two ways with love. You can hold one love, knowing that, if it is a living thing, it must develop and change. That takes maturity, and care, and a consciousness of the other person. That was Thalia's way. Or you enjoy the beginning of love and, once you're past that, you have to hunt for a new love, because the excitement seems to be gone. Men like Winchester who use all their brains on their jobs, never grow up; they go on thinking that preliminary stir and snap is love itself. Cut flowers, that was Winchester's idea, while to Thalia love was a tree.

But I said Brooklyn Bridge was the point at which the affair had its start. It seems impossible to begin there, or anywhere, as I try to account for what happened. Ten years after the summer when Winchester made himself such a nuisance—that last summer the Corsons spent at the Cape—I went down at the end of the season for a week with Thalia and the children at the Long Island place. Winchester drove out for the week-end. The children were mournful because they didn't wish to leave the shore for school; a sharp September wind brought rain and fog down the Sound, and Winchester nourished all that Sunday a disagreeable grouch. I had seen nothing of them for most of the ten intervening years, as I had been first in France and then in China, after feature-article stuff. The week had been pleasant: good servants, comfortable house, a half-moon of white beach below the drop of lawn; Thalia a stimulating listener, with Fletcher, a thin, eager boy of twelve, like her in his intensity of interest. Dorothy, a plump, pink child of ten, had no use for stories of French villages or Chinese temples. Nug, the wire-haired terrier, and her dolls were more immediate and convincing. Thalia was thin and non-committal, except for her interest in what I had seen and done. I couldn't, for all my affection, establish any real contact. She spoke casually of the town house, of dinners she gave for Winchester, of his absorption in business affairs. But she was sheathed in polished aloofness and told me nothing of herself. She did say, one evening, that she was glad I was to be in New York that winter. Winchester, like his daugher Dorothy, had no interest in foreign parts once he had ascertained that I hadn't even seen the Chinese quarters of the motor company in which he was concerned. He had an amusing attitude toward me: careful indifference, no doubt calculated to put me in my place as no longer alluring. Thalia tried to coax him into listening to some of my best stories. "Tell him about the bandits, Mary"—but his sulkiness brought, after dinner, a casual explanation from her, untinged with apology. "He's working on an enormous project, a merging of several companies, and he's so soaked in it he can't come up for a breath."

In the late afternoon the maid set out high tea for us, before our departure for New York. Thalia suggested that perhaps one highball was enough if Winchester intended to drive over the wet roads. Win immediately mixed a second, asking if she had ever seen him in the least affected. "Be better for you than tea before a long damp drive, too." He clinked the ice in his glass. "Jazz you up a bit." Nug was begging for food and Thalia, bending to give him a corner of her sandwich, apparently did not hear Winchester. He looked about the room, a smug, owning look. The fire and candlelight shone in the heavy waxed rafters, made silver beads of the rain on the French windows. I watched him—heavier, more dominant, his prominent dark eyes and his lips sullen, as if the whiskey banked up his temper rather than appeased it.

Then Jim, the gardener, brought the car to the door; the children scrambled in. Dorothy wanted to take Nug, but her father said not if she wanted to sit with him and drive.

"How about chains, sir?" Jim held the umbrella for Thalia.

"Too damned noisy. Don't need them." Winchester slammed the door and slid under the wheel. Thalia and I, with Fletcher between us, sat comfortably in the rear.

"I like it better when Walter drives, don't you, Mother?" said Fletcher as we slid down the drive out to the road.

"Sh—Father likes to drive. And Walter likes Sunday off, too." Thalia's voice was cautious.

"It's too dark to see anything."

"I can see lots," announced Dorothy, whereupon Fletcher promptly turned the handle that pushed up the glass between the chauffeur's seat and the rear.

The heavy car ran smoothly over the wet narrow road, with an occasional rumble and flare of headlights as some car swung past. Not till we reached the turnpike was there much traffic. There Winchester had to slacken his speed for other shiny beetles slipping along through the rain. Sometimes he cut past a car, weaving back into line in the glaring teeth of a car rushing down on him, and Fletcher would turn inquiringly toward his mother. The gleaming, wet darkness and the smooth motion made me drowsy, and I paid little heed until we slowed in a congestion of cars at the approach to the bridge. Far below on the black river, spaced red and white stars suggested slow-moving tugs, and beyond, faint lights splintered in the rain hinted at the city.

"Let's look for the cliff dwellers, Mother."

Thalia leaned forward, her fine, sharp profile dimly outlined against the shifting background of arches, and Fletcher slipped to his feet, his arm about her neck. "There!"

We were reaching the New York end of the bridge, and I had a swift glimpse of their cliff dwellers—lights in massed buildings, like ancient camp fires along a receding mountain side. Just then Winchester nosed out of the slow line, Dorothy screamed, the light from another car tunnelled through our windows, the car trembled under the sudden grip of brakes, and like a crazy top spun sickeningly about, with a final thud against the stone abutment. A shatter of glass, a confusion of motor horns about us, a moment while the tautness of shock held me rigid.

Around me that periphery of turmoil—the usual recriminations, "what the hell you think you're doing?"—the shriek of a siren on an approaching motorcycle. Within the circle I tried to move across the narrow space of the car. Fletcher was crying; vaguely I knew that the door had swung open, that Thalia was crouching on her knees, the rain and the lights pouring on her head and shoulders; her hat was gone, her wide fur collar looked like a drenched and lifeless animal. "Hush, Fletcher." I managed to force movement into my stiff body. "Are you hurt? Thalia—" Then outside Winchester, with the bristling fury of panic, was trying to lift her drooping head. "Thalia! My God, you aren't hurt!" Someone focussed a searchlight on the car as Winchester got his arms about her and lifted her out through the shattered door.

Over the springing line of the stone arch I saw the cliff dwellers' fires and I thought as I scrambled out to follow Winchester, "She was leaning forward, looking at those, and that terrific spin of the car must have knocked her head on the door as it lurched open."

"Lay her down, man!" An important little fellow had rushed up, a doctor evidently. "Lay her down, you fool!" Someone threw down a robe, and Winchester, as if Thalia were a drowned feather, knelt with her, laid her there on the pavement. I was down beside her and the fussy little man also. She did look drowned, drowned in that beating sea of tumult, that terrific honking of motors, unwilling to stop an instant even for—was it death? Under the white glare of headlights her lovely face had the empty shallowness, the husklikeness of death. The little doctor had his pointed beard close to her breast; he lifted one of her long eyelids. "She's just fainted, eh, doctor?" Winchester's angry voice tore at him.

The little man rose slowly. "She your wife? I'm sorry. Death must have been instantaneous. A blow on the temple."

With a kind of roar Winchester was down there beside Thalia, lifting her, her head lolling against his shoulder, his face bent over her. "Thalia! Thalia! Do you hear? Wake up!" I think he even shook her in his baffled fright and rage. "Thalia, do you hear me? I want you to open your eyes. You weren't hurt. That was nothing." And then, "Dearest, you must!" and more words, frantic, wild words, mouthed close to her empty face. I touched his shoulder, sick with pity, but he staggered up to his feet, lifting her with him. Fletcher pressed shivering against me, and I turned for an instant to the child. Then I heard Thalia's voice, blurred and queer, "You called me, Win?" and Winchester's sudden, trium phant laugh. She was standing against his shoulder, still with that husklike face, but she spoke again, "You did call me?"

"Here, let's get out of this." Winchester was again the efficient, competent man of affairs. The traffic cops were shouting, the lines of cars began to move. Winchester couldn't start his motor. Something had smashed. His card and a few words left responsibility with an officer, and even as an ambulance shrilled up, he was helping Thalia into a taxi. "You take the children, will you?" to me, and "Get her another taxi, will you?" to the officer. He had closed the taxi door after himself, and was gone, leaving us to the waning curiosity of passing cars. As we rode off in a second taxi, I had a glimpse of the little doctor, his face incredulous, his beard wagging, as he spoke to the officer.

Dorothy was, characteristically, tearfully indignant that her father had left her to me. Fletcher was silent as we bumped along under the elevated tracks, but presently he tugged at my sleeve, and I heard his faint whisper. "What is it?" I asked.

"Is my mother really dead?" he repeated.

"Of course not, Fletcher. You saw her get into the cab with your father."

"Why didn't Daddy take us too?" wailed Dorothy, and I had to turn to her, although my nerves echoed her question.

The house door swung open even as the taxi bumped the curb, and the butler hurried out with an umbrella which we were too draggled to need.

"Mr. Corson instructed me to pay the man, madam." He led us into the hall, where a waiting maid popped the children at once into the tiny elevator.

"Will you wait for the elevator, madam? The library is one flight." The butler led me up the stairs, and I dropped into a low chair near the fire, vaguely aware of the long narrow room, with the discreet gold of the walls giving back light from soft lamps. "I'll tell Mr. Corson you have come."

"Is Mrs. Corson—does she seem all right?" I asked.

"Quite, madam. It was a fortunate accident, with no one hurt."

Well, perhaps it had addled my brain! I waited in a kind of numbness for Winchester to come.

Presently he strode in, his feet silent on the thick rugs.

"Sorry," he began, abruptly. "I wanted to look the children over. Not a scratch on them. You're all right, of course?"

"Oh, yes. But Thalia—"

"She won't even have a doctor. I put her straight to bed—she's so damned nervous, you know. Hot-water bottles . . . she was cold. I think she's asleep now. Said she'd see you in the morning. You'll stay here, of course." He swallowed in a gulp the whiskey he had poured. "Have some, Mary? Or would you like something hot?"

"No, thanks. If you're sure she's all right I'll go to bed."

"Sure?" His laugh was defiant. "Did that damn fool on the bridge throw a scare into you? He gave me a bad minute, I'll say. If that car hadn't cut in on me—I told Walter last week the brakes needed looking at. They shouldn't grab like that. Might have been serious."

"Since it wasn't—" I rose, wearily, watching him pour amber liquid slowly into his glass—"if you'll have someone show me my room—"

"After Chinese bandits, a little skid ought not to matter to you." His prominent eyes gleamed hostilely at me; he wanted some assurance offered that the skidding wasn't his fault, that only his skill had saved all our lives.

"I can't see Thalia?" I said.

"She's asleep. Nobody can see her." His eyes moved coldly from my face, down to my muddy shoes. "Better give your clothes to the maid for a pressing. You're smeared quite a bit."

I woke early, with clear September sun at the windows of the room, with blue sky behind the sharp city contours beyond the windows. There was none too much time to make the morning train for Albany, where I had an engagement that day, an interview for an article. The maid who answered my ring insisted on serving breakfast to me in borrowed elegance of satin negligée. Mrs. Corson was resting, and would see me before I left. Something—the formality and luxury, the complicated household so unlike the old days at the Cape—accented the queer dread which had filtered all night through my dreams.

I saw Thalia for only a moment. The heavy silk curtains were drawn against the light and in the dimness her face seemed to gather shadows.

"Are you quite all right, Thalia?" I hesitated beside her bed, as if my voice might tear apart the veils of drowsiness in which she rested.

"Why, yes—" as if she wondered. Then she added, so low that I wasn't sure what I heard, "It is hard to get back in."

"What, Thalia?" I bent toward her.

"I'll be myself once I've slept enough." Her voice was clearer. "Come back soon, won't you, Mary?" Then her eyelids closed and her face merged into the shadows of the room. I tiptoed away, thinking she slept.

It was late November before I returned to New York. Freelancing has a way of drawing herrings across your trail and, when I might have drifted back in early November, a younger sister wanted me to come home to Arlington for her marriage. I had written to Thalia, first a note of courtesy for my week with her, and then a letter begging for news. Like many people of charm, she wrote indifferent letters, stiff and childlike, lacking in her personal quality. Her brief reply was more unsatisfactory than usual. The children were away in school, lots of cold rainy weather, everything was going well. At the end, in writing unlike hers, as if she scribbled the line in haste, "I am lonely. When are you coming?" I answered that I'd show up as soon as the wedding was over.

The night I reached Arlington was rainy, too, and I insisted upon a taxi equipped with chains. My brother thought that amusing, and at dinner gave the family an exaggerated account of my caution. I tried to offer him some futile sisterly advice and, to point up my remarks, told about that drive in from Long Island with the Corsons. I had never spoken of it before; I found that an inexplicable inhibition kept me from making much of a story.

"Well, nothing happened, did it?" Richard was triumphant.

"A great deal might have," I insisted. "Thalia was stunned, and I was disagreeably startled."

"Thalia was stunned, was she?" An elderly cousin of ours from New Jersey picked out that item. I saw her fitting it into some pigeonhole, but she said nothing until late that evening when she stopped at the door of my room.

"Have you seen Thalia Corson lately?" she asked.

"I haven't been in New York since September."

She closed the door and lowered her voice, a kind of avid curiosity riding astride the decorous pity she expressed.

"I called there, one day last week. I didn't know what was the matter with her. I hadn't heard of that accident."

I waited, an old antagonism for my proper cousin blurring the fear that shot up through my thoughts.

"Thalia was always *individual*, of course." She used the word like a reproach. "But she had *savoir faire*. But now she's—well—queer. Do you suppose her head was affected?"

"How is she queer?"

"She looks miserable, too. Thin and white."

"But how—"

"I am telling you, Mary. She was quite rude. First she didn't come down for ever so long, although I sent up word that I'd come up to her room if she was resting. Then her whole manner—well, I was really offended. She scarcely heard a word I said to her, just sat with her back to a window so I couldn't get a good look at her. When I said, 'You don't look like yourself,' she actually sneered. 'Myself?' she said. 'How do you know?' Imagine! I tried to chatter along as if I noticed nothing. I flatter myself I can manage awkward moments rather well. But Thalia sat there and I am sure she muttered under her breath. Finally I rose to go and I said, meaning well, 'You'd better take a good rest. You look half dead.' Mary, I wish you'd seen the look she gave me! Really I was frightened. Just then their dog came in, you know, Dorothy's little terrier. Thalia used to be silly about him. Well, she actually tried to hide in the folds of the curtain, and I don't wonder. The dog was terrified at her. He crawled on his belly out of the room. Now she must have been cruel to him if he acts like that. I think Winchester should have a specialist. I didn't know how to account for any of it; but of course a blow on the head can affect a person."

Fortunately my mother interrupted us just then, and I didn't, by my probable rudeness, give my cousin reason to suppose that the accident had affected me, too. I sifted through her remarks and decided they might mean only that Thalia found her more of a bore than usual. As for Nug, perhaps he retreated from the cousin! During the next few days the house had so much wedding turmoil that she found a chance only for a few more dribbles: one that Thalia had given up all her clubs—she had belonged to several—the other that she had sent the children to boarding schools instead of keeping them at home. "Just when her husband is doing so well, too!"

I was glad when the wedding party had departed, and I could plan to go back to New York. Personally I think a low-caste Chinese wedding is saner and more interesting than a modern American affair. My cousin "should think I could stay home with the family," and "couldn't we go to New York together, if I insisted upon gadding off?" We couldn't. I saw to that. She hoped that I'd look up Thalia. Maybe I could advise Winchester about a specialist.

I did telephone as soon as I got in. That sentence "I am lonely," in her brief note kept recurring. Her voice sounded thin and re- mote, a poor connection, I thought. She was sorry. She was giving a dinner for Winchester that evening. The next day.

I had piles of proof to wade through that next day, and it was late afternoon when I finally went to the Corson house. The butler looked doubtful but I insisted, and he left me in the hall while he went off with my card. He returned, a little smug in his mes- sage: Mrs. Corson was resting and had left word she must not be disturbed. Well, you can't protest to a perfect butler, and I started down the steps, indignant, when a car stopped in front of the house, a liveried chauffeur opened the door, and Winchester emerged. He glanced at me in the twilight and extended an abrupt hand.

"Would Thalia see you?" he asked.

"No." For a moment I hoped he might convoy me past the butler. "Isn't she well? She asked me to come today."

"I hoped she'd see you." Winchester's hand smoothed at his little mustache. "She's just tired from her dinner last night. She overexerted herself, was quite the old Thalia." He looked at me slowly in the dusk, and I had a brief feeling that he was really looking at me, no, for me, for the first time in all our meetings, as if he considered me without relation to himself for once. "Come in again, will you?" He thrust away whatever else he thought of saying. "Thalia really would like to see you. Can I give you a lift?"

"No, thanks. I need a walk." As I started off I knew the mo- ment had just missed some real significance. If I had ventured a question . . . but, after all, what could I ask him? He had said that Thalia was "just tired." That night I sent a note to her, say- ing I had called and asked when I might see her.

She telephoned me the next day. Would I come in for Thanks- giving? The children would be home, and she wanted an old- fashioned day, everything but the sleigh ride New York couldn't furnish. Dinner would be at six, for the children; perhaps I could come in early. I felt a small grievance at being put off for almost a week, but I promised to come.

That was the week I heard gossip about Winchester, in the curious devious way of gossip. Atlantic City, and a gaudy lady. Someone having an inconspicuous fortnight of convalescence there had seen them. I wasn't surprised, except perhaps that Winchester chose Atlantic City. Thalia was too fine; he couldn't grow up to her. I wondered how much she knew. She must, years ago, with her sensitiveness, have discovered that Winchester was stationary so far as love went and, being stationary himself, was inclined to move the object toward which he directed his passion.

On Thursday, as I walked across Central Park, gaunt and deserted in the chilly afternoon light, I decided that Thalia probably knew more about Winchester's affairs than gossip had given me. Perhaps that was why she had sent the children away. He had always been conventionally discreet, but discretion would be a tawdry coin among Thalia's shining values.

I was shown up to the nursery, with a message from Thalia that she would join me there soon. Fletcher seemed glad to see me, in a shy, excited way, and stood close to my chair while Dorothy wound up her phonograph for a dance record and pirouetted about us with her doll.

"Mother keeps her door tight locked all the time," whispered Fletcher doubtfully. "We can't go in. This morning I knocked and knocked but no one answered."

"Do you like your school?" I asked cheerfully.

"I like my home better." His eyes, so like Thalia's with their long, arched lids, had young bewilderment under their lashes.

"See me!" called Dorothy. "Watch me do this!"

While she twirled I felt Fletcher's thin body stiffen against my arm, as if a kind of panic froze him. Thalia stood in the doorway. Was the boy afraid of her? Dorothy wasn't. She cried, "See me, Mother! Look at me!" and in her lusty confusion, I had a moment to look at Thalia before she greeted me. She was thin, but she had always been that. She did not heed Dorothy's shrieks, but watched Fletcher, a kind of slanting dread on her white, proud face. I had thought, that week on Long Island, that she shut herself away from me, refusing to restore the intimacy of ten years earlier. But now a stiff loneliness hedged her as if she were rimmed in ice and snow. She smiled. "Dear Mary," she said. At the sound of her voice I lost my slightly cherished injury that she had refused earlier to see me. "Let's go down to the library," she went on. "It's almost time for the turkey." I felt Fletcher break his intent watchfulness with a long sigh, and as the children went ahead of us, I caught at Thalia's arm. "Thalia—" She drew away, and her arm, under the soft flowing sleeve of dull blue stuff, was so slight it seemed brittle. I thought suddenly that she must have chosen that gown because it concealed so much beneath its lovely embroidered folds. "You aren't well, Thalia. What *is* it?"

"Well enough! Don't fuss about me." And even as I stared reproachfully she seemed to gather vitality, so that the dry pallor of her face became smooth ivory, and her eyes were no longer hollow and distressed. "Come."

The dinner was amazingly like one of our old holidays. Winchester wore his best mood, the children were delighted and happy. Thalia, under the gold flames of the tall black candles, was a gracious and lovely hostess. I almost forgot my troublesome anxiety, wondering whether my imagination hadn't been playing me tricks.

We had coffee by the library fire and some of Winchester's old Chartreuse. Then he insisted upon exhibiting his new radio. Thalia demurred, but the children begged for a concert. "This is their party, Tally!" Winchester opened the doors of the old teakwood cabinet which housed the apparatus. Thalia sank back into the shadows of a wing chair, and I watched her over my cigarette. Off guard, she had relaxed into strange apathy. Was it the firelight or my unaccustomed Chartreuse? Her features seemed blurred as if a clumsy hand trying to trace a drawing made uncertain outlines. Strange groans and whirrs from the radio.

"Win, I can't stand it!" Her voice dragged from some great distance. "Not tonight." She swayed to her feet, her hands restless under the loose sleeves.

"Static," growled Winchester. "Wait a minute."

"No!" Again it was as if vitality flowed into her. "Come, children. You have had your party. Time to go upstairs. I'll go with you."

They were well trained, I thought. Kisses for their father, a curtsy from Dorothy for me, and a grave little hand extended by Fletcher. Then Winchester came toward the fire as the three of them disappeared.

"You're good for Thalia," he said, in an undertone. "She's—well, what do you make of her?"

"Why?" I fenced, unwilling to indulge him in my vague anxieties.

"You saw how she acted about the radio. She has whims like that. Funny, she was herself at dinner. Last week she gave a dinner for me, important affair, pulled it off brilliantly. Then she shuts herself up and won't open her door for days. I can't make it out. She's thin—"

"Have you had a doctor?" I asked, banally.

"That's another thing. She absolutely refuses. Made a fool of me when I brought one here. Wouldn't unlock her door. Says she just wants to rest. But"—he glanced toward the door—"do you know that fool on the bridge . . . that little runt? The other night, I swear I saw him rushing down the steps as I came home. Thalia just laughed when I asked about it."

Something clicked in my thoughts, a quick suspicion, drawing a parallel between her conduct and that of people I had seen in the East. Was it some drug? That lethargy, and the quick spring into vitality? Days behind a closed door—

"I wish you'd persuade her to go off for a few weeks. I'm frightfully pressed just now, in an important business matter, but if she'd go off—maybe you'd go with her?"

"Where, Winchester?" We both started, with the guilt of conspirators. Thalia came slowly into the room. "Where shall I go? Would you suggest—Atlantic City?"

"Perhaps. Although some place farther south this time of year—" Winchester's imperturbability seemed to me far worse than some slight sign of embarrassment; it marked him as so rooted in successful deceit, whether Thalia's inquiry were innocent or not. "If Mary would go with you. I can't get away just now."

"I shall not go anywhere until your deal goes through. Then—" Thalia seated herself again in the wing chair. The hand she lifted to her cheek, fingers just touching her temple beneath the soft drift of hair, seemed transparent against the firelight. "Have you told Mary about your deal? Winchester plans to be the most important man on Automobile Row." Was there mockery in her tone? "I can't tell you the details, but he's buying out all the rest."

"Don't be absurd. Not all of them. It's a big merging of companies, that's all."

"We entertain the lords at dinner, and in some mysterious way that smooths the merging. It makes a wife almost necessary."

"Invite Mary to the next shebang, and let her see how well you do it." Winchester was irritated. "For all your scoffing, there's as much politics to being president of such a concern as of the United States."

"Yes, I'll invite Mary. Then she'll see that you don't really want to dispense with me—yet."

"Good God, I meant for a week or two."

As Winchester, lighting a cigarette, snapped the head from several matches in succession, I moved my chair a little backward, distressed. There was a thin wire of significance drawn so taut between the two that I felt at any moment it might splinter in my face.

"It's so lucky"—malice flickered on her thin face—"that you

weren't hurt in that skid on the bridge, Mary. Winchester would just have tossed you in the river to conceal your body."

"If you're going over that again!" Winchester strode out of the room. As Thalia turned her head slightly to watch him, her face and throat had the taut rigidity of pain so great that it congeals the nerves.

I was silent. With Thalia I had never dared intrude except when she admitted me. In another moment she too had risen. "You'd better go home, Mary," she said, slowly. "I might tell you things you wouldn't care to live with."

I tried to touch her hand, but she retreated. If I had been wiser or more courageous, I might have helped her. I shall always have that regret, and that can't be much better to live with than whatever she might have told me. All I could say was stupidly, "Thalia, if there's anything I can do! You know I love you."

"Love? That's a strange word," she said, and her laugh in the quiet room was like the shrilling of a grasshopper on a hot afternoon. "One thing I will tell you." (She stood now on the stairway above me.) "Love has no power. It never shouts out across great space. Only fear and self-desire are strong."

Then she had gone, and the butler appeared silently, to lead me to the little dressing room.

"The car is waiting for you, madam," he assured me, opening the door. I didn't want it, but Winchester was waiting, too, hunched angrily in a corner.

"That's the way she acts," he began. "Now you've seen her I'll talk about it. Thalia never bore grudges, you know that."

"It seems deeper than a grudge," I said cautiously.

"That reference to the . . . the accident. That's a careless remark I made. I don't even remember just what I said. Something entirely inconsequential. Just that it was damned lucky no one was hurt when I was putting this merger across. You know if it'd got in the papers it would have queered me. Wrecking my own car . . . there's always a suspicion you've been drinking. She picked it up and won't drop it. It's like a fixed idea. If you can suggest something. I want her to see a nerve specialist. What does she do behind that locked door?"

"What about Atlantic City?" I asked, abruptly. I saw his dark eyes bulge, trying to ferret out my meaning, there in the dusky interior of the car.

"A week there with you might do her good." That was all he would say, and I hadn't courage enough to accuse him, even in Thalia's name.

"At least you'll try to see her again," he said, as the car stopped in front of my apartment house.

I couldn't sleep that night. I felt that just over the edge of my squirming thoughts there lay clear and whole the meaning of it all, but I couldn't reach past thought. And then, stupidly enough, I couldn't get up the next day. Just a feverish cold, but the doctor insisted on a week in bed and subdued me with warnings about influenza.

I had begun to feel steady enough on my feet to consider venturing outside my apartment when the invitation came, for a formal dinner at the Corsons'. Scrawled under the engraving was a line, "Please come. T." I sent a note, explaining that I had been ill, and that I should come—the dinner was a fortnight away—unless I stayed too wobbly.

I meant that night to arrive properly with the other guests, but my watch, which had never before done anything except lose a few minutes a day, had gained an unsuspected hour. Perhaps the hands stuck—perhaps— Well, I was told I was early, Thalia was dressing, and only the children, home for the Christmas holidays, were available. So I went again to the nursery. Dorothy was as plump and unconcerned as ever, but Fletcher had a strained, listening effect, and he looked too thin and white for a little boy. They were having their supper on a small table, and Fletcher kept going to the door, looking out into the hall. "Mother promised to come up," he said.

The maid cleared away their dishes, and Dorothy, who was in a beguiling mood, chose to sit on my lap and entertain me with stories. One was about Nug the terrier; he had been sent out to the country because Mother didn't like him any more.

"I think," interrupted Fletcher, "she likes him, but he has a queer notion about her."

"She doesn't like him," repeated Dorothy. Then she dismissed that subject, and Fletcher too, for curiosity about the old silver chain I wore. I didn't notice that the boy had slipped away, but he must have gone down stairs; for presently his fingers closed over my wrist, like a frightened bird's claw, and I turned to see him, trembling, his eyes dark with terror. He couldn't speak but he clawed at me, and I shook Dorothy from my knees and let him pull me out to the hall.

"What is it, Fletcher?" He only pointed down the stairway, toward his mother's door, and I fled down those stairs. What had the child seen?

"The door wasn't locked—" he gasped behind me—"I opened it very still and went in—"

I pushed it ajar. Thalia sat before her dressing table, with the three-fold mirrors reiterating like a macabre symphony her rigid, contorted face. Her gown, burnished blue and green like peacock's feathers, sheathed her gaudily, and silver, blue, and green chiffon clouded her shoulders. Her hands clutched at the edge of the dressing table. For an instant I could not move, thrust through with a terror like the boy's. Then I stumbled across the room. Before I reached her, the mirrors echoed her long shudder, her eyelids dragged open, and I saw her stare at my reflection wavering toward her. Then her hands relaxed, moved quickly toward the crystal jars along the heavy glass of the table and, without a word, she leaned softly forward, to draw a scarlet line along her white lips.

"How cold it is in here," I said, stupidly, glancing toward the windows, where the heavy silk damask, drawn across, lay in motionless folds. "Fletcher said—" I was awkward, an intruder.

"He startled me." Her voice came huskily. She rouged her hollow cheeks. It was as if she drew another face for herself. "I didn't have time to lock the door." Then turning, she sought him out, huddled at the doorway, like a moth on a pin of fear. "It wasn't nice of you, Son. It's all right now. You see?" She rose, drawing her lovely scarf over her shoulders. "You should never open closed doors." She blew him a kiss from her finger tips. "Now run along and forget you were so careless."

The icy stir of air against my skin had ceased. I stared at her, my mind racing back over what I knew of various drugs and the stigmata of their victims. But her eyes were clear and undilated, a little piteous. "This," she said, "is the last time. I can't endure it." And then, with that amazing flood of vitality, as if a sudden connection had been made and current flowed again, "Come, Mary. It is time we were down stairs."

I thought Fletcher peered over the railing as we went down. But a swift glance failed to detect him.

The dinner itself I don't remember definitely except that it glittered and sparkled, moving with slightly alcoholic wit through elaborate courses, while I sat like an abashed poor relation at a feast, unable to stop watching Thalia, wondering whether my week of fever had given me a tendency to hallucinations. At the end a toast was proposed, to Winchester Corson and his extraordinary success. "It's done, then?" Thalia's gaiety had sudden malice—as she looked across at Winchester, seating himself after a slightly pompous speech. "Sealed and cemented forever?"

"Thanks to his charming wife, too," cried a plump, bald man, waving his glass. "A toast to Mrs. Corson!"

Thalia rose, her rouge like flecked scarlet on white paper. One hand drew her floating scarf about her throat, and her painted lips moved without a sound. There was an instant of agitated discomfort, as the guests felt their mood broken so abruptly, into which her voice pierced, thin, high. "I . . . deserve . . . such a toast—"

I pushed back my chair and reached her side.

"I'll take her—" I saw Winchester's face, wine-flushed, angry rather than concerned. "Come, Thalia."

"Don't bother. I'll be all right—now." But she moved ahead of me so swiftly that I couldn't touch her. I thought she tried to close her door against me, but I was too quick for that. The silver candelabra still burned above the mirrors. "Mary!" Her voice was low again as she spoke a telephone number. "Tell him *at once.*" She stood away from me, her face a white mask with spots of scarlet, her peacock dress ashimmer. I did as I was bid and when I had said, "Mrs. Corson wishes you at once," there was an emptiness where a man's voice had come which suggested a sudden leap out of a room somewhere.

"I can never get in again!" Her fingers curled under the chiffon scarf. "Never! The black agony of fighting back— If he—" She bent her head, listening. "Go down to the door and let him in," she said.

I crept down the stairs. Voices from the drawing-room. Winchester was seeing the party through. Almost as I reached the door and opened it I found him there: the little doctor with the pointed beard. He brushed past me up the stairs. He knew the way, then! I was scarcely surprised to find Thalia's door fast shut when I reached it. Behind it came not a sound. Fletcher, like an unhappy sleepwalker, his eyes heavy, slipped down beside me, clinging to my hand. I heard farewells, churring of taxis and cars. Then Winchester came up the stairs.

"She's shut you out?" He raised his fist and pounded on the door. "I'm going to stop this nonsense!"

"I sent for a doctor," I said. "He's in there."

"Is it"—his face was puffy and gray—"that same fool?" Then the door opened, and the man confronted us.

"It is over," he said.

"What have you done to her?" Winchester lunged toward the

door, but the little man's lifted hand had dignity enough somehow to stop him.

"She won't come back again." He spoke slowly. "You may look
if you care to."

"She's dead?"

"She died—months ago. There on the bridge. But you called to
her, and she thought you wanted—her."

Winchester thrust him aside and strode into the room. I dared
one glance and saw only pale hair shining on the pillow. Then
Fletcher flung himself against me, sobbing, and I knelt to hold
him close against the fear we both felt.

What Winchester saw I never knew. He hurled himself past us,
down the stairs. And Thalia was buried with the coffin lid fast
closed under the flowers.

Reprinted by permission of the author.

1. Why, do you feel, is the writer unable to remember
   Thalia Corson with detailed clarity?
2. What does the author mean by saying, "This affair
   won't add to itself"?
3. What is the vocation of the narrator? Is it displayed
   in the description of the actual crash?
4. What is the significance of Thalia's line to Mary, "It is
   hard to get back in."
5. Symbolically, what may "the little doctor with the
   pointed beard" represent?

# III. HISTORY

# III. HISTORY

SIR WALTER SCOTT created historical fiction. Not that he was the first to turn to the past for his stories; merely that he was the first novelist to bring to his portrayal of the past the antiquarian knowledge which enabled him to show how it differed from the present. The older treatment of historical themes is typified by the Elizabethan custom of acting plays, whatever their time or place, in contemporary English dress. Shakespeare himself has been accused of filling "Ilion, Rome, or any town you like of olden time with timeless Englishmen"; certainly neither he nor his audience saw any incongruity in putting clocks in Caesar's Rome or corsets on Cleopatra. The educated knew, as a matter of information, that clothes and weapons and houses were different in the past, but they assumed that the men and women were not.

Sir Walter changed all that. His antiquarian studies had familiarized him with all the details of medieval life. The eighteenth century, says G. M. Trevelyan, "had forgotten, among other things, what a revolutionist or a religious fanatic was really like. . . . Gibbon had traced in his cold, clear outline, the procession of fourteen calamitous centuries, that move past us with slow and stately pace, each as like to the one that it follows as are the figures in the frieze of the Parthenon. That was how Scott found history; he left it what it has been ever since, an eager aspiration, destined to perpetual change, doomed to everlasting imperfection, but living, complex, broad as humanity itself. To the calm eye of Gibbon mankind remained from the age of the Antonines to the age of Rienzi, essentially the same, divided up in each succeeding era into a number of formulae—the magistrates, the philosophers, the priests, the nobles, the plebeians, the Barbarians—each class retaining the same generalized character throughout the piece. It was Sir Walter who first showed us how not only clothes and weapons, but thought and morals vary according to the period, the province, the class, the man. To him the pageant of history was more like a Walpurgis night than a Parthenon procession."

Since Scott's day, knowledge of the past has widened and deepened. Modern writers show somewhat higher resistance than Sir Walter and George Eliot did to the temptation to include *all* they have learned about their period; they dwell more on ideas and less on clothes. The good novelist must know how people thought, even more than how they dressed. He soon learns to avoid crude physical anachronism, such as putting Robert Lee on the telephone. (Yet even in these matters the careless writer slips: in *The Challenge to Sirius*, for instance, Sheila Kaye-Smith put Idaho troops into the battle of Lookout Mountain.) But anachronism of thought is harder to escape, especially when it conflicts with his own deeper convictions. Yet to show an ante-bellum Southern planter repudiating slavery, an Elizabethan scorning witchcraft or admiring Alpine scenery, is a worse historical boner than putting Cleopatra in corsets. The historical novelist must be true to thought as well as fact.

This principle determines certain conventions of historical fiction. It is difficult and dangerous to use real people as the central figures. If they are well known, the reader will resent any serious tampering with the facts; if they are obscure, they have no pictorial value. Hence the novelist usually invents his main characters and keeps the real people to secondary roles. The exceptions are more apparent than real. Stevenson can center "A Lodging for the Night" on François Villon because so little is known of the poet's life that the possibility of such an episode cannot be denied. We know Villon's character from his poetry; Stevenson invents action that fits the character. With Rahere, in "The Tree of Justice," Kipling follows the converse course. All we know about Rahere is an action: after being court jester to King Henry I he became a monk and founded the church and hospital of St. Bartholomew in London. Kipling invents a character to fit the action. But the use of real people as protagonists is seldom satisfactory beyond the limits of a short story, and even within those limits it may mean headaches for the conscientious author.

In an article written soon after he completed *Drums Along the Mohawk* Mr. Edmonds discussed some of those headaches. His first object, he explained, in writing about the Revolution in up-state New York, was to show how it affected, not the leaders, but the ordinary men and women of the region. After inventing a fictional couple about whom to center his story, he had to establish them among real people who had performed historic acts. This raised a new problem:

In some cases, from the exigencies of story or space, it was necessary to compress two or more persons' experiences into the life of one. The question was, where I had falsified the facts of a real person's life, . . . ought I to change his name? . . . I . . . finally decided that where my real character in the book performed some act for which he was locally famous I should call him by his real name.

In . . . Adam Helmer, for instance, I had a man who performed one of the great feats of valor of the Revolution, yet in the book I wanted him to be a younger man, unmarried—for I did not have space for his family life,—and also, to wind up my story, I wanted him to marry someone he never married at all! But if I called him Heinrich Smith and let him run his race against the best runners of the Iroquois and save German Flats by winning it I should be robbing a great reputation of one of its best deeds. . . .

Perhaps Mr. Edmonds worried too much. In historical narrative, as in everything else that lives, the letter kills; it is the spirit that makes alive. When once the author has realized his people as people, not as figures in a pageant, he has done the main thing necessary to make them convincing to the reader. As in most other types of fiction, character counts most.

*John Buchan*

# THE COMPANY OF THE MARJOLAINE

I CAME down from the mountains and into the pleasing valley of the Adige in as pelting a heat as ever mortal suffered under. The way underfoot was parched and white; I had newly come out of a wilderness of white limestone crags, and a sun of Italy blazed blindingly in an azure Italian sky. You are to suppose, my dear aunt, that I had had enough and something more of my craze for foot-marching. A fortnight ago I had gone to Belluno in a postchaise, dismissed my fellow to carry my baggage by way of Verona, and with no more than a valise on my back plunged into the fastnesses of those mountains. I had a fancy to see the little sculptured hills which made backgrounds for Gianbellin, and there were rumours of great mountains built wholly of marble which shone like the battlements of the Celestial City. So at any rate reported young Mr. Wyndham, who had travelled with me from Milan to Venice. I lay the first night at Pieve, where Titian had the fortune to be born, and the landlord at the inn displayed a set of villainous daubs which he swore were the early works of that master. Thence up a toilsome valley I journeyed to the Ampezzan country, where indeed I saw my white mountains, but, alas! no longer Celestial. For it rained like Westmoreland for five endless days, while I kicked my heels in an inn and turned a canto of Ariosto into halting English couplets. By-and-by it cleared, and I headed westward towards Bozen, among the tangle of wild rocks, where the Dwarf King had once his rose-garden. The first night I had no inn, but slept in the vile cabin of a forester, who spoke a tongue half Latin, half Dutch, which I failed to master. The next day was a blaze of heat, the mountain-paths lay thick with dust, and I had no wine from sunrise to sunset. Can you wonder that, when the following noon I saw Santa Chiara sleeping in its green circlet of meadows, my thought was only of a deep draught and a cool chamber? I protest that I am a great lover of natural beauty, of rock and cascade, and all the properties of the poet; but the enthusiasm of M. Rousseau himself would sink from the stars to earth if he had marched since breakfast in a cloud of dust with a throat like the nether millstone.

Yet I had not entered the place before Romance revived. The little town—a mere wayside halting-place on the great mountain-road to the North—had the air of mystery which foretells adventure. Why is it that a dwelling or a countenance catches the fancy with the promise of some strange destiny? I have houses in my mind which I know will some day and somehow be intertwined oddly with my life; and I have faces in memory of which I know nothing save that I shall undoubtedly cast eyes again upon them. My first glimpses of Santa Chiara gave me this earnest of romance. It was walled and fortified, the streets were narrow pits of shade, old tenements with bent fronts swayed to meet each other. Melons lay drying on flat roofs, and yet now and then would come a high-pitched northern gable. Latin and Teuton met and mingled in the place, and, as Mr. Gibbon has taught us, the offspring of this admixture is something fantastic and unpredictable. I forgot my grievous thirst and my tired feet in admiration and a certain vague expectation of wonders. Here, ran my thought, it is fated, maybe, that Romance and I shall at last compass a meeting. Perchance some princess is in need of my arm, or some affair of high policy is afoot in this jumble of old masonry. You will laugh at my folly, but I had an excuse for it. A fortnight in strange mountains disposes a man to look for something at his next encounter with his kind, and the sight of Santa Chiara would have fired the imagination of a judge in Chancery.

I strode happily into the courtyard of the Tre Croci, and presently had my expectation confirmed. For I found my fellow, Gianbattista,—a faithful rogue I got in Rome on a Cardinal's recommendation,—hot in dispute with a lady's-maid. The woman was old, harsh-featured—no Italian clearly, though she spoke fluently in the tongue. She rated my man like a pickpocket, and the dispute was over a room.

"The signor will bear me out," said Gianbattista. "Was not I sent to Verona with his baggage, and thence to this place of ill manners? Was I not bidden engage for him a suite of apartments? Did I not duly engage these fronting on the gallery, and dispose therein the signor's baggage? And lo! an hour ago I found it all turned into the yard and this woman installed in its place. It is monstrous, unbearable! Is this an inn for travellers, or haply the private mansion of those Magnificences?"

"My servant speaks truly," I said firmly yet with courtesy, having no mind to spoil adventure by urging rights. "He had orders to take these rooms for me, and I know not what higher power can countermand me."

The woman had been staring at me scornfully, for no doubt in my dusty habit I was a figure of small dignity; but at the sound of my voice she started, and cried out, "You are English, signor?"

I bowed an admission.

"Then my mistress shall speak with you," she said, and dived into the inn like an elderly rabbit.

Gianbattista was for sending for the landlord and making a riot in that hostelry; but I stayed him, and bidding him fetch me a flask of white wine, three lemons, and a glass of eau de vie, I sat down peaceably at one of the little tables in the courtyard and prepared for the quenching of my thirst. Presently, as I sat drinking that excellent compound of my own invention, my shoulder was touched, and I turned to find the maid and his mistress. Alas for my hopes of a glorious being, young and lissom and bright with the warm riches of the south! I saw a short, stout little lady, well on the wrong side of thirty. She had plump red cheeks, and fair hair dressed indifferently in the Roman fashion. Two candid blue eyes redeemed her plainness, and a certain grave and gentle dignity. She was notably a gentlewoman, so I got up, doffed my hat, and waited her commands.

She spoke in Italian. "Your pardon, signor, but I fear my good Cristine has done you unwittingly a wrong."

Cristine snorted at this premature plea of guilty, while I hastened to assure the fair apologist that any rooms I might have taken were freely at her service.

I spoke unconsciously in English, and she replied in a halting parody of that tongue. "I understand him," she said, "but I do not speak him happily. I will discourse, if the signor pleases, in our first speech."

She and her father, it appeared, had come over the Brenner, and arrived that morning at the Tre Croci, where they purposed to lie for some days. He was an old man, very feeble, and much depending upon her constant care. Wherefore it was necessary that the rooms of all the party should adjoin, and there was no suite of the size in the inn save that which I had taken. Would I therefore consent to forego my right, and place her under an eternal debt?

I agreed most readily, being at all times careless where I sleep, so the bed be clean, or where I eat, so the meal be good. I bade my servant see the landlord and have my belongings carried to other rooms. Madame thanked me sweetly, and would have gone, when a thought detained her.

"It is but courteous," she said, "that you should know the names of those whom you have befriended. My father is called the Count d'Albani, and I am his only daughter. We travel to Florence, where we have a villa in the environs."

"My name," said I, "is Hervey-Townshend, an Englishman travelling abroad for his entertainment."

"Hervey?" she repeated. "Are you one of the family of Miladi Hervey?"

"My worthy aunt," I replied, with a tender recollection of that preposterous woman.

Madame turned to Cristine, and spoke rapidly in a whisper.

"My father, sir," she said, addressing me, "is an old frail man, little used to the company of strangers; but in former days he has had kindness from members of your house, and it would be a satisfaction to him, I think, to have the privilege of your acquaintance."

She spoke with the air of a vizier who promises a traveller a sight of the Grand Turk. I murmured my gratitude, and hastened after Gianbattista. In an hour I had bathed, rid myself of my beard, and arrayed myself in decent clothing. Then I strolled out to inspect the little city, admired an altar-piece, chaffered with a Jew for a cameo, purchased some small necessaries, and returned early in the afternoon with a noble appetite for dinner.

The Tre Croci had been in happier days a bishop's lodging, and possessed a dining-hall ceiled with black oak and adorned with frescoes. It was used as a general *salle à manger* for all dwellers in the inn, and there accordingly I sat down to my long-deferred meal. At first there were no other diners, and I had two maids, as well as Gianbattista, to attend on my wants. Presently Madame d'Albani entered, escorted by Cristine and by a tall gaunt serving-man, who seemed no part of the hostelry. The landlord followed, bowing civilly, and the two women seated themselves at the little table at the farther end. "Il Signor Conte dines in his room," said Madame to the host, who withdrew to see to that gentleman's needs.

I found my eyes straying often to the little party in the cool twilight of that refectory. The man-servant was so old and battered, and yet of such a dignity, that he lent a touch of intrigue to the thing. He stood stiffly behind Madame's chair, handing dishes with an air of silent reverence—the lackey of a great noble, if ever I had seen the type. Madame never glanced towards me, but conversed sparingly with Cristine, while she pecked delicately at her food. Her name ran in my head with a tantalising flavour of the familiar. Albani! D'Albani! It was a name not uncommon in the Roman States, but I had never heard it linked to a noble family. And yet I had, somehow, somewhere, and in the vain effort at recollection I had almost forgotten my hunger. There was nothing bourgeois in the little lady. The austere servants, the high manner of condescension, spake of a stock used to deference, though, maybe, pitifully decayed in its fortunes. There was a mystery in these quiet folk which tickled my curiosity. Romance after all was not destined to fail me at Santa Chiara.

My doings of the afternoon were of interest to myself alone. Suffice it to say that when I returned at nightfall I found Gianbattista the trustee of a letter. It was from Madame, written in a fine thin hand on a delicate paper, and it invited me to wait upon the signor, her father, that evening at eight o'clock. What caught my eye was a coronet stamped in a corner. A coronet, I say, but in truth it was a crown, the same as surmounts the Arms Royal of England on the signboard of a Court tradesman. I marvelled at the ways of foreign heraldry. Either this family of d'Albani had higher pretensions than I had given it credit for, or it employed an unlearned and imaginative stationer. I scribbled a line of acceptance and went to dress.

The hour of eight found me knocking at the Count's door. The grim serving-man admitted me to the pleasant chamber which should have been mine own. A dozen wax candles burned in sconces, and on the table among fruits and the relics of supper stood a handsome candelabra of silver. A small fire of logs had been lit on the hearth, and before it in an armchair sat a strange figure of a man. He seemed not so much old as aged. I should have put him at sixty, but the marks he bore were clearly less those of Time than of Life. There sprawled before me the relics of noble looks. The fleshy nose, the pendulous cheek, the drooping mouth, had once been cast in the lines of manly beauty. Heavy eyebrows above and heavy bags beneath spoiled the effect of a choleric blue eye, which age had not dimmed. The man was gross and yet haggard; it was not the padding of good living which clothed his bones, but a heaviness as of some dropsical malady. I could picture him in health a gaunt loose-limbed being, high-featured and swift and eager. He was dressed wholly in black velvet, with fresh ruffles and wristbands, and he wore heeled shoes with antique silver buckles. It was a figure of an older age which rose slowly to greet me, in one hand a snuff-box and a purple handkerchief, and in the other a book with finger marking place. He made me a great bow as Madame uttered my name, and held out a hand with a kindly smile.

"Mr. Hervey-Townshend," he said, "we will speak English, if you please. I am fain to hear it again, for 'tis a tongue I love. I make you welcome, sir, for your own sake and for the sake of your kin. How is her honourable ladyship, your aunt? A week ago she sent me a letter."

I answered that she did famously, and wondered what cause of correspondence my worthy aunt could have with wandering nobles of Italy.

He motioned me to a chair between Madame and himself, while a servant set a candle on a shelf behind him. Then he proceeded to catechise me in excellent English, with now and then a phrase of French, as to the doings in my own land. Admirably informed this Italian gentleman proved himself. I defy you to find in Almack's more intelligent gossip. He inquired as to the chances of my Lord North and the mind of my Lord Rockingham. He had my Lord Shelburne's foibles at his finger's ends. The habits of the Prince, the aims of their ladyships of Dorset and Buckingham, the extravagance of this noble Duke and that right honourable gentleman were not hid from him. I answered discreetly yet frankly, for there was no ill-breeding in his curiosity. Rather it seemed like the inquiries of some fine lady, now buried deep in the country, as to the doings of a forsaken Mayfair. There was humour in it and something of pathos.

"My aunt must be a voluminous correspondent, sir," I said.

He laughed. "I have many friends in England who write to me, but I have seen none of them for long, and I doubt I may never see them again. Also in my youth I have been in England." And he sighed as at a sorrowful recollection.

Then he showed the book in his hand. "See," he said, "here is one of your English writings, the greatest book I have ever happened on." It was a volume of Mr. Fielding.

For a little he talked of books and poets. He admired Mr. Fielding profoundly, Dr. Smollett somewhat less, Mr. Richardson not at all. But he was clear that England had a monopoly of good writers, saving only my friend M. Rousseau, whom he valued, yet with reservations. Of the Italians he had no opinion. I instanced against him the plays of Signor Alfieri. He groaned, shook his head, and grew moody.

"Know you Scotland?" he asked suddenly.

"I replied that I had visited Scotch cousins, but had no great estimation for the country. "It is too poor and jagged," I said, "for the taste of one who loves colour and sunshine and suave outlines."

He sighed. "It is indeed a bleak land, but a kindly. When the sun shines at all he shines on the truest hearts in the world. I love its bleakness too. There is a spirit in the misty hills and the harsh seawind which inspires men to great deeds. Poverty and courage go often together, and my Scots, if they are poor, are as untameable as their mountains."

"You know the land, sir?" I asked.

"I have seen it, and I have known many Scots. You will find

them in Paris and Avignon and Rome, with never a plack in their pockets. I have a feeling for exiles, sir, and I have pitied these poor people. They gave their all for the cause they followed."

Clearly the Count shared my aunt's views of history, those views which have made such sport for us often at Carteron. Stalwart Whig as I am, there was something in the tone of the old gentleman which made me feel a certain majesty in the lost cause.

"I am Whig in blood and Whig in principle," I said, "but I have never denied that those Scots who followed the Chevalier were too good to waste on so trumpery a leader."

I had no sooner spoken the words than I felt that somehow I had been guilty of a *bêtise*.

"It may be so," said the Count. "I did not bid you here, sir, to argue on politics, on which I am assured we should differ. But I will ask you one question. The King of England is a stout upholder of the right of kings. How does he face the defection of his American possessions?"

"The nation takes it well enough, and as for his Majesty's feelings there is small inclination to inquire into them. I conceive of the whole war as a blunder out of which we have come as we deserved. The day is gone by for the assertion of monarchic rights against the will of a people."

"May be. But take note that the King of England is suffering to-day as—how do you call him?—the Chevalier suffered forty years ago. 'The wheel has come full circle,' as your Shakespeare says. Time has wrought his revenge."

He was staring into a fire, which burned small and smokily.

"You think the day for kings is ended. I read it differently. The world will ever have need of kings. If a nation cast out one it will have to find another. And mark you, those later kings, created by the people, will bear a harsher hand than the old race who ruled as of right. Some day the world will regret having destroyed the kindly and legitimate line of monarchs and put in their place tyrants who govern by the sword or by flattering an idle mob."

This belated dogma would at other times have set me laughing, but the strange figure before me gave no impulse to merriment. I glanced at Madame, and saw her face grave and perplexed, and I thought I read a warning gleam in her eye. There was a mystery about the party which irritated me, but good breeding forbade me to seek a clue.

"You will permit me to retire, sir," I said. "I have but this morning come down from a long march among the mountains east of this valley. Sleeping in wayside huts and tramping those sultry paths make a man think pleasantly of bed."

The Count seemed to brighten at my words. "You are a marcher, sir, and love the mountains? Once I would gladly have joined you, for in my youth I was a great walker in hilly places. Tell me, now, how many miles will you cover in a day?"

I told him thirty at a stretch.

"Ah," he said, "I have done fifty, without food, over the roughest and mossiest mountains. I lived on what I shot, and for drink I had spring water. Nay, I am forgetting. There was another beverage, which I assume you have never tasted. Heard you ever, sir, of that *eau de vie* which the Scots call *usquebagh?* It will comfort a traveller as no thin Italian wine will comfort him. By my soul, you shall taste it. Charlotte, my dear, bid Oliphant fetch glasses and hot water and lemons. I will give Mr. Hervey-Townshend a sample of the brew. You English are all *têtes-de-fer*, sir, and are worthy of it."

The old man's face had lighted up, and for the moment his air had the jollity of youth. I would have accepted the entertainment had I not again caught Madame's eye. It said, unmistakably and with serious pleading, "Decline." I, therefore, made my excuses, urged fatigue, drowsiness, and a delicate stomach, bade my host good-night, and in deep mystification left the room.

Enlightenment came upon me as the door closed. There on

the threshold stood the man-servant whom they called Oliphant, erect as a sentry on guard. The sight reminded me of what I had once seen at Basle when by chance a Rhenish Grand Duke had shared the inn with me. Of a sudden a dozen clues linked together—the crowned notepaper, Scotland, my aunt Hervey's politics, the tale of old wanderings.

"Tell me," I said in a whisper, "who is the Count d'Albani, your master?" and I whistled softly a bar of "Charlie is my darling."

"Ay," said the man, without relaxing a muscle of his grim face. "It is the King of England—my king and yours."

## II

In the small hours of the next morning I was awoke by a most unearthly sound. It was as if all the cats on all the roofs of Santa Chiara were sharpening their claws and wailing their battle-cries. Presently out of the noise came a kind of music—very slow, solemn, and melancholy. The notes ran up in great flights of ecstasy, and sunk anon to the tragic deeps. In spite of my sleepiness I was held spell-bound, and the musician had concluded with certain barbaric grunts before I had the curiosity to rise. It came from somewhere in the gallery of the inn, and as I stuck my head out of my door I had a glimpse of Oliphant, nightcap on head and a great bagpipe below his arm, stalking down the corridor.

The incident, for all the gravity of the music, seemed to give a touch of farce to my interview of the past evening. I had gone to bed with my mind full of sad stories of the deaths of kings. Magnificence in tatters has always affected my pity more deeply than tatters with no such antecedent, and a monarch out at elbows stood for me as the last irony of our mortal life. Here was a king whose misfortunes could find no parallel. He had been in his youth the hero of a high adventure, and his middle age had been spent in fleeting among the courts of Europe, and waiting—

a pensioner on the whims of his foolish but regnant brethren. I
had heard tales of a growing sottishness, a decline in spirit, a
squalid taste in pleasures. Small blame, I had always thought, to
so ill-fated a princeling. And now I had chanced upon the gentleman in his dotage, travelling with a barren effort at mystery, attended by a sad-faced daughter and two ancient domestics. It was
a lesson in the vanity of human wishes which the shallowest
moralist would have noted. Nay, I felt more than the moral. Something human and kindly in the old fellow had caught my fancy.
The decadence was too tragic to prose about, the decadent too
human to moralise on. I had left the chamber of the—shall I say
*de jure* King of England?—a sentimental adherent of the cause.
But this business of the bagpipes touched the comic. To harry an
old valet out of bed and set him droning on pipes in the small
hours smacked of a theatrical taste, or at least of an undignified
fancy. Kings in exile, if they wish to keep the tragic air, should
not indulge in such fantastic serenades.

My mind changed again when after breakfast I fell in with
Madame on the stair. She drew aside to let me pass, and then
made as if she would speak to me. I gave her good-morning, and,
my mind being full of her story, addressed her as "Excellency."

"I see, sir," she said, "that you know the truth. I have to ask
your forbearance for the concealment I practised yesterday. It was
a poor requital for your generosity, but it is one of the shifts of
our sad fortune. An uncrowned king must go in disguise, or risk
the laughter of every stableboy. Besides, we are too poor to travel
in state, even if we desired it."

Honestly, I knew not what to say. I was not asked to sympa-
thise, having already revealed my politics, and yet the case cried
out for sympathy. You remember, my dear aunt, the good Lady
Culham, who was our Dorsetshire neighbour, and tried hard to
mend my ways at Carteron? This poor Duchess—for so she called
herself—was just such another. A woman made for comfort, house-
wifery, and motherhood, and by no means for racing about Europe

.in charge of a disreputable parent. I could picture her settled equably on a garden seat with a lap-dog and needle-work, blinking happily over green lawns and mildly rating an errant gardener. I could fancy her sitting in a summer parlour, very orderly and dainty, writing lengthy epistles to a tribe of nieces. I could see her marshalling a household in the family pew, or riding serenely in the family coach behind fat bay horses. But here, on an inn staircase, with a false name and a sad air of mystery, she was wofully out of place. I noted little wrinkles forming in the corners of her eyes, and the ravages of care beginning in the plump rosiness of her face. Be sure there was nothing appealing in her mien. She spoke with the air of a great lady, to whom the world is matter only for an after-thought. It was the facts that appealed and grew poignant from her courage.

"There is another claim upon your good-nature," she said. "Doubtless you were awoke last night by Oliphant's playing upon the pipes. I rebuked the landlord for his insolence in protesting, but to you, a gentleman and a friend, an explanation is due. My father sleeps ill, and your conversation seems to have cast him into a train of sad memories. It has been his habit on such occasions to have the pipes played to him, since they remind him of friends and happier days. It is a small privilege for an old man, and he does not claim it often."

I declared that the music had only pleased, and that I would welcome its repetition. Whereupon she left me with a little bow and an invitation to join them that day at dinner, while I departed into the town on my own errands. I returned before midday, and was seated at an arbour in the garden, busy with letters, when there hove in sight the gaunt figure of Oliphant. He hovered around me, if such a figure can be said to hover, with the obvious intention of addressing me. The fellow had caught my fancy, and I was willing to see more of him. His face might have been hacked out of grey granite, his clothes hung loosely on his spare bones, and his stockinged shanks would have done no discredit to Don

Quixote. There was no dignity in his air, only a steady and enduring sadness. Here, thought I, is the one of the establishment
who most commonly meets the shock of the world's buffets. I
called him by name and asked him his desires.

It appeared that he took me for a Jacobite, for he began a rig-
marole about loyalty and hard fortune. I hastened to correct him,
and he took the correction with the same patient despair with
which he took all things. 'Twas but another of the blows of Fate.

"At any rate," he said in a broad Scotch accent, "ye come of
kin that has helpit my maister afore this. I've many times heard
tell o' Herveys and Townshends in England, and a' folk said they
were on the richt side. Ye're maybe no a freend, but ye're a
freend's freend, or I wadna be speirin' at ye."

I was amused at the prologue, and waited on the tale. It soon
came. Oliphant, it appeared, was the purse-bearer of the household, and woful straits that poor purse-bearer must have been
often put to. I questioned him as to his master's revenues, but
could get no clear answer. There were payments due next month
in Florence which would solve the difficulties for the winter, but
in the meantime expenditure had beaten income. Travelling had
cost much, and the Count must have his small comforts. The
result in plain words was that Oliphant had not the wherewithal
to frank the company to Florence; indeed I doubted if he could
have paid the reckoning in Santa Chiara. A loan was therefore
sought from a friend's friend, meaning myself.

I was very really embarrassed. Not that I would not have given
willingly, for I had ample resources at the moment and was mightily concerned about the sad household. But I knew that the little
Duchess would take Oliphant's ears from his head if she guessed
that he had dared to borrow from me, and that if I lent, her back
would for ever be turned against me. And yet, what would follow
on my refusal? In a day or two there would be a pitiful scene
with mine host, and as like as not some of their baggage detained
as security for payment. I did not love the task of conspiring

behind the lady's back, but if it could be contrived 'twas indubitably the kindest course. I glared sternly at Oliphant, who met me with his pathetic dog-like eyes.

"You know that your mistress would never consent to the request you have made of me?"

"I ken," he said humbly. "But payin' is my job, and I simply havena the siller. It's no the first time it has happened, and it's a sair trial for them both to be flung out o' doors by a foreign hostler because they canna meet his charges. But, sir, if ye can lend to me, ye may be certain that her leddyship will never hear a word o't. Puir thing, she takes nae thocht o' where the siller comes frae, ony mair than the lilies o' the field."

I became a conspirator. "You swear, Oliphant, by all you hold sacred, to breathe nothing of this to your mistress, and if she should suspect, to lie like a Privy Councillor?"

A flicker of a smile crossed his face. "I'll lee like a Scotch packman, and the Father o' lees could do nae mair. You need have no fear for your siller, sir. I've aye repaid when I borrowed, though you may have to wait a bittock." And the strange fellow strolled off.

At dinner no Duchess appeared till long after the appointed hour, nor was there any sign of Oliphant. When she came at last with Cristine, her eyes looked as if she had been crying, and she greeted me with remote courtesy. My first thought was that Oliphant had revealed the matter of the loan, but presently I found that the lady's trouble was far different. Her father, it seemed, was ill again with his old complaint. What that was I did not ask, nor did the Duchess reveal it.

We spoke in French, for I had discovered that this was her favourite speech. There was no Oliphant to wait on us, and the inn servants were always about, so it was well to have a tongue they did not comprehend. The lady was distracted and sad. When I inquired feelingly as to the general condition of her father's health she parried the question, and when I offered my services she disregarded my words. It was in truth a doleful meal, while the faded Cristine sat like a sphinx staring into vacancy. I spoke of England and of her friends, of Paris and Versailles, of Avignon where she had spent some years, and of the amenities of Florence, which she considered her home. But 'twas like talking to a nunnery door. I got nothing but "It is indeed true, sir," or "Do you say so, sir?" till my energy began to sink. Madame perceived my discomfort, and as she rose murmured an apology. "Pray forgive my distraction, but I am poor company when my father is ill. I have a foolish mind, easily frightened. Nay, nay!" she went on when I again offered help, "the illness is trifling. It will pass off by to-morrow, or at the latest the next day. Only I had looked forward to some ease at Santa Chiara, and the promise is belied."

As it chanced that evening, returning to the inn, I passed by the north side where the windows of the Count's rooms looked over a little flower garden abutting on the courtyard. The dusk was falling, and a lamp had been lit which gave a glimpse into the interior. The sick man was standing by the window, his figure flung into relief by the lamplight. If he was sick, his sickness was of a curious type. His face was ruddy, his eye wild, and, his wig being off, his scanty hair stood up oddly round his head. He seemed to be singing, but I could not catch the sound through the shut casement. Another figure in the room, probably Oliphant, laid a hand on the Count's shoulder, drew him from the window, and closed the shutter.

It needed only the recollection of stories which were the property of all Europe to reach a conclusion on the gentleman's illness. The legitimate King of England was very drunk.

As I went to my room that night I passed the Count's door. There stood Oliphant as sentry, more grim and haggard than ever, and I thought that his eye met mine with a certain intelligence. From inside the room came a great racket. There was the sound of glasses falling, then a string of oaths, English, French, and for all I know, Irish, rapped out in a loud drunken voice. A pause, and then came the sound of maudlin singing. It pursued me along the gallery, an old childish song, delivered as if 'twere a pot-house catch—

> "Qu'est-c' qui passe ici si tard,
> Compagnons de la Marjolaine—"

One of the late-going company of the Marjolaine hastened to bed. This king in exile, with his melancholy daughter, was becoming too much for him.

### III

It was just before noon the next day that the travellers arrived. I was sitting in the shady loggia of the inn, reading a volume of De Thou, when there drove up to the door two coaches. Out of the first descended very slowly and stiffly four gentlemen; out of the second four servants and a quantity of baggage. As it chanced there was no one about, the courtyard slept its sunny noontide sleep, and the only movement was a lizard on the wall and a buzz of flies by the fountain. Seeing no sign of the landlord, one of the travellers approached me with a grave inclination.

"This is the inn called the Tre Croci, sir?" he asked.

I said it was, and shouted on my own account for the host. Presently that personage arrived with a red face and a short wind, having ascended rapidly from his own cellar. He was awed by the dignity of the travellers, and made none of his usual protests of incapacity. The servants filed off solemnly with the baggage, and the four gentlemen sat themselves down beside me in the loggia and ordered each a modest flask of wine.

At first I took them for our countrymen, but as I watched them the conviction vanished. All four were tall and lean beyond the average of mankind. They wore suits of black, with antique starched frills to their shirts; their hair was their own and un-powdered. Massive buckles of an ancient pattern adorned their square-toed shoes, and the canes they carried were like the yards of a small vessel. They were four merchants, I had guessed, of Scotland may be, or of Newcastle, but their voices were not Scotch, and their air had no touch of commerce. Take the heavy-browed preoccupation of a Secretary of State, add the dignity of a bishop, the sunburn of a fox-hunter, and something of the disciplined erectness of a soldier, and you may perceive the manner of these four gentlemen. By the side of them my assurance vanished. Compared with their Olympian serenity my person seemed fussy and servile. Even so, I mused, must Mr. Franklin have looked when baited in Parliament by the Tory pack. The reflection gave me the cue. Presently I caught from their conversation the word "Washington," and the truth flashed upon me. I was in the presence of four of Mr. Franklin's countrymen. Having never seen an American in the flesh, I rejoiced at the chance of enlarging my acquaintance.

They brought me into the circle by a polite question as to the length of road to Verona. Soon introductions followed. My name intrigued them, and they were eager to learn of my kinship to Uncle Charles. The eldest of the four, it appeared, was Mr. Galloway out of Maryland. Then came two brothers, Sylvester by name, of Pennsylvania, and last Mr. Fish, a lawyer of New York. All four had campaigned in the late war, and all four were members of the Convention, or whatever they call their rough-and-ready parliament. They were modest in their behaviour, much disinclined to speak of their past, as great men might be whose reputation was world-wide. Somehow the names stuck in my memory. I was certain that I had heard them linked with some stalwart fight or some moving civil deed or some defiant manifesto. The making of history was in their steadfast eyes and the grave lines of the mouth. Our friendship flourished mightily in a brief hour, and brought me the invitation, willingly accepted, to sit with them at dinner.

There was no sign of the Duchess or Cristine or Oliphant. Whatever had happened, that household to-day required all hands on deck, and I was left alone with the Americans. In my day I have supped with the Macaronies, I have held up my head at the Cocoa Tree, I have avoided the floor at hunt dinners, I have drunk glass to glass with Tom Carteron. But never before have I seen such noble consumers of good liquor as those four gentlemen from beyond the Atlantic. They drank the strong red Cyprus as if it had been spring-water. "The dust of your Italian roads takes some cleansing, Mr. Townshend," was their only excuse, but in truth none was needed. Without any surcease of dignity they grew communicative, and passed from lands to peoples and from peoples to constitutions. Before we knew it we were embarked upon high politics.

Naturally we did not differ on the war. Like me, they held it to have been a grievous necessity. They had no bitterness against England, only regrets for her blunders. Of his Majesty they spoke with respect, of his Majesty's advisers with dignified condemnation. They thought highly of our troops in America; less highly of our generals.

"Look you, sir," said Mr. Galloway, "in a war such as we have witnessed the Almighty is the only strategist. You fight against the forces of Nature, and a newcomer little knows that the success or failure of every operation he can conceive depends not upon generalship, but upon the conformation of a vast country. Our generals, with this in mind and with fewer men, could make all your schemes miscarry. Had the English soldiery not been of such stubborn stuff, we should have been victors from the first. Our leader was not General Washington, but General America, and his brigadiers were forests, swamps, lakes, rivers, and high mountains."

"And now," I said, "having won, you have the greatest of human experiments before you. Your business is to show that the Saxon stock is adaptable to a republic."

It seemed to me that they exchanged glances.

"We are not pedants," said Mr. Fish, "and have no desire to

dispute about the form of a constitution. A people may be as free under a king as under a senate. Liberty is not the lackey of any type of government."

These were strange words from a member of a race whom I had thought wedded to the republicanism of Helvidius Priscus.

"As a loyal subject of a monarchy," I said, "I must agree with you. But your hands are tied, for I cannot picture the establishment of a House of Washington, and—if not, where are you to turn for your sovereign?"

Again a smile seemed to pass among the four.

"We are experimenters, as you say, sir, and must go slowly. In the meantime we have an authority which keeps peace and property safe. We are at leisure to cast our eyes round and meditate on the future."

"Then, gentlemen," said I, "you take an excellent way of meditation in visiting this museum of old sovereignties. Here you have the relics of any government you please—a dozen republics, tyrannies, theocracies, merchant confederations, kingdoms, and more than one empire. You have your choice. I am tolerably familiar with the land, and if I can assist you I am at your service."

They thanked me gravely. "We have letters," said Mr. Galloway; "one in especial is to a gentleman whom we hope to meet in this place. Have you heard in your travels of the Count of Albany?"

"He has arrived," said I, "two days ago. Even now he is in the chamber above us at dinner."

The news interested them hugely.

"You have seen him?" they cried. "What is he like?"

"An elderly gentleman in poor health, a man who has travelled much, and, I judge, has suffered something from fortune. He has a fondness for the English, so you will be welcome, sirs; but he was indisposed yesterday, and may still be unable to receive you. His daughter travels with him and tends his old age."

"And you—you have spoken with him?"

"The night before last I was in his company. We talked of

many things, including the late war. He is somewhat of your opinion on matters of government."

The four looked at each other, and then Mr. Galloway rose.

"I ask your permission, Mr. Townshend, to consult for a moment with my friends. The matter is of some importance, and I would beg you to await us." So saying, he led the others out of doors, and I heard them withdraw to a corner of the loggia. Now, thought I, there is something afoot, and my long-sought romance approaches fruition. The company of the Marjolaine, whom the Count had sung of, have arrived at last.

Presently they returned and seated themselves at the table.

"You can be of great assistance to us, Mr. Townshend, and we would fain take you into our confidence. Are you aware who is this Count of Albany?"

I nodded. "It is a thin disguise to one familiar with history."

"Have you reached any estimate of his character or capabilities? You speak to friends, and, let me tell you, it is a matter which deeply concerns the Count's interests."

"I think him a kindly and pathetic old gentleman. He naturally bears the mark of forty years' sojourn in the wilderness."

Mr. Galloway took snuff.

"We have business with him, but it is business which stands in need of an agent. There is no one in the Count's suite with whom we could discuss affairs?"

"There is his daughter."

"Ah, but she would scarcely suit the case. Is there no man—a friend, and yet not a member of the family—who can treat with us?"

I replied that I thought that I was the only being in Santa Chiara who answered the description.

"If you will accept the task, Mr. Townshend, you are amply qualified. We will be frank with you and reveal our business. We are on no less an errand than to offer the Count of Albany a crown."

I suppose I must have had some suspicion of their purpose, and yet the revelation of it fell on me like a thunderclap. I could only stare owlishly at my four grave gentlemen.

Mr. Galloway went on unperturbed. "I have told you that in America we are not yet Republicans. There are those among us who favour a republic, but they are by no means a majority. We have got rid of a king who misgoverned us, but we have no wish to get rid of kingship. We want a king of our own choosing, and we would get with him all the ancient sanctions of monarchy. The Count of Albany is of the most illustrious royal stock in Europe,—he is, if legitimacy goes for anything, the rightful King of Britain. Now, if the republican party among us is to be worsted, we must come before the nation with a powerful candidate for their favour. You perceive my drift? What more potent appeal to American pride than to say: 'We have got rid of King George; we choose of our own free will the older line and King Charles'?"

I said foolishly that I thought monarchy had had its day, and that 'twas idle to revive it.

"That is a sentiment well enough under a monarchical government; but we, with a clean page to write upon, do not share it. You know your ancient historians. Has not the repository of the chief power always been the rock on which republicanism was shipwrecked? If that power is given to the chief citizen, the way is prepared for the tyrant. If it abides peacefully in a royal house, it abides with cyphers who dignify, without obstructing, a popular constitution. Do not mistake me, Mr. Townshend. This is no whim of a sentimental girl, but the reasoned conclusion of the men who achieved our liberty. There is every reason to believe that General Washington shares our views, and Mr. Hamilton, whose name you may know, is the inspirer of our mission."

"But the Count is an old man," I urged; for I knew not where to begin in my exposition of the hopelessness of their errand.

"By so much the better. We do not wish a young king who

may be fractious. An old man tempered by misfortune is what our purpose demands."

"He has also his failings. A man cannot lead his life for forty years and retain all the virtues."

At that one of the Sylvesters spoke sharply. "I have heard such gossip, but I do not credit it. I have not forgotten Preston and Derby."

I made my last objection. "He has no posterity—legitimate posterity—to carry on his line."

The four gentlemen smiled. "That happens to be his chiefest recommendation," said Mr. Galloway. "It enables us to take the House of Stuart on trial. We need a breathing-space and leisure to look around; but unless we establish the principle of monarchy at once the republicans will forestall us. Let us get our king at all costs, and during the remaining years of his life we shall have time to settle the succession problem. We have no wish to saddle ourselves for good with a race who might prove burdensome. If King Charles fails he has no son, and we can look elsewhere for a better monarch. You perceive the reason of my view?"

I did, and I also perceived the colossal absurdity of the whole business. But I could not convince them of it, for they met my objections with excellent arguments. Nothing save a sight of the Count would, I feared, disillusion them.

"You wish me to make this proposal on your behalf?" I asked.

"We shall make the proposal ourselves, but we desire you to prepare the way for us. He is an elderly man, and should first be informed of our purpose."

"There is one person whom I beg leave to consult—the Duchess, his daughter. It may be that the present is an ill moment for approaching the Count, and the affair requires her sanction."

They agreed, and with a very perplexed mind I went forth to seek the lady. The irony of the thing was too cruel, and my heart ached for her. In the gallery I found Oliphant packing some very shabby trunks, and when I questioned him he told me that the family were to leave Santa Chiara on the morrow. Perchance the Duchess had awakened to the true state of their exchequer, or perchance she thought it well to get her father on the road again as a cure for his ailment.

I discovered Cristine, and begged for an interview with her mistress on an urgent matter. She led me to the Duchess's room, and there the evidence of poverty greeted me openly. All the little luxuries of the menage had gone to the Count. The poor lady's room was no better than a servant's garret, and the lady herself sat stitching a rent in a travelling cloak. She rose to greet me with alarm in her eyes.

As briefly as I could I set out the facts of my amazing mission. At first she seemed scarcely to hear me. "What do they want with him?" she asked. "He can give them nothing. He is no friend to the Americans or to any people who have deposed their sovereign." Then, as she grasped my meaning, her face flushed.

"It is a heartless trick, Mr. Townshend. I would fain think you no party to it."

"Believe me, dear madame, it is no trick. The men below are in sober earnest. You have but to see their faces to know that theirs is no wild adventure. I believe sincerely that they have the power to implement their promise."

"But it is madness. He is old and worn and sick. His day is long past for winning a crown."

"All this I have said, but it does not move them." And I told her rapidly Mr. Galloway's argument.

She fell into a muse. "At the eleventh hour! Nay, too late, too late! Had he been twenty years younger, what a stroke of fortune! Fate bears too hard on us, too hard!"

Then she turned to me fiercely. "You have no doubt heard, sir, the gossip about my father, which is on the lips of every fool in Europe. Let us have done with this pitiful make-believe. My father is a sot. Nay, I do not blame him. I blame his enemies and his miserable destiny. But there is the fact. Were he not old, he would still be unfit to grasp a crown and rule over a turbulent people. He flees from one city to another, but he cannot flee from himself. That is his illness on which you condoled with me yesterday."

The lady's control was at breaking-point. Another moment and I expected a torrent of tears. But they did not come. With a great effort she regained her composure.

"Well, the gentlemen must have an answer. You will tell them that the Count, my father—nay, give him his true title if you care—is vastly obliged to them for the honour they have done him, but would decline on account of his age and infirmities. You know how to phrase a decent refusal."

"Pardon me," said I, "but I might give them that answer till doomsday and never content them. They have not travelled many thousand miles to be put off by hearsay evidence. Nothing will satisfy them but an interview with your father himself."

"It is impossible," she said sharply.

"Then we must expect the renewed attentions of our American friends. They will wait till they see him."

She rose and paced the room.

"They must go," she repeated many times. "If they see him sober he will accept with joy, and we shall be the laughing-stock of the world. I tell you it cannot be. I alone know how immense is the impossibility. He cannot afford to lose the last rags of his dignity, the last dregs of his ease. They must not see him. I will speak with them myself."

"They will be honoured, madame, but I do not think they will be convinced. They are what we call in my land 'men of business.' They will not be content till they get the Count's reply from his own lips."

A new duchess seemed to have arisen, a woman of quick action and sharp words.

"So be it. They shall see him. Oh, I am sick to death of fine sentiments and high loyalty and all the vapouring stuff I have lived among for years. All I ask for myself and my father is a little peace, and, by Heaven! I shall secure it. If nothing will kill your gentlemen's folly but truth, why, truth they shall have. They shall see my father, and this very minute. Bring them up, Mr. Townshend, and usher them into the presence of the rightful King of England. You will find him alone." She stopped her walk and looked out of the window.

I went back in a hurry to the Americans. "I am bidden to bring you to the Count's chamber. He is alone and will see you. These are the commands of Madame, his daughter."

"Good!" said Mr. Galloway, and all four, grave gentlemen as they were, seemed to brace themselves to a special dignity as befitted ambassadors to a king. I led them upstairs, tapped at the Count's door, and, getting no answer, opened it and admitted them.

And this was what we saw. The furniture was in disorder, and on a couch lay an old man sleeping a heavy drunken sleep. His mouth was open and his breath came stertorously. The face was purple, and large purple veins stood out on the mottled forehead. His scanty white hair was draggled over his cheek. On the floor was a broken glass, wet stains still lay on the boards, and the place reeked of spirits.

The four looked for a second—I do not think longer—at him whom they would have made their king. They did not look at each other. With one accord they moved out, and Mr. Fish, who was last, closed the door very gently behind him.

In the hall below Mr. Galloway turned to me. "Our mission is ended, Mr. Townshend. I have to thank you for your courtesy." Then to the others. "If we order the coaches now, we may get well on the way to Verona ere sundown."

.    .    .    .    .    .    .

An hour later two coaches rolled out of the courtyard of the Tre Croci. As they passed, a window was half-opened on the upper floor, and a head looked out. A line of a song came down, a song sung in a strange quivering voice. It was the catch I had heard the night before:

> "Qu'est-c' qui passe ici si tard,
> Compagnons de la Marjolaine—e?"

It was true. The company came late indeed—too late by forty years.

1. Who were Ariosto, Mr. Gibbon, Mr. Fielding, Dr. Smollett, and Mr. Richardson?
2. Was Oliphant's piping an idiosyncrasy of the royal stranger or a custom elsewhere?
3. How, by means of words and attitudes, is the atmosphere of the eighteenth century suggested?
4. Why does the author change from the mood inspired by "sad stories of the deaths of kings" to "The legitimate king of England was very drunk"?
5. If he did not pointedly announce himself as such, how would you know that the story-teller is an Englishman?

## Robert Louis Stevenson

# A LODGING FOR THE NIGHT

I T WAS late in November, 1456. The snow fell over Paris with rigorous, relentless persistence; sometimes the wind made a sally and scattered it in flying vortices; sometimes there was a lull, and flake after flake descended out of the black night air, silent, circuitous, interminable. To poor people, looking up under moist eyebrows, it seemed a wonder where it all came from. Master Francis Villon had propounded an alternative that afternoon, at a tavern window: was it only Pagan Jupiter plucking geese upon Olympus? or were the holy angels moulting? He was only a poor Master of Arts, he went on; and as the question somewhat touched upon divinity, he durst not venture to conclude. A silly old priest from Montargis, who was among the company, treated the young rascal to a bottle of wine in honour of the jest and grimaces with which it was accompanied, and swore on his own white beard that he had been just such another irreverent dog when he was Villon's age.

The air was raw and pointed, but not far below freezing; and the flakes were large, damp, and adhesive. The whole city was sheeted up. An army might have marched from end to end and not a footfall given the alarm. If there were any belated birds in heaven, they saw the island like a large white patch, and the bridges like slim white spars, on the black ground of the river.

High up overhead the snow settled among the tracery of the cathedral towers. Many a niche was drifted full; many a statue wore a long white bonnet on its grotesque or sainted head. The gargoyles had been transformed into great false noses, drooping towards the point. The crockets were like upright pillows swollen on one side. In the intervals of the wind, there was a dull sound of dripping about the precincts of the church.

The cemetery of St. John had taken its own share of the snow. All the graves were decently covered; tall white housetops stood around in grave array; worthy burghers were long ago in bed, be-nightcapped like their domiciles; there was no light in all the neighbourhood but a little peep from a lamp that hung swinging in the church choir, and tossed the shadows to and fro in time to its oscillations. The clock was hard on ten when the patrol went by with halberds and a lantern, beating their hands; and they saw nothing suspicious about the cemetery of St. John.

Yet there was a small house, backed up against the cemetery wall, which was still awake, and awake to evil purpose, in that snoring district. There was not much to betray it from without; only a stream of warm vapour from the chimney-top, a patch where the snow melted on the roof, and a few half-obliterated footprints at the door. But within, behind the shuttered windows, Master Francis Villon the poet, and some of the thievish crew with whom he consorted, were keeping the night alive and pass-ing round the bottle.

A great pile of living embers diffused a strong and ruddy glow from the arched chimney. Before this straddled Dom Nicolas, the Picardy monk, with his skirts picked up and his fat legs bared to the comfortable warmth. His dilated shadow cut the room in half; and the firelight only escaped on either side of his broad person, and in a little pool between his outspread feet. His face had the beery, bruised appearance of the continual drinker's; it was covered with a network of congested veins; purple in ordinary circumstances, but now pale violet, for even with his back to the

fire the cold pinched him on the other side. His cowl had half
fallen back, and made a strange excrescence on either side of his
bull neck. So he straddled, grumbling, and cut the room in half
with the shadow of his portly frame.

On the right, Villon and Guy Tabary were huddled together
over a scrap of parchment; Villon making a ballade which he
was to call the "Ballade of Roast Fish," and Tabary spluttering
admiration at his shoulder. The poet was a rag of a man, dark,
little, and lean, with hollow cheeks and thin black locks. He
carried his four-and-twenty years with feverish animation. Greed
had made folds about his eyes, evil smiles had puckered his mouth.
The wolf and pig struggled together in his face. It was an eloquent, sharp, ugly, earthly countenance. His hands were small and
prehensile, with fingers knotted like a cord; and they were continually flickering in front of him in violent and expressive panto-
mime. As for Tabary, a broad, complacent, admiring imbecility
breathed from his squash nose and slobbering lips: he had become a thief, just as he might have become the most decent of
burgesses, by the imperious chance that rules the lives of human
geese and human donkeys.

At the monk's other hand, Montigny and Thevenin Pensete
played a game of chance. About the first there clung some flavour
of good birth and training, as about a fallen angel; something
long, lithe, and courtly in the person; something aquiline and
darkling in the face. Thevenin, poor soul, was in great feather:
he had done a good stroke of knavery that afternoon in the Faubourg St. Jacques, and all night he had been gaining from
Montigny. A flat smile illuminated his face; his bald head shone
rosily in a garland of red curls; his little protuberant stomach
shook with silent chucklings as he swept in his gains.

"Doubles or quits?" said Thevenin.

Montigny nodded grimly.

"Some may prefer to dine in state," wrote Villon, "On bread
and cheese on silver plate. Or, or—help me out, Guido!"

Tabary giggled.

"Or *parsley on a golden dish,*" scribbled the poet.

The wind was freshening without; it drove the snow before it, and sometimes raised its voice in a victorious whoop, and made sepulchral grumblings in the chimney. The cold was growing sharper as the night went on. Villon, protruding his lips, imitated the gust with something between a whistle and a groan. It was an eerie, uncomfortable talent of the poet's, much detested by the Picardy monk.

"Can't you hear it rattle in the gibbet?" said Villon. "They are all dancing the devil's jig on nothing, up there. You may dance, my gallants, you'll be none the warmer! Whew! what a gust! Down went somebody just now! A medlar the fewer on the three-legged medlar-tree!—I say, Dom Nicolas, it'll be cold to-night on the St. Denis Road?" he asked.

Dom Nicolas winked both his big eyes, and seemed to choke upon his Adam's apple. Montfaucon, the great grisly Paris gibbet, stood hard by the St. Denis Road, and the pleasantry touched him on the raw. As for Tabary, he laughed immoderately over the medlars; he had never heard anything more light-hearted; and he held his sides and crowed. Villon fetched him a fillip on the nose, which turned his mirth into an attack of coughing.

"Oh, stop that row," said Villon, "and think of rhymes to 'fish.'"

"Doubles or quits," said Montigny doggedly.

"With all my heart," quoth Thevenin.

"Is there any more in that bottle?" asked the monk.

"Open another," said Villon. "How do you ever hope to fill that big hogshead, your body, with little things like bottles? And how do you expect to get to heaven? How many angels, do you fancy, can be spared to carry up a single monk from Picardy? Or do you think yourself another Elias—and they'll send the coach for you?"

"*Hominibus impossibile,*" [1] replied the monk as he filled his glass.

Tabary was in ecstasies.

Villon filliped his nose again.

"Laugh at my jokes, if you like," he said.

"It was very good," objected Tabary.

Villon made a face at him. "Think of rhymes to 'fish,' " he said. "What have you to do with Latin? You'll wish you knew none of it at the great assizes, when the devil calls for Guido Tabary, clericus—the devil with the hump-back and red-hot finger-nails. Talking of the devil," he added in a whisper, "look at Montigny!"

All three peered covertly at the gamester. He did not seem to be enjoying his luck. His mouth was a little to a side; one nostril nearly shut, and the other much inflated. The black dog was on his back, as people say, in terrifying nursery metaphor; and he breathed hard under the gruesome burden.

"He looks as if he could knife him," whispered Tabary, with round eyes.

The monk shuddered, and turned his face and spread his open hands to the red embers. It was the cold that thus affected Dom Nicolas, and not any excess of moral sensibility.

"Come now," said Villon—"about this ballade. How does it run so far?" And beating time with his hand, he read it aloud to Tabary.

They were interrupted at the fourth rhyme by a brief and fatal movement among the gamesters. The round was completed, and Thevenin was just opening his mouth to claim another victory, when Montigny leaped up, swift as an adder, and stabbed him to the heart. The blow took effect before he had time to utter a cry, before he had time to move. A tremor or two convulsed his frame; his hands opened and shut, his heels rattled on the floor; then his head rolled backward over one shoulder with the

[1] Impossible to man [but possible to God].

eyes wide open; and Thevenin Pensete's spirit had returned to Him who made it.

Every one sprang to his feet; but the business was over in two twos. The four living fellows looked at each other in rather a ghastly fashion; the dead man contemplating a corner of the roof with a singular and ugly leer.

"My God!" said Tabary; and he began to pray in Latin.

Villon broke out into hysterical laughter. He came a step forward and ducked a ridiculous bow at Thevenin, and laughed still louder. Then he sat down suddenly, all of a heap, upon a stool, and continued laughing bitterly, as though he would shake himself to pieces.

Montigny recovered his composure first.

"Let's see what he has about him," he remarked, and he picked the dead man's pockets with a practised hand, and divided the money into four equal portions on the table. "There's for you," he said.

The monk received his share with a deep sigh, and a single stealthy glance at the dead Thevenin, who was beginning to sink into himself and topple sideways off the chair.

"We're all in for it," cried Villon, swallowing his mirth. "It's a hanging job for every man jack of us that's here—not to speak of those who aren't." He made a shocking gesture in the air with his raised right hand, and put out his tongue and threw his head on one side, so as to counterfeit the appearance of one who has been hanged. Then he pocketed his share of the spoil, and executed a shuffle with his feet as if to restore the circulation.

Tabary was the last to help himself; he made a dash at the money, and retired to the other end of the apartment.

Montigny stuck Thevenin upright in the chair, and drew out the dagger, which was followed by a jet of blood.

"You fellows had better be moving," he said, as he wiped the blade on his victim's doublet.

"I think we had," returned Villon, with a gulp. "Damn his fat head!" he broke out. "It sticks in my throat like phlegm. What right has a man to have red hair when he is dead?" And he fell all of a heap again upon the stool, and fairly covered his face with his hands.

Montigny and Dom Nicolas laughed aloud, even Tabary feebly chiming in.

"Cry baby," said the monk.

"I always said he was a woman," added Montigny, with a sneer. "Sit up, can't you?" he went on, giving another shake to the murdered body. "Tread out that fire, Nick!"

But Nick was better employed; he was quietly taking Villon's purse, as the poet sat, limp and trembling, on the stool where he had been making a ballade not three minutes before. Montigny and Tabary dumbly demanded a share of the booty, which the monk silently promised as he passed the little bag into the bosom of his gown. In many ways an artistic nature unfits a man for practical existence.

No sooner had the theft been accomplished than Villon shook himself, jumped to his feet, and began helping to scatter and extinguish the embers. Meanwhile Montigny opened the door and cautiously peered into the street. The coast was clear; there was no meddlesome patrol in sight. Still it was judged wiser to slip out severally; and as Villon was himself in a hurry to escape from the neighbourhood of the dead Thevenin, and the rest were in a still greater hurry to get rid of him before he should discover the loss of his money, he was the first by general consent to issue forth into the street.

The wind had triumphed and swept all the clouds from heaven. Only a few vapours, as thin as moonlight, fleeted rapidly across the stars. It was bitter cold; and by a common optical effect, things seemed almost more definite than in the broadest daylight. The sleeping city was absolutely still; a company of white hoods, a field full of little alps, below the twinkling stars. Villon cursed his fortune. Would it were still snowing! Now, wherever he went, he left an indelible trail behind him on the glittering streets; wherever he went he was still tethered to the house by the cemetery of St. John; wherever he went he must weave, with his own plodding feet, the rope that bound him to the crime and would bind him to the gallows. The leer of the dead man came back to him with a new significance. He snapped his fingers as if to pluck up his own spirits, and choosing a street at random, stepped boldly forward in the snow.

Two things preoccupied him as he went; the aspect of the gallows at Montfaucon in this bright, windy phase of the night's existence, for one; and for another, the look of the dead man with his bald head and garland of red curls. Both struck cold upon his heart, and he kept quickening his pace as if he could escape from unpleasant thoughts by mere fleetness of foot. Sometimes he looked back over his shoulder with a sudden nervous jerk; but he was the only moving thing in the white streets, except when the wind swooped round a corner and threw up the snow, which was beginning to freeze, in spouts of glittering dust.

Suddenly he saw, a long way before him, a black clump and a couple of lanterns. The clump was in motion, and the lanterns swung as though carried by men walking. It was a patrol. And though it was merely crossing his line of march he judged it wiser to get out of eyeshot as speedily as he could. He was not in the humour to be challenged, and he was conscious of making a very conspicuous mark upon the snow. Just on his left hand there stood a great hotel, with some turrets and a large porch before the door; it was half-ruinous, he remembered, and had long stood empty; and so he made three steps of it, and jumped into the shelter of the porch. It was pretty dark inside, after the glimmer of the snowy streets, and he was groping forward with outspread hands, when he stumbled over some substance which offered an indescribable mixture of resistances, hard and soft, firm and loose. His heart gave a leap, and he sprang two steps back and stared dreadfully at the obstacle. Then he gave a little laugh of relief.

It was only a woman, and she dead. He knelt beside her to make sure upon this latter point. She was freezing cold, and rigid like a stick. A little ragged finery fluttered in the wind about her hair, and her cheeks had been heavily rouged that same afternoon. Her pockets were quite empty; but in her stocking, underneath the garter, Villon found two of the small coins that went by the name of whites. It was little enough; but it was always something; and the poet was moved with a deep sense of pathos that she should have died before she had spent her money. That seemed to him a dark and pitiable mystery; and he looked from the coins in his hand to the dead woman, and back again to the coins, shaking his head over the riddle of man's life. Henry V. of England, dying at Vincennes just after he had conquered France, and this poor jade cut off by a cold draught in a great man's doorway, before she had time to spend her couple of whites—it seemed a cruel way to carry on the world. Two whites would have taken such a little while to squander; and yet it would have been one more good taste in the mouth, one more smack of the lips, before the devil got the soul, and the body was left to birds and vermin. He would like to use all his tallow before the light was blown out and the lantern broken.

While these thoughts were passing through his mind, he was feeling, half mechanically, for his purse. Suddenly his heart stopped beating; a feeling of cold scales passed up the back of his legs, and a cold blow seemed to fall upon his scalp. He stood petrified for a moment; then he felt again with one feverish movement; and then his loss burst upon him, and he was covered at once with perspiration. To spendthrifts money is so living and actual—it is such a thin veil between them and their pleasures! There is only one limit to their fortune—that of time; and a spendthrift with only a few crowns is the Emperor of Rome until they are spent. For such a person to lose his money is to suffer the most shocking reverse, and fall from heaven to hell, from all to nothing, in a breath. And all the more if he has put his head in the halter for it; if he may be hanged to-morrow for that same purse, so dearly earned, so foolishly departed! Villon stood and cursed; he threw the two whites into the street; he shook his fist at heaven; he stamped, and was not horrified to find himself trampling the poor corpse. Then he began rapidly to retrace his steps towards the house beside the cemetery. He had forgotten all fear of the patrol, which was long gone by at any rate, and had no idea but that of his lost purse. It was in vain that he looked right and left upon the snow: nothing was to be seen. He had not dropped it in the streets. Had it fallen in the house? He would have liked dearly to go in and see; but the idea of the grisly occupant unmanned him. And he saw besides, as he drew near, that their efforts to put out the fire had been unsuccessful; on the contrary, it had broken into a blaze, and a changeful light played in the chinks of door and window, and revived his terror for the authorities and Paris gibbet.

He returned to the hotel with the porch, and groped about upon the snow for the money he had thrown away in his childish passion. But he could only find one white; the other had prob ably struck sideways and sunk deeply in. With a single white in his pocket, all his projects for a rousing night in some wild tavern vanished utterly away. And it was not only pleasure that fled laughing from his grasp; positive discomfort, positive pain, attacked him as he stood ruefully before the porch. His perspiration had dried upon him; and although the wind had now fallen, a binding frost was setting in stronger with every hour, and he felt benumbed and sick at heart. What was to be done? Late as was the hour, improbable as was success, he would try the house of his adopted father, the chaplain of St. Benoît.

He ran there all the way, and knocked timidly. There was no answer. He knocked again and again, taking heart with every stroke; and at last steps were heard approaching from within. A barred wicket fell open in the iron-studded door, and emitted a gush of yellow light.

"Hold up your face to the wicket," said the chaplain from within.

"It's only me," whimpered Villon.

"Oh, it's only you, is it?" returned the chaplain; and he cursed him with foul unpriestly oaths for disturbing him at such an hour, and bade him be off to hell, where he came from.

"My hands are blue to the wrist," pleaded Villon; "my feet are dead and full of twinges; my nose aches with the sharp air; the cold lies at my heart. I may be dead before morning. Only this once, father, and before God, I will never ask again!"

"You should have come earlier," said the ecclesiastic coolly. "Young men require a lesson now and then." He shut the wicket and retired deliberately into the interior of the house.

Villon was beside himself; he beat upon the door with his hands and feet, and shouted hoarsely after the chaplain.

"Wormy old fox!" he cried. "If I had my hand under your twist, I would send you flying headlong into the bottomless pit."

A door shut in the interior, faintly audible to the poet down long passages. He passed his hand over his mouth with an oath. And then the humour of the situation struck him, and he laughed and looked lightly up to heaven, where the stars seemed to be winking over his discomfiture.

What was to be done? It looked very like a night in the frosty streets. The idea of the dead woman popped into his imagination, and gave him a hearty fright; what had happened to her in the early night might very well happen to him before morning. And he so young! and with such immense possibilities of disorderly amusement before him! He felt quite pathetic over the notion of his own fate, as if it had been some one else's, and made a little imaginative vignette of the scene in the morning when they should find his body.

He passed all his chances under review, turning the white between his thumb and forefinger. Unfortunately he was on bad terms with some old friends who would once have taken pity on him in such a plight. He had lampooned them in verses; he had beaten and cheated them; and yet now, when he was in so close a pinch, he thought there was at least one who might perhaps relent. It was a chance. It was worth trying at least, and he would go and see.

On the way, two little accidents happened to him which coloured his musings in a very different manner. For, first, he fell in with the track of a patrol, and walked in it for some hundred yards, although it lay out of his direction. And this spirited him up; at least he had confused his trail; for he was still possessed with the idea of people tracking him all about Paris over the snow, and collaring him next morning before he was awake. The other matter affected him quite differently. He passed a street corner, where, not so long before, a woman and her child had been devoured by wolves. This was just the kind of weather, he reflected, when wolves might take it into their heads to enter Paris again; and a lone man in these deserted streets would run the chance of something worse than a mere scare. He stopped and looked upon the place with an unpleasant interest—it was a centre where several lanes intersected each other; and he looked down them all, one after another, and held his breath to listen, lest he should detect some galloping black things on the snow or hear the sound of howling between him and the river. He remembered his mother telling him the story and pointing out the spot, while he was yet a child. His mother! if he only knew where she lived, he might make sure at least of shelter. He determined he would inquire upon the morrow; nay, he would go and see her too, poor old girl! So thinking, he arrived at his destination—his last hope for the night.

The house was quite dark, like its neighbours; and yet after a few taps, he heard a movement overhead, a door opening, and a cautious voice asking who was there. The poet named himself in a loud whisper, and waited, not without some trepidation, the result. Nor had he to wait long. A window was suddenly opened, and a pailful of slops splashed down upon the doorstep. Villon had not been unprepared for something of the sort, and had put himself as much in shelter as the nature of the porch admitted; but for all that, he was deplorably drenched below the waist. His hose began to freeze almost at once. Death from cold and exposure stared him in the face; he remembered he was of phthisical tendency, and began coughing tentatively. But the gravity of the danger steadied his nerves. He stopped a few hundred yards from the door where he had been so rudely used, and reflected with his finger to his nose. He could only see one way of getting a lodging, and that was to take it. He had noticed a house not far away, which looked as if it might be easily broken into, and thither he betook himself promptly, entertaining himself on the way with the idea of a room still hot, with a table still loaded with the remains of supper, where he might pass the rest of the black hours and whence he should issue, on the morrow, with an armful of valuable plate. He even considered on what viands and what wines he should prefer; and as he was calling the roll of his favourite dainties, roast fish presented itself to his mind with an odd mixture of amusement and horror.

"I shall never finish that ballade," he thought to himself; and then, with another shudder at the recollection, "Oh, damn his fat head!" he repeated fervently, and spat upon the snow.

The house in question looked dark at first sight; but as Villon made a preliminary inspection in search of the handiest point of attack, a little twinkle of light caught his eye from behind a curtained window.

"The devil!" he thought. "People awake! Some student or some saint, confound the crew! Can't they get drunk and lie in bed snoring like their neighbours! What's the good of curfew, and poor devils of bell-ringers jumping at a rope's end in bell-towers? What's the use of day, if people sit up all night? The gripes to them!" He grinned as he saw where his logic was leading him. "Every man to his business, after all," added he, "and if they're awake, by the Lord, I may come by a supper honestly for once, and cheat the devil."

He went boldly to the door and knocked with an assured hand. On both previous occasions, he had knocked timidly and with some dread of attracting notice; but now when he had just discarded the thought of a burglarious entry, knocking at a door seemed a mighty simple and innocent proceeding. The sound of his blows echoed through the house with thin, phantasmal reverberations, as though it were quite empty; but these had scarcely died away before a measured tread drew near, a couple of bolts were withdrawn, and one wing was opened broadly, as though no guile or fear of guile were known to those within. A tall figure of a man, muscular and spare, but a little bent, confronted Villon. The head was massive in bulk, but finely sculptured; the nose blunt at the bottom, but refining upward to where it joined a pair of strong and honest eyebrows; the mouth and eyes surrounded with delicate markings, and the whole face based upon a thick white beard, boldly and squarely trimmed. Seen as it was by the light of a flickering hand-lamp, it looked perhaps nobler than it had a right to do; but it was a fine face, honourable rather than intelligent, strong, simple, and righteous.

"You knock late, sir," said the old man in resonant, courteous tones.

Villon cringed and brought up many servile words of apology; at a crisis of this sort the beggar was uppermost in him, and the man of genius hid his head with confusion.

"You are cold," repeated the old man, "and hungry? Well, step in." And he ordered him into the house with a noble enough gesture.

"Some great seigneur," thought Villon, as his host, setting down the lamp on the flagged pavement of the entry, shot the bolts once more into their places.

"You will pardon me if I go in front," he said, when this was done; and he preceded the poet upstairs into a large apartment, warmed with a pan of charcoal and lit by a great lamp hanging from the roof. It was very bare of furniture: only some gold plate on a sideboard; some folios; and a stand of armour between the windows. Some smart tapestry hung upon the walls, representing the crucifixion of our Lord in one piece, and in another a scene of shepherds and shepherdesses by a running stream. Over the chimney was a shield of arms.

"Will you seat yourself," said the old man, "and forgive me if I leave you? I am alone in my house to-night, and if you are to eat I must forage for you myself."

No sooner was his host gone than Villon leaped from the chair on which he had just seated himself, and began examining the room, with the stealth and passion of a cat. He weighed the gold flagons in his hand, opened all the folios, and investigated the arms upon the shield, and the stuff with which the seats were lined. He raised the window curtains, and saw that the windows were set with rich stained glass in figures, so far as he could see, of martial import. Then he stood in the middle of the room, drew a long breath, and retaining it with puffed cheeks, looked round and round him, turning on his heels, as if to impress every feature of the apartment on his memory.

"Seven pieces of plate," he said. "If there had been ten, I would have risked it. A fine house, and a fine old master, so help me all the saints!"

And just then, hearing the old man's tread returning along the corridor, he stole back to his chair, and began humbly toasting his wet legs before the charcoal pan.

His entertainer had a plate of meat in one hand and a jug of wine in the other. He set down the plate upon the table, motioning Villon to draw in his chair, and going to the sideboard, brought back two goblets which he filled.

"I drink your better fortune," he said, gravely touching Villon's cup with his own.

"To our better acquaintance," said the poet, growing bold. A mere man of the people would have been awed by the courtesy of the old seigneur, but Villon was hardened in that matter; he had made mirth for great lords before now, and found them as black rascals as himself. And so he devoted himself to the viands with a ravenous gusto, while the old man, leaning backward, watched him with steady, curious eyes.

"You have blood on your shoulder, my man," he said.

Montigny must have laid his wet right hand upon him as he left the house. He cursed Montigny in his heart.

"It was none of my shedding," he stammered.

"I had not supposed so," returned his host quietly. "A brawl?"

"Well, something of that sort," Villon admitted with a quaver.

"Perhaps a fellow murdered?"

"Oh, no, not murdered," said the poet, more and more confused. "It was all fair play—murdered by accident. I had no hand in it, God strike me dead!" he added fervently.

"One rogue the fewer, I dare say," observed the master of the house.

"You may dare to say that," agreed Villon, infinitely relieved. "As big a rogue as there is between here and Jerusalem. He turned up his toes like a lamb. But it was a nasty thing to look at. I dare say you've seen dead men in your time, my lord?" he added, glancing at the armour.

"Many," said the old man. "I have followed the wars, as you imagine."

Villon laid down his knife and fork, which he had just taken up again.

"Were any of them bald?" he asked.

"Oh, yes, and with hair as white as mine."

"I don't think I should mind the white so much," said Villon. "His was red." And he had a return of his shuddering and tendency to laughter, which he drowned with a great draught of wine. "I'm a little put out when I think of it," he went on. "I knew him—damn him! And then the cold gives a man fancies—or the fancies give a man cold, I don't know which."

"Have you any money?" asked the old man.

"I have one white," returned the poet, laughing. "I got it out of a dead jade's stocking in a porch. She was as dead as Cæsar, poor wench, and as cold as a church, with bits of ribbon sticking in her hair. This is a hard world in winter for wolves and wenches and poor rogues like me."

"I," said the old man, "am Enguerrand de la Feuillée, seigneur de Brisetout, bailly du Patatrac. Who and what may you be?"

Villon rose and made a suitable reverence. "I am called Francis Villon," he said, "a poor Master of Arts of this university. I know some Latin, and a deal of vice. I can make chansons, ballades, lais, virelais, and roundels, and I am very fond of wine. I was born in a garret, and I shall not improbably die upon the gallows. I may add, my lord, that from this night forward I am your lordship's very obsequious servant to command."

"No servant of mine," said the knight; "my guest for this evening, and no more."

"A very grateful guest," said Villon politely, and he drank in dumb show to his entertainer.

"You are shrewd," began the old man, tapping his forehead, "very shrewd; you have learning; you are a clerk; and yet you take a small piece of money off a dead woman in the street. Is it not a kind of theft?"

"It is a kind of theft much practised in the wars, my lord."

"The wars are the field of honour," returned the old man proudly. "There a man plays his life upon the cast; he fights in the name of his lord the king, his Lord God, and all their lordships the holy saints and angels."

"Put it," said Villon, "that I were really a thief, should I not play my life also, and against heavier odds?"

"For gain but not for honour."

"Gain?" repeated Villon with a shrug. "Gain! The poor fellow wants supper, and takes it. So does the soldier in a campaign. Why, what are all these requisitions we hear so much about? If they are not gain to those who take them, they are loss enough to the others. The men-at-arms drink by a good fire, while the burgher bites his nails to buy them wine and wood. I have seen a good many ploughmen swinging on trees about the country; ay, I have seen thirty on one elm, and a very poor figure they made; and when I asked some one how all these came to be hanged, I was told it was because they could not scrape together enough crowns to satisfy the men-at-arms."

"These things are a necessity of war, which the low-born must endure with constancy. It is true that some captains drive over-hard; there are spirits in every rank not easily moved by pity; and indeed many follow arms who are no better than brigands."

"You see," said the poet, "you cannot separate the soldier from the brigand; and what is a thief but an isolated brigand with circumspect manners? I steal a couple of mutton chops, without so much as disturbing people's sleep; the farmer grumbles a bit, but sups none the less wholesomely on what remains. You come up blowing gloriously on a trumpet, take away the whole sheep, and beat the farmer pitifully into the bargain. I have no trumpet; I am only Tom, Dick, or Harry; I am a rogue and a dog, and hanging's too good for me—with all my heart; but just ask the farmer which of us he prefers, just find out which of us he lies awake to curse on cold nights."

"Look at us two," said his lordship. "I am old, strong, and honoured. If I were turned from my house to-morrow, hundreds would be proud to shelter me. Poor people would go out and pass the night in the streets with their children, if I merely hinted that I wished to be alone. And I find you up, wandering homeless, and picking farthings off dead women by the wayside! I fear no man and nothing; I have seen you tremble and lose countenance at a word. I wait God's summons contentedly in my own house, or, if it please the king to call me out again, upon the field of battle. You look for the gallows; a rough, swift death, without hope or honour. Is there no difference between these two?"

"As far as to the moon," Villon acquiesced. "But if I had been born lord of Brisetout, and you had been the poor scholar Francis, would the difference have been any the less? Should not I have been warming my knees at this charcoal pan, and would not you have been groping for farthings in the snow? Should not I have been the soldier, and you the thief?"

"A thief?" cried the old man. "I a thief! If you understand your words, you would repent them."

Villon turned out his hands with a gesture of inimitable impudence. "If your lordship had done me the honour to follow my argument!" he said.

"I do you too much honour in submitting to your presence," said the knight. "Learn to curb your tongue when you speak with old and honourable men, or some one hastier than I may reprove you in a sharper fashion." And he rose and paced the lower end of the apartment, struggling with anger and antipathy. Villon surreptitiously refilled his cup, and settled himself more comfortably in the chair, crossing his knees and leaning his head upon one hand and the elbow against the back of the chair. He was now replete and warm; and he was in nowise frightened for his host, having gauged him as justly as was possible between two such different characters. The night was far spent, and in a very comfortable fashion after all; and he felt morally certain of a safe departure on the morrow.

"Tell me one thing," said the old man, pausing in his walk. "Are you really a thief?"

"I claim the sacred rights of hospitality," returned the poet. "My lord, I am."

"You are very young," the knight continued.

"I should never have been so old," replied Villon, showing his fingers, "if I had not helped myself with these ten talents. They have been my nursing mothers and my nursing fathers."

"You may still repent and change."

"I repent daily," said the poet. "There are few people more given to repentance than poor Francis. As for change, let somebody change my circumstances. A man must continue to eat, if it were only that he may continue to repent."

"The change must begin in the heart," returned the old man solemnly.

"My dear lord," answered Villon, "do you really fancy that I steal for pleasure? I hate stealing, like any other piece of work or of danger. My teeth chatter when I see a gallows. But I must eat, I must drink, I must mix in society of some sort. What the devil! Man is not a solitary animal—*Cui Deus fæminam tradit.*[1] Make me king's pantler—make me abbot of St. Denis; make me bailly of the Patatrac; and then I shall be changed indeed. But as long as you leave me the poor scholar Francis Villon, without a farthing, why, of course, I remain the same."

"The grace of God is all-powerful."

"I should be a heretic to question it," said Francis. "It has made you lord of Brisetout and bailly of the Patatrac; it has given me nothing but the quick wits under my hat and these ten toes upon my hands. May I help myself to wine? I thank you respectfully. By God's grace, you have a very superior vintage."

The lord of Brisetout walked to and fro with his hands behind his back. Perhaps he was not yet quite settled in his mind about the parallel between thieves and soldiers; perhaps Villon had interested him by some cross-thread of sympathy; perhaps his wits were simply muddled by so much unfamiliar reasoning; but whatever the cause, he somehow yearned to convert the young man to a better way of thinking, and could not make up his mind to drive him forth again into the street.

"There is something more than I can understand in this," he said at length. "Your mouth is full of subtleties, and the devil has led you very far astray; but the devil is only a very weak spirit

[1] To whom God gave woman.

before God's truth, and all his subtleties vanish at a word of true honour, like darkness at morning. Listen to me once more. I learned long ago that a gentleman should live chivalrously and lovingly to God, and the king, and his lady; and though I have seen many strange things done, I have still striven to command my ways upon that rule. It is not only written in all noble histories, but in every man's heart, if he will take care to read. You speak of food and wine, and I know very well that hunger is a difficult trial to endure; but you do not speak of other wants; you say nothing of honour, of faith to God and other men, of courtesy, of love without reproach. It may be that I am not very wise—and yet I think I am—but you seem to me like one who has lost his mind and made a great error in life. You are attending to the little wants, and you have totally forgotten the great and only real ones, like a man who should be doctoring toothache on the Judgment Day. For such things as honour and love and faith are not only nobler than food and drink, but indeed I think we desire them more, and suffer more sharply for their absence. I speak to you as I think you will most easily understand me. Are you not, while careful to fill your belly, disregarding another appetite in your heart, which spoils the pleasure of your life and keeps you continually wretched?"

Villon was sensibly nettled under all this sermonizing. "You think I have no sense of honour!" he cried. "I'm poor enough, God knows! It's hard to see rich people with their gloves, and you blowing in your hands. An empty belly is a bitter thing, although you speak so lightly of it. If you had had as many as I, perhaps you would change your tune. Any way I'm a thief—make the most of that—but I'm not a devil from hell, God strike me dead. I would have you to know I've an honour of my own, as good as yours, though I don't prate about it all day long, as if it was a God's miracle to have any. It seems quite natural to me; I keep it in its box till it's wanted. Why now, look you here, how long have I been in this room with you? Did you not tell me you were alone in the house? Look at your gold plate! You're strong, if you like, but you're old and unarmed, and I have my knife. What did I want but a jerk of the elbow and here would have been you with the cold steel in your bowels, and there would have been me, linking in the streets, with an armful of golden cups! Did you suppose I hadn't wit enough to see that? And I scorned the action. There are your damned goblets, as safe as in a church; there are you, with your heart ticking as good as new; and here am I, ready to go out again as poor as I came in, with my one white that you threw in my teeth! And you think I have no sense of honour—God strike me dead!"

The old man stretched out his right arm. "I will tell you what you are," he said. "You are a rogue, my man, an impudent and black-hearted rogue and vagabond. I have passed an hour with you. Oh! believe me, I feel myself disgraced! And you have eaten and drunk at my table. But now I am sick at your presence; the day has come, and the night-bird should be off to his roost. Will you go before, or after?"

"Which you please," returned the poet, rising. "I believe you to be strictly honourable." He thoughtfully emptied his cup. "I wish I could add you were intelligent," he went on, knocking on his head with his knuckles. "Age! age! the brains stiff and rheumatic."

The old man preceded him from a point of self-respect. Villon followed, whistling, with his thumbs in his girdle.

"God pity you," said the lord of Brisetout at the door.

"Good-bye, papa," returned Villon with a yawn. "Many thanks for the cold mutton."

The door closed behind him. The dawn was breaking over the white roofs. A chill, uncomfortable morning ushered in the day. Villon stood and heartily stretched himself in the middle of the road.

"A very dull old gentleman," he thought. "I wonder what his goblets may be worth."

1. Which descriptive line most aptly describes François Villon?
2. Do you agree that the snowstorm is a character in the story?
3. What are the literary qualifications of the ballade?
4. What has made Villon cynical?
5. Which man has the better philosophy of life, the Seigneur de Brisetout or Villon?

*Walter D. Edmonds*

# ADAM HELMER'S RUN

HE sixteenth of September, 1778, was a day of haze and blistering dry heat. In the western part of the Mohawk Valley, beyond Little Falls, the men of German Flats were working in the fields, carting the last of the harvest to their log barns. They worked like men who were afraid of time.

Throughout the working day a man would stop to listen to some disturbance of the heavy air. It might be a dog barking a rabbit up one of the southern hills; it might be the creak of an overloaded cart across the river—each time, however, the man looked toward whichever fort was nearest to him to make sure that no smoke showed from the alarm gun.

Early in March, Fairfield had been destroyed. In May, there had been raiding of outlying cabins near the little lakes. In June, Springfield had been razed. In July, word had come to them of Major Butler's expedition against Wyoming, where the women and children had been turned into the woods, half naked, without provisions, most of them to starve. And then in August they had begun to see how the raids were closing in against themselves. Andrustown was burned, even to the haycocks in the fields.

It was impossible to catch these raiding parties. They had all the western and northern wildernesses to hide in. The militiamen were compelled to work their fields; their farms were their sole source of food. Congress, and the Continental high command, and the Albany government, all three turned deaf ears to their pleas for regular troops to garrison their own two forts. The answer always was the same, that Congress was maintaining Fort Stanwix at vast expense for their protection. But Fort Stanwix stood thirty miles farther west in the wilderness, and all the Indians and Tories had to do was march around it on their way to German Flats.

The people knew as surely as they knew that night would follow day that sooner or later the hostile forces must descend on them— the wonder was that they had not come sooner. A cannon from one of the forts, a shot on the hills, or the war whoop of the Indians would tell them that the time had come. Most of the men had fought at Oriskany, when Joseph Brant brought his red devils—Mohawks, Cayugas and Senecas—against the rear. They had seen them in the scrub like dogs, worrying the dead; and they had seen those men after the Indians had finished with them. That was why they kept their eyes on the dull brown stockades, with their blockhouses, in whose spy lofts a sentry always stood on watch, or on the steeple of the old stone church that pricked the haze higher than the Herkimer blockhouse roofs and in whose belfry the bell had been replaced by a brass three-pounder. They realized that their lives and the lives of their families depended on the sharp sight of these watchmen, and even more on the alertness of the scouting parties patrolling the Indian trails to west and south.

Fifteen miles to the south of German Flats, Adam Helmer lay on his back in the sumac scrub and considered Bellinger's hard treatment of him. He had his shoulders propped against a half-embedded, mossy log, so that he could comb his hair and, if he chose, look down the slope through the sumac leaves to the Indian trail. A mile and a half south of his post lay the little Tory settlement of Edmeston, unmolested, as safe from marauding Indians and destructives as Philadelphia City. It seemed ironical. The place didn't even have a stockade. Some days the scouts would go to the edge of the overhanging hill and stare down at the women in the bean patches, at the children playing along the stream. The men who worked in the fields did not even have their muskets with them.

The Indian trail that followed the Unadilla north branched off at Edmeston and passed the place where Adam lay, and a half mile back of him the hill with the hideout shanty which the scouts had built for rainy weather and in which now Adam had left the other three men playing with a pair of dice. Then the trail headed a little east of north, following the low lie of the land for eight miles into Andrustown, or what had been Andrustown; and from there its foot-deep, beaten slot became the road that led directly over the river hills to German Flats.

Adam passed the bone comb carefully through his hair and found a knot to labor over. He was proud of his hair; it was as near golden as a man's hair had any right to be, and he wore it long on his shoulders. Though it wasn't quite a match for the ruddier color of his beard, Adam himself rather fancied the contrast. He had never yet discovered a girl who objected to the combination.

At the moment, however, he was thinking of Andrustown. He had seen, as he came through the day before, the charred squarish heaps of embers that marked what had been barns and cabins, and the burnt spots through the hayfields where the cocks had been fired. The graves of three murdered men still showed bare. One had been disturbed by a fox or a roving dog. Adam remembered the place as it used to look, a double row of simple habitations, when he used to go there helling after Polly Bowers. With her family she had taken refuge in Fort Herkimer, and was now living in one of the sheds; but it was less than a year ago that he had visited her in the little hamlet. He had gone to attend the Bowers husking bee. He was glad she hadn't been in the haying party that had got caught there by the destructives. The women hadn't been killed—the Butler ranger in command had turned them loose—but then the Indians had chased them, knocked them down and stripped them. That was an Indian habit. They liked a woman's clothes to wear round their heads, a petticoat, or a shift, or anything that was thin and bright-colored. It was like the way they killed the horses at Oriskany to hear them scream. The women had had to walk the whole way back stark naked into German Flats.

It was funny, Adam thought, the way the Indians were. He'd never liked them himself, as some settlers claimed they did. He'd had trouble with some of them on his trap lines. But he didn't mind wrestling with them. They were always after a man to wrestle, but the same Indian seldom came after Adam a second time. He flexed his arm and admired his own muscle.

He was a man to look at, lying there in the sumac, combing his yellow hair. He had good straight features and deep blue eyes. His green-fringed hunting shirt of butternut-brown linen stretched tight over his chest, and his long legs lay straight and loose down the slope ahead of him. When he moved to get a better view of the trail, his action was soundless. Not a leaf seemed to be stirred. Not a leaf in all the woods was stirring. It was airless and hot, and the sultry haze hung between the trees like smoke.

Indians, thought Adam, smelled bad. That was another thing he disliked about them. They had a greasy, sweetish sort of smell. When one came into a tavern to drink on a cold afternoon, the heat of the fire would put his smell all over the room. And they were all thieves, even such few as he liked, as old Blue Back, the Oneida, who Bellinger had told him was scouting to the north of German Flats. It was queer that they were supposed to be such wonderful runners. He had heard stories told of Indians who could run eighty miles between sunrise and noon. A hundred miles a day was not uncommon. It was even queerer that the few Adam had ever raced for a gallon of rum could go as fast as they did. But in a hundred-yard sprint he had yet to find the man, red or white, who could keep up with him. Those same licked Indians always wanted him to race them thirty miles for another gallon, but what man in his natural senses would run thirty miles, or ten for that matter, for a gallon of rum?

Adam cleared the knot from his hair and examined the cause on the comb. Another bur—that was the worst of sleeping out. It made him indignant to consider his hard lot. Just because he didn't work a farm, they expected him to run scouts all the time. Here he was, not ten days in from a three weeks' trip toward Tioga Point, and they sent him out again to watch this place by Edmeston. It wouldn't have been so bad if Joe Boleo had been along, or even Blue Back. But the three men back there in the lodge were the damnedest fool set of farmers Adam had ever seen. It was astonishing how men you knew down around the flats for pretty sensible men turned out to be as crumbly as a lot of woodlice, once you got them away from home. One of them had a pair of dice in his pocket with which the three of them played all the time, leaving Adam to keep guard while they lay around throwing the things in the shade of the lodge. Adam would have booted them out on their rear ends and sent them off on daily beats east and west of the position, if he hadn't felt sure they would bring down the whole Six Nations with the blundering racket they made even on an open path. He preferred to have them where he could see and hear them. Besides, he was pretty certain that if an army came against the flats, it would be sure to come along the Indian trail he was now watching.

He was sure, because when Andrustown was being burned—it was just his luck not to have been around to get a pot at some of the destructives—he had been tailing Butler's army on its way back toward Niagara from Wyoming. He had picked them up on the Susquehanna and shadowed them in to Tioga Point, and there he had lain nearly ten days until Brant's army appeared from the east.

Adam had never itched to shoot anyone the way he itched to

take a pot shot at those men. They were the ones who had been
harrying Springfield and the Lakes and Andrustown. He had happened on them as they came in along the trail. Brant, the Mohawk, trying to look gentrified and white and Indian all at the
same time, with his Indian blanket and his red coat and his laced
hat; Caldwell in his green Ranger uniform looked unhuman as a
man of wood. Then Adam had picked out Casselman, the man
who had led the rape on Fairfield, the man's own home town,
and had taken as many scalps as the Indians with him.

The army itself was a motley bunch of men; Indians for the
most part, Cayugas, Senecas and Mohawks, in their paint and
feathers, and Eries with strange headdresses made of the dried
heads of animals; Green Coat soldiers, with their leather gaiters
and black leather skullcaps; a few scattered remnants of the old
Highland guard of Fort Johnson, dark limber men, wearing tartan
kilts and knee-length leggings of deerskin, and carrying long-
barreled smoothbores and Indian war clubs.

They came along the trail with the loose stride of woodsmen,
their tread light on the ground, dangling scalps from their belts,
those that had taken scalps, and speculating loudly whether the
bounty still held at eight dollars in Niagara. They had passed
Adam without order or without scouts, they were so sure of their
safety; but they herded up close to one another, like a pack of
dogs, running with the instinct to kill.

They were the same men whom Brant, a week later, took out
of Tioga Point, back toward the east, augmented by a hundred
from Butler's army. Adam had tailed them as far as the Susquehanna; making sure only that they were turning north before he
ran the news back to Fort Herkimer. He had thought, and so had
Bellinger, that they would come any time, for Brant and Casselman had often promised to kill every man in German Flats.

One of the three back in the lodge must have won a big one,
for he laughed. His voice came down to Adam, thin and nasal.

Adam roused angrily. Those fools acted like drunks at a wake. He thought grimly of going up and licking the noise out of them, but it was too hot for him to bother. Let them yell. He was hidden where he was and he didn't want to move.

He half wished something would happen, something that would give him an excuse to report back to the flats. If it did, he made up his mind he would get an evening off with Polly Bowers, orders or no orders.

It did him good to think of her as he lay in the heat. It helped to take the eternal dry droning of the locusts out of his ears. He had had his eye on her from the time she was thirteen. A little slim-legged, dark-haired, brown-eyed, coltish girl, she looked ready to prance if you said boo to her. She had had knees like a colt, too, lumpy and round. Adam thought sentimentally, that that was the damnedest part in her growing up, the way her knees had fitted into the general scheme of her legs when the time came. He thought she had the best-looking legs in German Flats, even though they were still thinnish. But the taper was there now, below the hem of the skirt, and the knees, when she let you see them, were as smooth as Adam had figured out they would be. Being a timber beast, he didn't know much about horseflesh, but he surely had an eye for girls. He had always taken pride in picking the good ones before they were grown.

Polly Bowers, though, was a skittish proposition and lately she had taken to shying off from him. He did not know how much stock to take of her notionalness; but the three bezabors up in the lodge had got talking one night about the way she went out when Adam was scouting. He had cornered her with the question one night himself. He had asked her right out whether she was carrying any other men besides himself along.

She had just laughed.

She had acted frisky and uppish as a red squirrel full of cherries. Standing right up to him, too, though her head didn't come to his armpit, and sticking her chin in the air just to tantalize him, so he couldn't keep his eyes on her own.

"What if I do?" she had said. "I ain't married to you, am I?"

"Polly, you can't act that way with me."

"Who are you to talk?" she had demanded hotly. "It would do you good with all the girls you've kiltered over."

"You better look out, Polly. Who do you expect would want to marry a girl that acted the way you do? Going with anybody," he had said virtuously.

She had laughed in his face, so gaily he had had to stop her mouth to keep her from calling attention to where they were. That was another thing he had against the destructives. If it hadn't been for them, Polly's family would still be in Andrustown and he could have acted like a free man instead of being careful as a preacher on a Sunday tour.

She had said to him, "I ain't wanted any man to marry me, yet, you or nobody else. And I'm not going to till the time comes either."

"You better watch your step, then," he had told her, and she had reached up and smacked his ear. It was like being hit by a fly, because she had to jump off the ground to reach the place.

And then she caught him around the neck and kissed him and told him how beautiful he was. She was the only girl who had ever called him beautiful. Others had said he was big, or handsome; but he didn't mind being called beautiful by Polly, and treated as if he were something that belonged to her and could be put on the shelf like a china pot when she wanted to, because she never actually put him there when he was round.

Remembering her kissing him like that, with her bare feet a good twelve inches off the ground, Adam grinned. He closed his eyes against the green, filtered sunlight and let his head fall back. He supposed it was natural for a good-looking young girl like her to look around a little, especially when he was out of reach for two and three weeks on a scout. All that troubled him was the idea of her running around with some fool farmer, like those three up in the lodge. Or like the young one—the other two were older and hitched tight to families of their own. Adam wondered how it would feel to be married and have a daughter, say like Polly Bowers. He couldn't figure it out. He was like Polly that way; he didn't intend to get married till he had to. It would be pretty near funny if it was to each other that they had to get hitched. His face sobered a little—it wouldn't be too bad, he thought.

That was the way a man thought when he was out on one of these watching scouts, lying around all day in the still woods, till a blue jay or a squirrel would light right over his head and wonder at him. It was partly the heat and the drowsy air that made you do it. It was a kind of habit of the brain, going round and round, not getting anywhere particular. Farming people, who had to work the guts out of themselves to grow crops, were scornful about it, and called you a loafer, the way those three fools up in the lodge would call him. But take them out here and they had to have something like dice to keep themselves from going crazy. He couldn't really blame them, Adam supposed. They didn't know what to do with themselves.

Then he had the thought, suppose Polly had been getting a fancy for somebody else. Suppose that was what made her act up the way she had the last time he was back. She had made it up at the last minute all right, but he had had the feeling that she was still looking round. Adam grunted and suddenly looked up at the branches over him.

He lay there very still. It was not that he had seen anything. There was nothing to see but the pendent, still green leaves on motionless twigs, against the hot blue of the sky. There was nothing on the trail either. He could look down over his moccasined toes and see the brown slot of it winding through the bottom grass of the glade. There was nothing to hear, except the continuing voice of the locusts—hot-weather birds, as Adam called them.

But that was what suddenly made him still. There was nothing. On a dry day like this the woods should have small sounds—the rustle of mice or small birds in the leaves, the tap of a woodpecker near by, a squirrel husking a green cone in a tree. The kind of sounds you hardly noticed till you noticed that they had stopped. The three fool farmers up in the lodge had not noticed anything. The low and distant mutter of their voices came with singular distinctness, arguing over a throw. But Adam did not listen to them:

Without a sound, he drew his feet back against the back of his hams and moved his hand out to grasp his gun. He did not lift it, but let it lie in its form along the leaves.

He could hear the Indians coming, but his first sight of them gave him a shock. Four had passed above him on the slope and were between him and the men in the lodge. They must have come over the back of the rise behind him, or he would surely have heard them before. Then he saw more of them on the trail. About forty of them, he judged, coming at a dog trot. That many meant that there were certainly more flankers out than the first four he had seen. It meant that the men in the lodge would be surrounded in another minute.

Still lying on his back, Adam thought swiftly. He could let the first push of Indians get by and try to cut behind them. He didn't care personally what happened to the three fools in the lodge. But he realized that if they could get off, the better chance there would be of warning the flats. He hadn't a doubt in his mind that at last Brant was on the way. And he was enraged with himself for allowing them to come up on him as if he were a fifteen-year-old lad on his first scout.

He figured that there was only one chance of those three fools getting away now, and he acted instantly. He rolled forward onto the balls of his feet, dropped one knee and took the leading Indian on the trail a clean shot under the wishbone. The man dropped like a sack of meal and the feet of those behind balled up over his body. Then, while they milled, Adam burst down the slope and over the trail less than a hundred feet ahead of them. He didn't stop to look at them, but took the opposite bank at full speed. He made it so fast that the first shots the Indians fired at him, he was dodging through the scrub.

The musket fire crackled like dry sticks and the stink of black powder reached out in the still air, so that he smelled it as he ran. But he paid no attention to the shooting and yelling on the trail. He dodged into some heavier timber and wheeled down the bank again. He had judged his course exactly. He hit the trail three hundred yards from his first crossing and around a bend from the main body of Indians.

He ran lightly, listening to the surge of voices he had left behind. Up at the lodge, a sudden burst of three shots sounded sharp and dry. The crazy fools hadn't even had the sense to cut and run when he gave them the diversion. He knew, as sure as he knew which end of himself he ate with, that the three men were being killed. He was sure it was the young lad's voice that kept yelping. The Indians hadn't even bothered to shoot back at them.

It left himself alone to carry the warning into German Flats.

That didn't bother him just then. He had been hoping all day for an excuse to get back home. He had it now all right.

Up in the Mohawk Valley no one had heard of Paul Revere. If Adam had, he would probably have used some of the words he generally used when he met a Yankee in a tavern. All he thought about was the fact that German Flats lay fifteen miles to the north and that he would, in half a minute, have probably the pick of Brant's Indians on his tail. It seemed queer that he should have been wondering how good an Indian runner really was in a long race.

Adam knew that he could run himself, but he knew also that he would have to run on an open trail. Once the Indians settled on his track, they would know he had to stick to it and that they wouldn't be bothered by tracking him. It didn't occur to Adam to cut into the woods and hide. He figured it as a race. The stakes, however, weren't a gallon of rum.

He eased up slightly, listening behind him. The first surge of yelling had overshot the eastern ridge; now it returned. It would be only a minute before they brought his tracks down to the trail. He began to put on a little pressure to make the next bend; but just before he rounded it, he heard the war whoop slide up to its inhuman pitch and a wild shot cut the air high over his head.

His wind had come back from that first crazy burst up and down the ridge. He lengthened his stride. His yellow hair, fresh from the combing he had given it, whipped up and down on his shoulders like a short flapping blanket. His mouth opened as he reached his full pace and he took the slight grade with the rush of a running buck deer.

The Indians had stopped yelling. At the end of the next straight stretch, Adam flung a look over his shoulder and saw the leading brave running, bent over, coming smooth and quick and soundless. The Indian knew that Adam had seen him, but he didn't lift his gun. He wasn't carrying a gun. He had only his tomahawk, which was a great deal more deadly weapon if he could pull up within forty feet.

Adam thought that the Indian must have been gaining, or else he was the leader of a group, adopting the old Mohawk dodge for running down a man by sprinting to make the fugitive travel at top speed. The others would take a steadier pace, swift enough to overhaul the leader as he tired without burning out themselves, and as soon as they had pulled the leader back, a fresh man would sprint out after the fugitive. By maintaining pressure on him in this way, they claimed they could run down any man in four or five hours of open going. Adam, to escape, would have not only to keep ahead of the press, he would have to run the heart completely out of them.

He sprinted now; not blindly, but picking his next easing point beforehand. He knew the trail, every stone and root of it, from Edmeston to German Flats, as well as he knew Polly Bowers. He figured that his easing point would be the ford through Licking Brook. Half a mile.

At any time it was worth while to see Adam Helmer run. He was the biggest man in the flats, six feet three in his moccasins. With his long yellow hair he seemed yet taller. He weighed over two hundred pounds, without an ounce of fat on him.

He began to draw away from the Indian as soon as he started to sprint. Glancing back again, he saw that the Indian had straightened up a little. He got the feeling that the Indian's face was surprised. Probably the Indian fancied himself as quite a runner. Maybe he was champion of some lousy set of lodges somewhere. Adam could have laughed at the notion if he had not needed his wind, but the laughter went on in his inside, sending the blood into his hands. His head felt fine and clear. He figured he had gained thirty yards on the Indian when he hit the brook.

He jumped the ford. It was too early to risk wetting his feet and going sore. But as he cleared the water, he threw his gun from him. It splashed into the pool below the ford and sank. Some day he would come back and get it; he would rather have it rust than have an Indian find it.

Now that his hands were free, Adam began unlacing his hunting shirt. He had to slow up to get it over his head, but he got it off without stopping and threw it behind a butternut tree with his powder flask and shot pouch. Then he tightened his belt and stuck his hatchet through it behind him where the handle would not keep smacking against his legs.

He was now naked from the waist up, and the wind of his running felt good on his chest, cooling the sweat as it trickled down through the short golden mane. He was a wonderful man to see; his skin white as a woman's, except for his hands and face, which were deeply burned. His long legs gave him a tremendous stride and he ran with his back straight, not crouched over like an Indian. He was feeling fine and going well. He felt so fine he thought he might almost let the leading Indian pull up and maybe have a throw at him with his tomahawk. He eased a little, enough to let the Indian pull up into sight.

When the buck appeared behind him, Adam saw that he was a new man. He was taller. His face was painted black and white instead of red and yellow, as the first man's had been. He did not come quite so fast, but Adam's trained eye saw that he had better staying powers. And he didn't bother to study Adam. He was putting all his mind on the running, as if all he was there for was to kill Adam's wind. He came with a limber long jounce in his trot, and to Adam his black face was like something dirty, unnatural, and so intent it seemed emotionless. Adam had seen a weasel once, pursuing a squirrel through the woods. It was like that weasel that the Indian came after him, a big, ugly-looking weasel. And chasing a big squirrel.

But Adam did not grin at his own cockeyed notion. Like the squirrel, then and there he put all idea of a quick fight clean out of his mind. The Indians meant to get him, and he wouldn't get away from them except by running. He settled down.

For the next three miles the chase continued with only a slight variation of pace, for instead of running blind and full speed, as the Indians figured on his doing, Adam adapted himself to the man behind. He had begun to feel the pressure, the feeling that there was no chance of slackening, but he was running with greater canniness. He kept his eyes glued to the trail, for he did not dare risk a blind step. His ankles wouldn't hold up as well if he lit on a rolling stone or a slippery root. He had a feeling that the climax of the race was still to come, and though he ran strongly, strong enough to lick most men in a hundred yards straightaway, he knew that these Indians were good.

One after another they came up behind him. The main pack of them he had not seen since the wild rush across the trail at the beginning. But he felt that he knew each man when he was done with him. Each had his trick of running. One never changed stride, another had a hop when he cleared a stone, one weaved a little.

They were all silent. That seemed strange. Adam was used to Indians yelling when he raced them. Indians were always noisy. But this race was run in silence, except for the thud of his feet on the trail and the thud of his heart in his chest.

His chest was wet now. It showed scars where he had burst through overhanging branches. The white shiny skin was crossed with red welts and brier scratches.

He felt the blood in his head, pounding like his feet. The sweat kept getting into his eyes, and the only break in his running was when he had to lift a hand to wipe them. It wasn't like running on a plainly marked road. He had to see.

His breathing, however, was still excellent. He had no fear of giving out; he could run till sundown, he thought. Then it came upon him that it would be a fact, if he managed to clear the Indians, that he would hit the flats just about sundown. Even while he ran he reasoned it out that Brant must have figured on reaching the valley after dark and striking in the morning.

Adam wondered what Brant would do when he found out that the word had gone ahead of him. He doubted whether Brant would get up his main army, anyway, much before he had planned to. But it didn't matter much. The only thing in the world that Adam could do was to reach the flats. If he got there, some people, anyway, would have a chance of getting to the forts.

His eyes kept checking in his landmarks and he realized that the site of Andrustown was only a mile, or a little more, ahead. He must have outdistanced most of even the first pursuit. He expected there would not be more than half a dozen who could have held on as long as this. If that were so, they would be sending up another man pretty soon. Adam wondered how fresh he would be.

Adam figured that if he could get through Andrustown clearing, it might be better for him now to try and lose them on the other side, for he would have gained as much time as anyone could have on the main body. As he chanced a backward glance, he saw that, as he had expected, the Indians were going to try to finish him. The new man had appeared and it was evident that he must be the best they had. He was not tall. He was thickset and had short legs. He was entirely naked except for the ankle moccasins and breechclout, and he was oiled and painted. He looked like a Mohawk. He wore two feathers. It seemed impossible that so short a man could have held the pace for seven miles, for he had a belly that showed in front of him. But his belly did not bounce at all. After a minute Adam got the idea that it must be an enlarged place where the Indian kept his wind.

The Indian's legs moved with incredible rapidity. He had already taken his tomahawk from his clout string, as if he were confident of being able to haul up on the white man. Already he had gained. But his appearance of confidence gave Adam the incentive he needed. It enraged him and he took his rage out in his running.

He was gulping air through his mouth. His beard stuck to the curve of his jaw with sweat. His eyes were bloodshot and his face flamed. The stride of his long legs had shortened considerably, but the pace held even and gradually quickened. He began to draw away.

When the Indian entered Andrustown clearing, Adam was already down past the black ruins of the houses and going away with every step. It was the greatest running the Indian had ever looked at. He knew he was licked, and he started slowing up. By the time Adam had hit the woods on the other side, the Indian had stopped and sat down by the road.

When Adam looked back from the woods, the Indian wasn't even looking after him. He was all alone in the clearing and he

was futilely banging the ground between his legs with his tomahawk. Adam knew he had made it.

He did not stop, nor even let down quickly on his pace. He
did not want to stop. He wanted to hold up all the way to German Flats. But all he had to race against now was time. He would
have laughed if he had had the breath for it. Time, he thought.
Time, hell!

The sunset was fading when Adam breasted the south shoulder
of Shoemaker Hill. He came round the curve of the road, going
slower. He wasn't quite sure any more of what he was racing and
he couldn't have seen well enough now to follow the slot of an
Indian trail. But a slight breath of wind from the north cleared
his eyes for the race down the hill, and he saw the valley.

The sky was like a great silken sheet over all the world, misty
in the north, but edged with sunset to the west. Under it, on a
level with his bloodshot eyes, the wilderness rolled northward—
mile upon mile, ridge upon ridge, until the mountains lifted
against the sky itself. The color of it in the fading light was like
water, gray-green, with darker shades where the evergreens marked
the long pine ridges or the balsam swamps. As the light waned,
and Adam's feet felt the ground dropping out from under them,
the whole panorama conveyed a sense of motion, the ridges rolling higher and higher as the hollows of the balsam swamps deepened with darkness.

But the valley itself was like a crystal under his feet through
which he might look down on a picture painted in miniature.
The bright line of the river was still tinged with the sunset; the
two forts—from this elevation they looked close together—were
geometrical shapes in the irregular fields; the fences were small
stitches painstakingly made to patch the surface of the earth. But
the houses and barns alone at the edges of the clearings were like
infinitesimal blocks in the crooked fingers of the wilderness, and
moving in toward them, Adam saw the antlike shapes of horses

pulling carts to barns, and children bringing the cattle in, and women standing on the doorsteps, having got supper.

Then it was all out of sight and he was once more pounding down the steep slope of the road. But he realized now what he had been running for. It was not to get away from the Indians, not even to prove to them that there was a white man who could lick them on a long run, nor to tell Bellinger; it was to give these poor fool farmers and their women and children a chance to get to the forts. It was ironical.

The ground leveled again as he came down on the flats, and the road stretched straight ahead to Fort Herkimer. The church steeple rose up above the stockade to quite a height when you saw it from the level ground. The light was on it now. The setting sun was picking out shadows between the sticks of the stockade and the sticks that made the wall of the blockhouse. The watchman in the blockhouse was leaning far out, staring toward Adam, but Adam could not see him. He was running half blind.

A dog scrambled under a fence and began barking at his heels. A man yelled at Adam from the far side of the fence. Adam worked his dry mouth and his voice answered hoarsely: "Brant's coming!" It sounded like a whisper. But behind him the man was shouting to his wife. He heard the cart rattle as it lurched round from the barn, and the children began to yell shrilly.

He gave the word at the next farm and the next. But after that he did not have to warn them. The watchman had understood. The three-pounder in the church belfry let off a cloud of smoke and a deep, sullen roar, a single shot, the warning for all people to get into the stockades. Before Adam reached the gates, he heard the second thud as the Fort Dayton alarm gun went off across the river, and then a third from Eldridge Blockhouse three miles to the east.

The valley was warned!

He wheeled in through the gates and gave his report to Colonel Bellinger.

There was nothing more to do.

All over the valley, people were thronging toward the forts by road and river. Those who had already reached Fort Herkimer stood in front of the church and stared down at Adam's naked chest. It was a mass of blood from the whipping it had had from branches. His eyes were red and half closed. But he was breathing easily again, grinning a little at Polly Bowers, who stood beside him as if he were her private property.

He had never, Adam thought, felt finer in his life.

From *Drums Along the Mohawk*, by Walter D. Edmonds, an Atlantic Monthly Press publication. Reprinted by permission of Little, Brown & Company.

1. What is the locale of the story?
2. What purpose is served in the story by the general account which precedes the appearance of Helmer?
3. List the observations made by Helmer which indicate his familiarity with Indians and other aspects of the frontier.
4. Do you think that Helmer would be able to get his rifle and other discarded possessions later?
5. How do the Indians compare or contrast with the Indians you have read of elsewhere?

# IV. HUMOR

# IV. HUMOR

A SURE way to start an argument is to define humor. Prefix "American" to the noun, and the argument becomes a brawl. And like most brawls, it proves nothing, for the roots of humor are not national but human, and even its flowers in different lands frequently are almost indistinguishable. Little is gained, therefore, by carrying the definition beyond the simple statement that humorous effect depends on incongruity, on unexpected associations which produce a pleasurable shock in the reader's mind.

Basically, all humor is probably dramatic. In the simple form of a humorous character in a play or novel, the dramatic quality is obvious. The author develops a character whose personality, either by intrinsic oddity or by its contrast with the rest of the dramatis personae, produces the pleasurable shock just mentioned. To maintain this effect demands careful selection of detail. All aspects of personality which do not contribute to this single effect must be kept out of the picture. In stories of back-stage life the clown may have a broken heart, but he cannot exhibit it behind the footlights and still do his job. The reader, furthermore, must co-operate; if he does not share the author's view of what is comic, the effect is lost. In the *Odyssey*, the immortal gods howl with laughter at the limping of crippled Hephaestus; in Elizabethan drama, idiots are comic characters; the modern reader flinches from both. Up to the end of the eighteenth century, Shylock was acted as a comic figure; today he is interpreted as tragic. Whether we ourselves find a drunken man amusing or disgusting depends on our point of view and our knowledge of the individual.

In other words, humorous treatment of character or action requires selective vision, the maintenance of a subtle but consistent

228

distortion of the total effect. When the distortion is primarily of action, we have farce; when it is of character we have comedy. Pure farce seldom evokes the thoughtful laughter which George Meredith defined as the purpose of comedy; we need to see our own absurdities, and our friends', dramatized before we achieve the higher levels of humor.

But the dramatic element in humor is not confined to plays and novels. The familiar essayist or the humorous commentator begins by creating for himself a dramatic personality which is a projection or intensification of one facet of his own temperament. The literary self of Mark Twain, or Robert Benchley, or James Thurber, or Stephen Leacock, is not the whole man. On meeting a humorist we may be disappointed to find his total personality serious, or even dull. When a man writes in his own person, the quality of his humor depends on the richness and variety of the personality he has to draw on; when he writes of other people, it depends on his insight into character.

The attempt to distinguish between humor of exaggeration and humor of understatement, and to label the former as character-istically American, is a favorite blind alley of discussion. Exaggera-tion and understatement are both distortion, and show a bewilder-ing tendency to merge into each other. In the Dorothy Parker story which follows, for instance, the incongruity between the ac-tions described and the terms describing them might be called understatement, but the total effect is to exaggerate their impres-sion. Mark Twain's yarn is a typical tall story, yet it owes at least as much to the lovable simplicity of Jim Baker's character as it does to its exaggerations. And Don Marquis's story is a parody of a real place, the Players Club in New York, of which Marquis was a member and in which Sargent's portrait of Edwin Booth, the founder, is held in much the same reverence as Henry Arlington's in the story.

The three stories together are almost a liberal education in the fine art of humor. Jim Baker's yarn, like Jim Bridger's tale of the peetrified forest and the Virginian's frog story in Owen Wister's classic, illustrates the skillfully built up climax. Starting at rational level with an apparently serious discussion of animal speech, it leads the reader by subtly contrived turns and detours down the garden of absurdity. Dorothy Parker's story might so easily be mere slap-stick farce, yet is so much more because the characters are three-dimensional figures and not just outlines in black and white. Don Marquis, within his limited frame, achieves a double layer of character portrayal: the head waiter revealed through his own words, and Henry Arlington and James Wilson as he interprets them. All the easy pitfalls of exaggeration are avoided. Nothing would have been simpler, for instance, than to carry John's misuse of words to the point of burlesque. But John has absorbed too much of the club atmosphere to stumble often; hence his slips are all the funnier when they come. All three stories owe their effectiveness far more to accurately observed character than to mere verbal cleverness or absurdity of situation. All three should make the reader ask himself, "I wonder if *I* look as funny as that to my friends?" Probably he should hope that he does.

*Mark Twain*

# JIM BAKER'S BLUE-JAY YARN

NIMALS talk to each other, of course. There can be no question about that; but I suppose there are very few people who can understand them. I never knew but one man who could. I knew he could, however, because he told me so himself. He was a middle-aged, simple-hearted miner who had lived in a lonely corner of California, among the woods and mountains, a good many years, and had studied the ways of his only neighbors, the beasts and the birds, until he believed he could accurately translate any remark which they made. This was Jim Baker. According to Jim Baker, some animals have only a limited education, and use only very simple words, and scarcely ever a comparison or a flowery figure; whereas, certain other animals have a large vocabulary, a fine command of language and a ready and fluent delivery; consequently these latter talk a great deal; they like it, they are conscious of their talent, and they enjoy "showing off." Baker said, that after long and careful observation, he had come to the conclusion that the blue-jays were the best talkers he had found among birds and beasts. Said he:—

"There's more to a blue-jay than any other creature. He has got more moods, and more different kinds of feelings than other creatures; and mind you, whatever a blue-jay feels, he can put into language. And no mere commonplace language, either, but rattling, out-and-out book-talk—and bristling with metaphor, too—just bristling! And as for command of language—why you never see a blue-jay get stuck for a word. No man ever did. They just boil out of him! And another thing: I've noticed a good deal, and there's no bird, or cow, or anything that uses as good grammar as a blue-jay. You may say a cat uses good grammar. Well, a cat does—but you let a cat get excited, once; you let a cat get to pulling fur with another cat on a shed, nights, and you'll hear grammar that will give you the lockjaw. Ignorant people think it's the *noise* which fighting cats make that is so aggravating, but it ain't so; it's the sickening grammar they use. Now I've never heard a jay use bad grammar but very seldom; and when they do, they are as ashamed as a human; they shut right down and leave.

"You may call a jay a bird. Well, so he is, in a measure—because he's got feathers on him, and don't belong to no church, perhaps; but otherwise he is just as much a human as you be. And I'll tell you for why. A jay's gifts, and instincts, and feelings, and interests, cover the whole ground. A jay hasn't got any more principle than a Congressman. A jay will lie, a jay will steal, a jay will deceive, a jay will betray; and four times out of five, a jay will go back on his solemnest promise. The sacredness of an obligation is a thing which you can't cram into no blue-jay's head. Now on top of all this, there's another thing: a jay can out-swear any gentleman in the mines. You think a cat can swear. Well, a cat can; but you give a blue-jay a subject that calls for his reserve-powers, and where is your cat? Don't talk to me—I know too much about this thing. And there's yet another thing: in the one little particular of scolding—just good, clean, out-and-out scolding—a blue-jay can lay over anything, human or divine. Yes, sir, a jay is everything that a man is. A jay can cry, a jay can laugh, a jay can feel shame, a jay can reason and plan and discuss, a jay likes gossip and scandal, a jay has got a sense of humor, a jay knows when he is an ass just as well as you do—maybe better. If a jay ain't human, he better take in

his sign, that's all. Now I'm going to tell you a perfectly true fact
about some blue-jays.

"When I first begun to understand jay language correctly, there
was a little incident happened here. Seven years ago, the last man
in this region but me, moved away. There stands his house—been
empty ever since; a log house, with a plank roof—just one big
room, and no more; no ceiling—nothing between the rafters and
the floor. Well, one Sunday morning I was sitting out here in
front of my cabin, with my cat, taking the sun, and looking at
the blue hills, and listening to the leaves rustling so lonely in the
trees, and thinking of the home away yonder in the States, that I
hadn't heard from in thirteen years, when a blue-jay lit on that
house, with an acorn in his mouth, and says, 'Hello, I reckon I've
struck something.' When he spoke, the acorn dropped out of his
mouth and rolled down the roof, of course, but he didn't care;
his mind was all on the thing he had struck. It was a knot-hole in
the roof. He cocked his head to one side, shut one eye and put
the other one to the hole, like a 'possum looking down a jug; then
he glanced up with his bright eyes, gave a wink or two with his
wings—which signifies gratification, you understand,—and says, 'It
looks like a hole, it's located like a hole,—blamed if I don't believe
it *is* a hole!'

"Then he cocked his head down and took another look; he
glances up perfectly joyful, this time; winks his wings and his tail
both, and says, 'O, no, this ain't no fat thing, I reckon! If I ain't
in luck!—why, it's a perfectly elegant hole!' So he flew down and
got that acorn, and fetched it up and dropped it in, and was just
tilting his head back, with the heavenliest smile on his face, when
all of a sudden he was paralyzed into a listening attitude and that
smile faded gradually out of his countenance like a breath off'n a
razor, and the queerest look of surprise took its place. Then he
says, 'Why, I didn't hear it fall!' He cocked his eye at the hole
again, and took a long look; raised up and shook his head; stepped
around to the other side of the hole and took another look from

that side; shook his head again. He studied a while, then he just went into the details—walked round and round the hole and spied into it from every point of the compass. No use. Now he took a thinking attitude on the comb of the roof and scratched the back of his head with his right foot a minute, and finally says, 'Well, it's too many for me, that's certain; must be a mighty long hole; however, I ain't got no time to fool around here, I got to 'tend to business; I reckon it's all right—chance it, anyway.'

"So he flew off and fetched another acorn and dropped it in, and tried to flirt his eye to the hole quick enough to see what become of it, but he was too late. He held his eye there as much as a minute; then he raised up and sighed, and says, 'Consound it, I don't seem to understand this thing, no way; however, I'll tackle her again.' He fetched another acorn, and done his level best to see what become of it, but he couldn't. He says, 'Well, I never struck no such a hole as this, before; I'm of the opinion it's a totally new kind of a hole.' Then he begun to get mad. He held in for a spell, walking up and down the comb of the roof and shaking his head and muttering to himself; but his feelings got the upper hand of him, presently, and he broke loose and cussed himself black in the face. I never see a bird take on so about a little thing. When he got through he walks to the hole and looks in again for half a minute; then he says, 'Well, you're a long hole, and a deep hole, and a mighty singular hole altogether—but I've started in to fill you, and I'm d—d if I *don't* fill you, if it takes a hundred years!'

"And with that, away he went. You never see a bird work so since you was born. He laid into his work like a nigger, and the way he hove acorns into that hole for about two hours and a half was one of the most exciting and astonishing spectacles I ever struck. He never stopped to take a look any more—he just hove 'em in and went for more. Well, at last he could hardly flop his wings, he was so tuckered out. He comes a-drooping down, once more, sweating like an ice-pitcher, drops his acorn in and says,

'Now I guess I've got the bulge on you by this time!' So he bent down for a look. If you'll believe me, when his head come up again he was just pale with rage. He says, 'I've shoveled acorns enough in there to keep the family thirty years, and if I can see a sign of one of 'em I wish I may land in a museum with a belly full of sawdust in two minutes!'

"He just had strength enough to crawl up on the comb and lean his back agin the chimbly, and then he collected his impressions and begun to free his mind. I see in a second that what I had mistook for profanity in the mines was only just the rudiments, as you may say.

"Another jay was going by, and heard him doing his devotions, and stops to inquire what was up. The sufferer told him the whole circumstance, and says, 'Now yonder's the hole, and if you don't believe me, go and look for yourself.' So this fellow went and looked, and comes back and says, 'How many did you say you put in there?' 'Not any less than two tons,' says the sufferer. The other jay went and looked again. He couldn't seem to make it out, so he raised a yell, and three more jays come. They all examined the hole, they all made the sufferer tell it over again, then they all discussed it, and got off as many leather-headed opinions about it as an average crowd of humans could have done.

"They called in more jays; then more and more, till pretty soon this whole region 'peared to have a blue flush about it. There must have been five thousand of them; and such another jawing and disputing and ripping and cussing, you never heard. Every jay in the whole lot put his eye to the hole and delivered a more chuckle-headed opinion about the mystery than the jay that went there before him. They examined the house all over, too. The door was standing half open, and at last one old jay happened to go and light on it and look in. Of course that knocked the mystery galley-west in a second. There lay the acorns, scattered all over the floor. He flopped his wings and raised a whoop. 'Come here!' he says, 'Come here, everybody; hang'd if this fool hasn't been trying to fill up a house with acorns!' They all came a-swooping down like a blue cloud, and as each fellow lit on the door and took a glance, the whole absurdity of the contract that that first jay had tackled hit him home and he fell over backwards suffocating with laughter, and the next jay took his place and done the same.

"Well, sir, they roosted around here on the house-top and the trees for an hour, and guffawed over that thing like human beings. It ain't any use to tell me a blue-jay hasn't got a sense of humor, because I know better. And memory, too. They brought jays here from all over the United States to look down that hole, every summer for three years. Other birds too. And they could all see the point except an owl that come from Nova Scotia to visit the Yo Semite, and he took this thing in on his way back. He said he couldn't see anything funny in it. But then he was a good deal disappointed about Yo Semite, too."

From A *Tramp Abroad,* copyright 1879 by Samuel L. Clemens, and reprinted by permission of Harper & Bros., New York, the authorized publishers.

1. *What attributes give this story its sustained manner?*
2. *How does an acceptance of the first sentence affect the reader's credulity? Is the very baldness of the statement a phase of Mark Twain's technique?*
3. *What part does Jim Baker play in developing the convincing air of the story?*
4. *Is this a particularly American story?*
5. *When does possibility leave off in the story and impossibility begin?*

*Don Marquis*

# A KEEPER OF TRADITION

"YOU could probably be sent to prison for life for what you've just done, in your careless fashion, and if it wasn't so hard to get waiters, I'd see as that happened to you. Not that you're really a waiter, or ever will be a waiter. When I'm dead, and one other man in this club, and five or six more in New York City, there won't be a waiter, as should be called a waiter, left in this here hemisphere. You bloody well ought to have your neck broke for what you just done—desecrating the shrine, so to speak, of the two greatest artists of any kind this country ever saw. Maybe I won't tell on you, and maybe I will tell on you; and maybe nobody will ever need to tell on you—maybe Fate will just take charge of you for what you've done, and curl you up into a horrible and poisonous ending, as will be a warning to a lot of brash young bolsheviks that call themselves waiters these days."

It was a sunny spring morning, and I was sitting on the back veranda of The Painters Club in New York City, eating a very late breakfast, when I heard this tirade uttered in a low, intense voice. Every one else had had his breakfast; it was too early for lunch; I was alone in the veranda. I moved my chair without noise, and peeped into the dining-room through the open window. The Oldest Waiter and the Youngest Waiter were polishing silverware at a serving-table just within the window. Horror was stamped upon the stern aquiline visage of the Oldest Waiter, as he looked alternately at a silver platter in his hands, and at the Youngest Waiter. And the face of the Youngest Waiter—a pimply, anemic youth, whom I recognized as having been recently promoted from the position of hat-check boy—was a mask of terror.

"What I done that's so awful, John?" quavered the Youngest Waiter.

"Mr. Watson, please," said John. "What you have done, Herbert, is almost inexpressible; and if it was to be found out on you, you'd never leave this club alive. You'd leave here in sections, in the trash-cans, and no questions asked, and no satisfaction given to any family of yours that might inquire. And the city gover'ment and the Supreme Court of the United States would back the club up in not answering questions, for this club ain't any ordinary club, Herbert. You got to be in this club eight or ten years, either as a servant or a member, before you realize the influence this club has got, through its employees and members, on the fate of this country."

"But what have I done, Mr. Watson, please?" trembled Herbert, a gentle dew breaking out on his pallid features.

"I can't tell you what you've done so you would understand how terrible it is," said Old Watson, "without I tell you the true story of how this club got started. And you ain't got the intelligence ever to understand what this club stands for. But what you've done is a good deal worse than if you was to go down to Mt. Vernon on the Fourth of July and insult the tomb of George Washington. But I'll try and give you an idea so that, if what you done to-day don't get found out on you, and you don't suddenly disappear off the face of the earth, you will know how to conduct yourself around here in the future, and who to look to for guidance and instructions."

I settled myself out of sight behind the angle of the window, to listen; and the Oldest Waiter continued:

The man who founded this club was the greatest oil-painter that ever lived, bar none, and it has been recognized and proved time and again. Put one of his paintings alongside one of Michael Angelo's or Rembrandt's, whether it is a human painting, or an ocean painting, or a landscape with sheep in it, and all rivals pale and fade into insignificance. And as far as Whistler's Mother is concerned, when put beside his painting of his own Mother, she becomes just merely an old lady, and nothing more.

His painting of himself, in the library up-stairs, is the greatest painting of any kind ever painted in the world. The next time you are in that room just notice how the eyes follow you about, wherever you stand, and you will see what I mean. That painting in the library being the greatest painting of the greatest painter that ever lived, done by himself in the studio at the top of this very building, is priceless. This club has been offered untold sums of money for it, up toward a million dollars; but we wouldn't sell it for all the money in the world, and people come from all over the world just to get one look at it, and worship it. And the last Ladies' Day here, there was a young woman who was a painter herself come into the club, and got one look at it, and expired; for it had been a lifelong ambition of hers just to look at it, and the excitement was too much for her. We carried her out through the kitchen, and got her into a cab, and her death was kept from the papers, for nothing as transpires in this club ever gets into any newspaper.

Young Herbert, what you have done today is worse, far worse, than if you was to take that world-famous painting out of its frame and burn it, in the face of all the membership of the club. And if it was to get out on you, even I could not save you from your fate, as much influence as I have got around these precincts.

This here great painter, I hope I don't need to tell you, was Mr. Henry Arlington, and there was five whole years of his life he would never have any hand but mine touch his Welsh rabbits.

"Cooks may come and cooks may go," he used often to say,

"but John here is the greatest artist the world has ever known in making a Welsh rabbit."

And I never said to him that one great artist always recognizes another. For I know what is due, from me and to me, too well to ever get familiar with a member; or encourage one to get familiar with me, but nevertheless that is the truth, as you will know, Young Herbert, if you should be allowed to remain in this club, and hearken to the old employees.

Well, Mr. Arlington, he started painting young, and he kept at it hard, and when he was forty years old he was getting incredulous amounts of money every time he put his brush to the canvas. And all the world was worshipping at his feet, and kings and queens, and princes of Wales and other places, when they would come to this country incognito, would crave permission to have their pictures painted. And if his engagements was such as he couldn't receive them personal, he would say they could send him a photograph, and he would dash off something from that for a memento for them.

And when he was about forty, and had no more worlds to conquer, he says to himself he will found the most exclusive club in the world, where painters can meet up with other artists, such as writers and sculptors and architects and actors and playwrights, and a sprinkling of very wealthy gentlemen who would be patrons of the arts and interested in purchasing art works. And now and then he would let in a President of the United States, or a senator even, if he was truly a gentleman and not merely a politician, and once I think there was a mayor of New York got in as a member. But he never come here but once or twice, for he saw at a glance he was outclassed, and didn't feel comfortable. Well, Young Herbert, this is perhaps the most exclusive club that the world has ever seen that you have desecrated down to its foundation-stones to-day; and I don't know how you got in here, even as a hat-check boy; but times ain't what they was thirty years ago, among either servants or members. All the same, if I ever was to hear you or any other young waiter takin' advantage of the laxness of the times, and repeatin' any of the remarks you may hear from new members down in the billiard-room on certain wet evenings, out you would go. For the difference between a servant and a member is that the latter may forget himself at rare intervals and tell a yarn that wouldn't wash in a drawing-room, but a servant has got to be an example always.

Mr. Arlington, after he founded the club, lived in the top story, and had his studio there, and it was often my privilege to wait upon him. But the one who was his favorite servant was James Wilson; and outside of Mr. Arlington himself, the greatest man in the world, and the most gentlemanly gentleman, was James Wilson, and James Wilson, Young Herbert, was the best servant this club or any other club has ever seen, for a good servant in a club like this has to start with being a gentleman, and if he ain't it will bloody well show up on him sooner or later and he will be consigned to outer darkness.

James Wilson had the most remarkable life of any man that was ever known; even, in some ways, as remarkable as Mr. Arlington's himself. He come into the club when it was founded, and he wasn't no more than eighteen years old, which I take to be about your age now, Young Herbert, to judge from your pimples and your not having any sense or any background. And whether you'll ever survive to see nineteen or not, depends on whether I'll take pity on you for what you done to-day, and, in a measure, on how you conduct yourself to me personal.

James Wilson, at eighteen, was as quiet and respectable and gentlemanly as if he'd been born a servant; and he knew his place too well ever to let it be seen by one of the members that he was, himself, full of the makings of a great artist. But when he got to waiting on Mr. Arlington almost exclusive, it begun to come out, little by little, amongst an inner circle of us servants and members, that James Wilson had been imbibing art from his surroundings here. Four or five of us knew it, and we said nothing. It was getting into James Wilson through the pores of his skin, as you might say; and the only question was whether it would take the turn of his being a great painter, or a great actor, or a great writer, or a great sculptor. For something gets into the pores of this club, if you stay here long enough—which you, probably, will not, Young Herbert, unless I get one of my good-natured streaks and don't report you. There probably ain't an old employee in this club that don't know more about the arts, through imbibing the talk through his pores, than almost any other collection of human beings in the world. But with most of them, it makes critics of them. That is the turn it has taken with me. I could not rhyme poetry together, like some of the members, and I could not paint oil-paintings any better than these cubists, and I could not architect, but I am a critic. With Old Gaffney, the superintendent, what it has turned into is making him just like a patron of the arts; and since Mr. Arlington and James Wilson passed away there is no more cultured gentleman in the world than Old Gaffney.

Well, by the time he was twenty-five, James Wilson had become head waiter, and at twenty-seven he was superintendent; and Mr. Arlington and me, and two or three others of the charter members and charter servants, knew secretly that his art had now taken a final turn, and he was secretly a great painter, second in all the world only to Mr. Arlington himself. And more and more he was the personal servant of Mr. Arlington, and more and more he was the gentleman. You couldn't look at Mr. Arlington and James Wilson without realizing how much difference there was between ordinary men and them two.

Only Mr. Arlington, as president of the club, and an artist, had his moments when he was a Bohemian, too. But James Wilson, whilst he was a servant, never permitted himself to be a Bohemian.

One day Old Gaffney, who was Young Gaffney then, says to me: "Mr. Watson, I heard a remarkable conversation this morning."

"What was it, Mr. Gaffney?" I says to him.

"It was between our president and Mr. Wilson," he says. "Mr. Arlington says to him: 'James, you show more promise than any young painter I have ever known. The amount of work you have done on my recent canvases is something that would startle the public, if they knew of it. Why don't you resign as a servant, and join the club as a member?'

" 'Mr. Henry,' says Mr. Wilson, 'I wouldn't consider it quite respectful to you, sir.' "

Gaffney told me that Mr. Arlington pooh-poohed this, and coaxed James Wilson, but James Wilson was firm. He said that if he ever became a painter, publicly, it would have to be under an assumed name; and it would also be under an assumed name that he would join the club. He had too much respect for the club and the gentlemen in it, ever to come in under the name as he had been a servant under.

Well, it was three or four years after this that Mr. Henry Arlington made that fatal trip to the South Sea Islands, and was reputed to be lost forever, and was never heard of but once again here nor anywheres else.

James Wilson lingered on at the club for several years after Mr. Arlington disappeared, and the club was getting older then, and it was James Wilson, as superintendent, who established the traditions of it almost as much as the memory of Henry Arlington, the founder and first president. For it ain't like any other club, Young Herbert. All us older servants and older members has always kept those traditions alive, and sometimes it has been bloody hard work for us, too, what with younger members coming in as has no background to speak of socially, though competent in the arts, and what with you dam bolsheviks as is sent us to train from the employment agencies.

It was about five years after Mr. Arlington disappeared that James Wilson suddenly left, and Old Gaffney became superintendent, and has been ever since. And it came, I always thought, through Gaffney imbibing the ideas of a patron of the arts; whereas I would naturally have been superintendent myself now, instead of head waiter, if I had imbibed those ideas instead of becoming a critic. Well, the Board of Governors is the Board of Governors, and no human being in this world can kick against what they decide on, but there has been times when the rest of us was bloody well disgusted with Old Gaffney as superintendent. But if I ever hear you speak disrespectful of him, or to him, Young Herbert, my lips will unseal themselves about the crime you committed to-day.

It was about a year after James Wilson left that all us people at the art-center of the country, which is right here, Young Herbert, begun to hear about a new painter who called himself Mr. Arlen Henderton; and we went to view his exhibitions, and we all says to each other that he has got to be a member of The Painters Club. For it was nothing short of genius that he showed. I says myself, one evening late, when I was serving a Welsh rabbit to Mr. De Casanova, the great art critic:

"I beg your pardon, Mr. De Casanova, but is it true, as I overheard some gentlemen saying at dinner to-night, that Mr. Arlen Henderton's work has the same wonderful touch as the late Mr. Henry Arlington's work?"

"It is true, John," says Mr. De Casanova.

Well, I hadn't heard any one say so; I had seen it in the work myself; but I wouldn't take the liberty to say so to a member. Nevertheless, I was glad Mr. De Casanova agreed with me.

It was only a year later that Mr. Arlen Henderton joined the club—and, as you would have guessed, Young Herbert, if you wasn't a born idiot, he was no less a person really than James Wilson. In his modest gentlemanly way he had thought it would be a tribute to our first president, the man from whom he had imbibed his painting, to take as near his name as he could on joining our club . . . being also, as he had said previously, determined not to join with his name as a servant. And I will say this for the gentlemanliness of this club, that neither member nor servant ever so far forgot himself as to call him James Wilson until a certain great day came when he himself requested that he be called that once more.

In a way of speaking, Mr. Arlen Henderton took the whole world by storm with his art, and he become more and more popular around the club; and now he permitted himself to be quite a little Bohemian at times, but never any more Bohemian than Mr. Arlington had been. And in five years more he had become the president of the club. And the day he was elected, he made a little talk to the club, and he says:

"Gentlemen, many of you have known for some years that my real name is James Wilson, and that I started in life as a hat-check boy in this club, of which to-day I have become the president; and you have kept the secret well, as was to have been expected of you. You know my motives for concealing my real name. But last night it suddenly occurred to me that my modesty might be misconstrued as snobbishness, and I said to myself: 'If I am elected president to-morrow I will return to the real name under which my fellow members knew me as a servant.' I think, gentlemen, that Mr. Arlington himself would like it."

Well, the members liked it, anyhow; and they cheered, and some was seen to wipe away a tear; and one or two of us old servants well-nigh forgot ourselves—but not quite, Young Herbert, not quite.

And the next fifteen years after that James Wilson was president of this club, and they was the halligan days. Often us old servants and old members think back upon that time, and sigh and say to ourselves: "Yes, those were the halligan days." More and more traditions of culturedness and arts and letters and background and Bohemianism and gentlemanliness was built up around here in those days, Young Herbert, than a dam bolshevik like you could bloody well comprehend in a million years, and that might well apply to some of the new members, too. After all, it's us old servants that eases the new members into conformity with the customs and traditions; there's some of us in every room all the time, a pattern and a model to them of what they should be.

And then, one night, twelve years ago last Christmas Eve it was, there happened one of the most remarkable things even this club has ever seen. And it's a secret to the world yet; there was twenty newspaper editors present, but it never got into any paper; and if you was to breathe one word of it, inside this club or outside, it would get back to me within twenty-four hours, and you would never even be heard of again, Young Herbert. You never have seen a Christmas Eve in this club—and it ain't likely you ever will see one, for you may be in prison, if not in the electric chair, before next Christmas, for the sacrilege and bolshevism you have performed here to-day. Christmas Eve is our big night here; for it was on Christmas Eve that Mr. Arlington turned over the club to the members. There's always a big dinner, with the president and the Board of Governors at the head of the long table there, and there's always a ceremony, which I will not desecrate by describing to a bloody little guttersnipe like you, but which you may live to witness yourself if you manage to make your peace with me.

This night we was short of waiters, and an old fellow we had picked off the streets a couple of weeks before, and used as a scullion, was drafted in at the last minute to help at the big dinner, first having been taken and trimmed up as to his hair and beard, and stuck into a proper shirt and suit. He was a bent old gray-haired fellow, who never said anything to anybody, and quiet and gentle, with misty blue eyes and a mind that seemingly wandered, but Gaffney had to take a chance on him.

Well, the whole club stood by their chairs, ready to sit down, as soon as president James Wilson and the Board of Governors took their seats, and all of a sudden this old scullion steps up to the head of the table, and looks around the dining-room with a queer look on his face.

"Gentlemen," he says, "I am glad to be with you once again."

And then he sits down in the president's chair.

You could have heard a pin drop, but before any one could say or do anything, or even breathe, he turns and says to the president of the club, James Wilson, sort of gentle and smiling and reproachful:

"James! James! This isn't my tankard!"

For every Christmas Eve things always started off by a toast, which every one drunk from his own pewter mug.

The president of the club, something come over him; and he turned without a word to the place on the wall where Mr. Henry Arlington's tankard always hung, like something sacred, and he reached it down, and filled it with ale, and handed it to the old man.

The old man raised it, and then full human understanding came over him like a flood, and it was too much for him—he raised himself up, and he gave a wild look around the room, and then he clutched at himself and fell dead. And James Wilson took the liberty of falling dead across him.

How Mr. Henry Arlington came not to be lost in that shipwreck we never knew; nor how many years he spent on some terrible island, nor how long he wandered crazy around the world before he came back to be a scullion here where he had been president. But when we cremated the body we saw he was tattooed all over.

And his ashes and James Wilson's ashes was put in that urn over the fireplace, and have been there all but worshipped through all the years since. And the next time I say to you to go to the fireplace and get me some ashes to help clean the silverware, go to the fire part of the fireplace, and not to the mantelpiece. For you could be bloody well executed for what you have done to-day. Now, then, fill the urn up again with wood ashes, and set it on the mantelpiece, and maybe I won't say anything. But you better remember, Young Herbert, who it was that saved you from a fate worse than death; and the next you come onto a pint of liquor in the locker-room, where it's got no legal right to be, you bring it to me to dispose of legal; don't you take it to Old Gaffney.

Ten minutes later I said to the Oldest Waiter: "John! It seems to me you have been embroidering a little, to call it that, on the history and traditions of the club."

"You heard me talking to Young Herbert?" inquired John, with a grin and a wink. "Well, you know, sir, you've got to impress these young bolsheviks some way, right from the start!"

> From *When the Turtles Sing and Other Unusual Tales*, by Don Marquis, copyright 1928 by Doubleday, Doran & Company, Inc.

1. *Do you object to the style of the introduction?*
2. *Is the Oldest Waiter an individual or a generalized type?*
3. *Would it have improved the story to have Young Herbert further aggravate the Oldest Waiter by conversational defenses?*
4. *Do you suppose the urn had been refilled before?*
5. *How much of the Oldest Waiter's story was solely to "impress these young bolsheviks"?*

*Dorothy Parker*

# YOU WERE PERFECTLY FINE

THE pale young man eased himself carefully into the low chair, and rolled his head to the side, so that the cool chintz comforted his cheek and temple.

"Oh, dear," he said. "Oh, dear, oh, dear, oh, dear. Oh."

The clear-eyed girl, sitting light and erect on the couch, smiled brightly at him.

"Not feeling so well today?" she said.

"Oh, I'm great," he said. "Corking, I am. Know what time I got up? Four o'clock this afternoon, sharp. I kept trying to make it, and every time I took my head off the pillow, it would roll under the bed. This isn't my head I've got on now. I think this is something that used to belong to Walt Whitman. Oh, dear, oh, dear, oh, dear."

"Do you think maybe a drink would make you feel better?" she said.

"The hair of the mastiff that bit me?" he said. "Oh, no, thank you. Please never speak of anything like that again. I'm through. I'm all, all through. Look at that hand; steady as a humming-bird. Tell me, was I very terrible last night?"

"Oh, goodness," she said, "everybody was feeling pretty high. You were all right."

"Yeah," he said. "I must have been dandy. Is everybody sore at me?"

"Good heavens, no," she said. "Everyone thought you were terribly funny. Of course, Jim Pierson was a little stuffy, there for a minute at dinner. But people sort of held him back in his chair, and got him calmed down. I don't think anybody at the other tables noticed it at all. Hardly anybody."

"He was going to sock me?" he said. "Oh, Lord. What did I do to him?"

"Why, you didn't do a thing," she said. "You were perfectly fine. But you know how silly Jim gets, when he thinks anybody is making too much fuss over Elinor."

"Was I making a pass at Elinor?" he said. "Did I do that?"

"Of course you didn't," she said. "You were only fooling, that's all. She thought you were awfully amusing. She was having a marvelous time. She only got a little tiny bit annoyed just once, when you poured the clam-juice down her back."

"My God," he said. "Clam-juice down that back. And every vertebra a little Cabot. Dear God. What'll I ever do?"

"Oh, she'll be all right," she said. "Just send her some flowers, or something. Don't worry about it. It isn't anything."

"No, I won't worry," he said. "I haven't got a care in the world. I'm sitting pretty. Oh, dear, oh, dear. Did I do any other fascinating tricks at dinner?"

"You were fine," she said. "Don't be so foolish about it. Everybody was crazy about you. The maître d'hôtel was a little worried because you wouldn't stop singing, but he really didn't mind. All he said was, he was afraid they'd close the place again, if there was so much noise. But he didn't care a bit, himself. I think he loved seeing you have such a good time. Oh, you were just singing away, there, for about an hour. It wasn't so terribly loud, at all."

"So I sang," he said. "That must have been a treat. I sang."

"Don't you remember?" she said. "You just sang one song after another. Everybody in the place was listening. They loved it. Only you kept insisting that you wanted to sing some song about some kind of fusiliers or other, and everybody kept shushing you, and you'd keep trying to start it again. You were wonderful. We were all trying to make you stop singing for a minute, and eat something, but you wouldn't hear of it. My, you were funny."

"Didn't I eat any dinner?" he said.

"Oh, not a thing," she said. "Every time the waiter would offer you something, you'd give it right back to him, because you said that he was your long-lost brother, changed in the cradle by a gypsy band, and that anything you had was his. You had him simply roaring at you."

"I bet I did," he said. "I bet I was comical. Society's Pet, I must have been. And what happened then, after my overwhelming success with the waiter?"

"Why, nothing much," she said. "You took a sort of dislike to some old man with white hair, sitting across the room, because you didn't like his necktie and you wanted to tell him about it. But we got you out, before he got really mad."

"Oh, we got out," he said. "Did I walk?"

"Walk! Of course you did," she said. "You were absolutely all right. There was that nasty stretch of ice on the sidewalk, and you did sit down awfully hard, you poor dear. But good heavens, that might have happened to anybody."

"Oh, surely," he said. "Mrs. Hoover or anybody. So I fell down on the sidewalk. That would explain what's the matter with my— Yes. I see. And then what, if you don't mind?"

"Ah, now, Peter!" she said. "You can't sit there and say you don't remember what happened after that! I did think that maybe you were just a little tight at dinner—oh, you were perfectly all right, and all that, but I did know you were feeling pretty gay. But you were so serious, from the time you fell down—I never knew you to be that way. Don't you know, how you told me I had never seen your real self before? Oh, Peter, I just couldn't bear it, if you didn't remember that lovely long ride we took to-

gether in the taxi! Please, you do remember that, don't you? I
think it would simply kill me, if you didn't."

"Oh, yes," he said. "Riding in the taxi. Oh, yes, sure. Pretty
long ride, hmm?"

"Round and round and round the park," she said. "Oh, and the
trees were shining so in the moonlight. And you said you never
knew before that you really had a soul."

"Yes," he said. "I said that. That was me."

"You said such lovely, lovely things," she said. "And I'd never
known, all this time, how you had been feeling about me, and I'd
never dared to let you see how I felt about you. And then last
night—oh, Peter dear, I think that taxi ride was the most important thing that ever happened to us in our lives."

"Yes," he said. "I guess it must have been."

"And we're going to be so happy," she said. "Oh I just want
to tell everybody! But I don't know—I think maybe it would be
sweeter to keep it all to ourselves."

"I think it would be," he said.

"Isn't it lovely?" she said.

"Yes," he said. "Great."

"Lovely!" she said.

"Look here," he said, "do you mind if I have a drink? I mean,
just medicinally, you know. I'm off the stuff for life, so help me.
But I think I feel a collapse coming on."

"Oh, I think it would do you good," she said. "You poor boy,
it's a shame you feel so awful. I'll go make you a highball."

"Honestly," he said, "I don't see how you could ever want to
speak to me again, after I made such a fool of myself, last night.
I think I'd better go join a monastery in Thibet."

"You crazy idiot!" she said. "As if I could ever let you go away
now! Stop talking like that. You were perfectly fine."

She jumped up from the couch, kissed him quickly on the forehead, and ran out of the room.

The pale young man looked after her and shook his head long and slowly, then dropped it in his damp and trembling hands.

"Oh, dear," he said. "Oh, dear, oh, dear, oh, dear."

From *Laments for the Living*, by Dorothy Parker. Copyright 1930. Published by the Viking Press, Inc., New York.

1. Is the girl being satirical when she says, "You were perfectly fine"?
2. Why do you think people laugh at persons who are drunk?
3. Should there have been more description in the story?
4. Analyze the girl's unspoken emotions.
5. What is the funniest joke on the young man? Is it the realization behind his final "Oh, dear"?

# V. DETECTION

# V. DETECTION

A CERTAIN type of highbrow speaks scornfully of the detective story, calling it a merely mechanical form of narrative. So it is; but so is the love story with its eternal triangle. The writer of love stories cannot escape the fact that there are only two sexes, and that the only possible situation is the rivalry of two members of one for the love of one member of the other. Yet within that narrow frame the possibilities of variation are as limitless as the number of people in the world, and so long as hate and greed lead men to crime the writer of detective fiction will find no dearth of problems.

The creation of the modern detective story is rightly credited to Poe, but it is important to remember just what Poe really did. He invented neither the reasoning process nor its application to the solution of ciphers or the exposure of crime. From the days when Stone Age man studied the spoor of his game or his enemies people have always applied their intelligence to the interpretation of evidence. The detection and exposure of evil-doers plays a large part in the world's literature. Joseph and Naboth were framed, and retribution finally overtook those who wronged them. In English literature before Poe the theme ranges from *Othello* and *Much Ado About Nothing* through *Tom Jones* to *Rob Roy* and *Eugene Aram*. Poe's creation was not a new theme but a new emphasis.

Instead of centering the reader's attention upon the dramatic tableau of the exposure, Poe reserved the chief place in the story for an exposition of the reasoning process by which the exposure was achieved. In his three chief stories in this genre, "The Gold Bug," "The Murders in the Rue Morgue," and "The Purloined Letter," the climax in the old dramatic sense occurs when the story is only half or two-thirds over. The closing section turns its back on the emotional and dramatic elements, and concentrates on a detailed report of the intellectual process by which the climax was reached. Poe's description of these stories as tales of the reasoning process—ratiocination—is thus precisely accurate.

A by-product of Poe's development of the detective story was the convention of the confidant-narrator. The nature of the form makes this convention almost inescapable. Everything depends on the interpretation of the evidence. The conscientious writer will not trick the reader by withholding essential facts, but if the detective himself told the story the interpretation of the facts could not be delayed without trickery. Yet running interpretation would destroy all suspense, so we must use the interested but slightly obtuse eye-witness who sees the facts but fails to draw the right inference from them. Today the English-speaking world names these two primary characters, the detective and his confidant, not Dupin and his friend but Sherlock Holmes and Dr. Watson.

The reason is simple. Dupin remains a shadowy person, and his stooge is scarcely even a shadow. In Holmes and Watson, on the other hand, Conan Doyle created two recognizable people who by force of their personalities have usurped in the popular mind the place that belongs by priority to Poe's figures. Dupin was only a vague projection of Poe's own intellect; Sherlock Holmes was modeled on a real man, Professor Bell of Edinburgh University, and was supplied with a strongly individualized array of traits and eccentricities.

This was one of Doyle's two major contributions to the detective story as a literary form. His detective is indeed so strongly individualized that most of the detectives in fiction since his day are obviously based on him even when their physical attributes are wholly different. It is not too much to say, for instance, that Reggie Fortune and Nero Wolf are fat and indolent because Holmes was lean and active. Doyle also succeeded, at his best, in individualizing Holmes's clients—a difficult task within the limits of the short story, since the posing and solution of the problem leaves neither time nor space for leisurely analysis of character. Yet it is only as it combines plot with plausible and recognizable people that the detective story can be taken seriously as a literary form.

Doyle's second contribution to the form was applying special knowledge to the detection of crime. Where Dupin solves his mysteries by pure analytical reasoning, Holmes more often does so by his recognition of the ashes of a particular kind of tobacco or by some other out-of-the-way bit of information. He seeks the neglected or misunderstood clue. Thus he foreshadows the work of the modern scientific detective in both fact and fiction. H. C. Bailey's Reggie Fortune and Austin Freeman's Dr. Thorndike both apply in literature the same sort of accurate special knowledge which was so effectively used by the experts on wood and handwriting in convicting Hauptmann of the murder of the Lindbergh baby.

In the hands of such modern masters as Dorothy Sayers the full-length detective novel shows an increasing tendency to return to the Victorian school of Wilkie Collins, where the setting and solution of the problem is accomplished in a gallery of highly individualized characters. Within the limits of the short story such full development is not possible, though Miss Sayers shows that characters can be clearly sketched, if not painted. The modern detective story, indeed, gives scope for everything from pure reason to the application of the most recondite special knowledge, and at its best offers the most tightly and logically constructed plots to be found in current fiction.

*Edgar Allan Poe*

# THE PURLOINED LETTER

AT PARIS, just after dark one gusty evening in the autumn of 18—, I was enjoying the twofold luxury of meditation and a meerschaum, in company with my friend, C. Auguste Dupin, in his little back library, or bookcloset, *au troisième*, No. 33 Rue Dunôt, Faubourg St. Germain. For one hour at least we had maintained a profound silence, while each, to any casual observer, might have seemed intently and exclusively occupied with the curling eddies of smoke that oppressed the atmosphere of the chamber. For myself, however, I was mentally discussing certain topics which had formed matter for conversation between us at an earlier period of the evening; I mean the affair of the Rue Morgue, and the mystery attending the murder of Marie Rogêt. I looked upon it, therefore, as something of a coincidence, when the door of our apartment was thrown open and admitted our old acquaintance, Monsieur G——, the Prefect of the Parisian police.

We gave him a hearty welcome; for there was nearly half as much of the entertaining as of the contemptible about the man, and we had not seen him for several years. We had been sitting in the dark, and Dupin now arose for the purpose of lighting a lamp, but sat down again, without doing so, upon G——'s saying that he had called to consult us, or rather to ask the opinion of my friend, about some official business which had occasioned a great deal of trouble.

"If it is any point requiring reflection," observed Dupin, as he forebore to enkindle the wick, "we shall examine it to better purpose in the dark."

"That is another of your odd notions," said the Prefect, who had the fashion of calling everything "odd" that was beyond his comprehension, and thus lived amid an absolute legion of "oddities."

"Very true," said Dupin, as he supplied his visitor with a pipe, and rolled toward him a comfortable chair.

"And what is the difficulty now?" I asked. "Nothing more in the assassination way, I hope?"

"Oh, no, nothing of that nature. The fact is, the business is very simple indeed, and I make no doubt that we can manage it sufficiently well ourselves; but then I thought Dupin would like to hear the details of it, because it is so excessively *odd*."

"Simple and odd," said Dupin.

"Why, yes; and not exactly that, either. The fact is, we have all been a good deal puzzled because the affair *is* so simple, and yet baffles us altogether."

"Perhaps it is the very simplicity of the thing which puts you at fault," said my friend.

"What nonsense you *do* talk!" replied the Prefect, laughing heartily.

"Perhaps the mystery is a little *too* plain," said Dupin.

"Oh, good heavens! who ever heard of such an idea?"

"A little *too* self-evident."

"Ha! ha! ha!—ha! ha! ha!—ho! ho! ho!" roared our visitor, profoundly amused. "Oh, Dupin, you will be the death of me yet!"

"And what, after all, *is* the matter on hand?" I asked.

"Why, I will tell you," replied the Prefect, as he gave a long, steady, and contemplative puff, and settled himself in his chair. "I will tell you in a few words; but, before I begin, let me caution you that this is an affair demanding the greatest secrecy, and that I should most probably lose the position I now hold were it known that I confided it to any one."

"Proceed," said I.

"Or not," said Dupin.

"Well, then; I have received personal information, from a very high quarter, that a certain document of the last importance has been purloined from the royal apartments. The individual who purloined it is known; this beyond a doubt; he was seen to take it. It is known, also, that it still remains in his possession."

"How is this known?" asked Dupin.

"It is clearly inferred," replied the Prefect, "from the nature of the document, and from the non-appearance of certain results which would at once arise from its passing out of the robber's possession—that is to say, from his employing it as he must design in the end to employ it."

"Be a little more explicit," I said.

"Well, I may venture so far as to say that the paper gives its holder a certain power in a certain quarter where such power is immensely valuable." The Prefect was fond of the cant of diplomacy.

"Still I do not quite understand," said Dupin.

"No? Well, the disclosure of the document to a third person, who shall be nameless, would bring in question the honor of a personage of the most exalted station, and this fact gives the holder of the document an ascendancy over the illustrious personage whose honor and peace are so jeopardized."

"But this ascendancy," I interposed, "would depend upon the robber's knowledge of the loser's knowledge of the robber. Who would dare—"

"The thief," said G——, "is the Minister D——, who dares all things, those unbecoming as well as those becoming a man. The method of the theft was not less ingenious than bold. The document in question—a letter, to be frank—had been received by the personage robbed while alone in the royal *boudoir.* During its perusal she was suddenly interrupted by the entrance of the other exalted personage from whom especially it was her wish to conceal it. After a hurried and vain endeavor to thrust it in a drawer, she was forced to place it, open as it was, upon a table. The address, however, was uppermost, and, the contents thus unexposed, the letter escaped notice. At this juncture, enters the Minister D——. His lynx eye immediately perceives the paper, recognizes the hand-writing of the address, observes the confusion of the personage ad-dressed, and fathoms her secret. After some business transactions, hurried through in his ordinary manner, he produces a letter some-what similar to the one in question, opens it, pretends to read it, and then places it in close juxtaposition to the other. Again he converses, for some fifteen minutes, upon the public affairs. At length, in taking leave, he takes also from the table the letter to which he had no claim. Its rightful owner saw, but, of course, dared not call attention to the act, in the presence of the third personage who stood at her elbow. The Minister decamped, leav-ing his own letter—one of no importance—upon the table."

"Here, then," said Dupin to me, "you have precisely what you demand to make the ascendancy complete—the robber's knowl-edge of the loser's knowledge of the robber."

"Yes," replied the Prefect, "and the power thus attained has, for some months past, been wielded, for political purposes, to a very dangerous extent. The personage robbed is more thoroughly convinced, every day, of the necessity of reclaiming her letter. But this, of course, cannot be done openly. In fine, driven to despair, she has committed the matter to me."

"Than whom," said Dupin, amid a perfect whirlwind of smoke, "no more sagacious agent could, I suppose, be desired, or even imagined."

"You flatter me," replied the Prefect; "but it is possible that some such opinion may have been entertained."

"It is clear," said I, "as you observe, that the letter is still in the possession of the Minister; since it is this possession, and not any employment of the letter, which bestows the power. With the employment the power departs."

"True," said G——; "and upon this conviction I proceeded. My first care was to make thorough search of the Minister's hotel; and here my chief embarrassment lay in the necessity of searching without his knowledge. Beyond all things, I have been warned of the danger which would result from giving him reason to suspect our design."

"But," said I, "you are quite au *fait* in these investigations. The Parisian police have done this thing often before."

"Oh, yes, and for this reason I did not despair. The habits of the Minister gave me, too, a great advantage. He is frequently absent from home all night. His servants are by no means numerous. They sleep at a distance from their master's apartment, and, being chiefly Neapolitans, are readily made drunk. I have keys, as you know, with which I can open any chamber or cabinet in Paris. For three months a night has not passed during the greater part of which I have not been engaged, personally, in ransacking the D—— Hotel. My honor is interested, and, to mention a great secret, the reward is enormous. So I did not abandon the search until I had become fully satisfied that the thief is a more astute man than myself. I fancy that I have investigated every nook and corner of the premises in which it is possible that the paper can be concealed."

"But is it not possible," I suggested, "that although the letter may be in the possession of the Minister, as it unquestionably is, he may have concealed it elsewhere than upon his own premises?"

"This is barely possible," said Dupin. "The present peculiar condition of affairs at court, and especially of those intrigues in which D—— is known to be involved, would render the instant availability of the document—its susceptibility of being produced at a moment's notice—a point of nearly equal importance with its possession."

"Its susceptibility of being produced?" said I.

"That is to say, of being *destroyed*," said Dupin.

"True," I observed; "the paper is clearly, then, upon the premises. As for its being upon the person of the Minister, we may consider that as out of the question."

"Entirely," said the Prefect. "He has been twice waylaid, as if by footpads, and his person rigidly searched under my own inspection."

"You might have spared yourself this trouble," said Dupin. "D——, I presume, is not altogether a fool; and, if not, must have anticipated these waylayings, as a matter of course."

"Not *altogether* a fool," said G——; "but, then, he is a poet, which I take to be only one remove from a fool."

"True," said Dupin, after a long and thoughtful whiff from his meerschaum, "although I have been guilty of certain doggerel myself."

"Suppose you detail," said I, "the particulars of your search."

"Why, the fact is, we took our time, and we searched *everywhere*. I have had long experience in these affairs. I took the entire building, room by room, devoting the nights of a whole week to each. We examined, first, the furniture of each apartment. We opened every possible drawer; and I presume you know that, to a properly trained police-agent, such a thing as a 'secret' drawer is impossible. Any man is a dolt who permits a 'secret' drawer to escape him in a search of this kind. The thing is so plain. There is a certain amount of bulk—of space—to be accounted for in every cabinet. Then we have accurate rules. The fiftieth part of a line could not escape us. After the cabinets we took the chairs. The cushions we probed with the fine long needles you have seen me employ. From the tables we removed the tops."

"Why so?"

"Sometimes the top of a table, or other similarly arranged piece of furniture, is removed by the person wishing to conceal an article; then the leg is excavated, the article deposited within the cavity, and the top replaced. The bottoms and tops of bedposts are employed in the same way."

"But could not the cavity be detected by sounding?" I asked.

"By no means, if, when the article is deposited, a sufficient wadding of cotton be placed around it. Besides, in our case, we were obliged to proceed without noise."

"But you could not have removed—you could not have taken to pieces *all* articles of furniture in which it would have been possible to make a deposit in the manner you mention. A letter may be compressed into a thin spiral roll, not differing much in shape or bulk from a large knitting-needle, and in this form it might be inserted into the rung of a chair, for example. You did not take to pieces all the chairs?"

"Certainly not; but we did better—we examined the rungs of every chair in the hotel, and, indeed, the jointings of every description of furniture, by the aid of a most powerful microscope. Had there been any traces of recent disturbance we should not have failed to detect it instantly. A single grain of gimlet-dust, for example, would have been as obvious as an apple. Any disorder in the gluing—any unusual gaping in the joints—would have sufficed to insure detection."

"I presume you looked to the mirrors, between the boards and the plates, and you probed the beds and the bedclothes, as well as the curtains and carpets."

"That, of course; and when we had absolutely completed every particle of the furniture in this way, then we examined the house itself. We divided its entire surface into compartments, which we numbered, so that none might be missed; then we scrutinized each individual square inch throughout the premises, including the two houses immediately adjoining, with the microscope, as before."

"The two houses adjoining!" I exclaimed. "You must have had a great deal of trouble."

"We had; but the reward offered is prodigious."

"You include the *grounds* about the houses?"

"All the grounds are paved with brick. They gave us comparatively little trouble. We examined the moss between the bricks, and found it undisturbed."

"You looked among D——'s papers, of course, and into the books of the library?"

"Certainly; we opened every package and parcel; we not only opened every book, but we turned over every leaf in each volume, not contenting ourselves with a mere shake, according to the fashion of some of our police officers. We also measured the thickness of every book-cover, with the most accurate admeasurement, and applied to each the most jealous scrutiny of the microscope. Had any of the bindings been recently meddled with, it would have been utterly impossible that the fact should have escaped observation. Some five or six volumes, just from the hands of the binder, we carefully probed, longitudinally, with the needles."

"You explored the floors beneath the carpets?"

"Beyond doubt. We removed every carpet, and examined the boards with the microscope."

"And the paper on the walls?"

"Yes."

"You looked into the cellars?"

"We did."

"Then," I said, "you have been making a miscalculation, and the letter is not upon the premises, as you suppose."

"I fear you are right there," said the Prefect. "And now, Dupin, what would you advise me to do?"

"To make a thorough research of the premises."

"That is absolutely needless," replied G——. "I am not more sure that I breathe than I am that the letter is not at the hotel."

"I have no better advice to give you," said Dupin. "You have, of course, an accurate description of the letter?"

"Oh, yes!" And here the Prefect, producing a memorandum book, proceeded to read aloud a minute account of the internal, and especially of the external, appearance of the missing document. Soon after finishing the perusal of this description, he took his departure, more entirely depressed in spirits than I had ever known the good gentleman before.

In about a month afterward he paid us another visit, and found us occupied very nearly as before. He took a pipe and a chair, and entered into some ordinary conversation. At length I said:

"Well, but, G——, what of the purloined letter? I presume you have at last made up your mind that there is no such thing as overreaching the Minister?"

"Confound him, say I—yes; I made the re-examination, however, as Dupin suggested—but it was all labor lost, as I knew it would be."

"How much was the reward offered, did you say?" asked Dupin.

"Why, a very great deal—a very liberal reward—I don't like to say how much, precisely; but one thing I *will* say, that I wouldn't mind giving my individual check for fifty thousand francs to any one who could obtain me that letter. The fact is, it is becoming of more and more importance every day; and the reward has been lately doubled. If it were trebled, however, I could do no more than I have done."

"Why, yes," said Dupin, drawling, between the whiffs of his meerschaum, "I really—think, G——, you have not exerted yourself—to the utmost in this matter. You might—do a little more, I think, eh?"

"How?—in what way?"

"Why"—puff, puff—"you might"—puff, puff—"employ counsel in the matter, eh"—puff, puff, puff. "Do you remember the story they tell of Abernethy?"

"No; hang Abernethy!"

"To be sure! Hang him and welcome. But, once upon a time, a certain miser conceived the design of spunging upon this Abernethy for a medical opinion. Getting up, for this purpose, an ordinary conversation in a private company, he insinuated his case to the physician as that of an imaginary individual.

" 'We will suppose,' said the miser, 'that his symptoms are such and such; now, doctor, what would you have directed him to take?'

" 'Take!' said Abernethy. 'Why, take *advice*, to be sure.' "

"But," said the Prefect, a little discomposed, "*I* am *perfectly* willing to take advice, and to pay for it. I would *really* give fifty thousand francs to any one who would aid me in the matter."

"In that case," replied Dupin, opening a drawer, and producing a check-book, "you may as well fill me up a check for the amount mentioned. When you have signed it, I will hand you the letter."

I was astounded. The Prefect appeared absolutely thunder-stricken. For some minutes he remained speechless and motion-less, looking incredulously at my friend with open mouth, and eyes that seemed starting from their sockets; then apparently re-covering himself in some measure, he seized a pen, and after sev-eral pauses and vacant stares, finally filled up and signed a check for fifty thousand francs, and handed it across the table to Dupin. The latter examined it carefully and deposited it in his pocket-book; then, unlocking an *escritoire*, took thence a letter and gave it to the Prefect. This functionary grasped it in a perfect agony of joy, opened it with a trembling hand, cast a rapid glance at its contents, and then, scrambling and struggling to the door, rushed at length unceremoniously from the room and from the house, without having uttered a syllable since Dupin had requested him to fill up the check.

When he had gone, my friend entered into some explanation.

"The Parisian police," he said, "are exceedingly able in their way. They are persevering, ingenious, cunning, and thoroughly versed in the knowledge which their duties seem chiefly to de-mand. Thus, when G—— detailed to us his mode of searching the premises at the Hotel D——, I felt entire confidence in his having made a satisfactory investigation—so far as his labors ex-tended."

"So far as his labors extended?" said I.

"Yes," said Dupin. "The measures adopted were not only the best of their kind, but carried out to absolute perfection. Had the letter been deposited within the range of their search, these fellows would, beyond a question, have found it."

I merely laughed—but he seemed quite serious in all that he said.

"The measures, then," he continued, "were good in their kind, and well executed; their defect lay in their being inapplicable to the case and to the man. A certain set of highly ingenious resources are, with the Prefect, a sort of Procrustean bed, to which he forcibly adapts his designs. But he perpetually errs by being too deep or too shallow for the matter in hand, and many a school-boy is a better reasoner than he. I knew one about eight years of age, whose success at guessing in the game of 'even and odd' attracted universal admiration. This game is simple, and is played with marbles. One player holds in his hand a number of these toys, and demands of another whether that number is even or odd. If the guess is right, the guesser wins one; if wrong, he loses one. The boy to whom I allude won all the marbles of the school. Of course, he had some principle of guessing; and this lay in mere observation and admeasurement of the astuteness of his opponents. For example, an arrant simpleton is his opponent, and, holding up his closed hand, asks, 'Are they even or odd?' Our school-boy replies, 'Odd,' and loses; but upon the second trial he wins, for he then says to himself: 'The simpleton had them even upon the first trial, and his amount of cunning is just sufficient to make him have them odd upon the second; I will therefore guess odd'; he guesses odd, and wins. Now, with a simpleton a degree above the first, he would have reasoned thus: 'This fellow finds that in the first instance I guessed odd, and, in the second, he will propose to himself, upon the first impulse, a simple variation from even to odd, as did the first simpleton; but then a second thought will suggest that this is too simple a variation, and finally he will decide upon putting it even as before. I will therefore guess even';

he guesses even, and wins. Now this mode of reasoning in the school-boy, whom his fellows termed 'Lucky,' what, in its last analysis, is it?"

"It is merely," I said, "an identification of the reasoner's intellect with that of his opponent."

"It is," said Dupin; "and, upon inquiring of the boy by what means he effected the *thorough* identification in which his success consisted, I received answer as follows: 'When I wish to find out how wise, or how stupid, or how good, or how wicked, is any one, or what are his thoughts at the moment, I fashion the expression of my face, as accurately as possible, in accordance with the expression of his, and then wait to see what thoughts or sentiments arise in my mind or heart, as if to match or correspond with the expression.' This response of the school-boy lies at the bottom of all the spurious profundity which has been attributed to Rochefoucault, to La Bougive, to Machiavelli, and to Campanella."

"And the identification," I said, "of the reasoner's intellect with that of his opponent, depends, if I understand you aright, upon the accuracy with which the opponent's intellect is admeasured."

"For its practical value it depends upon this," replied Dupin; "and the Prefect and his cohort fail so frequently, first, by default of this identification, and, secondly, by ill-admeasurement, or rather through non-admeasurement, of the intellect with which they are engaged. They consider only their own ideas of ingenuity; and, in searching for anything hidden, advert only to the modes in which *they* would have hidden it. They are right in this much—that their own ingenuity is a faithful representative of that of *the mass*; but when the cunning of the individual felon is diverse in character from their own, the felon foils them of course. This always happens when it is above their own, and very usually when it is below. They have no variation of principle in their investigations; at best, when urged by some unusual emergency—by some extraordinary reward—they extend or exaggerate their old modes of *practice*, without touching their principles. What, for example, in this case of D——, has been done to vary the principle of action? What is all this boring, and probing, and sounding, and scrutinizing with the microscope, and dividing the surface of the building into registered square inches—what is it all but an exaggeration of the application of the one principle or set of principles of search, which are based upon the one set of notions regarding human ingenuity, to which the Prefect, in the long routine of his duty, has been accustomed? Do you not see he had taken it for granted that *all* men proceed to conceal a letter, not exactly in a gimlet-hole bored in a chair-leg, but, at least, in *some* out-of-the-way hole or corner suggested by the same tenor of thought which would urge a man to secrete a letter in a gimlet-hole bored in a chair-leg? And do you not see, also, that such *recherché* nooks for concealment are adapted only for ordinary occasions, and would be adopted only by ordinary intellects; for, in all cases of concealment, a disposal of the article concealed—a disposal of it in this *recherché* manner—is, in the very first instance, presumable and presumed; and thus its discovery depends, not at all upon the acumen, but altogether upon the mere care, patience, and determination of the seekers; and where the case is of importance—or, when the reward is of magnitude—the qualities in question have *never* been known to fail. You will now understand what I meant in suggesting that, had the purloined letter been hidden anywhere within the limits of the Prefect's examination—in other words, had the principle of its concealment been comprehended within the principles of the Prefect—its discovery would have been a matter altogether beyond question. This functionary, however, has been thoroughly mystified; and the remote source of his defeat lies in the supposition that the Minister is a fool, because he has acquired renown as a poet. All fools are poets; this the Prefect *feels*; and he is merely guilty of a *non distributio medii* in thence inferring that all poets are fools. I mean to say, that if the Minister had been no more than a mathematician, the Prefect would have been under no necessity of giving me this check. I knew him, however, as both mathematician and poet, and my measures were adapted to his capacity, with reference to the circumstances by which he was surrounded. I knew him as a courtier, too, and as a bold *intriguant*. Such a man, I considered, could not fail to be aware of the ordinary political modes of action. He could not have failed to anticipate—and events have proved that he did not fail to anticipate—the waylayings to which he was subjected. He must have foreseen, I reflected, the secret investigations of his premises. His frequent absences from home at night, which were hailed by the Prefect as certain aids to his success, I regarded only as ruses, to afford opportunity for thorough search to the police, and thus the sooner to impress them with the conviction to which G——, in fact, did finally arrive—the conviction that the letter was not upon the premises. I felt, also, that the whole train of thought, which I was at some pains in detailing to you just now, concerning the invariable principle of political action in searches for articles concealed—I felt that this whole train of thought would necessarily pass through the mind of the Minister. It would imperatively lead him to despise all the ordinary nooks of concealment. He could not, I reflected, be so weak as not to see that the most intricate and remote recess of his hotel would be as open as his commonest closets to the eyes, to the probes, to the gimlets, and to the microscopes of the Prefect. I saw, in fine, that he would be driven, as a matter of course, to *simplicity*, if not deliberately induced to it as a matter of choice. You will remember, perhaps, how desperately the Prefect laughed when I suggested, upon our first interview, that it was just possible this mystery troubled him so much on account of its being so very self-evident."

"Yes," said I, "I remember his merriment well. I really thought he would have fallen into convulsions."

"The material world," continued Dupin, "abounds with very strict analogies to the immaterial; and thus some color of truth has been given to the rhetorical dogma that metaphor, or simile, may be made to strengthen an argument as well as to embellish a description. The principle of the *vis inertiae*, for example, seems to be identical in physics and metaphysics. It is not more true, in the former, that a large body is with more difficulty set in motion than a smaller one, and that its subsequent *momentum* is commensurate with this difficulty, than it is, in the latter, that intellects of the vaster capacity, while more forcible, more constant, and more eventful in their movements than those of inferior grade, are yet the less readily moved, and more embarrassed, and full of hesitation in the first few steps of their progress. Again: have you ever noticed which of the street signs, over the shop doors, are the most attractive of attention?"

"I have never given the matter a thought," I said.

"There is a game of puzzles," he resumed, "which is played upon a map. One party playing requires another to find a given word—the name of town, river, state, or empire—any word, in short, upon the motley and perplexed surface of the chart. A novice in the game generally seeks to embarrass his opponents by giving them the most minutely lettered names; but the adept selects such words as stretch, in large characters, from one end of the chart to the other. These, like the over-largely lettered signs and placards of the street, escape observation by dint of being excessively obvious; and here the physical oversight is precisely analogous with the moral inapprehension by which the intellect suffers to pass unnoticed those considerations which are too obtrusively and too palpably self-evident. But this is a point, it appears, somewhat above or beneath the understanding of the Prefect. He never once thought it probable, or possible, that the Minister had deposited the letter immediately beneath the nose of the whole world, by way of best preventing any portion of that world from perceiving it.

"But the more I reflected upon the daring, dashing, and discriminating ingenuity of D——; upon the fact that the document must always have been *at hand*, if he intended to use it to good purpose; and upon the decisive evidence, obtained by the Prefect, that it was not hidden within the limits of that dignitary's ordinary search, the more satisfied I became that, to conceal this letter, the Minister had resorted to the comprehensive and sagacious expedient of not attempting to conceal it.

"Full of these ideas, I prepared myself with a pair of green spectacles, and called one fine morning, quite by accident, at the Ministerial hotel. I found D—— at home, yawning, lounging, and dawdling, as usual, and pretending to be in the last extremity of *ennui*. He is, perhaps, the most really energetic human being now alive—but that is only when nobody sees him.

"To be even with him, I complained of my weak eyes, and lamented the necessity of the spectacles, under cover of which I cautiously and thoroughly surveyed the whole apartment, while seemingly intent only upon the conversation of my host.

"I paid especial attention to a large writing-table near which he sat, and upon which lay confusedly some miscellaneous letters and other papers, with one or two musical instruments and a few books. Here, however, after a long and very deliberate scrutiny, I saw nothing to excite particular suspicion.

"At length my eyes, in going the circuit of the room, fell upon a trumpery filigree card-rack of pasteboard that hung dangling by a dirty blue ribbon from a little brass knob just beneath the middle of the mantelpiece. In this rack, which had three or four compartments, were five or six soiled cards and a solitary letter. This last was much soiled and crumpled. It was torn nearly in two, across the middle—as if a design, in the first instance, to tear it entirely up as worthless had been altered or stayed in the second. It had a large black seal, bearing the D—— cipher very conspicuously, and was addressed, in a diminutive female hand, to D——, the Minister, himself. It was thrust carelessly, and even, as it seemed, contemptuously, into one of the uppermost divisions of the rack.

"No sooner had I glanced at this letter than I concluded it to be that of which I was in search. To be sure, it was, to all appearance, radically different from the one of which the Prefect had read us so minute a description. Here the seal was large and black, with the D—— cipher; there it was small and red, with the ducal arms of the S—— family. Here the address, to the Minister, was diminutive and feminine; there the superscription, to a certain royal personage, was markedly bold and decided; the size alone formed a point of correspondence. But, then, the *radicalness* of these differences, which was excessive; the dirt; the soiled and torn condition of the paper, so inconsistent with the *true* methodical habits of D——, and so consistent of a design to delude the be- holder into an idea of the worthlessness of the document—these things, together with the hyperobtrusive situation of this docu- ment, full in the view of every visitor, and thus exactly in accord- ance with the conclusions to which I had previously arrived—these things, I say, were strongly corroborative of suspicion in one who came with the intention to suspect.

"I protracted my visit as long as possible, and, while I main- tained a most animated discussion with the Minister upon a topic which I knew well had never failed to interest and excite him, I kept my attention riveted upon the letter. In this examination I committed to memory its external appearance and arrangement in the rack, and also fell, at length, upon a discovery which set at rest whatever trivial doubt I might have entertained. In scrutiniz- ing the edges of the paper, I observed them to be more *chafed* than seemed necessary. They presented the *broken* appearance which is manifested when a stiff paper, having been once folded and pressed with a folder, is refolded in a reversed direction, in the same creases or edges which formed the original fold. This discovery was sufficient. It was clear to me that the letter had been turned, as a glove, inside out, re-directed and re-sealed. I bade the Minister good-morning, and took my departure at once, leaving a gold snuff-box upon the table.

"The next morning I called for the snuff-box, when we resumed, quite eagerly, the conversation of the preceding day. While thus engaged, however, a loud report, as if of a pistol, was heard immediately beneath the windows of the hotel, and was succeeded by a series of fearful screams and the shoutings of a terrified mob. D—— rushed to a casement, threw it open, and looked out. In the meantime I stepped to the card-rack, took the letter, put it in my pocket, and replaced it by a *facsimile* (so far as regards externals), which I had carefully prepared at my lodgings—imitating the D—— cipher, very readily, by means of a seal formed of bread.

"The disturbance in the street had been occasioned by the frantic behavior of a man with a musket. He had fired it among a crowd of women and children. It proved, however, to have been without ball, and the fellow was suffered to go his way as a lunatic or a drunkard. When he had gone, D—— came from the window, whither I had followed him immediately upon securing the object in view. Soon afterward I bade him farewell. The pretended lunatic was a man in my own pay."

"But what purpose had you," I asked, "in replacing the letter by a *facsimile?* Would it not have been better, at the first visit, to have seized it openly and departed?"

"D——," replied Dupin, "is a desperate man and a man of nerve. His hotel, too, is not without attendants devoted to his interests. Had I made the wild attempt you suggest, I might never have left the Ministerial presence alive. The good people of Paris might have heard of me no more. But I had an object apart from these considerations. You know my political prepossessions. In this matter I act as a partisan of the lady concerned. For eighteen months the Minister has had her in his power. She has now him in hers—since, being unaware that the letter is not in his possession, he will proceed with his exactions as if it was. Thus will he inevitably commit himself, at once, to his political destruction. His downfall, too, will not be more precipitate than awkward. It is all very well to talk about the *facilis descensus Averni;* but in all kinds of climbing, as Catalani said of singing, it is far more easy to get up than to come down. In the present instance I have no sympathy—

at least no pity—for him who descends. He is that *monstrum hor-rendum*, an unprincipled man of genius. I confess, however, that I should like very well to know the precise character of his thoughts, when, being defied by her whom the Prefect terms 'a certain personage,' he is reduced to opening the letter I left for him in the card-rack."

"How? Did you put anything particular in it?"

"Why—it did not seem altogether right to leave the interior blank—that would have been insulting. D——, at Vienna once, did me an evil turn, which I told him, quite good-humoredly, that I should remember. So, as I knew he would feel some curiosity in regard to the identity of the person who had outwitted him, I thought it a pity not to give him a clew. He is well acquainted with my MS., and I just copied into the middle of the blank sheet the words:

> "'—— Un dessein si funeste,
> S'il n'est digne d'Atrée, este digne de Thyeste.'

They are to be found in Crébillon's Atrée."

1. What points of detection are involved in "the robber's knowledge of the loser's knowledge of the robber"?
2. The "personage robbed" is a woman. Does this add anything to the story?
3. What is the connection between the crime and the fact that the Minister D—— is a poet and a mathematician?
4. What do you think of Poe's simulated French atmosphere?
5. Translate the couplet at the close of the story.

# Sir Arthur Conan Doyle

# THE RED-HEADED LEAGUE

I HAD called upon my friend, Mr. Sherlock Holmes, one day in the autumn of last year, and found him in deep conversation with a very stout, florid-faced elderly gentleman, with fiery red hair. With an apology for my intrusion, I was about to withdraw, when Holmes pulled me abruptly into the room and closed the door behind me.

"You could not possibly have come at a better time, my dear Watson," he said, cordially.

"I was afraid that you were engaged."

"So I am. Very much so."

"Then I can wait in the next room."

"Not at all. This gentleman, Mr. Wilson, has been my partner and helper in many of my most successful cases, and I have no doubt that he will be of the utmost use to me in yours also."

The stout gentleman half rose from his chair and gave a bob of greeting, with a quick little questioning glance from his small, fat-encircled eyes.

"Try the settee," said Holmes, relapsing into his armchair, and putting his finger-tips together, as was his custom when in judicial moods. "I know, my dear Watson, that you share my love of all that is bizarre and outside the conventions and humdrum routine of everyday life. You have shown your relish for it by the enthusiasm which has prompted you to chronicle, and, if you will excuse my saying so, somewhat to embellish so many of my own little adventures."

"Your cases have indeed been of the greatest interest to me," I observed.

"You will remember that I remarked the other day, just before we went into the very simple problem presented by Miss Mary Sutherland, that for strange effects and extraordinary combinations we must go to life itself, which is always far more daring than any effort of the imagination."

"A proposition which I took the liberty of doubting."

"You did, doctor, but none the less you must come round to my view, for otherwise I shall keep on piling fact upon fact on you, until your reason breaks down under them and acknowledges me to be right. Now, Mr. Jabez Wilson here has been good enough to call upon me this morning, and to begin a narrative which promises to be one of the most singular which I have listened to for some time. You have heard me remark that the strangest and most unique things are very often connected not with the larger but with the smaller crimes, and occasionally, indeed, where there is room for doubt whether any positive crime has been committed. As far as I have heard, it is impossible for me to say whether the present case is an instance of crime or not, but the course of events is certainly among the most singular that I have ever listened to. Perhaps, Mr. Wilson, you would have the great kindness to recommence your narrative. I ask you, not merely because my friend, Dr. Watson, has not heard the opening part, but also because the peculiar nature of the story makes me anxious to have every possible detail from your lips. As a rule, when I have heard some slight indication of the course of events I am able to guide myself by the thousands of other similar cases which occur to my memory. In the present instance I am forced to admit that the facts are, to the best of my belief, unique."

The portly client puffed out his chest with an appearance of some little pride, and pulled a dirty and wrinkled newspaper from the inside pocket of his greatcoat. As he glanced down the advertisement column, with his head thrust forward, and the paper flattened out upon his knee, I took a good look at the man, and endeavored, after the fashion of my companion, to read the indications which might be presented by his dress or appearance.

I did not gain very much, however, by my inspection. Our visitor bore every mark of being an average commonplace British tradesman, obese, pompous, and slow. He wore rather baggy gray shepherd's check trousers, a not over-clean black frock-coat, unbuttoned in the front, and a drab waistcoat with a heavy brassy Albert chain, and a square pierced bit of metal dangling down as an ornament. A frayed top hat and a faded brown overcoat with a wrinkled velvet collar lay upon a chair beside him. Altogether, look as I would, there was nothing remarkable about the man save his blazing red head and the expression of extreme chagrin and discontent upon his features.

Sherlock Holmes's quick eye took in my occupation, and he shook his head with a smile as he noticed my questioning glances. "Beyond the obvious facts that he has at some time done manual labor, that he takes snuff, that he is a Freemason, that he has been in China, and that he has done a considerable amount of writing lately, I can deduce nothing else."

Mr. Jabez Wilson started up in his chair, with his forefinger upon the paper, but his eyes upon my companion.

"How, in the name of good fortune, did you know all that, Mr. Holmes?" he asked. "How did you know, for example, that I did manual labor? It's as true as gospel, for I began as a ship's carpenter."

"Your hands, my dear sir. Your right hand is quite a size larger than your left. You have worked with it and the muscles are more developed."

"Well, the snuff, then, and the Freemasonry?"

"I won't insult your intelligence by telling you how I read that, especially as, rather against the strict rules of your order, you use an arc and compass breastpin."

"Ah, of course, I forgot that. But the writing?"

"What else can be indicated by that right cuff so very shiny for five inches, and the left one with the smooth patch near the elbow where you rest it upon the desk."

"Well, but China?"

"The fish which you have tattooed immediately above your wrist could only have been done in China. I have made a small study of tattoo marks, and have even contributed to the literature of the subject. That trick of staining the fishes' scales of a delicate pink is quite peculiar to China. When, in addition, I see a Chinese coin hanging from your watch-chain, the matter becomes even more simple."

Mr. Jabez Wilson laughed heavily. "Well, I never!" said he. "I thought at first that you had done something clever, but I see that there was nothing in it after all."

"I begin to think, Watson," said Holmes, "that I make a mistake in explaining. 'Omne ignotum pro magnifico,' you know, and my poor little reputation, such as it is, will suffer shipwreck if I am so candid. Can you not find the advertisement, Mr. Wilson?"

"Yes, I have got it now," he answered, with his thick, red finger planted half-way down the column. "Here it is. This is what began it all. You just read it for yourself, sir."

I took the paper from him and read as follows:

"To the Red-headed League: On account of the bequest of the late Ezekiah Hopkins, of Lebanon, Pa., U. S. A., there is now another vacancy open which entitles a member of the League to a salary of four pounds a week for purely nominal services. All red-headed men who are sound in body and mind and above the age of twenty-one years are eligible. Apply in person on Monday, at eleven o'clock, to Duncan Ross, at the offices of the League, 7 Pope's Court, Fleet Street."

"What on earth does this mean?" I ejaculated, after I had twice read over the extraordinary announcement.

Holmes chuckled and wriggled in his chair, as was his habit when in high spirits. "It is a little off the beaten track, isn't it?" said he. "And now, Mr. Wilson, off you go at scratch, and tell us all about yourself, your household, and the effect which this advertisement had upon your fortunes. You will first make a note, doctor, of the paper and the date."

"It is *The Morning Chronicle* of April 27, 1890. Just two months ago."

"Very good. Now, Mr. Wilson."

"Well, it is just as I have been telling you, Mr. Sherlock Holmes," said Jabez Wilson, mopping his forehead. "I have a small pawnbroker's business at Coburg Square, near the City. It's not a very large affair, and of late years it has not done more than just give me a living. I used to be able to keep two assistants, but now I only keep one; and I would have a job to pay him but that he is willing to come for half wages, so as to learn the business."

"What is the name of this obliging youth?" asked Sherlock Holmes.

"His name is Vincent Spaulding, and he's not such a youth either. It's hard to say his age. I should not wish a smarter assistant, Mr. Holmes; and I know very well that he could better himself, and earn twice what I am able to give him. But, after all, if he is satisfied, why should I put ideas in his head?"

"Why, indeed? You seem most fortunate in having an employee who comes under the full market price. It is not a common experience among employers in this age. I don't know that your assistant is not as remarkable as your advertisement."

"Oh, he has his faults, too," said Mr. Wilson. "Never was such a fellow for photography. Snapping away with a camera when he ought to be improving his mind, and then diving down into the cellar like a rabbit into its hole to develop his pictures. That is his main fault; but, on the whole, he's a good worker. There's no vice in him."

"He is still with you, I presume?"

"Yes, sir. He and a girl of fourteen, who does a bit of simple cooking, and keeps the place clean—that's all I have in the house, for I am a widower, and never had any family. We live very quietly, sir, the three of us; and we keep a roof over our heads, and pay our debts, if we do nothing more.

"The first thing that put us out was that advertisement. Spaulding, he came down into the office just this day eight weeks, with this very paper in his hand, and he says:

" 'I wish to the Lord, Mr. Wilson, that I was a red-headed man.'

" 'Why that?' I asks.

" 'Why,' says he, 'here's another vacancy on the League of the Red-headed Men. It's worth quite a little fortune to any man who gets it, and I understand that there are more vacancies than there are men, so that the trustees are at their wits' end what to do with the money. If my hair would only change color here's a nice little crib all ready for me to step into.'

" 'Why, what is it, then?' I asked. You see, Mr. Holmes, I am a very stay-at-home man, and, as my business came to me instead of my having to go to it, I was often weeks on end without putting my foot over the door-mat. In that way I didn't know much of what was going on outside, and I was always glad of a bit of news.

" 'Have you never heard of the League of the Red-headed Men?' he asked, with his eyes open.

" 'Never.'

" 'Why, I wonder at that, for you are eligible yourself for one of the vacancies.'

" 'And what are they worth?' I asked.

" 'Oh, merely a couple of hundred a year, but the work is slight, and it need not interfere very much with one's other occupations.'

"Well, you can easily think that that made me prick up my

ears, for the business has not been over good for some years, and
an extra couple of hundred would have been very handy.

" 'Tell me all about it,' said I.

" 'Well,' said he, showing me the advertisement, 'you can see
for yourself that the League has a vacancy, and there is the address where you should apply for particulars. As far as I can make
out, the League was founded by an American millionaire, Ezekiah
Hopkins, who was very peculiar in his ways. He was himself red-
headed, and he had a great sympathy for all red-headed men;
so, when he died, it was found that he had left his enormous
fortune in the hands of trustees, with instructions to apply the
interest to the providing of easy berths to men whose hair is of
that color. From all I hear it is splendid pay, and very little to do.'

" 'But,' said I, 'there would be millions of red-headed men who
would apply.'

" 'Not so many as you might think,' he answered. 'You see it
is really confined to Londoners, and to grown men. This American
had started from London when he was young, and he wanted to
do the old town a good turn. Then, again, I have heard it is no
use your applying if your hair is light red, or dark red, or anything but real, bright, blazing, fiery red. Now, if you cared to
apply, Mr. Wilson, you would just walk in; but perhaps it would
hardly be worth your while to put yourself out of the way for the
sake of a few hundred pounds.'

"Now it is a fact, gentlemen, as you may see for yourselves, that
my hair is of a very full and rich tint, so that it seemed to me
that, if there was to be any competition in the matter, I stood as
good a chance as any man that I had ever met. Vincent Spaulding
seemed to know so much about it that I thought he might prove
useful, so I just ordered him to put up the shutters for the day,
and to come right away with me. He was very willing to have a
holiday, so we shut the business up, and started off for the address
that was given us in the advertisement.

"I never hope to see such a sight as that again, Mr. Holmes.

From north, south, east, and west every man who had a shade of red in his hair had tramped into the City to answer the advertisement. Fleet Street was choked with red-headed folk, and Pope's Court looked like a coster's orange barrow. I should not have thought there were so many in the whole country as were brought together by that single advertisement. Every shade of color they were—straw, lemon, orange, brick, Irish-setter, liver, clay; but, as Spaulding said, there were not many who had the real vivid flame-colored tint. When I saw how many were waiting, I would have given it up in despair; but Spaulding would not hear of it. How he did it I could not imagine, but he pushed and pulled and butted until he got me through the crowd, and right up to the steps which led to the office. There was a double stream upon the stair, some going up in hope, and some coming back dejected; but we wedged in as well as we could, and soon found ourselves in the office."

"Your experience has been a most entertaining one," remarked Holmes, as his client paused and refreshed his memory with a huge pinch of snuff. "Pray continue your very interesting statement."

"There was nothing in the office but a couple of wooden chairs and a deal table, behind which sat a small man, with a head that was even redder than mine. He said a few words to each candidate as he came up, and then he always managed to find some fault in them which would disqualify them. Getting a vacancy did not seem to be such a very easy matter after all. However, when our turn came, the little man was much more favorable to me than to any of the others, and he closed the door as we entered, so that he might have a private word with us.

" 'This is Mr. Jabez Wilson,' said my assistant, 'and he is willing to fill a vacancy in the League.'

" 'And he is admirably suited for it,' the other answered. 'He has every requirement. I cannot recall when I have seen anything so fine.' He took a step backward, cocked his head on one side, and gazed at my hair until I felt quite bashful. Then suddenly he plunged forward, wrung my hand, and congratulated me warmly on my success.

" 'It would be injustice to hesitate,' said he. 'You will, however, I am sure, excuse me for taking an obvious precaution.' With that he seized my hair in both his hands, and tugged until I yelled with the pain. 'There is water in your eyes,' said he, as he released me. 'I perceive that all is as it should be. But we have to be careful, for we have twice been deceived by wigs and once by paint. I could tell you tales of cobbler's wax which would disgust you with human nature.' He stepped over to the window and shouted through it at the top of his voice that the vacancy was filled. A groan of disappointment came up from below, and the folk all trooped away in different directions, until there was not a red head to be seen except my own and that of the manager.

" 'My name,' said he, 'is Mr. Duncan Ross, and I am myself one of the pensioners upon the fund left by our noble benefactor. Are you a married man, Mr. Wilson? Have you a family?'

"I answered that I had not.

"His face fell immediately.

" 'Dear me!' he said, gravely, 'that is very serious indeed! I am sorry to hear you say that. The fund was, of course, for the propagation and spread of the red-heads as well as for their maintenance. It is exceedingly unfortunate that you should be a bachelor.'

"My face lengthened at this, Mr. Holmes, for I thought that I was not to have the vacancy after all; but, after thinking it over for a few minutes, he said that it would be all right.

" 'In the case of another,' said he, 'the objection might be fatal, but we must stretch a point in favor of a man with such a head of hair as yours. When shall you be able to enter upon your new duties?'

" 'Well, it is a little awkward, for I have a business already,' said I.

" 'Oh, never mind about that, Mr. Wilson!' said Vincent Spaulding. 'I shall be able to look after that for you.'

" 'What would be the hours?' I asked.

" 'Ten to two.'

"Now a pawnbroker's business is mostly done of an evening, Mr. Holmes, especially Thursday and Friday evenings, which is just before pay-day; so it would suit me very well to earn a little in the mornings. Besides, I knew that my assistant was a good man, and that he would see to anything that turned up.

" 'That would suit me very well,' said I. 'And the pay?'

" 'Is four pounds a week.'

" 'And the work?'

" 'Is purely nominal.'

" 'What do you call purely nominal?'

" 'Well, you have to be in the office, or at least in the building, the whole time. If you leave, you forfeit your whole position forever. The will is very clear upon that point. You don't comply with the conditions if you budge from the office during that time.'

" 'It's only four hours a day, and I should not think of leaving,' said I.

" 'No excuse will avail,' said Mr. Duncan Ross, 'neither sickness, nor business, nor anything else. There you must stay, or you lose your billet.'

" 'And the work?'

" 'Is to copy out the "Encyclopædia Britannica." There is the first volume of it in that press. You must find your own ink, pens, and blotting-paper, but we provide this table and chair. Will you be ready to-morrow?'

" 'Certainly,' I answered.

" 'Then, good-by, Mr. Jabez Wilson, and let me congratulate you once more on the important position which you have been fortunate enough to gain.' He bowed me out of the room, and I went home with my assistant hardly knowing what to say or do, I was so pleased at my own good fortune.

"Well, I thought over the matter all day, and by evening I was in low spirits again; for I had quite persuaded myself that the whole affair must be some great hoax or fraud, though what its object might be I could not imagine. It seemed altogether past belief that anyone could make such a will, or that they would pay such a sum for doing anything so simple as copying out the 'Encyclopædia Britannica.' Vincent Spaulding did what he could to cheer me up, but by bed-time I had reasoned myself out of the whole thing. However, in the morning I determined to have a look at it anyhow, so I bought a penny bottle of ink, and with a quill pen and seven sheets of foolscap paper I started off for Pope's Court.

"Well, to my surprise and delight everything was as right as possible. The table was set out ready for me, and Mr. Duncan Ross was there to see that I got fairly to work. He started me off upon the letter A, and then he left me; but he would drop in from time to time to see that all was right with me. At two o'clock he bade me good-day, complimented me upon the amount that I had written, and locked the door of the office after me.

"This went on day after day, Mr. Holmes, and on Saturday the manager came in and planked down four golden sovereigns for my week's work. It was the same next week, and the same the week after. Every morning I was there at ten, and every afternoon I left at two. By degrees Mr. Duncan Ross took to coming in only once of a morning, and then, after a time, he did not come in at all. Still, of course, I never dared to leave the room for an instant, for I was not sure when he might come, and the billet was such a good one, and suited me so well, that I would not risk the loss of it.

"Eight weeks passed away like this, and I had written about Abbots, and Archery, and Armor, and Architecture, and Attica, and hoped with diligence that I might get on to the B's before very long. It cost me something in foolscap, and I had pretty nearly filled a shelf with my writings. And then suddenly the whole business came to an end."

"To an end?"

"Yes, sir. And no later than this morning. I went to my work as usual at ten o'clock, but the door was shut and locked, with a little square of cardboard hammered onto the middle of the panel with a tack. Here it is, and you can read for yourself."

He held up a piece of white cardboard, about the size of a sheet of note-paper. It read in this fashion:

> "THE RED-HEADED LEAGUE IS DISSOLVED.
> Oct. 9, 1890."

Sherlock Holmes and I surveyed this curt announcement and the rueful face behind it, until the comical side of the affair so completely overtopped every consideration that we both burst out into a roar of laughter.

"I cannot see that there is anything very funny," cried our client, flushing up to the roots of his flaming head. "If you can do nothing better than laugh at me, I can go elsewhere."

"No, no," cried Holmes, shoving him back into the chair from which he had half risen. "I really wouldn't miss your case for the world. It is most refreshingly unusual. But there is, if you will excuse my saying so, something just a little funny about it. Pray what steps did you take when you found the card upon the door?"

"I was staggered, sir. I did not know what to do. Then I called at the offices round, but none of them seemed to know anything about it. Finally, I went to the landlord, who is an accountant living on the ground floor, and I asked him if he could tell me what had become of the Red-headed League. He said that he had never heard of any such body. Then I asked him who Mr. Duncan Ross was. He answered that the name was new to him.

" 'Well,' said I, 'the gentleman at No. 4.'

" 'What, the red-headed man?'

" 'Yes.'

" 'Oh,' said he, 'his name was William Morris. He was a solicitor, and was using my room as a temporary convenience until his new premises were ready. He moved out yesterday.'

" 'Where could I find him?'

" 'Oh, at his new offices. He did tell me the address. Yes, 17 King Edward Street, near St. Paul's.'

"I started off, Mr. Holmes, but when I got to that address it was a manufactory of artificial knee-caps, and no one in it had ever heard of either Mr. William Morris, or Mr. Duncan Ross."

"And what did you do then?" asked Holmes.

"I went home to Saxe-Coburg Square, and I took the advice of my assistant. But he could not help me in any way. He could only say that if I waited I should hear by post. But that was not quite good enough, Mr. Holmes. I did not wish to lose such a place without a struggle, so, as I had heard that you were good enough to give advice to poor folk who were in need of it, I came right away to you."

"And you did very wisely," said Holmes. "Your case is an exceedingly remarkable one, and I shall be happy to look into it. From what you have told me I think that it is possible that graver issues hang from it than might at first sight appear."

"Grave enough!" said Mr. Jabez Wilson. "Why, I have lost four pound a week."

"As far as you are personally concerned," remarked Holmes, "I do not see that you have any grievance against this extraordinary league. On the contrary, you are, as I understand, richer by some thirty pounds, to say nothing of the minute knowledge which you have gained on every subject which comes under the letter A. You have lost nothing by them."

"No, sir. But I want to find out about them, and who they are, and what their object was in playing this prank—if it was a prank—upon me. It was a pretty expensive joke for them, for it cost them two-and-thirty pounds."

"We shall endeavor to clear up these points for you. And, first, one or two questions, Mr. Wilson. This assistant of yours who first called your attention to the advertisement—how long had he been with you?"

"About a month then."

"How did he come?"

"In answer to an advertisement."

"Was he the only applicant?"

"No, I had a dozen."

"Why did you pick him?"

"Because he was handy and would come cheap."

"At half wages, in fact."

"Yes."

"What is he like, this Vincent Spaulding?"

"Small, stout-built, very quick in his ways, no hair on his face, though he's not short of thirty. Has a white splash of acid upon his forehead."

Holmes sat up in his chair in considerable excitement. "I thought as much," said he. "Have you ever observed that his ears are pierced for earrings?"

"Yes, sir. He told me that a gypsy had done it for him when he was a lad."

"Hum!" said Holmes, sinking back in deep thought. "He is still with you?"

"Oh, yes, sir; I have only just left him."

"And has your business been attended to in your absence?"

"Nothing to complain of, sir. There's never very much to do of a morning."

"That will do, Mr. Wilson. I shall be happy to give you an opinion upon the subject in the course of a day or two. To-day is Saturday, and I hope that by Monday we may come to a conclusion.

"Well, Watson," said Holmes, when our visitor had left us, "what do you make of it all?"

"I make nothing of it," I answered, frankly. "It is a most mysterious business."

"As a rule," said Holmes, "the more bizarre a thing is the less mysterious it proves to be. It is your commonplace, featureless crimes which are really puzzling, just as a commonplace face is the most difficult to identify. But I must be prompt over this matter."

"What are you going to do, then?" I asked.

"To smoke," he answered. "It is quite a three-pipe problem, and I beg that you won't speak to me for fifty minutes." He curled himself up in his chair, with his thin knees drawn up to his hawk-like nose, and there he sat with his eyes closed and his black clay pipe thrusting out like the bill of some strange bird. I had come to the conclusion that he had dropped asleep, and indeed was nodding myself, when he suddenly sprang out of his chair with the gesture of a man who has made up his mind, and put his pipe down upon the mantelpiece.

"Sarasate plays at St. James's Hall this afternoon," he remarked. "What do you think, Watson? Could your patients spare you for a few hours?"

"I have nothing to do to-day. My practice is never very absorbing."

"Then put on your hat and come. I am going through the City first, and we can have some lunch on the way. I observe that there is a good deal of German music on the programme, which is rather more to my taste than Italian or French. It is introspective, and I want to. introspect. Come along!"

We traveled by the Underground as far as Aldersgate; and a short walk took us to Saxe-Coburg Square, the scene of the singular story which we had listened to in the morning. It was a poky, little, shabby-genteel place, where four lines of dingy, two-storied brick houses looked out into a small railed-in inclosure, where a lawn of weedy grass, and a few clumps of faded laurel bushes made a hard fight against a smoke-laden and uncongenial atmosphere.

Three gilt balls and a brown board with JABEZ WILSON in white letters, upon a corner house, announced the place where our red-headed client carried on his business. Sherlock Holmes stopped in front of it with his head on one side, and looked it all over, with his eyes shining brightly between puckered lids. Then he walked slowly up the street, and then down again to the corner, still looking keenly at the houses. Finally he returned to the pawn-broker's and, having thumped vigorously upon the pavement with his stick two or three times, he went up to the door and knocked. It was instantly opened by a bright-looking, clean-shaven young fellow, who asked him to step in.

"Thank you," said Holmes, "I only wished to ask you how you would go from here to the Strand."

"Third right, fourth left," answered the assistant, promptly, closing the door.

"Smart fellow, that," observed Holmes as we walked away. "He is, in my judgment, the fourth smartest man in London, and for daring I am not sure that he has not a claim to be third. I have known something of him before."

"Evidently," said I, "Mr. Wilson's assistant counts for a good deal in this mystery of the Red-headed League. I am sure that you inquired your way merely in order that you might see him."

"Not him."

"What then?"

"The knees of his trousers."

"And what did you see?"

"What I expected to see."

"Why did you beat the pavement?"

"My dear doctor, this is a time for observation, not for talk. We are spies in an enemy's country. We know something of Saxe-Coburg Square. Let us now explore the parts which lie behind it."

The road in which we found ourselves as we turned round the corner from the retired Saxe-Coburg Square presented as great a contrast to it as the front of a picture does to the back. It was one of the main arteries which convey the traffic of the City to the north and west. The roadway was blocked with the immense stream of commerce flowing in a double tide inward and outward, while the footpaths were black with the hurrying swarm of pedestrians. It was difficult to realize, as we looked at the line of fine shops and stately business premises, that they really abutted on the other side upon the faded and stagnant square which we had just quitted.

"Let me see," said Holmes, standing at the corner, and glancing along the line, "I should like just to remember the order of the houses here. It is a hobby of mine to have an exact knowledge of London. There is Mortimer's, the tobacconist; the little newspaper shop, the Coburg branch of the City and Suburban Bank, the Vegetarian Restaurant, and McFarlane's carriage-building depot. That carries us right on to the other block. And now, doctor, we've done our work, so it's time we had some play. A sandwich and a cup of coffee, and then off to violin-land, where all is sweetness, and delicacy, and harmony, and there are no red-headed clients to vex us with their conundrums."

My friend was an enthusiastic musician, being himself not only a very capable performer, but a composer of no ordinary merit. All the afternoon he sat in the stalls wrapped in the most perfect happiness, gently waving his long thin fingers in time to the music, while his gently smiling face and his languid, dreamy eyes were as unlike those of Holmes the sleuth-hound, Holmes the relentless, keen-witted, ready-handed criminal agent, as it was possible to conceive. In his singular character the dual nature alternately asserted itself, and his extreme exactness and astuteness represented, as I have often thought, the reaction against the poetic and contemplative mood which occasionally predominated in him. The swing of his nature took him from extreme languor to devouring energy; and, as I knew well, he was never so truly formidable as when, for days on end, he had been lounging in his armchair amid his improvisations and his black-letter editions.

Then it was that the lust of the chase would suddenly come upon him, and that his brilliant reasoning power would rise to the level of intuition, until those who were unacquainted with his methods would look askance at him as on a man whose knowledge was not that of other mortals. When I saw him that afternoon so en-wrapped in the music at St. James's Hall, I felt that an evil time might be coming upon those whom he had set himself to hunt down.

"You want to go home, no doubt, doctor," he remarked, as we emerged.

"Yes, it would be as well."

"And I have some business to do which will take some hours. This business at Coburg Square is serious."

"Why serious?"

"A considerable crime is in contemplation. I have every reason to believe that we shall be in time to stop it. But to-day being Saturday rather complicates matters. I shall want your help to-night."

"At what time?"

"Ten will be early enough."

"I shall be at Baker Street at ten."

"Very well. And, I say, doctor! there may be some little danger, so kindly put your army revolver in your pocket." He waved his hand, turned on his heel, and disappeared in an instant among the crowd.

I trust that I am not more dense than my neighbors, but I was always oppressed with a sense of my own stupidity in my dealings with Sherlock Holmes. Here I had heard what he had heard, I had seen what he had seen, and yet from his words it was evident that he saw clearly not only what had happened, but what was about to happen, while to me the whole business was still confused and grotesque. As I drove home to my house in Kensington I thought over it all, from the extraordinary story of the red-headed copier of the "Encyclopædia" down to the visit to Saxe-

Coburg Square, and the ominous words with which he had parted from me. What was this nocturnal expedition, and why should I go armed? Where were we going, and what were we to do? I had the hint from Holmes that this smooth-faced pawnbroker's assistant was a formidable man—a man who might play a deep game. I tried to puzzle it out, but gave it up in despair, and set the matter aside until night should bring an explanation.

It was a quarter-past nine when I started from home and made my way across the Park, and so through Oxford Street to Baker Street. Two hansoms were standing at the door, and, as I entered the passage, I heard the sound of voices from above. On entering his room, I found Holmes in animated conversation with two men, one of whom I recognized as Peter Jones, the official police agent; while the other was a long, thin, sad-faced man, with a very shiny hat and oppressively respectable frock-coat.

"Ha! our party is complete," said Holmes, buttoning up his pea-jacket, and taking his heavy hunting crop from the rack. "Watson, I think you know Mr. Jones, of Scotland Yard? Let me introduce you to Mr. Merryweather, who is to be our companion in to-night's adventure."

"We're hunting in couples again, doctor, you see," said Jones, in his consequential way. "Our friend here is a wonderful man for starting a chase. All he wants is an old dog to help him do the running down."

"I hope a wild goose may not prove to be the end of our chase," observed Mr. Merryweather, gloomily.

"You may place considerable confidence in Mr. Holmes, sir," said the police agent, loftily. "He has his own little methods, which are, if he won't mind my saying so, just a little too theoretical and fantastic, but he has the makings of a detective in him. It is not too much to say that once or twice, as in that business of the Sholto murder and the Agra treasure, he has been more nearly correct than the official force."

"Oh, if you say so, Mr. Jones, it is all right!" said the stranger, with deference. "Still, I confess that I miss my rubber. It is the first Saturday night for seven-and-twenty years that I have not had my rubber."

"I think you will find," said Sherlock Holmes, "that you will play for a higher stake to-night than you have ever done yet, and that the play will be more exciting. For you, Mr. Merryweather, the stake will be some thirty thousand pounds; and for you, Jones, it will be the man upon whom you wish to lay your hands."

"John Clay, the murderer, thief, smasher, and forger. He's a young man, Mr. Merryweather, but he is at the head of his profession, and I would rather have my bracelets on him than on any criminal in London. He's a remarkable man, is young John Clay. His grandfather was a Royal Duke, and he himself has been to Eton and Oxford. His brain is as cunning as his fingers, and though we meet signs of him at every turn, we never know where to find the man himself. He'll crack a crib in Scotland one week, and be raising money to build an orphanage in Cornwall the next. I've been on his track for years, and have never set eyes on him yet."

"I hope that I may have the pleasure of introducing you to-night. I've had one or two little turns also with Mr. John Clay, and I agree with you that he is at the head of his profession. It is past ten, however, and quite time that we started. If you two will take the first hansom, Watson and I will follow in the second."

Sherlock Holmes was not very communicative during the long drive, and lay back in the cab humming the tunes which he had heard in the afternoon. We rattled through an endless labyrinth of gas-lit streets until we emerged into Farringdon Street.

"We are close there now," my friend remarked. "This fellow Merryweather is a bank director and personally interested in the matter. I thought it as well to have Jones with us also. He is not a bad fellow, though an absolute imbecile in his profession. He has one positive virtue. He is as brave as a bulldog, and as tenacious as a lobster if he gets his claws upon anyone. Here we are, and they are waiting for us."

We had reached the same crowded thoroughfare in which we had found ourselves in the morning. Our cabs were dismissed, and following the guidance of Mr. Merryweather, we passed down a narrow passage, and through a side door which he opened for us. Within there was a small corridor, which ended in a very massive iron gate. This also was opened, and led down a flight of winding stone steps, which terminated at another formidable gate. Mr. Merryweather stopped to light a lantern, and then conducted us down a dark, earth-smelling passage, and so, after opening a third door, into a huge vault or cellar, which was piled all round with crates and massive boxes.

"You are not very vulnerable from above," Holmes remarked, as he held up the lantern and gazed about him.

"Nor from below," said Mr. Merryweather, striking his stick upon the flags which lined the floor. "Why, dear me, it sounds quite hollow!" he remarked, looking up in surprise.

"I must really ask you to be a little more quiet," said Holmes, severely. "You have already imperiled the whole success of our expedition. Might I beg that you would have the goodness to sit down upon one of those boxes, and not to interfere?"

The solemn Mr. Merryweather perched himself upon a crate, with a very injured expression upon his face while Holmes fell upon his knees upon the floor, and, with the lantern and a magnifying lens, began to examine minutely the cracks between the stones. A few seconds sufficed to satisfy him, for he sprang to his feet again, and put his glass in his pocket.

"We have at least an hour before us," he remarked, "for they can hardly take any steps until the good pawnbroker is safely in bed. Then they will not lose a minute, for the sooner they do their work the longer time they will have for their escape. We are at present, doctor—as no doubt you have divined—in the cellar of the City branch of one of the principal London banks. Mr.

Merryweather is the chairman of directors, and he will explain to you that there are reasons why the more daring criminals of London should take a considerable interest in this cellar at present."

"It is our French gold," whispered the director. "We have had several warnings that an attempt might be made upon it."

"Your French gold?"

"Yes. We had occasion some months ago to strengthen our resources, and borrowed, for that purpose, thirty thousand napoleons from the Bank of France. It has become known that we have never had occasion to unpack the money, and that it is still lying in our cellar. The crate upon which I sit contains two thousand napoleons packed between layers of lead foil. Our reserve of bullion is much larger at present than is usually kept in a single branch office, and the directors have had misgivings upon the subject."

"Which were very well justified," observed Holmes. "And now it is time that we arranged our little plans. I expect that within an hour matters will come to a head. In the meantime, Mr. Merryweather, we must put the screen over that dark lantern."

"And sit in the dark?"

"I am afraid so. I had brought a pack of cards in my pocket, and I thought that, as we were a *partie carrée*, you might have your rubber after all. But I see that the enemy's preparations have gone so far that we cannot risk the presence of a light. And, first of all, we must choose our positions. These are daring men, and, though we shall take them at a disadvantage, they may do us some harm, unless we are careful. I shall stand behind this crate, and do you conceal yourself behind those. Then, when I flash a light upon them, close in swiftly. If they fire, Watson, have no compunction about shooting them down."

I placed my revolver, cocked, upon the top of the wooden case behind which I crouched. Holmes shot the slide across the front of his lantern, and left us in pitch darkness—such an absolute darkness as I have never before experienced. The smell of hot metal remained to assure us that the light was still there, ready to flash out at a moment's notice. To me, with my nerves worked up to a pitch of expectancy, there was something depressing and subduing in the sudden gloom, and in the cold, dank air of the vault.

"They have but one retreat," whispered Holmes. "That is back through the house into Saxe-Coburg Square. I hope that you have done what I asked you, Jones?"

"I have an inspector and two officers waiting at the front door."

"Then we have stopped all the holes. And now we must be silent and wait."

What a time it seemed! From comparing notes afterwards, it was but an hour and a quarter, yet it appeared to me that the night must have almost gone, and the dawn be breaking above us. My limbs were weary and stiff, for I feared to change my position, yet my nerves were worked up to the highest pitch of tension, and my hearing was so acute that I could not only hear the gentle breathing of my companions, but I could distinguish the deeper, heavier inbreath of the bulky Jones from the thin, sighing note of the bank director. From my position I could look over the case in the direction of the floor. Suddenly my eyes caught the glint of a light.

At first it was but a lurid spark upon the stone pavement. Then it lengthened out until it became a yellow line, and then, without any warning or sound, a gash seemed to open and a hand appeared, a white, almost womanly hand, which felt about in the center of the little area of light. For a minute or more the hand, with its writhing fingers, protruded out of the floor. Then it was withdrawn as suddenly as it appeared, and all was dark again save the single lurid spark, which marked a chink between the stones.

Its disappearance, however, was but momentary. With a rending, tearing sound, one of the broad white stones turned over upon its side, and left a square, gaping hole, through which streamed the light of a lantern. Over the edge there peeped a clean-cut, boyish face, which looked keenly about it, and then, with a hand on either side of the aperture, drew itself shoulder-high and waist-high, until one knee rested upon the edge. In another instant he stood at the side of the hole, and was hauling after him a companion, lithe and small like himself, with a pale face and a shock of very red hair.

"It's all clear," he whispered. "Have you the chisel and the bags? Great Scott! Jump, Archie, jump, and I'll swing for it!"

Sherlock Holmes had sprung out and seized the intruder by the collar. The other dived down the hole, and I heard the sound of rending cloth as Jones clutched at his skirts. The light flashed upon the barrel of a revolver, but Holmes's hunting crop came down on the man's wrist, and the pistol clinked upon the stone floor.

"It's no use, John Clay," said Holmes, blandly, "you have no chance at all."

"So I see," the other answered, with the utmost coolness. "I fancy that my pal is all right, though I see you have got his coat-tails."

"There are three men waiting for him at the door," said Holmes.

"Oh, indeed. You seem to have done the thing very completely. I must compliment you."

"And I you," Holmes answered. "Your red-headed idea was very new and effective."

"You'll see your pal again presently," said Jones. "He's quicker at climbing down holes than I am. Just hold out while I fix the derbies."

"I beg that you will not touch me with your filthy hands," remarked our prisoner, as the handcuffs clattered upon his wrists. "You may not be aware that I have royal blood in my veins. Have the goodness also, when you address me, always to say 'sir' and 'please.' "

"All right," said Jones, with a stare and a snigger. "Well, would you please, sir, march upstairs where we can get a cab to carry your highness to the police station."

"That is better," said John Clay, serenely. He made a sweeping bow to the three of us, and walked quietly off in the custody of the detective.

"Really, Mr. Holmes," said Mr. Merryweather, as we followed them from the cellar, "I do not know how the bank can thank you or repay you. There is no doubt that you have detected and defeated in the most complete manner one of the most determined attempts at bank robbery that have ever come within my experience."

"I have had one or two little scores of my own to settle with Mr. John Clay," said Holmes. "I have been at some small expense over this matter, which I shall expect the bank to refund, but beyond that I am amply repaid by having had an experience which is in many ways unique, and by hearing the very remarkable narrative of the Red-headed League."

"You see, Watson," he explained, in the early hours of the morning, as we sat over a glass of whisky and soda in Baker Street, "it was perfectly obvious from the first that the only possible object of this rather fantastic business of the advertisement of the League, and the copying of the 'Encyclopædia,' must be to get this not over-bright pawnbroker out of the way for a number of hours every day. It was a curious way of managing it, but really it would be difficult to suggest a better. The method was no doubt suggested to Clay's ingenious mind by the color of his accomplice's hair. The four pounds a week was a lure which must draw him, and what was it to them, who were playing for thousands? They put in the advertisement, one rogue has the temporary office, the other rogue incites the man to apply for it, and together they manage to secure his absence every morning in the week. From the time that I heard of the assistant having come for half wages, it was obvious to me that he had some strong motive for securing the situation."

"But how could you guess what the motive was?"

"Had there been women in the house, I should have suspected a mere vulgar intrigue. That, however, was out of the question. The man's business was a small one, and there was nothing in his house which could account for such elaborate preparations, and such an expenditure as they were at. It must then be something out of the house. What could it be? I thought of the assistant's fondness for photography, and his trick of vanishing into the cellar. The cellar! There was the end of this tangled clew. Then I made inquiries as to this mysterious assistant, and found that I had to deal with one of the coolest and most daring criminals in London. He was doing something in the cellar—something which took many hours a day for months on end. What could it be, once more? I could think of nothing save that he was running a tunnel to some other building.

"So far I had got when we went to visit the scene of action. I surprised you by beating upon the pavement with my stick. I was ascertaining whether the cellar stretched out in front or behind. It was not in front. Then I rang the bell, and, as I hoped, the assistant answered it. We have had some skirmishes, but we had never set eyes upon each other before. I hardly looked at his face. His knees were what I wished to see. You must yourself have remarked how worn, wrinkled, and stained they were. They spoke of those hours of burrowing. The only remaining point was what they were burrowing for. I walked round the corner, saw that the City and Suburban Bank abutted on our friend's premises, and felt that I had solved my problem. When you drove home after the concert I called upon Scotland Yard, and upon the chairman of the bank directors, with the result that you have seen."

"And how could you tell that they would make their attempt to-night?" I asked.

"Well, when they closed their League offices that was a sign that they cared no longer about Mr. Jabez Wilson's presence; in other words, that they had completed their tunnel. But it was essential that they should use it soon, as it might be discovered, or the bullion might be removed. Saturday would suit them better than any other day, as it would give them two days for their escape. For all these reasons I expected them to come to-night."

"You reasoned it out beautifully," I exclaimed, in unfeigned admiration. "It is so long a chain, and yet every link rings true."

"It saved me from ennui," he answered, yawning. "Alas! I already feel it closing in upon me. My life is spent in one long effort to escape from the commonplaces of existence. These little problems help me to do so."

"And you are a benefactor of the race," said I. He shrugged his shoulders. "Well, perhaps, after all, it is of some little use," he remarked. " 'L'homme c'est rien—l'œuvre c'est tout,' as Gustave Flaubert wrote to George Sand."

1. What is Holmes's attitude toward Watson?
2. What is Watson's exact purpose in the story?
3. At what points do you first suspect the villain and the type of crime?
4. Does the old-fashioned air, with its hansoms, gas lamps, and dark lanterns, lessen your enjoyment of the story?
5. How real does Holmes appear to you?

*Dorothy Sayers*

# THE ENTERTAINING EPISODE OF
# THE ARTICLE IN QUESTION

THE unprofessional detective career of Lord Peter Wimsey was regulated (though the word has no particular propriety in this connection) by a persistent and undignified inquisitiveness. The habit of asking silly questions—natural, though irritating, in the immature male—remained with him long after his immaculate man, Bunter, had become attached to his service to shave the bristles from his chin and see to the due purchase and housing of Napoleon brandies and Villar y Villar cigars. At the age of thirty-two his sister Mary christened him Elephant's Child. It was his idiotic enquiries (before his brother, the Duke of Denver, who grew scarlet with mortification) as to what the Woolsack was really stuffed with that led the then Lord Chancellor idly to investigate the article in question, and to discover, tucked deep within its recesses, that famous diamond necklace of the Marchioness of Writtle, which had disappeared on the day Parliament was opened and been safely secreted by one of the cleaners. It was by a continual and personal badgering of the Chief Engineer at 2LO on the question of "Why is Oscillation and How is it Done?" that his lordship incidentally unmasked the great Ploffsky gang of Anarchist conspirators, who were accustomed to converse in code by a methodical system of howls, superimposed (to the great annoyance of listeners in British and European stations) upon the London wave-length and duly relayed by 5XX over a radius of some five or six hundred miles. He annoyed persons of more leisure than decorum by suddenly taking into his head to descend to the Underground by way of the stairs, though the only exciting things he ever actually found there were the bloodstained boots of the Sloane Square murderer; on the other hand when the drains were taken up at Glegg's Folly, it was by hanging about and hindering the plumbers at their job that he accidentally made the discovery which hanged that detestable poisoner, William Girdlestone Chitty.

Accordingly, it was with no surprise at all that the reliable Bunter, one April morning, received the announcement of an abrupt change of plan.

They had arrived at the Gare St. Lazare in good time to register the luggage. Their three months' trip to Italy had been purely for enjoyment, and had been followed by a pleasant fortnight in Paris. They were now intending to pay a short visit to the Duc de Sainte-Croix in Rouen on their way back to England. Lord Peter paced the Salle des Pas Perdus for some time, buying an illustrated paper or two and eyeing the crowd. He bent an appreciative eye on a slim, shingled creature with the face of a Paris *gamin*, but was forced to admit to himself that her ankles were a trifle on the thick side; he assisted an elderly lady who was explaining to the bookstall clerk that she wanted a map of Paris and not a *carte postale*, consumed a quick cognac at one of the little green tables at the far end, and then decided he had better go down and see how Bunter was getting on.

In half an hour Bunter and his porter had worked themselves up to the second place in the enormous queue—for, as usual, one of the weighing-machines was out of order. In front of them stood an agitated little group—the young woman Lord Peter had noticed in the Salle des Pas Perdus, a sallow-faced man of about thirty, their porter, and the registration official, who was peering eagerly through his little *guichet.*

"*Mais je te répéte que je ne les ai pas,*" said the sallow man heatedly. "*Voyons, voyons. C'est bien toi qui les as pris, n'est-ce pas? Eh bien, alors, comment veux-tu que je les aie, moi?*"

"*Mais non, mais non, je te les ai bien donnés là-haut, avant d'aller chercher les journaux.*"

"*Je t'assure que non. Enfin, c'est évident! J'ai cherché partout, que diable! Tu ne m'as rien donné, du tout, du tout.*"

"*Mais puisque je t'ai dit d'aller faire enrégistrer les bagages! Ne faut-il pas que je t'aie bien remis les billets? Me prends-tu pour un imbécile? Va! On n'est pas dépourvu de sens! Mais regarde l'heure! Le train part à 11 h. 20 m. Cherche un peu, au moins.*"

"*Mais puisque j'ai cherché partout—le gilet, rien! Le jacquet rien, rien! Le pardessus—rien! rien! rien! C'est toi—*"

Here the porter, urged by the frantic cries and stamping of the queue, and the repeated insults of Lord Peter's porter, flung himself into the discussion.

"*P't-être qu' m'sieur a bouté les billets dans son pantalon,*" he suggested.

"*Triple idiot!*" snapped the traveller, "*je vous le demande—est-ce qu'on a jamais entendu parler de mettre des billets dans son pantalon? Jamais—*"

The French porter is a Republican, and, moreover, extremely ill-paid. The large tolerance of his English colleague is not for him.

"*Ah!*" said he, dropping two heavy bags and looking round for moral support. "*Vous dites? En voilà du joli! Allons, mon p'tit, ce n'est pas parcequ'on porte un faux-col qu'on a le droit d'insulter les gens.*"

The discussion might have become a full-blown row, had not the young man suddenly discovered the missing tickets—incidentally, they were in his trousers-pocket after all—and continued the registration of his luggage, to the undisguised satisfaction of the crowd.

"Bunter," said his lordship, who had turned his back on the group and was lighting a cigarette, "I am going to change the tickets. We shall go straight on to London. Have you got that snapshot affair of yours with you?"

"Yes, my lord."

"The one you can work from your pocket without anyone noticing?"

"Yes, my lord."

"Get me a picture of those two."

"Yes, my lord."

"I will see to the luggage. Wire to the Duc that I am unexpectedly called home."

"Very good, my lord."

Lord Peter did not allude to the matter again till Bunter was putting his trousers in the press in their cabin on board the *Normannia*. Beyond ascertaining that the young man and woman who had aroused his curiosity were on the boat as second-class passengers, he had sedulously avoided contact with them.

"Did you get that photograph?"

"I hope so, my lord. As your lordship knows, the aim from the breast-pocket tends to be unreliable. I have made three attempts, and trust that one at least may prove to be not unsuccessful."

"How soon can you develop them?"

"At once, if your lordship pleases. I have all the materials in my suit case."

"What fun!" said Lord Peter, eagerly tying himself into a pair of mauve silk pyjamas. "May I hold the bottles and things?"

Mr. Bunter poured 3 ounces of water into an 8-ounce measure, and handed his master a glass rod and a minute packet.

"If your lordship would be so good as to stir the contents of the white packet slowly into the water," he said, bolting the door, "and, when dissolved, add the contents of the blue packet."

"Just like a Seidlitz powder," said his lordship happily. "Does it fizz?"

"Not much, my lord," replied the expert, shaking a quantity of hypo crystals into the hand-basin.

"That's a pity," said Lord Peter. "I say, Bunter, it's no end of a bore to dissolve."

"Yes, my lord," returned Bunter sedately. "I have always found that part of the process exceptionally tedious, my lord."

Lord Peter jabbed viciously with the glass rod.

"Just you wait," he said, in a vindictive tone, "till we get to Waterloo."

.     .     .     .     .     .     .

Three days later Lord Peter Wimsey sat in his book-lined sitting-room at 110A Piccadilly. The tall bunches of daffodils on the table smiled in the spring sunshine, and nodded to the breeze which danced in from the open window. The door opened, and his lordship glanced up from a handsome edition of the Contes de la Fontaine, whose handsome hand-coloured Fragonard plates he was examining with the aid of a lens.

"Morning, Bunter. Anything doing?"

"I have ascertained, my lord, that the young person in question has entered the service of the elder Duchess of Medway. Her name is Célestine Berger."

"You are less accurate than usual, Bunter. Nobody off the stage is called Célestine. You should say 'under the name of Célestine Berger.' And the man?"

"He is domiciled at this address in Guilford Street, Bloomsbury, my lord."

"Excellent, my Bunter. Now give me *Who's Who*. Was it a very tiresome job?"

"Not exceptionally so, my lord."

"One of these days I suppose I shall give you something to do which you will jib at," said his lordship, "and you will leave me and I shall cut my throat. Thanks. Run away and play. I shall lunch at the club."

The book which Bunter had handed his employer indeed bore the words *Who's Who* engrossed upon its cover, but it was to be found in no public library and in no bookseller's shop. It was a bulky manuscript, closely filled, in part with the small print-like handwriting of Mr. Bunter, in part with Lord Peter's neat and altogether illegible hand. It contained biographies of the most unexpected people, and the most unexpected facts about the most obvious people. Lord Peter turned to a very long entry under the name of the Dowager Duchess of Medway. It appeared to make satisfactory reading, for after a time he smiled, closed the book, and went to the telephone.

"Yes—this is the Duchess of Medway. Who is it?"

The deep, harsh old voice pleased Lord Peter. He could see the imperious face and upright figure of what had been the most famous beauty in the London of the 'sixties.

"It's Peter Wimsey, duchess."

"Indeed, and how do you do, young man? Back from your Continental jaunting?"

"Just home—and longing to lay my devotion at the feet of the most fascinating lady in England."

"God bless my soul, child, what do you want?" demanded the duchess. "Boys like you don't flatter an old woman for nothing."

"I want to tell you my sins, duchess."

"You should have lived in the great days," said the voice appreciatively. "Your talents are wasted on the young fry."

"That is why I want to talk to you, duchess."

"Well, my dear, if you've committed any sins worth hearing I shall enjoy your visit."

"You are as exquisite in kindness as in charm. I am coming this afternoon."

"I will be at home to you and to no one else. There."

"Dear lady, I kiss your hands," said Lord Peter, and he heard a deep chuckle as the duchess rang off.

. . . . . . .

"You may say what you like, duchess," said Lord Peter from his reverential position on the fender-stool, "but you are the youngest grandmother in London, not excepting my own mother."

"Dear Honoria is the merest child," said the duchess. "I have twenty years more experience of life, and have arrived at the age when we boast of them. I have every intention of being a great-grandmother before I die. Sylvia is being married in a fortnight's time, to that stupid son of Attenbury's."

"Abcock?"

"Yes. He keeps the worst hunters I ever saw, and doesn't know still champagne from sauterne. But Sylvia is stupid, too, poor child, so I dare say they will get on charmingly. In my day one had to have either brains or beauty to get on—preferably both. Nowadays nothing seems to be required but a total lack of figure. But all the sense went out of society with the House of Lords' veto. I except you, Peter. You have talents. It is a pity you do not employ them in politics."

"Dear lady, God forbid."

"Perhaps you are right, as things are. There were giants in my day. Dear Dizzy. I remember so well, when his wife died, how hard we all tried to get him—Medway had died the year before—but he was wrapped up in that stupid Bradford woman, who had never even read a line of one of his books, and couldn't have understood 'em if she had. And now we have Abcock standing for Midhurst, and married to Sylvia!"

"You haven't invited me to the wedding, duchess dear. I'm so hurt," sighed his lordship.

"Bless you, child, I didn't send out the invitations, but I suppose your brother and that tiresome wife of his will be there. You must come, of course, if you want to. I had no idea you had a passion for weddings."

"Hadn't you?" said Peter. "I have a passion for this one. I want to see Lady Sylvia wearing white satin and the family lace and diamonds, and to sentimentalise over the days when my fox-terrier bit the stuffing out of her doll."

"Very well, my dear, you shall. Come early and give me your support. As for the diamonds, if it weren't a family tradition, Sylvia shouldn't wear them. She has the impudence to complain of them."

"I thought they were some of the finest in existence."

"So they are. But she says the settings are ugly and old-fashioned, and she doesn't like diamonds, and they won't go with her dress. Such nonsense. Whoever heard of a girl not liking diamonds? She wants to be something romantic and moonshiny in pearls. I have no patience with her."

"I'll promise to admire them," said Peter—"use the privilege of early acquaintance and tell her she's an ass and so on. I'd love to have a view of them. When do they come out of cold storage?"

"Mr. Whitehead will bring them up from the Bank the night before," said the duchess, "and they'll go into the safe in my room. Come round at twelve o'clock and you shall have a private view of them."

"That would be delightful. Mind they don't disappear in the night, won't you?"

"Oh, my dear, the house is going to be over-run with policemen. Such a nuisance. I suppose it can't be helped."

"Oh, I think it's a good thing," said Peter. "I have rather an unwholesome weakness for policemen."

On the morning of the wedding-day, Lord Peter emerged from Bunter's hands a marvel of sleek brilliance. His primrose-coloured hair was so exquisite a work of art that to eclipse it with his glossy hat was like shutting up the sun in a shrine of polished jet; his spats, light trousers, and exquisitely polished shoes formed a tone-symphony in monochrome. It was only by the most impassioned pleading that he persuaded his tyrant to allow him to place two small photographs and a thin, foreign letter in his breast-pocket. Mr. Bunter, likewise immaculately attired, stepped into the taxi after him. At noon precisely they were deposited beneath the striped awning which adorned the door of the Duchess of Medway's house in Park Lane. Bunter promptly disappeared in the direction of the back entrance, while his lordship mounted the steps and asked to see the dowager.

The majority of the guests had not yet arrived, but the house was full of agitated people, flitting hither and thither, with flowers and prayer-books, while a clatter of dishes and cutlery from the dining-room proclaimed the laying of a sumptuous breakfast. Lord Peter was shown into the morning-room while the footman went to announce him, and here he found a very close friend and devoted colleague, Detective-Inspector Parker, mounting guard in plain clothes over a costly collection of white elephants. Lord Peter greeted him with an affectionate hand-grip.

"All serene so far?" he enquired.

"Perfectly O.K."

"You got my note?"

"Sure thing. I've got three of our men shadowing your friend in Guilford Street. The girl is very much in evidence here. Does the old lady's wig and that sort of thing. Bit of a coming-on disposition, isn't she?"

"You surprise me," said Lord Peter. "No"—as his friend grinned sardonically—"you really do. Not seriously? That would throw all my calculations out."

"Oh, no! Saucy with her eyes and her tongue, that's all."

"Do her job well?"

"I've heard no complaints. What put you on to this?"

"Pure accident. Of course I may be quite mistaken."

"Did you receive any information from Paris?"

"I wish you wouldn't use that phrase," said Lord Peter peevishly. "It's so of the Yard—yardy. One of these days it'll give you away."

"Sorry," said Parker. "Second nature, I suppose."

"Those are the things to beware of," returned his lordship, with an earnestness that seemed a little out of place. "One can keep guard on everything but just those second-nature tricks." He moved across to the window, which overlooked the tradesmen's entrance. "Hullo!" he said, "here's our bird."

Parker joined him, and saw the neat, shingled head of the French girl from the Gare St. Lazare, topped by a neat black bandeau and bow. A man with a basket full of white narcissi had rung the bell, and appeared to be trying to make a sale. Parker gently opened the window, and they heard Célestine say with a marked French accent, "No, nossing to-day, sank you." The man insisted in the monotonous whine of his type, thrusting a big bunch of the white flowers upon her, but she pushed them back into the basket with an angry exclamation and flirted away, tossing her head and slapping the door smartly to. The man moved off muttering. As he did so a thin, unhealthy-looking lounger in a check cap detached himself from a lamp-post opposite and mouched along the street after him, at the same time casting a glance up at the window. Mr. Parker looked at Lord Peter, nodded, and made a slight sign with his hand. At once the man in the check cap removed his cigarette from his mouth, extinguished it, and, tucking the stub behind his ear, moved off without a second glance.

"Very interesting," said Lord Peter, when both were out of sight. "Hark!"

There was a sound of running feet overhead—a cry—and a general commotion. The two men dashed to the door as the bride, rushing frantically downstairs with her bevy of bridesmaids after her, proclaimed in a hysterical shriek: "The diamonds! They're stolen! They're gone!"

Instantly the house was in an uproar. The servants and the caterers' men crowded into the hall; the bride's father burst out from his room in a magnificent white waistcoat and no coat; the Duchess of Medway descended upon Mr. Parker, demanding that something should be done; while the butler, who never to the day of his death got over the disgrace, ran out of the pantry with a corkscrew in one hand and a priceless bottle of crusted port in the other, which he shook with all the vehemence of a town-crier ringing a bell. The only dignified entry was made by the dowager duchess, who came down like a ship in sail, dragging Célestine with her, and admonishing her not to be so silly.

"Be quiet, girl," said the dowager. "Anyone would think you were going to be murdered."

"Allow me, your grace," said Mr. Bunter, appearing suddenly from nowhere in his usual unperturbed manner, and taking the agitated Célestine firmly by the arm. "Young woman, calm yourself."

"But what is to be done?" cried the bride's mother. "How did it happen?"

It was at this moment that Detective-Inspector Parker took the floor. It was the most impressive and dramatic moment in his whole career. His magnificent calm rebuked the clamorous nobility surrounding him.

"Your grace," he said, "there is no cause for alarm. Our measures have been taken. We have the criminals and the gems, thanks to Lord Peter Wimsey, from whom we received inf—"

"Charles!" said Lord Peter in an awful voice.

"Warning of the attempt. One of our men is just bringing in the male criminal at the front door, taken red-handed with your grace's diamonds in his possession." (All gazed round, and perceived indeed the check-capped lounger and a uniformed constable entering with the flower-seller between them.) "The female criminal, who picked the lock of your grace's safe, is—here! No, you don't," he added, as Célestine, amid a torrent of apache language which nobody, fortunately, had French enough to understand, attempted to whip out a revolver from the bosom of her demure black dress. "Célestine Berger," he continued, pocketing the weapon, "I arrest you in the name of the law, and I warn you that anything you say will be taken down and used as evidence against you."

"Heaven help us," said Lord Peter; "the roof would fly off the court. And you've got the name wrong, Charles. Ladies and gentlemen, allow me to introduce to you Jacques Lerouge, known as Sans-culotte—the youngest and cleverest thief, safe-breaker, and female impersonator that ever occupied a dossier in the Palais de Justice."

There was a gasp. Jacques Sans-culotte gave vent to a low oath and cocked a *gamin* grimace at Peter.

"*C'est parfait*," said he; "*toutes mes félicitations, milord*, what you call a fair cop, *hein?* And now I know him," he added, grinning at Bunter, "the so-patient Englishman who stand behind us in the queue at St. Lazare. But tell me, please, how you know me, that I may correct it, *next time*."

"I have mentioned to you before, Charles," said Lord Peter, "the unwisdom of falling into habits of speech. They give you away. Now, in France, every male child is brought up to use masculine adjectives about himself. He says: *Que je suis beau!* But a little girl has it rammed home to her that she is female; she must say: *Que je suis belle!* It must make it beastly hard to be a female impersonator. When I am at a station and I hear an excited young woman say to her companion, "*Me prends-tu pour un imbécile*—the masculine article arouses curiosity. And that's that!" he concluded briskly. "The rest was merely a matter of getting Bunter to take a photograph and communicating with our friends of the Sûreté and Scotland Yard."

Jacques Sans-culotte bowed again.

"Once more I congratulate milord. He is the only Englishman I have ever met who is capable of appreciating our beautiful language. I will pay great attention in future to the article in question."

With an awful look, the Dowager Duchess of Medway advanced upon Lord Peter.

"Peter," she said, "do you mean to say you *knew* about this, and that for the last three weeks you have allowed me to be dressed and undressed and put to bed by a *young man?*"

His lordship had the grace to blush.

"Duchess," he said humbly, "on my honour I didn't know absolutely for certain till this morning. And the police were so anxious to have these people caught red-handed. What can I do to show my penitence? Shall I cut the privileged beast in pieces?"

The grim old mouth relaxed a little.

"After all," said the dowager duchess, with the delightful consciousness that she was going to shock her daughter-in-law, "there are very few woman of my age who could make the same boast. It seems that we die as we have lived, my dear."

For indeed the Dowager Duchess of Medway had been notable in her day.

> From *Lord Peter Views the Body*. Reprinted by permission of Ann Watkins, Inc., the author's literary agent.

> 1. Lord Peter Wimsey is set down as an unprofessional detective; what is "unprofessional" about the story?
> 2. From the standpoint of style, what word would you use to describe the manner of writing?
> 3. What British ways of expression, such as "that snapshot affair," can you discern?
> 4. Why is there so much French in the story?
> 5. Is Lord Peter the sort of person of whose "further adventures" you would like to hear more?

# VI. COUNTRY

# VI. COUNTRY

A SYMPTOM of complex urban civilization has always been the glorification of country life. In classical times, Theocritus in Alexandria and Virgil in Rome sang of the simple pleasures and simple virtues of shepherds and farmers, and the tradition has continued down to the present day. Artificiality, hypocrisy, and greed were supposed to thrive in the city; rural folk lived close to nature and drew strength and virtue from the soil. La Fontaine's fable of the town rat and the country rat summed up the whole convention—the more so as La Fontaine, like Theocritus and Virgil, had never the slightest real desire to live the simple life of which he sang.

Like so many other European literary conventions, this one was adopted early in America, and figures equally in Royal Tyler's comedy, *The Contrast* (1787), and in tales like "The Wife" and "The Pride of the Village" in Irving's *Sketch Book*. A century later it was still going strong in such popular dramas as *Way Down East* and *Shore Acres*. Meantime, it had been powerfully reinforced by the earlier novels and short stories of the local color school.

Local color as a deliberate and self-conscious element in American fiction is generally held to begin with the publication of Bret Harte's "The Luck of Roaring Camp" in 1868. In the following year Mrs. Stowe's *Oldtown Folks* broke Down East soil, and during the next twenty years Georgia Negroes, Tennessee mountaineers, Louisiana Creoles, and the loggers and farmers of the Upper Lakes all furnished their quotas of picturesque detail, quaint dialect, and eccentric character. Before 1890, however, a new note of rebellion and social criticism began to sound in local color fiction. On the surface, the stories of Sarah Orne Jewett and Mary Wilkins Freeman are simple tales of simple New England folk. Implicit in them, nevertheless, is criticism of the narrow environment and harsh living conditions which warp or thwart the lives of so many of the characters. Both Miss Jewett and Mrs. Freeman were too clear-eyed to pretend that all was well with a New England drained of its most vigorous manhood by the Civil War and by the lure of factory towns and Western farms.

What these women merely suggested was spoken out, and underscored, by Hamlin Garland in the series of stories which he collected under the title of *Main-Traveled Roads*. Bred up in struggles against nature and economic forces on a succession of newly broken prairie farms, Garland at last rebelled. A pilgrimage to the East, followed by a winter in Boston, gave the young farmer a glimpse of the arts and graces of life which his prairie environment had robbed him of in his boyhood. At the same time, acquaintance with the single-tax doctrines of Henry George awakened him to the nature of the economic forces against which he had seen his father and his neighbors struggling. This combination of economic doctrine with personal rebellion enabled him to make explicit—sometimes too explicit—the social criticism which Miss Jewett and Mrs. Freeman had merely implied. Garland gave the rural story of America the tone which has dominated it ever since. From being a simple narrative of homely virtues in a homely setting, it became a social document.

In most of his rural characters, Garland still clung to the remnants of the romantic tradition. His real villains are bankers and city folk; most of his farmers, he seems to say, would have been generous and upright if their harsh environment had not warped them. Infuriated by stories which ignored the physical muck and sweat and smells of the farm, Garland used them in full measure. But the next generation of story writers went further than he had in depicting moral stenches. From Willa Cather's early stories, through Sherwood Anderson's *Winesburg, Ohio* (1919), Sinclair Lewis's *Main Street* (1920), and Ruth Suckow's *Country People* (1924), down to William Faulkner and Erskine Caldwell, the dominant tone has been anger or despair. Rural and small town life at best is depicted as narrow, boresome, and stultifying; at worst, it concentrates all the phases of physical, mental, and moral degeneracy.

Essentially, of course, such an attitude is nothing but inverted romanticism. In revolting against the pretty-pretty glorification of rural life the rebels have swung to an even more extreme denigration. It is a good thing to remember that country people, like other human beings, may be mean and petty and cruel, but it is not necessary to forget that they may also have their fair allotment of human virtues. The time must be almost ripe for a return to cheerfulness in the portrayal of the village and the farm—or, if not to cheerfulness, at least to a steadier and better balanced view of the people who live there.

*David Grayson*

# THE COUNTRY DOCTOR

Sunday afternoon, June 9.

WE HAD a funeral to-day in this community and the longest funeral procession, Charles Baxter says, he has seen in all the years of his memory among these hills. A good man has gone away—and yet remains. In the comparatively short time I have been here I never came to know him well personally, though I saw him often in the country roads, a ruddy old gentleman with thick, coarse, iron-gray hair, somewhat stern of countenance, somewhat shabby of attire, sitting as erect as a trooper in his open buggy, one muscular hand resting on his knee, the other holding the reins of his familiar old white horse. I said I did not come to know him well personally, and yet no one who knows this community can help knowing Doctor John North. I never so desired the gift of moving expression as I do at this moment, on my return from his funeral, that I may give some faint idea of what a good man means to a community like ours—as the more complete knowledge of it has come to me to-day.

In the district school that I attended when a boy we used to love to leave our mark, as we called it, wherever our rovings led us. It was a bit of boyish mysticism, unaccountable now that we have grown older and wiser (perhaps); but it had its meaning. It was an instinctive outreaching of the young soul to perpetuate the knowledge of its existence upon this forgetful earth. My mark, I remember, was a notch and a cross. With what secret fond diligence I carved it in the gray bark of beech trees, on fence posts, or on barn doors, and once, I remember, on the roof-ridge of our home, and once, with high imaginings of how long it would remain, I spent hours chiseling it deep in a hard-headed old boulder in the pasture, where, if man has been as kind as Nature, it remains to this day. If you should chance to see it you would not know of the boy who carved it there.

So Doctor North left his secret mark upon the neighbourhood— as all of us do, for good or for ill, upon our neighbourhoods, in accordance with the strength of that character which abides within us. For a long time I did not know that it was he, though it was not difficult to see that some strong good man had often passed this way. I saw the mystic sign of him deep-lettered in the hearthstone of a home; I heard it speaking bravely from the weak lips of a friend; it is carved in the plastic heart of many a boy. No, I do not doubt the immortalities of the soul; in this community, which I have come to love so much, dwells more than one of John North's immortalities—and will continue to dwell. I, too, live more deeply because John North was here.

He was in no outward way an extraordinary man, nor was his life eventful. He was born in this neighbourhood: I saw him lying quite still this morning in the same sunny room of the same house where he first saw the light of day. Here among these common hills he grew up, and save for the few years he spent at school or in the army, he lived here all his life long. In old neighbourhoods and especially farm neighbourhoods people come to know one another—not clothes knowledge, or money knowledge—but that sort of knowledge which reaches down into the hidden springs of human character. A country community may be deceived by a stranger, too easily deceived, but not by one of its own people. For it is not a studied knowledge; it resembles that slow geologic uncovering before which not even the deep buried bones of the prehistoric saurian remain finally hidden.

I never fully realised until this morning what a supreme triumph it is, having grown old, to merit the respect of those who know us best. Mere greatness offers no reward to compare with it, for greatness compels that homage which we freely bestow upon goodness. So long as I live I shall never forget this morning. I stood in the door-yard outside of the open window of the old doctor's home. It was soft, and warm, and very still—a June Sunday morning. An apple tree not far off was still in blossom, and across the road on a grassy hillside sheep fed unconcernedly. Occasionally, from the roadway where the horses of the countryside were waiting, I heard the clink of a bit-ring or the low voice of some new-comer seeking a place to hitch. Not half those who came could find room in the house: they stood uncovered among the trees. From within, wafted through the window, came the faint odour of flowers, and the occasional minor intonation of someone speaking—and finally our own Scotch Preacher! I could not see him, but there lay in the cadences of his voice a peculiar note of peacefulness, of finality. The day before he died Doctor North had said:

"I want McAlway to conduct my funeral, not as a minister but as a man. He has been my friend for forty years; he will know what I mean."

The Scotch Preacher did not say much. Why should he? Everyone there knew: and speech would only have cheapened what we knew. And I do not now recall even the little he said, for there was so much all about me that spoke not of the death of a good man, but of his life. A boy who stood near me—a boy no longer, for he was as tall as a man—gave a more eloquent tribute than any preacher could have done. I saw him stand his ground for a time with that grim courage of youth which dreads emotion more than a battle: and then I saw him crying behind a tree! He was not a relative of the old doctor's; he was only one of many into whose deep life the doctor had entered.

They sang "Lead, Kindly Light," and came out through the narrow doorway into the sunshine with the coffin, the hats of the pall-bearers in a row on top, and there was hardly a dry eye among us.

And as they came out through the narrow doorway, I thought how the Doctor must have looked out daily through so many, many years upon this beauty of hills and fields and of sky above, grown dearer from long familiarity—which he would know no more. And Kate North, the Doctor's sister, his only relative, followed behind, her fine old face gray and set, but without a tear in her eye. How like the Doctor she looked: the same stern control!

In the hours which followed, on the pleasant winding way to the cemetery, in the groups under the trees, on the way homeward again, the community spoke its true heart, and I have come back with the feeling that human nature, at bottom, is sound and sweet. I knew a great deal before about Doctor North, but I knew it as knowledge, not as emotion, and therefore it was not really a part of my life.

I heard again the stories of how he drove the country roads, winter and summer, how he had seen most of the population into the world and had held the hands of many who went out! It was the plain, hard life of a country doctor, and yet it seemed to rise in our community like some great tree, its roots deep buried in the soil of our common life, its branches close to the sky. To those accustomed to the outward excitements of city life it would have seemed barren and uneventful. It was significant that the talk was not so much of what the Doctor did as of *how* he did it, not so much of his actions as of the natural expression of his character. And when we come to think of it, goodness *is* uneventful. It does not flash, it glows. It is deep, quiet and very simple. It passes not with oratory, it is commonly foreign to riches, nor does it often sit in the places of the mighty: but may be felt in the touch of a friendly hand or the look of a kindly eye.

Outwardly, John North often gave the impression of brusqueness. Many a woman, going to him for the first time, and until she learned that he was in reality as gentle as a girl, was frightened by his manner. The country is full of stories of such encounters. We laugh yet over the adventure of a woman who formerly came to spend her summers here. She dressed very beautifully and was "nervous." One day she went to call on the Doctor. He made a careful examination and asked many questions. Finally he said, with portentous solemnity:

"Madam, you're suffering from a very common complaint."

The Doctor paused, then continued, impressively:

"You haven't enough work to do. This is what I would advise. Go home, discharge your servants, do your own cooking, wash your own clothes and make your own beds. You'll get well."

She is reported to have been much offended, and yet to-day there was a wreath of white roses in Doctor North's room sent from the city by that woman.

If he really hated anything in this world the Doctor hated whimperers. He had a deep sense of the purpose and need of punishment, and he despised those who fled from wholesome discipline.

A young fellow once went to the Doctor—so they tell the story—and asked for something to stop his pain.

"Stop it!" exclaimed the Doctor: "why, it's good for you. You've done wrong, haven't you? Well, you're being punished; take it like a man. There's nothing more wholesome than good honest pain."

And yet how much pain he alleviated in this community—in forty years!

The deep sense that a man should stand up to his fate was one of the key-notes of his character; and the way he taught it, not only by word but by every action of his life, put heart into many a weak man and woman. Mrs. Patterson, a friend of ours, tells of a reply she once had from the Doctor to whom she had gone with a new trouble. After telling him about it she said:

"I've left it all with the Lord."

"You'd have done better," said the Doctor, "to keep it yourself. Trouble is for your discipline: the Lord doesn't need it."

It was thus out of his wisdom that he was always telling people what they knew, deep down in their hearts, to be true. It sometimes hurt at first, but sooner or later, if the man had a spark of real manhood in him, he came back, and gave the Doctor an abiding affection.

There were those who, though they loved him, called him intolerant. I never could look at it that way. He *did* have the only kind of intolerance which is at all tolerable, and that is the intolerance of intolerance. He always set himself with vigour against that unreason and lack of sympathy which are the essence of intolerance; and yet there was a rock of conviction on many subjects behind which he could not be driven. It was not intolerance: it was with him a reasoned certainty of belief. He had a phrase to express that not uncommon state of mind, in this age particularly, which is politely willing to yield its foothold within this universe to almost any reasoner who suggests some other universe, however shadowy, to stand upon. He called it a "mush of concession." He might have been wrong in his convictions, but he, at least, never floundered in a "mush of concession." I heard him say once:

"There are some things a man can't concede, and one is, that a man who has broken a law, like a man who has broken a leg, has got to suffer for it."

It was only with the greatest difficulty that he could be prevailed upon to present a bill. It was not because the community was poor, though some of our people are poor, and it was certainly not because the Doctor was rich and could afford such philanthropy, for, saving a rather unproductive farm which during the last ten years of his life lay wholly uncultivated, he was as poor as any man in the community. He simply seemed to forget that people owed him.

It came to be a common and humorous experience for people to go to the Doctor and say:

"Now, Doctor North, how much do I owe you? You remember you attended my wife two years ago when the baby came—and John when he had the diphtheria—"

"Yes, yes," said the Doctor, "I remember."

"I thought I ought to pay you."

"Well, I'll look it up when I get time."

But he wouldn't. The only way was to go to him and say:

"Doctor, I want to pay ten dollars on account."

"All right," he'd answer, and take the money.

To the credit of the community I may say with truthfulness that the Doctor never suffered. He was even able to supply himself with the best instruments that money could buy. To him nothing was too good for our neighbourhood. This morning I saw in a case at his home a complete set of oculist's instruments, said to be the best in the county—a very unusual equipment for a country doctor. Indeed, he assumed that the responsibility for the health of the community rested upon him. He was a sort of self-constituted health officer. He was always sniffing about for old wells and damp cellars—and somehow, with his crisp humour and sound sense, getting them cleaned. In his old age he even grew querulously particular about these things—asking a little more of human nature than it could quite accomplish. There were innumerable other ways—how they came out to-day all glorified now that he is gone!—in which he served the community.

Horace tells how he once met the Doctor driving his old white horse in the town road.

"Horace," called the Doctor, "why don't you paint your barn?"

"Well," said Horace, "it *is* beginning to look a bit shabby."

"Horace," said the Doctor, "you're a prominent citizen. We look to you to keep up the credit of the neighbourhood."

Horace painted his barn.

I think Doctor North was fonder of Charles Baxter than of anyone else, save his sister. He hated sham and cant: if a man had a single reality in him the old Doctor found it; and Charles Baxter in many ways exceeds any man I ever knew in the downright quality of genuineness. The Doctor was never tired of telling—and with humour—how he once went to Baxter to have a table made for his office. When he came to get it he found the table upside down and Baxter on his knees finishing off the under part of the drawer slides. Baxter looked up and smiled in the engaging way he has, and continued his work. After watching him for some time the Doctor said:

"Baxter, why do you spend so much time on that table? Who's going to know whether or not the last touch has been put on the under side of it?"

Baxter straightened up and looked at the Doctor in surprise.

"Why, I will," he said.

How the Doctor loved to tell that story! I warrant there is no boy who ever grew up in this country who hasn't heard it.

It was a part of his pride in finding reality that made the Doctor such a lover of true sentiment and such a hater of sentimentality. I prize one memory of him which illustrates this point. The district school gave a "speaking" and we all went. One boy with a fresh young voice spoke a "soldier piece"—the soliloquy of a one-armed veteran who sits at a window and sees the troops go by with dancing banners and glittering bayonets, and the people cheering and shouting. And the refrain went something like this:

> "Never again call 'Comrade'
>     To the men who were comrades for years;
> Never again call 'Brother'
>     To the men we think of with tears."

I happened to look around while the boy was speaking, and there sat the old Doctor with the tears rolling unheeded down his ruddy face; he was thinking, no doubt, of *his* war time and the comrades *he* knew.

On the other hand, how he despised fustian and bombast. His "Bah!" delivered explosively, was often like a breath of fresh air in a stuffy room. Several years ago, before I came here—and it is one of the historic stories of the county—there was a semi-political Fourth of July celebration with a number of ambitious orators. One of them, a young fellow of small worth who wanted to be elected to the legislature, made an impassioned address on "Patriotism." The Doctor was present, for he liked gatherings: he liked people. But he did not like the young orator, and did not want him to be elected. In the midst of the speech, while the audience was being carried through the clouds of oratory, the Doctor was seen to be growing more and more uneasy. Finally he burst out: "Bah!"

The orator caught himself, and then swept on again.

"Bah!" said the Doctor.

By this time the audience was really interested. The orator stopped. He knew the Doctor, and he should have known better than to say what he did. But he was very young and he knew the Doctor was opposing him.

"Perhaps," he remarked sarcastically, "the Doctor can make a better speech than I can."

The Doctor rose instantly, to his full height—and he was an impressive-looking man.

"Perhaps," he said, "I can, and what is more, I will." He stood up on a chair and gave them a talk on Patriotism—real patriotism —the patriotism of duty done in the small concerns of life. That speech, which ended the political career of the orator, is not forgotten to-day.

One thing I heard to-day about the old Doctor impressed me deeply. I have been thinking about it ever since: it illuminates his character more than anything I have heard. It is singular, too, that I should not have known the story before. I don't believe it was because it all happened so long ago; it rather remained untold out of deference to a sort of neighbourhood delicacy.

I had, indeed, wondered why a man of such capacities, so many qualities of real greatness and power, should have escaped a city career. I said something to this effect to a group of men with whom I. was talking this morning. I thought they exchanged glances; one said:

"When he first came out of the army he'd made such a fine record as a surgeon that everyone urged him to go to the city and practice—"

A pause followed which no one seemed inclined to fill.

"But he didn't go," I said.

"No, he didn't go. He was a brilliant young fellow. He *knew* a lot, and he was popular, too. He'd have had a great success—"

Another pause.

"But he didn't go?" I asked promptingly.

"No; he staid here. He was better educated than any man in this county. Why, I've seen him more'n once pick up a book of Latin and read it *for pleasure*."

I could see that all this was purposely irrelevant, and I liked them for it. But walking home from the cemetery Horace gave me the story; the community knew it to the last detail. I suppose it is a story not uncommon among men, but this morning, told of the old Doctor we had just laid away, it struck me with a tragic poignancy difficult to describe.

"Yes," said Horace, "he was to have been married, forty years ago, and the match was broken off because he was a drunkard."

"A drunkard!" I exclaimed, with a shock I cannot convey.

"Yes, sir," said Horace, "one o' the worst you ever see. He got it in the army. Handsome, wild, brilliant—that was the Doctor. I was a little boy but I remember it mighty well."

He told me the whole distressing story. It was all a long time ago and the details do not matter now. It was to be expected that a man like the old Doctor should love, love once, and love as few men do. And that is what he did—and the girl left him because he was a drunkard!

"They all thought," said Horace, "that he'd up an' kill himself. He said he would, but he didn't. Instid o' that he put an open bottle on his table and he looked at it and said: 'Which is stronger, now, you or John North? We'll make that the test,' he said, 'we'll live or die by that.' Them was his exact words. He couldn't sleep nights and he got haggard like a sick man, but he left the bottle there and never touched it."

How my heart throbbed with the thought of that old silent struggle! How much it explained; how near it brought all these people around him! It made him so human. It is the tragic necessity (but the salvation) of many a man that he should come finally to an irretrievable experience, to the assurance that everything is lost. For with that moment, if he be strong, he is saved. I wonder if anyone ever attains real human sympathy who has not passed through the fire of some such experience. Or to humour either! For in the best laughter do we not hear constantly that deep minor note which speaks of the ache in the human heart? It seems to me I can understand Doctor North!

He died Friday morning. He had been lying very quiet all night; suddenly he opened his eyes and said to his sister: "Good-bye, Kate," and shut them again. That was all. The last call had come and he was ready for it. I looked at his face after death. I saw the iron lines of that old struggle in his mouth and chin; and the humour that it brought him in the lines around his deep-set eyes.

—And as I think of him this afternoon, I can see him—curiously, for I can hardly explain it—carrying a banner as in battle right here among our quiet hills. And those he leads seem to be the people we know, the men, and the women, and the boys! He is the hero of a new age. In olden days he might have been a pioneer, carrying the light of civilisation to a new land; here he has been a sort of moral pioneer—a pioneering far more difficult than any we have ever known. There are no heroics connected with it, the name of the pioneer will not go ringing down the ages; for it is a silent leadership and its success is measured by victories in other lives. We see it now, only too dimly, when he is gone. We reflect sadly that we did not stop to thank him. How busy we were with our own affairs when he was among us! I wonder is there anyone here to take up the banner he has laid down!

—I forgot to say that the Scotch Preacher chose the most impressive text in the Bible for his talk at the funeral:

"He that is greatest among you, let him be . . . as he that doth serve."

And we came away with a nameless, aching sense of loss, thinking how, perhaps, in a small way, we might do something for somebody else—as the old Doctor did.

> From *Adventures in Contentment*, by David Grayson (Ray Stannard Baker), copyright, 1907, 1935, by Doubleday, Doran & Company, Inc.

1. Why did a brilliant doctor stay in so small a town? Was it wholly because of his unhappy love affair?
2. Do doctors know more about human nature than other men?
3. What is meant by "a deep sense of the purpose and need of punishment"?
4. Do you think that David Grayson's portrayal of rural ways of thought and action is sound?
5. What sort of a man do you picture as the teller of the story?

*Meridel LeSueur*

# THE TRAP

I T WAS really frightening to go out doors with that raw spring
wind blowing up from the river. Mrs. Darling stood at the
side door of her house peeking out, her bare arms across her
breast, and she could feel the chill go right through her. A
bright, wide, pale sky shone above and the rather wild country
around was black and wet-looking. It was two lots to another
house, and nothing at all stood between Mrs. Darling's house and
the river bluffs. She peeked across the river chasm at the view. It
really rather frightened her, but the doctor did think the view so
fine.

After a good dinner with his friends he would stand at the window overlooking the valley with the lights twinkling below them
in the dark abyss and the cliff rising a sheer bank of darkness and
terror on the other side of the river, and he would light his cigar
or his pipe and throw out his chest a little and balance himself
on his toes and say with a sweep of his hand, "See what a view!"
"What a view!" all the guests would say, peeking out the window,
and at such times she herself would sing out, "Isn't it a wonderful
view? Oh, we do enjoy it so much."

And then the doctor would turn and look at her as if she too
were a splendid view. She was called by all his friends "a splendid
woman . . . a splendid wife."

The doctor would be proud of her and glad she hadn't cut her hair, which was piled in a thick knot on her head just as it had been when he had married her, a young girl, and she was so young seeming yet with the body of a young woman, though she had been married twenty years.

It is true that she had had no children. It was frightening having children. She had put it off. "I couldn't be having them and then losing them. I'm afraid of the sorrow," she said to her friends.

"Oh, the Dr. has built another brush-heap trying to catch a thrush," she said to herself, peering out the half-open door. She always called her husband the "Dr." even to herself, and to her friends at bridge parties she said, "The Dr. always likes his eggs just three and a half minutes."

There on the ground was a heap of brush. She had been uneasy the evening before when the doctor had been prowling around outside and had come in with black mud on his hands and shoes. "What were you doing?" she had asked uneasily. "Oh, just looking around," he had said, with that irritating vagueness; and later, when she had forgotten about it, he said, "I piled up some old brush outside the window. Maybe a thrush will build a nest there."

Oh, if they had built their house in a good suburb where the houses set close together and one's neighbors were close and one didn't have to see that great raw chasm of the Mississippi all the time, that gash in the golden cliffs, in winter so awful, so raw and exposed like bleaching bones, and the cliffs like wounds, so that she just kept the curtains pulled down most of the time.

She looked back into the warm darkened house, so snug, such a good house. "Oh, your house, Mrs. Darling, your gorgeous house."—"Yes, the Dr. and I like it."—"And, of course, the view!" —"Oh, yes, a marvellous view."—"What freedom . . . just like the country."—That was pleasant if only there weren't so much light about them, like a great shout. If only there were close houses, women coming and going up and down the steps, overhanging elms; but to be out in this bright light under so broad a sky—it was frightening.

She was always a little afraid even to stay in the house—it was so quiet, so absolutely noiseless. It always seemed that there was some presence just invisible to her. Like a child, she never had got used to being alone in a house. When her friend Sada was there, how nice it was to have a house and an absent, comfortable husband whom one spoke of so pleasantly and remotely as the "Dr."

But the sky was bright and there was something in the wind. Had she better get a scarf, that little woollen one? She hesitated, then she boldly stepped out the door just as she was and stood blinking in the bright light that fell from the broad pale sky, and the wind blew and blew about her. Everything seemed so white, and the wind moved all the stiff grasses and the stiff trees, as if shaking them, and she stood holding her chill arms in her hands and the wind shaking against her too. She walked over to a young tree she and the doctor had planted and gingerly put her hands on it and then wiped the wetness off on her dress with distaste.

She moved her lips, talking gently to herself, as she always did. "Now why does he want to drag that dirty brush into the yard? That's how he got his feet so muddy. What good is it? And birds" —she said in one of her rare moments of candor she had only by herself—"birds will only dirty the walk and the gables. . . ."

She stepped gingerly over the soft new lawn, lifting her high heels so they would not sink into the mud. She did hate so to squash into anything. Her face had a pouting look of displeasure. She gathered her short skirts together around her legs. She always felt herself in a swirl of skirts, and regretted the short mode. To herself she always rose amidst a swirl of skirts, as she did on her marriage-day. She was at the time of her girlhood and would never be in any other.

Just the same, she was going to take a peek into the black thicket of brush the doctor had piled up to catch a thrush—just to see if there could be a thrush there.

She stopped and peered at the little wren-house the doctor had built and put high on a pole to catch a wren. It was tiny and snug against the sky with a little door and little windows just like a human house. "It is cunning," she said, "cunning, so neat and snug, so closed away like a tiny doll's house. It would be snug to live in. . . ." She bent her face upward until the light showered so whitely on her and made her really blind, so that white spots were in her eyes and the grove of trees across the road looked far off and faint, as if they were not real.

Feeling rather dazzled, she tiptoed to the pile of brush and stood peering down. The twigs made a close weave, a jagged black twining, and as she looked she could see deeper into the maze of crisscross wintry twigs, far in, and she was shivering from the chill wind that kept blowing, exposing her. She thought she saw something far down in the maze, and then, with a start, a terrible fright that almost made her swoon, she realized that a tiny eye was looking up at her from far below, a round, shining black eye looking straight at her. She could not even scream. It was like a nightmare.

Then the eye seemed to roll away into blackness, and then suddenly, without warning, there was a flicking whirr, a quick sound, wings fanned her face, and there was a frightening contact of a black, quick body. She screamed and shielded her face in her hands. The bird winged up into the pale sky, letting out a shrill, scolding cry that struck the heart of the woman standing with her face covered. She began to sob. She didn't know why. A terrible hollow fright was in her. She could not move. She just covered her face in her hands and sobbed—like a child.

The cook came to the door and, seeing her, ran out. "Why, whatever is it?"

She could not say. She stood shaking and sobbing. She wished for her father, but he was long dead. The cook pulled her hands away, and she stood sobbing, her frightened face exposed in the white light, without maturity, dreadfully like the face of a child, as if nothing had touched her for many years.

"It was the bird," she sobbed. "I didn't expect . . ."

The cook led her into the house, wondering. Mrs. Darling could not stop sobbing. She felt exposed. All the exposures of the world welled in her, the fright of her girlhood, the fright of her marriage, all the strange fright and exposure she had suffered. It was too much. She could not bear it. She could not—

She pulled away from the cook and ran upstairs. She lay on the bed, her head buried in the pillow. She clung to the pillow as if it were a human being. She pressed her body against it. She sobbed with such violence, it was madness. She could not stop. The frightening world, the exposure and the terror. It was too much.

She tried to think of something she might get up and do. Oh, it was no use feather-stitching now, or what good was needle-point? What was there to do? What did it all amount to? She could not bear to get up and see out the window and feel her heart beat in that dreadful fright. She wanted to burrow into some dark place. Where was her father? She could always run to him when she was a child—the smell of him, the feel, the blind peace of his breast. Where was he now?

She could not think. She put her face in the pillow so she was blind. She felt it was her father near her, and at last she fell asleep.

## II

She woke to the sound of voices and a shattering light falling into the room from the sky without. The sun was shining directly across her bed in that bright way of early spring, so that the mole, like winter eyes, can scarcely bear it. She sprang up suddenly from her sleep and pulled down the blinds. That was Sada downstairs talking to the cook. Oh, good! Sada. Sada.

"Sada, Sada," she called at the stairs, "I'll be down. I'm so glad you've come."

Sada called up in her high singing voice like a young girl's, "Oh, are you sleeping? Heavens, what a lazy one."

"Oh, wait, I'll be down. Wait. Wait." Sada turned on the radio and a waltz came up the stairs. Mrs. Darling's heart sang. It was all right now. She washed her face and powdered it and put on the tiniest speck of rouge. She always felt a little wicked about rouge.

Then she ran down-stairs, imaginary skirts swirling about her, and Sada, with a little cry, ran to the door and they embraced, making little sounds in their throats as if they had not seen each other for years and years, as if they had not played bridge together only the afternoon before. They buried their faces in each other's necks and laughed and sniffed each other and held each other at arm's length and laughed more, a high, meaningless ripple of laughter.

Sada was a well-dressed woman who lived fashionably in an apartment hotel and indulged in illnesses simply out of boredom, as some women might indulge in love-affairs or dime novels. She had a little upturned nose and a very white skin and wide blue eyes. She must have been very pretty as a girl with her frailty and blonde goldness, but the frailty had gone a little stout and the blonde goldness was like a chrysanthemum after the first spring shower, not after a storm, just a light spring rain, one of the first. Her flesh was softening, her neck drying a little, and her eyes, so blue, were now a little washed out and vacant. This she could see in her mirror quite plainly, and her husband also could see it when he looked at her closely.

Neither woman was maturing. It seemed as if they had only been blighted a little by a too strong sun.

They clung together with this peculiar intimacy, as if it was a great relief for them to let down their game in an adult world. They had always this sense of strain and fright, almost of fear, but particularly that sense they never got over of going on a journey with a strange man away from home. It was as if they had simply gone from their father and mother to a husband—just changed hands. And they were constrained, in unfamiliar company. Together they were happy. It was an interlude.

Mrs. Darling pulled Sada to the sofa, and she stooped to poke the fire so it would burn up, turning her eyes back to Sada, listening to her chatter. She looked, crouching there stirring the fire, as if there was a woman power in her, but so unawakened, so slumbering. Perhaps that's what made her frightened sometimes, stop fixing the fire and lift her slumbering breast sharply and turn her eyes in fright and terror back into the snug room—perhaps it was a terror of never being used.

"I was so bored today," Sada was saying, opening her great blue eyes. And they almost filled with tears, because it was such a pity for her, of all people, to be bored. And she could make her eyes fill with tears which moved her husband to almost any lengths.

"Oh"—Mrs. Darling rose and clasped her hands with a naïve kind of ecstasy she had—"Sada, it's wicked to be bored. Think of all the people who haven't even enough to eat. Oh, I like my life. I have the pleasantest time!" She threw back her head with its heavy weight of hair. "Oh, I want to show you something." She went to the table and took out of the Bible an old picture, brown on the edges. "Sada, look, isn't this killing, simply killing?"

The two women sat on the sofa bending over the picture a moment. It was one of Mrs. Darling taken just before her marriage. They turned and looked into each other's eyes a moment solemnly, then they both burst into high hysterical laughter, dropping their heads together, leaning against each other in convulsive laughter.

"My dear, the plume . . ."

"The mutton sleeves . . . did you ever!"

"Imagine a hat like that . . . and the rats! Ohhhhh, dear!"

Mrs. Darling simply laughed until the tears came in her eyes.

But she saw that look in the eyes of the girl in the picture, that timid, expectant look, peering out on some mysterious future.

"Isn't that killing. . . ."

"Isn't it simply precious. . . ."

But the head was lifted a little proudly, with an expectant pride, and the breasts were arched in the tight bodice like a pouter pigeon's. Oh, that woman had almost flown out—had almost gone on a voyage—there had been the hope of setting sail, the excitement of a dangerous journey in which all would be risked. That girl had for a moment been looking out toward a strange sea.

"Where *did* you dig this up, Ellen?"

"I found it in an old Bible. It was taken just before the Dr. and I were married . . . really. I think it was just the week before."

They stopped laughing and looked down at the little blackened picture.

"Well, that's a long time. . . ."

"Twenty years."

They were silent. The clock on the mantel seemed just at that moment to begin to tick, and a log fell in the fire, the ash showering out a little.

Mrs. Darling got up and took a little broom and slowly swept the ashes back, making it neat.

Sada went restlessly to the window, her chic, round legs showing beneath the short skirt. "What is this, Ellen?" she cried. Almost anything excited her, so she cried out in that high voice, "That little house on the pole?"

Ellen went to the window and put her arm around the other woman. "That's for wrens. The Dr. built it himself and put it up. He wants to have a lot of birds."

"Is it a trap?" Sada asked.

"Oh, no. We wouldn't trap them, of course. It's just a nice, comfortable house already made for them, you see, and once they get used to the comforts, then they always come back. They get sort of domesticated."

"Isn't it cunning," Sada said. "So exactly like a little human house. I should think wrens would simply be delighted to find such a good house."

"Oh, I don't know," Ellen said vaguely, squinting a little as she did when looking any distance. She looked down at the pile of brush, thinking of the black eye that had looked up at her that morning and the frightening whirr of wings and the hard, swift body against her. She could hardly bear to think of it but she murmured politely, "Birds are very interesting." Then she suddenly said warmly, looking at the face of Sada, "My dear, you've no idea—learning about birds. I'm so *interested*. I never knew a thing about them before. The Dr. has gotten so interested in them. He tells me all about them."

"Oh, good heavens," Sada said, "I can't imagine George interested in birds."

"Well, birds are nice. You know the female is always a very drab color and the male is the one that dresses up."

"Really? Well, isn't that interesting . . . educational. . . ."

The two women, their arms intertwined, came away from the window and the shadow of a bird winged suddenly between the bright light and the room, a flying shadow for an instant flicked over them.

They sank down together and Sada opened a box of chocolates she had brought and they began talking together, that strange inconsequential talk yet fraught with all the meaning of life, possible only to women. It was hardly talk but like some primeval chatter, a chirping, with this high female laughter, senseless and hysterical. They told each other what had happened to them, what every one had said, what every one wore, what every one did.

"I don't feel like doing a thing," Sada said with a little breath of self-pity. "I'd like to give up one of my rooms." Then, with a gasp of laughter, "I only have one."

"Oh, Sada," Ellen laughed.

"I will have to move. I will. I can't bear it. Imagine what happened. I went up on the roof and one of the maids came up and hung out Judge Stoner's trousers. My dear, can you imagine how I felt sitting there and having her right before me hang up that old man's trousers! I'm not one to complain to authorities. I try to put up with things, but there were those trousers with the suspenders hanging down. It was disgusting, simply disgusting. And I went and complained and my husband said . . ."

Then Ellen Darling must relate a tale about a cat they had had at home when she was a girl, and the cat used to sit right in the middle of the table.

"What was it made of?"

"Oh, Sada, it was a real cat."

"A real cat. . . ." And they looked at each other and simply burst into nonsensical laughter.

The afternoon was pleasant and timeless, almost as it is when one is a little girl and one's best friend comes in and you have a corner where no one can molest you and before you can blink, the afternoon is gone, the sun is setting, and it is time for supper, time for the family to gather, and the close strange paradise is over.

"Good heavens, see the time." They looked at the clock and it seemed to tick again.

"Oh, Sada, stay; please stay for dinner. Phone George and have him come."

"Oh, no, he's grouchy. You've no idea."

"Oh, stay, anyhow."

"No. No. Call a taxi. I have to hurry. I'll just have time to dress."

"Please, please, don't go." Mrs. Darling clung to the quick blonde woman, who was putting on her coat. "I wish you'd stay."

She wished the other woman would stay all night—forever. She always wanted some third person to be with them. There was a sort of jolliness when three people were together—one could forget about that terrible fearful intimacy.

But Sada powdered her nose and chattered, and they lit the lights because the blue darkness was creeping up between the bare cliffs, and the birds chirped outside like something sharp being broken in the mid-air and tinkling around the house.

It would be an hour before the doctor came, and she had a terror of that last hour of the day. "Oh, Sada," she said, clinging to the other woman.

"There's the taxi. Good-by. Good-by."

Both women felt like crying, as if they wouldn't see each other the next afternoon at the bridge party. Sada ran on her voluptuously curved legs down the steps, then she stopped and turned back where Ellen stood with the door half shut and shivering. She ran back. "Good-by, dear." They hesitated, looking at each other.

"You've got too much powder on your nose, Sada."

"Oh, ye gods. Good-by, darling."

"Good-by. Good-by."

### III

Ellen Darling peeked through the door after the taxi had driven away. Opposite stood the grove of trees in the dusk. If only there were houses instead of the frightening grove of trees that always looked so dim at dusk, as if some presence slid behind the black trunks just as one looked away. She shut the door softly.

She could hear the cook moving in the kitchen. She wished she didn't have a cook, then she might get supper herself, and that would give her something to do that last hour. She went into the room where she and Sada had been all the afternoon. The little clock was ticking very loudly now. She found the picture in the Bible and stood looking at it for a long time, quite soberly, as if she were trying to see straight into it. She put it carefully in the Bible again. Then she stood listening. It was very still in the room and she did not know for what she was listening. She looked at the roses in the rug design.

Then her mind went all about the house—roamed about. She saw every crook and cranny of it and knew how they had planned it thus and so, every turn and crevice, the placement of every window looking out on the world. Now it was snug, an enviable house. Not a woman that did not envy her her house.

She stood very still, looking out of the eyes of that girl in the picture, that girl who lifted her breast and looked out and out.

She stood very still and the house shifted a little around her, and everything just shifted and broke up a little, and it was terrifying the way the house lay around her suddenly breathing, the living speech of her life.

She lifted her breast and her face and listened; so she looked for an instant very much like the girl in the picture—listening—

A pan was dropped in the kitchen. She went quickly to the window and pulled down the blinds, but not before she saw the blue darkness and the birds flying low around the brush-pile the doctor had made to lure a thrush.

She went to the front window to pull the blind, and she looked out across the thicket that stood in the rich, drifting duskiness. She saw a figure coming through the grove. A pang went through her. It was the doctor. She watched and watched, straining her eyes to see him coming through the thicket. Why didn't he take the road? His shoes would be muddy. It was annoying to have him come mysteriously like that through the thicket. She wanted to scream, to do something violent. But there he came walking nearer through the winter trees, and he looked like a lost boy to her. It was irritating to see him a little lost boy walking toward the house in the evening.

He came aimlessly, not firmly on his feet, but aimlessly. She thought for a moment he wasn't coming to the house at all, or perhaps it wasn't he. Oh, yes, she could not be mistaken in the droop of those shoulders, that shabby look; although, of course, he wasn't shabby in the ordinary sense; that is, his clothes were pressed and brushed, but for some reason shabby was the only word for it; he looked shabby, his body had a shabby, beaten look, and his face had a sharp pallor, and his nostrils flared up testily, and he was hard to live with of late.

Yes, he looked whipped, and it filled her with anger to see him look whipped and shabby. But there he was with his secretive eyes and his quietness and sudden tempers, and that was her husband. He came out of the thicket and was crossing the road. Then he stepped onto their lawn and stooped and touched the grass. What was he doing? She crouched now to the window, peeking out so he wouldn't see her. She thought she might discover something. She could scarcely breathe. What was he stooping to look at? Then he stood upright and looked around, looked over the river, and the dusk came thickly all around him, as if in a few moments it would blot him out, completely engulf him.

She felt like crying out to him, warning him of some danger, but she crouched at the window, shading her eyes. He came slowly down the walk through the thick dusk. Now she heard him step slowly on the porch, as if he were very tired. She had a moment of terror, as she always had at steps on the porch, dreading to see some strange person.

Then he opened the door with his key and she heard him in the hall. She moved away swiftly from the window. She felt guilty, as if she had betrayed him somehow watching him secretly. She stood wringing her hands a little in the room waiting for him to stand in the door.

Just as she thought, when he came in the door everything seemed natural again, habitual.

"Hello," he said, with that faint, caustic, withdrawn way he had.

"Hello," she said, and she went to him and he let her kiss him.

He went to the side window that overlooked the brush and the wren's nest. "I wonder if we got a bird today?" he said, shading his hand and putting his face close to the window so that his breath showed. She thought he would make a mark on the pane, and it had just been washed.

"Oh, well," he said, "it's too dark to see now. I can't see anything."

## IV

"I hope we get a thrush and his mate," the doctor said, eating his dessert, bending a little over the dish with that tired droop of his narrow shoulders.

"Oh," Mrs. Darling said, "why is it so important?" She pouted a little, flouncing her shoulders.

"Oh, I don't know," he said, looking up at her with that humorous, tired ease he had. "Why not, Ellen? I think it would be nice to have a couple of mating birds for the season and their young ones."

She looked at him sharply but he was eating again, his face lowered. She thought she might cry, as she had often done when he seemed to be rebuking her about not having children, but then she thought better of it and went on eating her dessert in little nibbles, tasting every bit. She did love blanc-mange, even if the whipped cream was fattening.

"Did you put oil in the car, Ellen?" he asked.

"Yes," she said childishly, "I told the garage man to do it. I told him to do it." Really, she had forgotten it completely; but if he found out, the garage man could be blamed.

"That's all right then," he said.

They went into the front room and she stooped to fix the fire, watching him anxiously. Why hadn't Sada stayed? Then she could have felt gay, like the doctor's wife. 'Oh, yes, that's the doctor's wife. Doctor Darling, you know. They live out on Victory Drive, in that stunning modern house. Haven't you noticed it? Aren't they an ideal couple? Oh, ideal, simply ideal.'

Doctor Darling stood by the table filling his pipe.

"Oh, look," she said, suddenly rising and going to the table.

"I've something simply killing to show you." She took the picture out of the Bible, hiding it behind her back. "Shut your eyes, shut them tight." She held up the picture, "Now open them."

He opened his eyes and blinked at the picture. A slow smile curved his thin lips and he lifted his hand and took the picture from her, then he lowered it slowly under the lamplight and lowered his head. She watched him anxiously but she knew nothing of what he was thinking. The little crow's feet at the corners of his eye told her nothing. He stood with his lean face over the picture. She got uneasy and leaned against him.

"Well, it's a long time," she said, laughing uneasily.

Why didn't he speak?

"Look at those mutton sleeves; isn't it killing?" she said, trying to laugh.

He laid the picture down. "That must have been taken just before we were married," he said.

"Yes," she cried eagerly. "Don't you remember we were married on the 14th of October, and the week before father thought I was tired and sent me down to visit Aunt Mary and a girl named Sally. I wonder where Sally is now? We went down-town one day and stopped in and had our pictures taken. Let's see, it must have been on the 9th—yes, it was the 9th. I remember that . . ."

She went on, "Isn't it killing?"

But he had laid the picture down and was filling his pipe. Then he closed the pouch, the string in his teeth, and put it in his pocket, and struck a match and lighted his pipe. He picked up the paper then and sat down before the fire and opened it carefully at the front page. Now he would read it—deaths, births, marriages, from first to last—so she got out her knitting, for she must be ready to listen and remark the various comments he would make about people, accidents, deaths. Perhaps something would remind him and he would tell of some conversation he had had that day at the office, or he would tell of some incident in his boyhood, perhaps, of which she very likely had heard already.

So she sat knitting.

Until he said it was time to go to bed and she went with him.

## V

It seemed to her it was only just light, and she felt uneasy and opened her eyes and saw him looking out the window through his binoculars down at the wren house, and at the thicket of brush he had put for the thrush. She hated him standing there, hated him in a sudden gust of hatred.

"What are you doing, darling?" she cried in a small voice, looking out over the blankets she held to her chin.

But he was looking down—leaning against the window looking down—seeing far down the little black eyes looking up at him and the two birds sitting in the thicket so silent and watchful. He thought he could see the little round breasts breathing softly.

"They're there. They've moved in," he said, looking down, watching the round warm breasts that seemed to be so near through the glasses.

"Have they really?" she said.

"Look, look," he said, turning around. real excitement on his face. "Take the glasses."

She got out of the bed shivering, and saw that his breast was uncovered, naked.

"Cover up," she said acridly. "You'll catch cold."

But he paid no attention.

"The little rascals have moved in."

"Oh, yes," she said, looking through the glasses and seeing absolutely nothing. "Now they'll have a safe, warm home."

"Oh, yes." He took the glasses and looked again. Yes, there they were. The male was looking around so proudly, curving his head, and his roving gay eye perked around.

"By Jove, a proud, a perky little fellow. Look, see him there."

She held the glasses up but she was seeing absolutely nothing.

She wished he would cover up his chest. It frightened her to see his naked chest exposed so near her. It was like the fright of that horrible little bird looking at her out of his round black eye.

She felt an obscure anger against him. Why be so excited about nesting-birds? Why didn't he cover up his chest?

She gave him the glasses and ran back to bed and snuggled down, covering up to her chin, and he stood looking out the window down at the birds.

From *Scribner's Magazine*, Jan., 1933. Reprinted by permission of the author.

1. What is meant by "that woman . . . had almost gone on a voyage"?
2. What is the connection between the natures of Mrs. Darling, the wren, and the thrush?
3. What do you conceive to have been the original cause of Mrs. Darling's state of mind?
4. What was she afraid of? Can you say definitely?
5. What do you think may have been Doctor Darling's mental devil, or don't you feel that he might have had one?

*Ring Lardner*

# THE MAYSVILLE MINSTREL

AYSVILLE was a town of five thousand inhabitants and its gas company served eight hundred homes, offices and stores.

The company's office force consisted of two men —Ed Hunter, trouble shooter and reader of meters, and Stephen Gale, whose title was bookkeeper, but whose job was a lot harder than that sounds.

From the first to the tenth of the month, Stephen stayed in the office, accepted checks and money from the few thrifty customers who wanted their discount of five percent, soft-soaped and argued with the many customers who thought they were being robbed, and tried to sell new stoves, plates and lamps to customers who were constantly complaining of defects in the stoves, plates and lamps they had bought fifteen or twenty years ago.

After the tenth, he kept the front door locked and went all over town calling on delinquents, many of whom were a year or more behind and had no intention of trying to catch up. This tiring, futile task usually lasted until the twenty-seventh, when Hunter started reading meters and Stephen copied the readings and made out the bills.

On the twenty-ninth, Hunter usually got drunk and Stephen had to hustle out and read the unread meters and hustle back and make out the rest of the bills.

When Townsend, the Old Man, who owned the business and five other gas businesses in larger towns, paid his semimonthly visit to Maysville, Stephen had to take a severe bawling out for failing to squeeze blood from Maysville's turnips and allowing Hunter to get drunk.

All in all, Stephen earned the $22.50 per week which he had been getting the eight years he had worked for the gas company.

He was now thirty-one. At twelve, he had been obliged to quit school and go to work as a Western Union messenger boy. His father was dead and his mother, who established herself, without much profit, as a dressmaker, easily could use the few dollars Stephen drew from the telegraph company. Later on he had jobs as driver of a grocery wagon, soda clerk in a drug store and freight wrestler at the Lackawanna depot.

The $22.50 offer from the gas office was manna from somewhere; it topped his highest previous salary by seven dollars and a half.

Stephen's mother died and Stephen married Stella Nichols, to whom lack of money was no novelty. But they had a couple of children and soon fell into debt, which made Stephen less efficient than ever as a collector of the company's back bills. He couldn't blame other people for not settling when he was stalling off creditors himself.

All he could do was wish to heaven that the Old Man would come across with a substantial raise, and he knew there was as much chance of that as of Stella's swimming the English Channel with a kid under each arm.

The Gales were too poor to go to picture shows; besides, there was no one to leave the children with. So Stephen and Stella stayed at home evenings and read books from the town library. The books Stephen read were books of poetry.

And often, after Stella had gone to bed, he wrote poetry of his own.

He wrote a poem to Stella and gave it to her on one of her birthdays and she said it was great and he ought to quit the darn old gas company and write poetry for a living.

He laughed that off, remarking that he was as poor now as he cared to be.

He didn't show Stella his other poems—poems about Nature, flowers, the Lackawanna Railroad, the beauties of Maysville, et cetera—but kept them locked in a drawer of his desk at the gas office.

There was a man named Charley Roberts who traveled out of New York for an instantaneous water-heater concern. For years he had been trying to sell old Townsend, but old Townsend said the heater ate up too much gas and would make the customers squawk. They squawked enough as it was. Roberts was a determined young man and kept after Townsend in spite of the latter's discouraging attitude.

Roberts was also a wise-cracking, kidding New Yorker, who, when at home, lunched where his heroes lunched, just to be near them, look at them and overhear some of their wise-cracks which he could repeat to his fellow drummers on the road. These heroes of his were comic-strip artists, playwrights and editors of humorous columns in the metropolitan press.

His favorite column was the one conducted by George Balch in the Standard and when he was in the small towns, he frequently clipped silly items from the local papers and sent them to George, who substituted his own captions for Charley's and pasted them up.

Charley had a tip that Old Man Townsend would be in Maysville on a certain day, and as he was in the neighborhood, he took an interurban car thither and called at the gas office. Stephen had just got back from a fruitless tour among the deadheads and was in the shop, behind the office, telling Ed Hunter that Mrs. Harper's pilot-light wouldn't stay lighted.

Roberts, alone in the office, looked idly at Stephen's desk and saw a book.

It was a volume of poems by Amy Lowell. A moment later Stephen reentered from the shop.

"Hello there, Gale," said Roberts.

"How are you, Mr. Roberts?" said Stephen.

"I heard the Old Man was here," said Roberts.

"You've missed him," said Stephen. "He was here yesterday afternoon and left for Haines City last night."

"Will he be here tomorrow?"

"I couldn't tell you. He's hard to keep track of."

"He's hard to sell, too. But I'll run over there and take a chance. I notice you've been reading highbrow poetry."

"I got this from the library."

"How do you like it?"

"I'm not strong for poetry that don't rhyme," said Stephen.

"I guess it's easier to write," said Roberts.

"I don't believe so. It isn't much trouble rhyming if you've got it in you. Look at Edgar Guest."

"How do you know he doesn't have trouble?"

"His works don't read like it," said Stephen, and after a pause: "Besides, I've tried it myself."

"Oh, so you're a poet, are you?" asked Roberts.

"I wouldn't exactly claim that, but I've written a few verses and it was more like fun than work. Maybe other people would think they were rotten, but I get pleasure writing them just the same."

"I'd like to read them, Gale," said Roberts eagerly.

"I don't know if I'd like you to or not. And I don't know if I've saved any. I wrote a poem to my wife on her birthday three years ago. She thought it was pretty good. I might let you read that, only I don't know if I've got a copy of it around here."

He knew very well he had a copy of it around there.

"See if you can find it," said Roberts.

Stephen looked in two or three drawers before he unlocked the one that contained his manuscripts.

"It's just a little thing I wrote for my wife on her birthday.

You'll probably think it's rotten. It's called 'To Stella.' That's my wife's first name."

Charley Roberts read the poem:

> Stella you today are twenty-three years old
> And yet your hair is still pure gold.
> Stella they tell me your name in Latin means a star
> And to me that is what you are
> With your eyes and your hair so yellow
> I rate myself a lucky fellow Stella.
> You know I cannot afford a costly gift
> As you know it costs us all I make to live
> And as you know we are already in debt,
> But if you will stay well and healthy
> Until I am rich and wealthy
> Maybe I will be more able then to give you a present
> Better than I can at present.
> So now Stella good-by for the present
> And I hope next year I can make things more pleasant.
> May you live to be old and ripe and mellow
> Is my kind birthday wish for you Stella.

"Do you mean to tell me," said Roberts, "that it was no trouble to write that?"

"It only took me less than a half-hour," said Stephen.

"Listen," said Roberts. "Let me have it."

"What do you want with it?"

"I can get it published for you."

"Where at?"

"In the New York Standard. I've got a friend, George Balch, who would run it in his column. He doesn't pay anything, but if this was printed and your name signed to it, it might attract attention from people who do pay for poetry. Then you could make a lot of money on the side."

"How much do they pay?"

"Well, some of the big magazines pay as high as a dollar a line."

"I forget how many lines there is in that."

Roberts counted them.

"Seventeen," he said. "And from what I've seen of old Townsend, I bet he doesn't pay you much more a week."

"And it only took me less than a half-hour to write," said Stephen.

"Will you let me send it to Balch?"

"I don't know if I've got another copy."

"Your wife must have a copy."

"I guess maybe she has."

He wasn't just guessing.

"I'll mail this to Balch tonight, along with a note. If he prints it, I'll send you the paper."

"I've got one that's even longer than that," said Stephen.

"Well, let's have it."

"No, I guess I'd better hang onto it—if your friend don't pay for them."

"You're absolutely right. A man's a sucker to work for nothing. You keep your other stuff till this is published and you hear from some magazine editor, as I'm sure you will. Then you can sell what you've already written, and write more, till you're making so much dough that you can buy the Maysville Gas Company from that old skinflint."

"I don't want any gas company. I want to get out of it. I just want to write."

"Why shouldn't you!"

"I've got to be sure of a living."

"Living! If you can make seventeen dollars in half an hour, that's thirty-four dollars an hour, or— How many hours do you put in here?"

"Ten."

"Three hundred and forty dollars a day! If that isn't a living, I'm selling manicure sets to fish."

"I couldn't keep up no such a pace. I have to wait for inspiration," said Stephen.

"A dollar a line would be enough inspiration for me. But the times when you didn't feel like doing it yourself, you could hire somebody to do it for you."

"That wouldn't be square, and people would know the difference anyway. It's hard to imitate another man's style. I tried once to write like Edgar Guest, but it wouldn't have fooled people that was familiar with his works."

"Nobody can write like Guest. And you don't need to. Your own style is just as good as his and maybe better. And speaking of Guest, do you think he's starving to death? He gives away dimes to the Fords."

Stephen was wild to tell Stella what had happened, but he was afraid this Balch might not like the poem as well as Roberts had; might not think it worth publishing, and she would be disappointed.

He would wait until he actually had it in print, if ever, and then show it to her.

He didn't have to wait long. In less than a week he received by mail from New York a copy of the Standard, and in George Balch's column was his verse with his name signed to it and a caption reading "To Stella—A Maysville Minstrel Gives His Mrs. a Birthday Treat."

For the first time in his career at the gas office, Stephen quit five minutes early and almost ran home. His wife was as excited as he had hoped she would be.

"But why does he call you a minstrel?" she asked. "He must have heard some way about that night at the Elks."

Stephen told her the rest of the story—how Roberts had predicted that the poem would attract the attention of magazine editors and create a demand for his verses at a dollar a line. And he confessed that he had other poems all ready to send when the call came.

He had brought two of them home from the office and he read them aloud for her approval:

"1. The Lackawanna Railroad.

"The Lackawanna Railroad where does it go?
It goes from Jersey City to Buffalo.
Some of the trains stop at Maysville but they are few
Most of them go right through
Except the 8:22
Going west but the 10:12 bound for Jersey City
That is the train we like the best
As it takes you to Jersey City
Where you can take a ferry or tube for New York City.
The Lackawanna runs many freights
Sometimes they run late
But that does not make so much difference with a freight
Except the people who have to wait for their freight.
Maysville people patronize the Interurban a specially the farmers
So the Interurban cuts into the business of the Lackawanna,
But if you are going to New York City or Buffalo
The Lackawanna is the way to go.
Will say in conclusion that we consider it an honor
That the City of Maysville is on the Lackawanna.

"2. The Gas Business.

"The Maysville Gas Co. has eight hundred meters
The biggest consumer in town is Mrs. Arnold Peters
Who owns the big house on Taylor Hill
And is always giving parties come who will.
Our collections amount to about $2600.00 per month
Five per cent discount if paid before the tenth of the month.
Mr. Townsend the owner considers people a fool
Who do not at least use gas for fuel.
As for lighting he claims it beats electricity
As electric storms often cut off the electricity
And then you have no light at night
And have to burn candles all night.
This is hardly right
A specially if you have company
Who will ask you what is the matter with the electricity.
So patronize the Gas Company which storms do not effect
And your friends will have no reason to object."

Stella raved over both the poems, but made a very practical suggestion.

"You are cheating yourself, dear," she said. "The poem about the railroad, for instance, the way you have got it, it is nineteen lines, or nineteen dollars if they really pay a dollar a line. But it would be almost double the amount if you would fix the lines different."

"How do you mean?"

She got a pencil and piece of paper and showed him:

> The Lackawanna Railroad
> Where does it go?
> It goes from Jersey City
> To Buffalo.

"You see," she said, "you could cut most of the lines in half and make thirty-eight dollars instead of nineteen."

But Stephen, with one eye on profit and the other on Art, could only increase the lines of "The Lackawanna" from nineteen to thirty and those of "The Gas Business" from seventeen to twenty one.

Three days later a special delivery came for Stephen.

It said:

Dear Mr. Gale:

On September second there was a poem entitled "To Stella" in the New York Standard. The poem was signed by you. It impressed me greatly and if you have written or will write others as good, our magazine will be glad to buy them, paying you one dollar a line.

Please let me hear from you and send along any poems you may have on hand.

Sincerely,

Wallace James,
Editor, "James's Weekly,"
New York City.

Stephen had never heard of "James's Weekly" and did not notice that the letter was postmarked Philadelphia and written on the stationery of a Philadelphia hotel.

He rushed to his house, addressed and mailed the railroad and gas verses, and after a brief and excited conference with Stella, decided to resign his job.

Old Man Townsend, dropping into Maysville the following morning, heard the decision and was not a bit pleased. He realized he never could get anyone else to do Stephen's work at Stephen's salary.

"I'll raise you to twenty-four dollars," he said.

"I'm not asking for a raise. I've got to quit so I can devote all my time to my poetry."

"Your poetry!"

"Yes, sir."

"Do you mean to say you're going to write poetry for a living?" asked the Old Man.

"Yes, sir."

"You'll starve to death."

"Edgar Guest is still alive."

"I don't care if he is or not," said the Old Man. "It's the twelfth of the month and Hunter can tend to his job and yours both for a couple of weeks. If you want to come back at the end of that time, I'll raise you to twenty-three dollars."

It was Stephen's intention to polish up some of his older poems and write one or two fresh ones so his supply would be ready for "James's" demand.

But he found it next to impossible to write while the fate of the two verses he had sent in was uncertain and, deciding to leave the old manuscripts as they were, he was able to make only a feeble start on a new one:

The Delaware River.

Not a great many miles from Maysville is the Delaware River
But there is no fish in this part of the River.
The upper part of the River is narrow and shallow
But they claim it is much wider near Philadelphia.

On the twentieth the envelope containing "The Lackawanna
Railroad" and "The Gas Business" was returned from New York.
There were several inscriptions stamped and written on it, such as
"Not Found" and "Not in Directory."

And it dawned on Stephen that he was the victim of quite a
joke.

To the accompaniment of Stella's sobs, he proceeded to tear up
all his manuscripts save "To Stella," which she had hidden away
where he couldn't find it.

"Mr. Townsend came in on the eight-thirty interurban," he
said. "I'll have to go see him."

"All right," said the Old Man when Stephen walked into the
office. "I'll take you back at your old salary, but don't let's have
no more foolishness. Get out now and try and coax a little money
out of that Harper woman. She ain't paid a nickel for eight
months."

"I wanted to speak to you about those instantaneous water-
heaters," said Stephen.

"What about them?"

"I was going to advise you not to buy them. They eat up too
much gas."

"Thanks for your advice, but I ordered some from Roberts in
Haines City. I told him to send half a dozen of them here," said
the Old Man.

"Will he be here to demonstrate them?" asked Stephen grimly.

"He said he would."

"I hope he will."

But even as he spoke, Stephen realized there was nothing he could do about it.

From *Round-up*, by Ring Lardner. Copyright, 1929, by Charles Scribner's Sons, New York. Reprinted by permission.

1. Ring Lardner was known as a writer of humorous stories. Do you find this story amusing?
2. What, do you think, was Lardner's opinion of Eddie Guest?
3. What is funny about Stephen's poetry?
4. Do you find a pattern of human behavior in this story?
5. This is a realistic story. Does it contain a moral?

# VII. CITY

# VII. CITY

I
T IS hard to be completely indifferent to a city. It either fascinates or repels. The result is that most fiction using urban settings is essentially romantic. The romance may be direct, the fruit of fascination; or it may be inverse, the fruit of exaggerated repulsion. From either angle, stories dealing with city life are likely to employ contrast as a motif—contrast between city and country, between the ranks of society, or between the individual and the crowd of which he is a component part.

In contrasting city and country, the urban story of older days was frequently indistinguishable, except in its setting, from the older type of rural story discussed in the previous section. City vice and sophistication were set against the simple virtues of the newcomer from the country. If rural virtue triumphed over fraud and temptation, the happy ending was ready made; if it succumbed, the tragedy was equally ready and obvious. And of course the Dickens-Harte device was ever available, to reveal beneath the hard or brutal exterior of the city dweller a heart unexpectedly stirred by the sight of virtue in distress. As already suggested in the Introduction, the majority of O. Henry's city stories are at bottom of this sturdy old romantic sort.

"The Furnished Room" is merely one of a series in which O. Henry employed the sure-fire plot of the parted lovers seeking each other in the wilderness of the city streets. As he himself admitted, little in his stories is fundamentally New York: change a few place-names and other surface details and the story might be transferred to Paris, London, or San Francisco. The theme is timeless and placeless, whether, as in "The Furnished Room," the lovers who are forever lost to each other in life are romantically united in death, or whether, as in "The Skylight Room" and

"Springtime à la Carte," they find each other and live happy ever after.

Almost equally timeless and placeless is the idea of social contrast, of the way saints and harlots, beggars and millionaires, racketeers and honest men, may rub elbows in the city and knowingly or unknowingly influence each other's lives. This idea, too, O. Henry repeatedly used for constructing plots, in stories like "Two Thanksgiving Day Gentlemen," "Brickdust Row," and "The Assessor of Success." More recent writers have applied it rather to the slice-of-life kind of narrative, in which glimpses and fragments of a dozen different stories come to light for an instant and then vanish again in the crowd. Such stories are Edna Ferber's "Hey, Taxi!", Katherine Brush's "Night Club," and to a less extent Faulkner's "Pennsylvania Station." No complete story, in the old sense, is told; the setting itself, with or without the character of the observer, supplies the unity.

A story like Ben Hecht's "The Pig" simply carries into sharper focus the same method of construction. Where the Ferber and Brush stories show a series of human situations in momentary glimpses, Hecht turns the spotlight for a brief space on a single situation. Two figures cease to be nameless units in the crowd, and appear as individuals in a tragedy of frustration wherein none of the really important facts are stated. Again the theme is timeless and placeless. Its setting need not even be urban, though were the story removed from the city the approach would have to be different, because it owes its present effect to the suggestion of the crowd out of which Anton and Sofie so briefly emerge.

When O. Henry in "A Municipal Report" took issue with Frank Norris's silly remark that New York, New Orleans, and San Francisco are the only "story cities" in the United States, that nothing could happen in Buffalo or Nashville, his challenge had wider implications than perhaps he realized. It is highly doubtful if there is such a thing as a New York subject or a Chicago subject; what could happen there could equally well happen in Philadelphia, Detroit, or Tacoma, for cities are composed of human beings, and human beings wherever they live get themselves into the same sort of jams. Purely political themes aside, it would not even matter much were the setting shifted to London, Berlin, or Moscow. But it could not be shifted to Pitcairn Island, John o' Groat's House, or Milan, Ohio. In country, village, or small town, every person stands out as an individual all the time, whereas the essence of the city is the crowd in which individuality is submerged until something happens to bring it out for an instant. "The crowd on the Appian Way is always the same age"; the function of the artist writing of the city is to pick individuals out of the crowd and against that background make us feel their common humanity. Whether the street be the Appian Way or Broadway, La Salle Street or Euclid Avenue, depends merely on the chance of which of them the author happens to know best.

# O. Henry

# THE FURNISHED ROOM

RESTLESS, shifting, fugacious as time itself is a certain vast bulk of the population of the red brick district of the lower West Side. Homeless, they have a hundred homes. They flit from furnished room to furnished room, transients forever—transients in abode, transients in heart and mind. They sing "Home, Sweet Home" in ragtime; they carry their *lares et penates* in a bandbox; their vine is entwined about a picture hat; a rubber plant is their fig tree.

Hence the houses of this district, having had a thousand dwellers, should have a thousand tales to tell, mostly dull ones, no doubt; but it would be strange if there could not be found a ghost or two in the wake of all these vagrant guests.

One evening after dark a young man prowled among these crumbling red mansions, ringing their bells. At the twelfth he rested his lean hand-baggage upon the step and wiped the dust from his hat-band and forehead. The bell sounded faint and far away in some remote, hollow depths.

To the door of this, the twelfth house whose bell he had rung, came a housekeeper who made him think of an unwholesome, surfeited worm that had eaten its nut to a hollow shell and now sought to fill the vacancy with edible lodgers.

He asked if there was a room to let.

"Come in," said the housekeeper. Her voice came from her throat; her throat seemed lined with fur. "I have the third floor back, vacant since a week back. Should you wish to look at it?"

The young man followed her up the stairs. A faint light from no particular source mitigated the shadows of the halls. They trod noiselessly upon a stair carpet that its own loom would have forsworn. It seemed to have become vegetable; to have degenerated in that rank, sunless air to lush lichen or spreading moss that grew in patches to the staircase and was viscid under the foot like organic matter. At each turn of the stairs were vacant niches in the wall. Perhaps plants had once been set within them. If so they had died in that foul and tainted air. It may be that statues of the saints had stood there, but it was not difficult to conceive that imps and devils had dragged them forth in the darkness and down to the unholy depths of some furnished pit below.

"This is the room," said the housekeeper, from her furry throat. "It's a nice room. It ain't often vacant. I had some most elegant people in it last summer—no trouble at all, and paid in advance to the minute. The water's at the end of the hall. Sprowls and Mooney kept it three months. They done a vaudeville sketch. Miss B'retta Sprowls—you may have heard of her—oh, that was just the stage names—right there over the dresser is where the marriage certificate hung, framed. The gas is here, and you see there is plenty of closet room. It's a room everybody likes. It never stays idle long."

"Do you have many theatrical people rooming here?" asked the young man.

"They comes and goes. A good proportion of my lodgers is connected with the theatres. Yes, sir, this is the theatrical district. Actor people never stays long anywhere. I get my share. Yes, they comes and they goes."

He engaged the room, paying for a week in advance. He was tired, he said, and would take possession at once. He counted out the money. The room had been made ready, she said, even to towels and water. As the housekeeper moved away he put, for the thousandth time, the question that he carried at the end of his tongue.

"A young girl—Miss Vashner—Miss Eloise Vashner—do you remember such a one among your lodgers? She would be singing on the stage, most likely. A fair girl, of medium height and slender, with reddish, gold hair and a dark mole near her left eyebrow."

"No, I don't remember the name. Them stage people has names they change as often as their rooms. They comes and they goes. No, I don't call that one to mind."

No. Always no. Five months of ceaseless interrogation and the inevitable negative. So much time spent by day in questioning managers, agents, schools and choruses; by night among the audiences of theatres from all-star casts down to music halls so low that he dreaded to find what he most hoped for. He who had loved her best had tried to find her. He was sure that since her disappearance from home this great, water-girt city held her somewhere, but it was like a monstrous quicksand, shifting its particles constantly, with no foundation, its upper granules of to-day buried to-morrow in ooze and slime.

The furnished room received its latest guest with a first glow of pseudo-hospitality, a hectic, haggard, perfunctory welcome like the specious smile of a demirep. The sophistical comfort came in reflected gleams from the decayed furniture, the ragged brocade upholstery of a couch and two chairs, a foot-wide cheap pier glass between the two windows, from one or two gilt picture frames and a brass bedstead in a corner.

The guest reclined, inert, upon a chair, while the room, confused in speech as though it were an apartment in Babel, tried to discourse to him of its divers tenantry.

A polychromatic rug like some brilliant-flowered rectangular, tropical islet lay surrounded by a billowy sea of soiled matting. Upon the gay-papered wall were those pictures that pursue the homeless one from house to house—The Huguenot Lovers, The

First Quarrel, The Wedding Breakfast, Psyche at the Fountain.
The mantel's chastely severe outline was ingloriously veiled behind
some pert drapery drawn rakishly askew like the sashes of the
Amazonian ballet. Upon it was some desolate flotsam cast aside
by the room's marooned when a lucky sail had borne them to a
fresh port—a trifling vase or two, pictures of actresses, a medicine
bottle, some stray cards out of a deck.

One by one, as the characters of a cryptograph become explicit,
the little signs left by the furnished room's procession of guests
developed a significance. The threadbare space in the rug in front
of the dresser told that lovely woman had marched in the throng.
The tiny finger prints on the wall spoke of little prisoners trying
to feel their way to sun and air. A splattered stain, raying like the
shadow of a bursting bomb, witnessed where a hurled glass or
bottle had splintered with its contents against the wall. Across
the pier glass had been scrawled with a diamond in staggering
letters the name "Marie." It seemed that the succession of dwellers
in the furnished room had turned in fury—perhaps tempted beyond forbearance by its garish coldness—and wreaked upon it their
passions. The furniture was chipped and bruised; the couch, distorted by bursting springs, seemed a horrible monster that had
been slain during the stress of some grotesque convulsion. Some
more potent upheaval had cloven a great slice from the marble
mantel. Each plank in the floor owned its particular cant and
shriek as from a separate and individual agony. It seemed incredible that all this malice and injury had been wrought upon the
room by those who had called it for a time their home; and yet
it may have been the cheated home instinct surviving blindly, the
resentful rage at false household gods that had kindled their wrath.
A hut that is our own we can sweep and adorn and cherish.

The young tenant in the chair allowed these thoughts to file,
soft-shod, through his mind, while there drifted into the room
furnished sounds and furnished scents. He heard in one room a
tittering and incontinent, slack laughter; in others the monologue

of a scold, the rattling of dice, a lullaby, and one crying dully; above him a banjo tinkled with spirit. Doors banged somewhere; the elevated trains roared intermittently; a cat yowled miserably upon a back fence. And he breathed the breath of the house—a dank savour rather than a smell—a cold, musty effluvium as from underground vaults mingled with the reeking exhalations of linoleum and mildewed and rotten woodwork.

Then, suddenly, as he rested there, the room was filled with the strong, sweet odour of mignonette. It came as upon a single buffet of wind with such sureness and fragrance and emphasis that it almost seemed a living visitant. And the man cried aloud: "What, dear?" as if he had been called, and sprang up and faced about. The rich odour clung to him and wrapped him around. He reached out his arms for it, all his senses for the time confused and commingled. How could one be peremptorily called by an odour? Surely it must have been a sound. But, was it not the sound that had touched, that had caressed him?

"She has been in this room," he cried, and he sprang to wrest from it a token, for he knew he would recognise the smallest thing that had belonged to her or that she had touched. This enveloping scent of mignonette, the odour that she had loved and made her own—whence came it?

The room had been but carelessly set in order. Scattered upon the flimsy dresser scarf were half a dozen hairpins—those discreet, indistinguishable friends of womankind, feminine of gender, infinite of mood and uncommunicative of tense. These he ignored, conscious of their triumphant lack of identity. Ransacking the drawers of the dresser he came upon a discarded, tiny, ragged handkerchief. He pressed it to his face. It was racy and insolent with heliotrope; he hurled it to the floor. In another drawer he found odd buttons, a theatre programme, a pawnbroker's card, two lost marshmallows, a book on the divination of dreams. In the last was a woman's black satin hair-bow, which halted him, poised between ice and fire. But the black satin hair-bow also is femininity's demure, impersonal, common ornament and tells no tales.

And then he traversed the room like a hound on the scent, skimming the walls, considering the corners of the bulging matting on his hands and knees, rummaging mantel and tables, the curtains and hangings, the drunken cabinet in the corner, for a visible sign, unable to perceive that she was there beside, around, against, within, above him, clinging to him, wooing him, calling him so poignantly through the finer senses that even his grosser ones became cognisant of the call. Once again he answered loudly: "Yes, dear!" and turned, wild-eyed, to gaze on vacancy, for he could not yet discern form and colour and love and outstretched arms in the odour of mignonette. Oh, God! whence that odour, and since when have odours had a voice to call? Thus he groped.

He burrowed in crevices and corners, and found corks and cigarettes. These he passed in passive contempt. But once he found in a fold of the matting a half-smoked cigar, and this he ground beneath his heel with a green and trenchant oath. He sifted the room from end to end. He found dreary and ignoble small records of many a peripatetic tenant; but of her whom he sought, and who may have lodged there, and whose spirit seemed to hover there, he found no trace.

And then he thought of the housekeeper.

He ran from the haunted room downstairs and to a door that showed a crack of light. She came out to his knock. He smothered his excitement as best he could.

"Will you tell me, madam," he besought her, "who occupied the room I have before I came?"

"Yes, sir. I can tell you again. 'Twas Sprowls and Mooney, as I said. Miss B'retta Sprowls it was in the theatres, but Missis Mooney she was. My house is well known for respectability. The marriage certificate hung, framed, on a nail over—"

"What kind of a lady was Miss Sprowls—in looks, I mean?"

"Why, black-haired, sir, short, and stout, with a comical face. They left a week ago Tuesday."

"And before they occupied it?"

"Why, there was a single gentleman connected with the draying business. He left owing me a week. Before him was Missis Crowder and her two children, that stayed four months; and back of them was old Mr. Doyle, whose sons paid for him. He kept the room six months. That goes back a year, sir, and further I do not remember."

He thanked her and crept back to his room. The room was dead. The essence that had vivified it was gone. The perfume of mignonette had departed. In its place was the old, stale odour of mouldy house furniture, of atmosphere in storage.

The ebbing of his hope drained his faith. He sat staring at the yellow, singing gaslight. Soon he walked to the bed and began to tear the sheets into strips. With the blade of his knife he drove them tightly into every crevice around windows and door. When all was snug and taut he turned out the light, turned the gas full on again and laid himself gratefully upon the bed.

.     .     .     .     .     .     .

It was Mrs. McCool's night to go with the can for beer. So she fetched it and sat with Mrs. Purdy in one of those subterranean retreats where housekeepers foregather and the worm dieth seldom.

"I rented out my third floor, back, this evening," said Mrs. Purdy, across a fine circle of foam. "A young man took it. He went up to bed two hours ago."

"Now, did ye, Mrs. Purdy, ma'am?" said Mrs. McCool, with intense admiration. "You do be a wonder for rentin' rooms of that kind. And did ye tell him, then?" she concluded in a husky whisper laden with mystery.

"Rooms," said Mrs. Purdy, in her furriest tones, "are furnished for to rent. I did not tell him, Mrs. McCool."

" 'Tis right ye are, ma'am; 'tis by renting rooms we kape alive.

Ye have the rale sense for business, ma'am. There be many people will rayjict the rentin' of a room if they be tould a suicide has been after dyin' in the bed of it."

"As you say, we has our living to be making," remarked Mrs. Purdy.

"Yis, ma'am; 'tis true. 'Tis just one wake ago this day I helped ye lay out the third floor, back. A pretty slip of a colleen she was to be killin' herself wid the gas—a swate little face she had, Mrs. Purdy, ma'am."

"She'd a-been called handsome, as you say," said Mrs. Purdy, assenting but critical, "but for that mole she had a-growin' by her left eyebrow. Do fill up your glass again, Mrs. McCool."

1. Define fugacious, lares et penates, demirep, polychromatic, flotsam, cryptograph, effluvium, and peripatetic.
2. Do you think that this story marks the author as a philosopher?
3. Why didn't the young man use the normal methods for locating missing persons?
4. Do you find the ending of the story inartistic?
5. Do you think O. Henry tells too much? Would the story have been better if slight suggestion had been made at the close instead of almost direct statement?

*Ben Hecht*

# THE PIG

"SOFIE POPAPOVITCH versus Anton Popapovitch," cries the clerk. A number of broken-hearted matrons awaiting their turn before the bar of justice in the Domestic Relations Court find time to giggle at the name Popapovitch. "Silence," cries the clerk. Very well, silence. Anton steps out. What's the matter with Anton? An indignant face, its chin raised, its eyes marching defiantly to the bar of justice. Sofie too, but weeping. And a lawyer, Sofie's lawyer.

Well, what's up? Why should the Popapovitches take up valuable time? Think of the taxpayers supporting this court and two Popapovitches marching up to have an argument on the taxpayers' money. Well, that's civilization.

Ah, ah! It appears that Anton, the rogue, went to a grand ball and raffle given by his lodge. What's wrong with that? Why must Sofie weep over that? Women are incredible. He went to the grand ball with his wife, as a man should. A very fine citizen, Anton. He belongs to a lodge that gives grand balls and he takes his wife.

Go on, says the judge, what happened? What's the complaint? Time is precious. Let's have it in a nutshell.

This is a good idea. People spend a frightful lot of unnecessary time weeping and mumbling in the courts. Mrs. Popapovitch will please stop weeping and get down to brass tacks. Very well, the complaint is, your honor, that Mr. Popapovitch got drunk at the grand ball. But that wasn't the end of it. There's some more. A paragraph of tears and then, your honor, listen to this: Mr. Popapovitch not only got drunk but he took a chance on the raffle which cost one dollar and he won.

But what did he win? Oh, oh! He won a pig. A live pig. That was the prize. A small, live pig with a ribbon round its neck. And, says Mrs. Popapovitch (there's humor in a long foreign-sounding name because it conjures up visions of bewildered, flat-faced people and bewildered flat-faced people are always humorous), and, says she, they had been married ten years. Happily married. She washed, scrubbed, tended house. There were no children. Well, what of that? Lots of people had no children.

Anyway, Anton worked, brought home his pay envelope O.K. And then he wins this pig. And what does he do? He takes it home. He won't leave it anywhere.

"What!" he says, "I leave this pig anywhere? Are you crazy? It's my pig. I win him. I take him home with me."

And then? Well, it's midnight, your honor. And Anton carries the pig upstairs into the flat. But there's no place to put him. Where can one put a pig in a flat, your honor? No place. The pig don't like to stand on carpets. And what pig likes to sleep on hard wood floors? A pig's a pig. And what's good for a pig? Aha! a pig pen.

So, your honor, Anton puts him in the bathtub. And he starts down stairs with a basket, and all night long he keeps bringing up basketfuls of dirt dug up from the alley. Dirt, cinders, more dirt. And he puts it in the bathtub. And what does the pig do? He squeals, grunts and wants to go home. He fights to get out of the bathtub. There's such a noise nobody can sleep. But Anton says, "Nice little pig. I fix you up fine. Nice little pig."

And so he fills the bathtub up with dirt. Then he turns on the water. And what does he say? He says, "Now, little pig, we have

fine mud for you. Nice fine mud." Yes, your honor, a whole bathtub full of mud. And when the pig sees this he gets happy and
lies down and goes to sleep. And Anton sits in the bathroom and
looks at the pig all night and says, "See. He's asleep. It's like home
for him."

But the next day Anton must go to work. All right, he'll go to
work. But first, understand everybody, he don't want this pig
touched. The pig stays in the bathtub and he must be there when
he comes home.

All right. The pig stays in the bathtub, your honor. Anton wants
it. Tomorrow the pig will be killed and that'll be an end for the
pig.

Anton comes home and he goes in the bathroom and he sits
and looks at the pig and complains the mud is dried up and why
don't somebody take care of his pig. His damn pig. He brings up
more dirt and makes more mud. And the pig tries to climb out
and throws mud all over the bathroom.

That's one day. And then there's another day. And finally a
third day. Will Anton let anybody kill his pig? Aha! He'll break
somebody's neck if he does. But, your honor, Mrs. Popapovitch
killed the pig. A terrible thing, isn't it, to kill a pig that keeps
squealing in the bathtub and splashing mud all day?

But what does Anton do when he comes home and finds his
pig killed? My God! He hits her, your honor. He hits her on the
head. His own wife whom he loves and lives with for ten years. He
throws her down and hollers, "You killed my little pig! You good
for nothing. I'll show you."

What a disgrace for the neighbors! Lucky there are no children,
your honor. Married ten years but no children. And it's lucky now.
Because the disgrace would have been worse. The neighbors come.
They pull him away from his wife. Her eye is black and blue. Her
nose is bleeding. That's all, your honor."

A very bad case for Anton Popapovitch. A decidedly bad case.
Step forward, Anton Popapovitch, and explain it, if you can. Did

you beat her up? Did you do this thing? And are you ashamed and willing to apologize and kiss and make up?

Anton, step forward and tell his honor. But be careful. Mrs. Popapovitch has a lawyer and it will go bad with you if you don't talk carefully.

All right. Here's Anton. He nods and keeps on nodding. What is this? What's he nodding about? Did this happen as your wife says, Anton? Anton blows out his cheeks and rubs his working-man's hand over his mouth. To think that you should beat your wife who has always been good to you, Anton. Who has cooked and been true to you! And there are no children to worry you. Not one. And you beat her. Bah, is that a man? Don't you love your wife? Yes. All right, then why did you do it?

Anton looks up surprised. "Because," says Anton, still surprised, "like she say. She kill my pig. You hear yourself, your honor. She say she kill him. And I put him in the bathtub and give him mud. And she kill him."

But is that a reason to beat your wife and nearly kill her? It is, says Anton. Well, then, why? Tell the judge, why you were so fond of this pig, Anton.

Ah, yes, Anton Popapovitch, tell the judge why you loved this little pig so much and made a home for him with mud in the bathtub. Why you dreamed of him as you stood working in the factory? Why you ran home to him and fed him and sat and looked at him and whispered, "Nice little pig?" Why?

God knows. But Anton Popapovitch can't explain it. It must remain one of the mysteries of our city, your honor. Call the next case. Put Anton Popapovitch on parole. Perhaps it was because . . . well, the matter is ended. Anton Popapovitch sighs and looks with accusing eyes at his wife Sofie, with accusing eyes that hint at evidence unheard.

From *A Thousand and One Afternoons in Chicago*. Copyright, 1927, by Pascal Covici, Publisher, Inc., and reprinted by permission of the author.

1. What do you think of Hecht's manner of handling the verbal confusion which customarily surrounds such people in court?
2. Is this story a portrayal of character or a problem?
3. Was the judge conscious of "the evidence unheard"?
4. What part does the city play in the lives of such people?
5. It was written for newspaper publication—"a human interest story," if you care to call it so; do you know of any other newspaper feature writer who commonly does as well?

*William Faulkner*

# PENNSYLVANIA STATION

THEY seemed to bring with them the smell of the snow falling in Seventh Avenue. Or perhaps the other people who had entered before them had done it, bringing it with them in their lungs and exhaling it, filling the arcade with a stale chill like that which might lie unwinded and spent upon the cold plains of infinity itself. In it the bright and serried shop-windows had a fixed and insomniac glare like the eyes of people drugged with coffee, sitting up with a strange corpse.

In the rotunda, where the people appeared as small and intent as ants, the smell and sense of snow still lingered, though high now among the steel girders, spent and vitiated too and filled here with a weary and ceaseless murmuring, like the voices of pilgrims upon the infinite plain, like the voices of all the travelers who had ever passed through it quiring and ceaseless as lost children.

They went on toward the smoking room. It was the old man who looked in the door. "All right," he said. He looked sixty, though he was probably some age like forty-eight or fifty-two or fifty-eight. He wore a long overcoat with a collar which had once been fur, and a cap with earflaps like the caricature of an up-State farmer. His shoes were not mates. "There ain't many here yet. It will be some time now." While they stood there three other men came and looked into the smoking room with that same air not quite diffident and not quite furtive, with faces and garments that seemed to give off that same effluvium of soup kitchens and Salvation Army homes. They entered; the old man led the way toward the rear of the room, among the heavy, solid benches on which still more men of all ages sat in attitudes of thought or repose and looking as transient as scarecrows blown by a departed wind upon a series of rock ledges. The old man chose a bench and sat down, making room for the young man beside him. "I used to think that if you sat somewhere about the middle, he might skip you. But I found out that it don't make much difference where you sit."

"Nor where you lie, either," the young man said. He wore an army overcoat, new, and a pair of yellow army brogans of the sort that can be bought from so-called army stores for a dollar or so. He had not shaved in some time. "And it don't make a hell of a lot of difference whether you are breathing or not while you are lying there. I wish I had a cigarette. I have got used to not eating but be damned if I don't hate to get used to not smoking."

"Sure now," the old man said. "I wish I had a cigarette to give you. I ain't used tobacco myself since I went to Florida. That was funny: I hadn't smoked in ten years, yet as soon as I got back to New York, that was the first thing I thought about. Isn't that funny?"

"Yes," the young man said. "Especially if you never had any tobacco when you thought about wanting it again."

"Wanting it and not having it couldn't have worried me then," the old man said. "I was all right then. Until I—" He settled himself. Into his face came that rapt expression of the talkative old, without heat or bewilderment or rancor. "What confused me was I thought all the time that the burying money was all right. As soon as I found out about Danny's trouble I come right back to New York—"

II

"Who is this Danny, anyway?" the young man said.

"Didn't I tell you? He's Sister's boy. There wasn't any of us left but Sister and Danny and me. Yet I was the weakly one. The one they all thought wouldn't live. I was give up to die twice before I was fifteen, yet I outlived them all. Outlived all eight of them when Sister died three years ago. That was why I went to Florida to live. Because I thought I couldn't stand the winters here. Yet I have stood three of them now since Sister died. But sometimes it looks like a man can stand just about anything if he don't believe he can stand it. Don't you think so?"

"I don't know," the young man said. "Which trouble was this?"

"Which?"

"Which trouble was Danny in now?"

"Don't get me wrong about Danny. He wasn't bad; just wild, like any young fellow. But not bad."

"All right," the young man said. "It wasn't any trouble then."

"No. He's a good boy. He's in Chicago now. Got a good job now. The lawyer in Jacksonville got it for him right after I come back to New York. I didn't know he had it until I tried to wire him that Sister was dead. Then I found that he was in Chicago, with a good job. He sent Sister a wreath of flowers that must have cost two hundred dollars. Sent it by air; that cost something, too. He couldn't come himself because he had just got the job and his boss was out of town and he couldn't get away. He was a good boy. That was why when that trouble come up about that woman on the floor below that accused him of stealing the clothes off her clothes-line, that I told Sister I would send him the railroad fare to Jacksonville, where I could look after him. Get him clean away from them low-life boys around the saloons and such. I come all the way from Florida to see about him. That was how I happened to go with Sister to see Mr. Pinckski, before she ever begun to pay on the coffin. She wanted me to go with her. Because you know

how an old woman is. Only she wasn't old, even if her and me had
outlived all the other seven. But you know how an old woman
seems to get comfort out of knowing she will be buried right in
case there isn't any of her kin there to 'tend to it. I guess maybe
that keeps a lot of them going.

"And especially with Danny already too busy to see if she was
buried at all, himself."

The old man, his mouth already shaped for further speech,
paused and looked at the young man. "What?"

"I say, if getting into the ground at last don't keep some of them
going, I don't know what it is that does."

"Oh. Maybe so. That ain't never worried me. I guess because I
was already give up to die twice before I was fifteen. Like now
every time a winter gets through, I just say to myself, 'Well, I'll
declare. Here I am again.' That was why I went to Florida: because of the winters here. I hadn't been back until I got Sister's
letter about Danny, and I didn't stay long then. And if I hadn't
got the letter about Danny, maybe I wouldn't ever have come
back. But I come back, and that was when she took me with her
to see Mr. Pinckski before she begun to pay on the coffin, for me
to see if it was all right like Mr. Pinckski said. He told her how
the insurance companies would charge her interest all the time.
He showed us with the pencil and paper how if she paid her
money to the insurance companies it would be the same as if she
worked six minutes longer every night and give the money for the
extra six minutes to the insurance company. But Sister said she
wouldn't mind that, just six minutes, because at three or four
o'clock in the morning six minutes wouldn't—"

"Three or four o'clock in the morning?"

"She scrubbed in them tall buildings down about Wall Street
somewhere. Her and some other ladies. They would help one another night about, so they could get done at the same time and
come home on the subway together. So Mr. Pinckski showed us
with the pencil and paper how if she lived fifteen years longer say

for instance Mr. Pinckski said, it would be the same as if she worked three years and eighty-five days without getting any pay for it. Like for three years and eighty-five days she would be working for the insurance companies for nothing. Like instead of living fifteen years, she would actually live only eleven years and two hundred and eight days. Sister stood there for a while, holding her purse under her shawl. Then she said, 'If I was paying the insurance companies to bury me instead of you, I would have to live three years and eighty-five days more before I could afford to die?'

" 'Well,' Mr. Pinckski said, like he didn't know what to say. 'Why, yes. Put it that way, then. You would work for the insurance companies three years and eighty-five days and not get any pay for it.'

" 'It ain't the work I mind,' Sister said. 'It ain't the working.' Then she took the first half a dollar out of her purse and put it down on Mr. Pinckski's desk."

## III

Now and then, with a long and fading reverberation, a subway train passed under their feet. Perhaps they thought momentarily of two green eyes tunneling violently through the earth without apparent propulsion or guidance, as though of their own unparalleled violence creating, like spaced beads on a string, lighted niches in whose wan and fleeting glare human figures like corpses set momentarily on end in a violated grave-yard leaned in one streaming and rigid direction and flicked away.

"Because I was a weak child. They give me up to die twice before I was fifteen. There was an insurance agent sold me a policy once, worried at me until I said all right, I would take it. Then they examined me and the only policy they would give me was a thousand dollars at the rate of fifty years old. And me just twenty-seven then. I was the third one of eight, yet when Sister died three years ago I had outlived them all. So when we got that trouble of

Danny's about the woman that said he stole the clothes fixed up, Sister could—"

"How did you get it fixed up?"

"We paid the money to the man that his job was to look after the boys that Danny run with. The alderman knew Danny and the other boys. It was all right then. So Sister could go on paying the fifty cents to Mr. Pinckski every week. Because we fixed it up for me to send the railroad fare for Danny as soon as I could, so he could be in Florida where I could look out for him. And I went back to Jacksonville and Sister could pay Mr. Pinckski the fifty cents without worrying. Each Sunday morning when her and the other ladies got through, they would go home by Mr. Pinckski's and wake him up and Sister would give him the fifty cents.

"He never minded what time it was because Sister was a good customer. He told her it would be all right, whatever time she got there, to wake him up and pay him. So sometimes it would be as late as four o'clock, especially if they had had a parade or something and the buildings messed up with confetti and maybe flags. Maybe four times a year the lady that lived next door to Sister would write me a letter telling me how much Sister had paid to Mr. Pinckski and that Danny was getting along fine, behaving and not running around with them tough boys any more. So when I could I sent Danny the railroad fare to Florida. I never expected to hear about the money.

"That was what confused me. Sister could read some. She could read the church weekly fine that the priest gave her, but she never was much for writing. She said if she could just happen to find a pencil the size of a broom handle that she could use both hands on, that she could write fine. But regular pencils were too small for her. She said she couldn't feel like she had anything in her hand. So I never expected to hear about the money. I just sent it and then I fixed up with the landlady where I was living for a place for Danny, just thinking that some day soon Danny would just come walking in with his suit-case. The landlady kept the room a week for me, and then a man come in to rent it, so there wasn't anything she could do but give me the refusal of it.

"That wasn't no more than fair, after she had already kept it open a week for me. So I begun to pay for the room and when Danny didn't come I thought maybe something had come up, with the hard winter and all, and Sister needed the money worse than to send Danny to Florida on it, or maybe she thought he was too young yet. So after three months I let the room go. Every three or four months I would get the letter from the lady next door to Sister, about how every Sunday morning Sister and the other ladies would go to Mr. Pinckski and pay him the fifty cents. After fifty-two weeks, Mr. Pinckski set the coffin aside, with her name cut on a steel plate and nailed onto the coffin, her full name: Mrs. Margaret Noonan Gihon.

"It was a cheap coffin at first, just a wooden box, but after she had paid the second fifty-two half a dollars he took the name plate off of it and nailed it onto a better coffin, letting her pick it out herself in case she died that year. And after the third fifty-two half a dollars he let her pick out a still finer one, and the next year one with gold handles on it. He would let her come in and look at it whenever she wanted and bring whoever she wanted with her, to see the coffin and her name cut in the steel plate and nailed onto it. Even at four o'clock in the morning he would come down in his night-shirt and unlock the door and turn the light on for Sister and the other ladies to go back and look at the coffin.

"Each year it got to be a better coffin, with Mr. Pinckski showing the other ladies with the pencil and paper how Sister would have the coffin paid out soon and then she would just be paying on the gold handles and the lining. He let her pick out the lining too that she wanted and when the lady next door wrote me the next letter, Sister sent me a sample of the lining and a picture of the handles. Sister drew the picture, but she never could use a pencil because she always said the handle was too small for her to hold, though she could read the church weekly the priest gave her, because she said the Lord illuminated it for her."

"Is that so," the young man said. "Jesus, I wish I either had a smoke or I would quit thinking about it."

"Yes. And a sample of the lining. But I couldn't tell much about it except that it suited Sister and that she liked it how Mr. Pinckski would let her bring in the other ladies to look at the trimmings and help her make up her mind. Because Mr. Pinckski said he would trust her because he didn't believe she would go and die on him to hurt his business like some did, and him not charging her a cent of interest like the insurance companies would charge. All she had to do was just to stop there every Sunday morning and pay him the half a dollar."

"Is that so?" the young man said. "He must be in the poorhouse now?"

"What?" The old man looked at the young man, his expression fixed. "Who in the poor-house now?"

### IV

"Where was Danny all this time? Still doing his settlement work?"

"Yes. He worked whenever he could get a job. But a high-spirited young fellow, without nobody but a widow woman mother, without no father to learn him how you have to give and take in this world. That was why I wanted him down in Florida with me."

Now his arrested expression faded; he went easily into narration again with a kind of physical and unlistening joy, like a checked and long-broken horse slacked off again.

"That was what got me confused. I had already sent the money for him to come to Jacksonville on and when I never heard about it I just thought maybe Sister needed it with the hard winter and all or maybe she thought Danny was too young, like women will.

And then about eight months after I let the room go I had a funny letter from the lady that lived next door to Sister. It said how Mr. Pinckski had moved the plate onto the next coffin and it said how glad Sister was that Danny was doing so well and she knew I would take good care of him because he was a good boy, beside being all Sister had. Like Danny was already in Florida, all the time.

"But I never knew he was there until I got the wire from him. It come from Augustine, not any piece away; I never found out until Sister died how Mrs. Zilich, that's the lady next door to her, that wrote the letters for Sister, had written me that Danny was coming to Florida the day he left, the day after the money come. Mrs. Zilich told how she had written the letter for Sister and give it to Danny himself to mail the night before he left. I never got it. I reckon Danny never mailed it. I reckon, being a young, high-spirited boy, he decided he wanted to strike out himself and show us what he could do without any help from us, like I did when I come to Florida.

"Mrs. Zilich said she thought of course Danny was with me and that she thought at the time it was funny that when I would write to Sister I never mentioned Danny. So when she would read the letters to Sister she would put in something about Danny was all right and doing fine. So when I got the wire from Danny in Augustine I telephoned Mrs. Zilich in New York. It cost eleven dollars. I told her that Danny was in a little trouble, not serious, and for her to not tell Sister it was serious trouble, to just tell her that we would need some money. Because I had sent money for Danny to come to Florida on and I had paid the three months for the room and I had just paid the premium on my insurance, and so the lawyer looked at Danny and Danny sitting there on the cot in the cell without no collar on and Danny said, 'Where would I get any money,' only it was jack he called it.

"And the lawyer said, 'Where would you get it?' and Danny said, 'Just set me down back home for ten minutes. I'll show you.'

'Seventy-five bucks,' he says, telling me that was all of it. Then the lawyer says that was neither here nor there and so I telephoned to Mrs. Zilich and told her to tell Sister to go to Mr. Pinckski and ask him to let her take back some of the coffin money; he could put the name plate back on the coffin she had last year or maybe the year before, and as soon as I could get some money on my insurance policy I would pay Mr. Pinckski back and some interest too. I telephoned from the jail, but I didn't say where I was telephoning from; I just said we would need some money quick."

"What was he in for this time?" the young man said.

"He wasn't in jail the other time, about them clothes off that line. That woman was lying about him. After we paid the money, she admitted she was probably mistaken."

"All right," the young man said. "What was he in for?"

"They called it grand larceny and killing a policeman. They framed him, them others did that didn't like him. He was just wild. That was all. He was a good boy. When Sister died he couldn't come to the funeral. But he sent a wreath that must have cost $200 if it cost a cent. By air mail, with the high postage in the . . ."

His voice died away; he looked at the young man with a kind of pleased astonishment. "I'll declare I made a joke. But I didn't mean—"

"Sure. I know you didn't mean to make a joke. What about the jail?"

"The lawyer was already there when I got there. Some friends had sent the lawyer to help him. And he swore to me on his mother's name that he wasn't even there when the cop got shot. He was in Orlando at the time. He showed me a ticket from Orlando to Waycross that he had bought and missed the train; that was how he happened to have it with him. It had the date punched in it, the same night the policeman got killed, showing that Danny wasn't even there and that them other boys had framed him. He was mad. The lawyer said how he would see the friends that had sent him to help Danny and get them to help. 'By God they better,' Danny said. 'If they think I'm going to take this laying down they better—'

"Then the lawyer got him quiet again, like he did when Danny was talking about that money the man he worked for or something had held out on him back in New York. And so I telephoned Mrs. Zilich, so as not to worry Sister, and told her to go to Mr. Pinckski. Two days later I got the telegram from Mrs. Zilich. I guess Mrs. Zilich hadn't never sent a telegram before and so she didn't know she had ten words without counting the address because it just said You and Danny come home quick Mrs. Sophie Zilich New York.

"I couldn't make nothing out of it and we talked it over and the lawyer said I better go and see, that he would take care of Danny till I got back. So we fixed up a letter from Danny to Sister, for Mrs. Zilich to read to her, about how Danny was all right and getting along fine—"

## V

At that moment there entered the room a man in the uniform of the railway company. As he entered, from about him some-where—behind, above—a voice came. Though it spoke human speech it did not sound like a human voice, since it was too big to have emerged from known man and it had a quality at once booming, cold, and forlorn, as though it were not interested in nor listening to what it said.

"There," the old man said.

He and the young man turned and looked back across the benches, as most of the other heads had done, as though they were all dummies moved by a single wire. The man in uniform ad-vanced slowly into the room, moving along the first bench. As he did so the men on that bench and on the others began to rise and depart, passing the man in uniform as though he were not there;

he too moving on into the room as if it were empty. "I guess we'll have to move."

"Hell," the young man said. "Let him come in and ask for them. They pay him to do it."

"He caught me the other night. The second time, too."

"What about that? This time won't make but three. What did you do then?"

"Oh yes," the old man said. "I knew that was the only thing to do, after that telegram. Mrs. Zilich wouldn't have spent the money to telegraph without good reason. I didn't know what she had told Sister. I just knew that Mrs. Zilich thought there wasn't time to write a letter and that she was trying to save money on the telegram, not knowing she had ten words and the man at the telegraph office not telling her better. So I didn't know what was wrong. I never suspicioned it at all. That was what confused me, you see."

He turned and looked back again toward the man in uniform moving from bench to bench while just before him the men in mismated garments, with that identical neatness of indigence, with that identical air of patient and indomitable forlornness, rose and moved toward the exit in a monstrous and outrageous analogy to flying fish before the advancing prow of a ship.

"What confused you?" the young man said.

"Mrs. Zilich told me. I left Danny in the jail. (Them friends that sent him the lawyer got him out the next day. When I heard from him again, he was already in Chicago, with a good job; he sent that wreath. I didn't know he was even gone from the jail until I tried to get word to him about Sister), and I come on to New York. I had just enough money for that, and Mrs. Zilich met me at the station and told me. At this station right here. It was snowing that night, too. She was waiting at the top of the steps.

" 'Where's Sister?' I said. 'She didn't come with you?'

" 'What is it now?' Mrs. Zilich said. 'You don't need to tell me he is just sick.'

" 'Did you tell Sister he ain't just sick?' I said. 'I didn't have to,' Mrs. Zilich said. 'I didn't have time to, even if I would have.' She told about how it was cold that night and so she waited up for Sister, keeping the fire going and a pot of coffee ready, and how she waited till Sister had took off her coat and shawl and was beginning to get warm, setting there with a cup of coffee; then Mrs. Zilich said, 'Your brother telephoned from Florida.' That's all she had time to say. She never even had to tell Sister how I said for her to go to Mr. Pinckski, because Sister said right off, 'He will want that money.' Just what I had said, you see.

"Mrs. Zilich noticed it too. 'Maybe it's because you are kin, both kin to that—' Then she stopped and said, 'Oh, I ain't going to say anything about him. Don't worry. The time to do that is past now.' Then she told me how she said to Sister, 'You can stop there on the way down this afternoon and see Mr. Pinckski.' But Sister was already putting on her coat and shawl again and her not an hour home from work and it snowing. She wouldn't wait."

"She had to take back the coffin money, did she?" the young man said.

"Yes. Mrs. Zilich said that her and Sister went to Mr. Pinckski and woke him up. And he told them that Sister had already taken the money back."

"What?" the young man said. "Already?"

"Yes. He said how Danny had come to him about a year back, with a note from Sister saying to give Danny the money that she had paid in to Mr. Pinckski and that Mr. Pinckski did it. And Sister standing there with her hands inside her shawl, not looking at anything until Mrs. Zilich said, 'A note? Mrs. Gihon never sent you a note because she can't write,' and Mr. Pinckski said, 'Should I know if she can't write or not when her own son brings me a note signed with her name?' and Mrs. Zilich says, 'Let's see it.'

"Sister hadn't said anything at all, like she wasn't even there, and Mr. Pinckski showed them the note. I saw it too. It said, 'Received of Mr. Pinckski a hundred and thirty dollars being the full amount deposited with him less interest. Mrs. Margaret N. Gihon.' And Mrs. Zilich said how she thought about that hundred and thirty dollars and she thought how Sister had paid twenty-six dollars a year for five years and seven months, and she said, 'Interest? What interest?' and Mr. Pinckski said, 'For taking the name off the coffin,' because that made the coffin second handed. And Mrs. Zilich said that Sister turned and went toward the door. 'Wait,' Mrs. Zilich said. 'We're going to stay right here until you get that money. There's something funny about this because you can't write to sign a note.' But Sister just went on toward the door until Mrs. Zilich said, 'Wait, Margaret.' And then Sister said, 'I signed it.'"

## VI

The voice of the man in uniform could be heard now as he worked slowly toward them: "Tickets. Tickets. Show your tickets."

"I guess it's hard enough to know what a single woman will do," the old man said. "But a widow woman with just one child. I didn't know she could write, either. I guess she picked it up cleaning up them offices every night. Anyway, Mr. Pinckski showed me the note, how she admitted she signed it, and he explained to me how the difference was; that he had to charge to protect himself in case the coffins ever were refused and become second hand; that some folks was mighty particular about having a brand new coffin.

"He had put the plate with Sister's name on it back onto the cheap coffin that she started off with, so she was still all right for a coffin, even if it never had any handles and lining. I never said anything about that; that twenty-six dollars she had paid in since she give the money to Danny wouldn't have helped any; I had already spent that much getting back to see about the money, and anyway, Sister still had a coffin—"

The voice of the man in uniform was quite near now, with a

quality methodical, monotonous, and implacable: "Tickets. Tickets. Show your tickets. All without railroad tickets."

The young man rose. "I'll be seeing you," he said. The old man rose too. Beyond the man in uniform the room was almost empty.

"I guess it's about time," the old man said. He followed the young man into the rotunda. There was an airplane in it, motionless, squatting, with a still, beetling look like a huge bug preserved in alcohol. There was a placard beside it, about how it had flown over mountains and vast wastes of snow.

"They might have tried it over New York," the young man said. "It would have been closer."

"Yes," the old man said. "It costs more, though. But I guess that's fair, since it is faster. When Sister died, Danny sent a wreath of flowers by air. It must have cost two hundred dollars. The wreath did, I mean. I don't know what it cost to send it by air."

Then they both looked up the ramp and through the arcade, toward the doors on Seventh Avenue. Beyond the doors lay a thick, moribund light that seemed to fill the arcade with the smell of snow and of cold, so that for a while longer they seemed to stand in the grip of a dreadful reluctance and inertia.

"So they went on back home," the old man said. "Mrs. Zilich said how Sister was already shaking and she got Sister to bed. And that night Sister had a fever and Mrs. Zilich sent for the doctor and the doctor looked at Sister and told Mrs. Zilich she had better telegraph if there was anybody to telegraph to. When I got home Sister didn't know me. The priest was already there, and we never could tell if she knew anything or not, not even when we read the letter from Danny that we had fixed up in the jail, about how he was all right. The priest read it to her, but we couldn't tell if she heard him or not. That night she died."

"Is that so," the young man said, looking up the ramp. He moved. "I'm going to the Grand Central."

Again the old man moved, with that same unwearying alacrity. "I guess that's the best thing to do. We might have a good while there." He looked up at the clock; he said with pleased surprise: "Half past one already. And a half an hour to get there. And if we're lucky, we'll have two hours before he comes along. Maybe three. That'll be five o'clock. Then it will be only two hours more till daylight."

From *The American Mercury*, Feb., 1934. Reprinted by permission of the editor and the author.

1. What handicaps beset, or what influences besides poverty work upon Danny and the two other members of his family?
2. Why was the pencil too small for Sister to hold?
3. What was Danny's business in Chicago?
4. What purpose does the young vagrant serve?
5. Why does Faulkner interrupt the tale of Sister and Mr. Pinckski with a definite break in the story form (Part III) and content?

# VIII.  WAR

# VIII. WAR

WAR as a theme figures largely in the English novel from Smollett to the present day. Sometimes, as in *Vanity Fair*, it is a mere episode in the development of a larger theme; again, as in the once popular romances of Charles Lever, it furnishes almost the whole setting. But however employed, the treatment is much the same. Almost without exception the emphasis is on what Shakespeare called "the pomp and circumstance of glorious war." It might, as in the death of George Osborne, involve personal tragedy, but not even in Thackeray is there any suggestion that war itself is tragedy, the tragedy of human stupidity and folly. Lever's soldiers all seem to have a glorious time; wounds and death are treated lightly, as chances of the game. When Henry Kingsley needed to get Charles Ravenshoe out of England for a time, he enlisted him in the cavalry and sent him to the Crimea to share in the charge of the Light Brigade. But Kingsley did not dwell on the fact that that charge was one of the most appalling blunders in military history prior to the World War, and even to Tennyson it seemed that the futile heroism of the troopers somehow consecrated the imbecility of their leaders.

A new tone is first noticeable in the stories of the British Army in India which Rudyard Kipling began to write in the 1880s. These stand midway between Lever and Kingsley and our own day. Kipling dismayed his contemporary critics by his greater frankness in reporting the violence and brutality of war. He shocked them even with a matter-of-fact picture of "Private Stanley Ortheris engaged in his business," which business happened at the moment to be obeying orders by shooting at long range a deserter from a native regiment. Kipling's tough, hard-fighting, hard-drinking privates were very different people from the dashing officers of Lever and Kingsley, but seen in perspective his stories, despite their greater frankness, belong more to the nineteenth than to the twentieth century tradition. Their psychological core is the oblique sentimentality which Kipling's early master, Bret Harte, had adapted from Dickens. Like Harte's miners, these hard-boiled soldiers have hearts of gold. Their roughness and brutality are justified because they are used against the enemies of the British Empire. Had Harte drawn his themes from the barracks instead of the mines, the result would not have been much different from "Only a Subaltern," or "The Drums of the Fore and Aft."

But the same decade which introduced *Soldiers Three* to a public outside of India saw the beginning of stories which broke completely with the traditions of sentiment and glory. Two Americans were responsible for the change: Ambrose Bierce, a veteran of the Civil War, and Stephen Crane, a young journalist who had never seen men in action until after he had written his greatest book. *In the Midst of Life*, Bierce's sole important volume of short stories, contains a dozen pictures of war as he remembered it. They are stories in the sense that Bierce contrived a dramatic situation for each, but their technical virtuosity is not their merit—rather, it is their defect. What counts is not the suggestion that Captain Coulter's orders to bombard his own home come from a jealous superior whose advances Coulter's wife has repulsed; it is the ungloved handling of violence, mutilation and death, with the underlying suggestion that patriotism is inadequate to overrule mean personal motives, that men's—and women's—lives may be sacrificed to no purpose beyond folly or spite.

What Bierce only suggested was fully stated by Stephen Crane in *The Red Badge of Courage*, the first book to depict the real dust and heat of conflict, the formlessness and futility of war as seen from below by the man in the ranks. Crane rejected all the conventional plot devices of climax and dramatic surprise. His Henry Fleming goes through the battle of Chancellorsville, suffers panic terror, runs away, regains control of himself, and at last rejoins his regiment an initiated soldier, all without having had any idea of the objectives of the fight. His own squad, at most his own regiment, were all he ever saw.

Between them, Bierce and Crane established the patterns and points of view of most of the fiction inspired by the World War. Where later writers tried to go beyond them they too often plunged, in their revulsion from patriotic platitudes, into something like hysteria. Crane struck the balance between the boredom of routine and the frenzy of action; a book like William March's *Company K* is all frenzy. Perhaps the result was inevitable. The World War brought casualties far outweighing in number and horror anything experienced even in our Civil War; this real concentration of shocks is trebly concentrated in the books. The vast scale of modern military operations, moreover, intensified the individual's sense of bewilderment and isolation which Crane had been the first to understand, and by magnifying the human inadequacy of the staff to manage their huge machine increased the feeling of futility. One reason why Lawrence of Arabia was the only individual hero of the World War to fire the popular imagination was because he was the only leader who conducted operations on a scale in which the individual had a chance to be observed. Modern war literature has this much in common with tales of city life, that it constantly emphasizes the disproportion between the individual and the unwieldy machine in which he is caught.

# Rudyard Kipling

# THE DRUMS OF THE FORE
# AND AFT

I N THE Army List they still stand as "The Fore and Fit
Princess Hohenzollern-Sigmaringen-Anspach's Merther-Tydfil-
shire Own Royal Loyal Light Infantry, Regimental District
329A," but the Army through all its barracks and canteens
knows them now as the "Fore and Aft." They may in time do
something that shall make their new title honorable, but at present they are bitterly ashamed, and the man who calls them "Fore
and Aft" does so at the risk of the head which is on his shoulders.

Two words breathed into the stables of a certain Cavalry Regiment will bring the men out into the streets with belts and mops
and bad language; but a whisper of "Fore and Aft" will bring out
this regiment with rifles.

Their one excuse is that they came again and did their best to
finish the job in style. But for a time all their world knows that
they were openly beaten, whipped, dumb-cowed, shaking and
afraid. The men know it; their officers know it; the Horse Guards
know it, and when the next war comes the enemy will know it
also. There are two or three regiments of the Line that have a
black mark against their names which they will then wipe out; and
it will be excessively inconvenient for the troops upon whom they
do their wiping.

The courage of the British soldier is officially supposed to be above proof, and, as a general rule, it is so. The exceptions are decently shoveled out of sight, only to be referred to in the freshet of unguarded talk that occasionally swamps a Mess-table at midnight. Then one hears strange and horrible stories of men not following their officers, of orders being given by those who had no right to give them, and of disgrace that, but for the standing luck of the British Army, might have ended in brilliant disaster. These are unpleasant stories to listen to, and the Messes tell them under their breath, sitting by the big wood fires, and the young officer bows his head and thinks to himself, please God, his men shall never behave unhandily.

The British soldier is not altogether to be blamed for occasional lapses; but this verdict he should not know. A moderately intelligent General will waste six months in mastering the craft of the particular war that he may be waging; a Colonel may utterly misunderstand the capacity of his regiment for three months after it has taken the field, and even a Company Commander may err and be deceived as to the temper and temperament of his own handful: wherefore the soldier, and the soldier of to-day more particularly, should not be blamed for falling back. He should be shot or hanged afterwards—to encourage the others; but he should not be vilified in newspapers, for that is want of tact and waste of space.

He has, let us say, been in the service of the Empress for, perhaps, four years. He will leave in another two years. He has no inherited morals, and four years are not sufficient to drive toughness into his fiber, or to teach him how holy a thing is his Regiment. He wants to drink, he wants to enjoy himself—in India he wants to save money—and he does not in the least like getting hurt. He has received just sufficient education to make him understand half the purport of the orders he receives, and to speculate on the nature of clean, incised, and shattering wounds. Thus, if he is told to deploy under fire preparatory to an attack, he knows that he runs a very great risk of being killed while he is deploying, and suspects that he is being thrown away to gain ten minutes' time. He may either deploy with desperate swiftness, or he may shuffle, or bunch, or break, according to the discipline under which he has lain for four years.

Armed with imperfect knowledge, cursed with the rudiments of an imagination, hampered by the intense selfishness of the lower classes, and unsupported by any regimental associations, this young man is suddenly introduced to an enemy who in eastern lands is always ugly, generally tall and hairy, and frequently noisy. If he looks to the right and the left and sees old soldiers—men of twelve years' service, who, he knows, know what they are about—taking a charge, rush, or demonstration without embarrassment, he is consoled and applies his shoulder to the butt of his rifle with a stout heart. His peace is the greater if he hears a senior, who has taught him his soldiering and broken his head on occasion, whispering: "They'll shout and carry on like this for five minutes. Then they'll rush in, and then we've got 'em by the short hairs!"

But, on the other hand, if he sees only men of his own term of service, turning white and playing with their triggers and saying: "What the Hell's up now?" while the Company Commanders are sweating into their sword-hilts and shouting: "Front-rank, fix bayonets. Steady there—steady! Sight for three hundred—no, for five! Lie down, all! Steady! Front-rank kneel!" and so forth, he becomes unhappy, and grows acutely miserable when he hears a comrade turn over with the rattle of fire-irons falling into the fender, and the grunt of a pole-axed ox. If he can be moved about a little and allowed to watch the effect of his own fire on the enemy he feels merrier, and may be then worked up to the blind passion of fighting, which is, contrary to general belief, controlled by a chilly Devil and shakes men like ague. If he is not moved about, and begins to feel cold at the pit of the stomach, and in that crisis is badly mauled and hears orders that were never given, he will break, and he will break badly, and of all things under the light of the Sun there is nothing more terrible than a broken British regiment.

When the worst comes to the worst and the panic is really epidemic, the men must be e'en let go, and the Company Commanders had better escape to the enemy and stay there for safety's sake. If they can be made to come again they are not pleasant men to meet; because they will not break twice.

About thirty years from this date, when we have succeeded in half-educating everything that wears trousers, our Army will be a beautifully unreliable machine. It will know too much and it will do too little. Later still, when all men are at the mental level of the officer of to-day, it will sweep the earth. Speaking roughly, you must employ either blackguards or gentlemen, or, best of all, blackguards commanded by gentlemen, to do butcher's work with efficiency and despatch. The ideal soldier should, of course, think for himself—the *Pocket-book* says so. Unfortunately, to attain this virtue, he has to pass through the phase of thinking of himself, and that is misdirected genius. A blackguard may be slow to think for himself, but he is genuinely anxious to kill, and a little punishment teaches him how to guard his own skin and perforate another's. A powerfully prayerful Highland Regiment, officered by rank Presbyterians, is, perhaps, one degree more terrible in action than a hard-bitten thousand of irresponsible Irish ruffians led by most improper young unbelievers. But these things prove the rule —which is that the midway men are not to be trusted alone. They have ideas about the value of life and an upbringing that has not taught them to go on and take the chances. They are carefully unprovided with a backing of comrades who have been shot over, and until that backing is re-introduced, as a great many Regimental Commanders intend it shall be, they are more liable to disgrace themselves than the size of the Empire or the dignity of the Army allows. Their officers are as good as good can be, because their training begins early, and God has arranged that a clean-run youth of the British middle classes shall, in the matter of backbone, brains, and bowels, surpass all other youths. For this reason a child of eighteen will stand up, doing nothing, with a tin sword in his hand and joy in his heart until he is dropped. If he dies, he dies like a gentleman. If he lives, he writes Home that he has been "potted," "sniped," "chipped," or "cut over," and sits down to besiege Government for a wound-gratuity until the next little war breaks out, when he perjures himself before a Medical Board, blarneys his Colonel, burns incense round his Adjutant, and is allowed to go to the Front once more.

Which homily brings me directly to a brace of the most finished little fiends that ever banged drum or tootled fife in the Band of a British Regiment. They ended their sinful career by open and flagrant mutiny and were shot for it. Their names were Jakin and Lew—Piggy Lew—and they were bold, bad drummer-boys, both of them frequently birched by the Drum-Major of the Fore and Aft.

Jakin was a stunted child of fourteen, and Lew was about the same age. When not looked after, they smoked and drank. They swore habitually after the manner of the barrack-room, which is cold-swearing and comes from between clinched teeth, and they fought religiously once a week. Jakin had sprung from some London gutter and may or may not have passed through Doctor Barnardo's hands ere he arrived at the dignity of drummer-boy. Lew could remember nothing except the Regiment and the delight of listening to the Band from his earliest years. He hid somewhere in his grimy little soul a genuine love for music, and was most mistakenly furnished with the head of a cherub: insomuch that beautiful ladies who watched the Regiment in church were wont to speak of him as a "darling." They never heard his vitriolic comments on their manners and morals, as he walked back to barracks with the Band and matured fresh causes of offence against Jakin.

The other drummer-boys hated both lads on account of their illogical conduct. Jakin might be pounding Lew, or Lew might be rubbing Jakin's head in the dirt, but any attempt at aggression on the part of an outsider was met by the combined forces of Lew and Jakin; and the consequences were painful. The boys were the Ishmaels of the corps, but wealthy Ishmaels, for they sold battles in alternate weeks for the sport of the barracks when they were not pitted against other boys; and thus amassed money.

On this particular day there was dissension in the camp. They had just been convicted afresh of smoking, which is bad for little boys who use plug-tobacco, and Lew's contention was that Jakin had "stunk so 'orrid bad from keepin' the pipe in pocket," that he and he alone was responsible for the birching they were both tingling under.

"I tell you I 'id the pipe back o' barracks," said Jakin pacifically.

"You're a bloomin' liar," said Lew without heat.

"You're a bloomin' little barstard," said Jakin, strong in the knowledge that his own ancestry was unknown.

Now there is one word in the extended vocabulary of barrack-room abuse that cannot pass without comment. You may call a man a thief and risk nothing. You may even call him a coward without finding more than a boot whiz past your ear, but you must not call a man a bastard unless you are prepared to prove it on his front teeth.

"You might ha' kep' that till I wasn't so sore," said Lew sorrowfully, dodging round Jakin's guard.

"I'll make you sorer," said Jakin genially, and got home on Lew's alabaster forehead. All would have gone well and this story, as the books say, would never have been written, had not his evil fate prompted the Bazar-Sergeant's son, a long, employless man of five-and-twenty, to put in an appearance after the first round. He was eternally in need of money, and knew that the boys had silver.

"Fighting again," said he. "I'll report you to my father, and he'll report you to the Color-Sergeant."

"What's that to you?" said Jakin with an unpleasant dilation of the nostrils.

"Oh! nothing to me. You'll get into trouble, and you've been up too often to afford that."

"What the Hell do you know about what we've done?" asked Lew the Seraph. "You aren't in the Army, you lousy, cadging civilian."

He closed in on the man's left flank.

"Jes' 'cause you find two gentlemen settlin' their diff'rences with their fistes you stick in your ugly nose where you aren't wanted. Run 'ome to your 'arf-caste slut of a Ma—or we'll give you what-for," said Jakin.

The man attempted reprisals by knocking the boys' heads together. The scheme would have succeeded had not Jakin punched him vehemently in the stomach, or had Lew refrained from kicking his shins. They fought together, bleeding and breathless, for half an hour, and, after heavy punishment, triumphantly pulled down their opponent as terriers pull down a jackal.

"Now," gasped Jakin, "I'll give you what-for." He proceeded to pound the man's features while Lew stamped on the outlying portions of his anatomy. Chivalry is not a strong point in the composition of the average drummer-boy. He fights, as do his betters, to make his mark.

Ghastly was the ruin that escaped, and awful was the wrath of the Bazar-Sergeant. Awful too was the scene in Orderly-room when the two reprobates appeared to answer the charge of half-murdering a "civilian." The Bazar-Sergeant thirsted for a criminal action, and his son lied. The boys stood to attention while the black clouds of evidence accumulated.

"You little devils are more trouble than the rest of the Regiment put together," said the Colonel angrily. "One might as well admonish thistledown, and I can't well put you in cells or under stoppages. You must be birched again."

"Beg y' pardon, Sir. Can't we say nothin' in our own defence, Sir?" shrilled Jakin.

"Hey! What? Are you going to argue with *me?*" said the Colonel.

"No, Sir," said Lew. "But if a man come to you, Sir, and said he was going to report you, Sir, for 'aving a bit of a turn-up with a friend, Sir, an' wanted to get money out o' you, Sir—"

The Orderly-room exploded in a roar of laughter. "Well?" said the Colonel.

"That was what that measly *jarnwar* there did, Sir, and 'e'd 'a' done it, Sir, if we 'adn't prevented 'im. We didn't 'it 'im much, Sir. 'E 'adn't no manner o' right to interfere with us, Sir. I don't mind bein' birched by the Drum-Major, Sir, nor yet reported by any Corp'ral, but I'm—but I don't think it's fair, Sir, for a civilian to come an' talk over a man in the Army."

A second shout of laughter shook the Orderly-room, but the Colonel was grave.

"What sort of characters have these boys?" he asked of the Regimental Sergeant-Major.

"Accordin' to the Bandmaster, Sir," returned that revered official —the only soul in the Regiment whom the boys feared—"they do everything *but* lie, Sir."

"Is it like we'd go for that man for fun, Sir?" said Lew, pointing to the plaintiff.

"Oh, admonished,—admonished!" said the Colonel testily, and when the boys had gone he read the Bazar-Sergeant's son a lecture on the sin of unprofitable meddling, and gave orders that the Bandmaster should keep the Drums in better discipline.

"If either of you come to practice again with so much as a scratch on your two ugly little faces," thundered the Bandmaster, "I'll tell the Drum-Major to take the skin off your backs. Understand that, you young devils."

Then he repented of his speech for just the length of time that Lew, looking like a seraph in red worsted embellishments, took the place of one of the trumpets—in hospital—and rendered the echo of a battle-piece. Lew certainly was a musician, and had often in his more exalted moments expressed a yearning to master every instrument of the Band.

"There's nothing to prevent your becoming a Bandmaster, Lew," said the Bandmaster, who had composed waltzes of his own, and worked day and night in the interests of the Band.

"What did he say?" demanded Jakin after practice.

" 'Said I might be a bloomin' Bandmaster, an' be asked in to 'ave a glass o' sherry-wine on Mess-nights."

"Ho! 'Said you might be a bloomin' non-combatant, did 'e! That's just about wot 'e would say. When I've put in my boy's service—it's a bloomin' shame that doesn't count for pension—I'll take on as a privit. Then I'll be a Lance in a year—knowin' what I know about the ins and outs o' things. In three years I'll be a bloomin' Sergeant. I won't marry then, not I! I'll 'old on and learn the orf'cers' ways an' apply for exchange into a reg'ment that doesn't know all about me. Then I'll be a bloomin' orf'cer. Then I'll ask you to 'ave a glass o' sherry-wine, Mister Lew, an' you'll bloomin' well 'ave to stay in the hanty-room while the Mess-Sergeant brings it to your dirty 'ands."

" 'S'pose I'm going to be a Bandmaster? Not I, quite. I'll be a orf'cer too. There's nothin' like takin' to a thing an' stickin' to it, the Schoolmaster says. The Reg'ment don't go 'ome for another seven years. I'll be a Lance then or near to."

Thus the boys discussed their futures, and conducted themselves piously for a week. That is to say, Lew started a flirtation with the Color-Sergeant's daughter, aged thirteen—"not," as he explained to Jakin, "with any intention of matrimony, but by way o' keepin' my 'and in." And the black-haired Cris Delighan enjoyed that flirtation more than previous ones, and the other drummer-boys raged furiously together, and Jakin preached sermons on the dangers of "bein' tangled along o' petticoats."

But neither love nor virtue would have held Lew long in the paths of propriety had not the rumor gone abroad that the Regiment was to be sent on active service, to take part in a war which, for the sake of brevity, we will call "The War of the Lost Tribes."

The barracks had the rumor almost before the Mess-room, and of all the nine hundred men in barracks, not ten had seen a shot fired in anger. The Colonel had, twenty years ago, assisted at a Frontier expedition; one of the Majors had seen service at the Cape; a confirmed deserter in E Company had helped to clear streets in Ireland; but that was all. The Regiment had been put by for many years. The overwhelming mass of its rank and file had from three to four years' service; the non-commissioned officers were under thirty years old; and men and sergeants alike had forgotten to speak of the stories written in brief upon the Colors—the New Colors that had been formally blessed by an Archbishop in England ere the Regiment came away.

They wanted to go to the Front—they were enthusiastically anxious to go—but they had no knowledge of what war meant, and there was none to tell them. They were an educated regiment, the percentage of school-certificates in their ranks was high, and most of the men could do more than read and write. They had been recruited in loyal observance of the territorial idea; but they themselves had no notion of that idea. They were made up of drafts from an over-populated manufacturing district. The system had put flesh and muscle upon their small bones, but it could not put heart into the sons of those who for generations had done overmuch work for over-scanty pay, had sweated in drying-rooms, stooped over looms, coughed among white-lead, and shivered on lime-barges. The men had found food and rest in the Army, and now they were going to fight "niggers"—people who ran away if you shook a stick at them. Wherefore they cheered lustily when the rumor ran, and the shrewd, clerkly non-commissioned officers speculated on the chances of batta and of saving their pay. At Headquarters, men said: "The Fore and Fit have never been under fire within the last generation. Let us, therefore, break them in easily by setting them to guard lines of communication." And this would have been done but for the fact that British Regiments were wanted—badly wanted—at the Front, and there were doubtful Native Regiments that could fill the minor duties. "Brigade 'em with two strong Regiments," said Headquarters. "They may be knocked about a bit, but they'll learn their business before they come through. Nothing like a night-alarm and a little cutting-up of stragglers to make a Regiment smart in the field. Wait till they've had half a dozen sentries' throats cut."

The Colonel wrote with delight that the temper of his men was excellent, that the Regiment was all that could be wished, and as sound as a bell. The Majors smiled with a sober joy, and the subalterns waltzed in pairs down the Mess-room after dinner, and nearly shot themselves at revolver-practice. But there was consternation in the hearts of Jakin and Lew. What was to be done with the Drums? Would the Band go to the Front? How many of the Drums would accompany the Regiment?

They took council together, sitting in a tree and smoking.

"It's more than a bloomin' toss-up they'll leave us be'ind at the Depot with the women. You'll like that," said Jakin sarcastically.

" 'Cause o' Cris, y' mean? Wot's a woman, or a 'ole bloomin' depôt o' women, 'longside o' the chanst of field-service? You know I'm as keen on going as you," said Lew.

" 'Wish I was a bloomin' bugler," said Jakin sadly. "They'll take Tom Kidd along, that I can plaster a wall with, an' like as not they won't take us."

"Then let's go an' make Tom Kidd so bloomin' sick 'e can't bugle no more. You 'old 'is 'ands an' I'll kick 'im," said Lew, wriggling on the branch.

"That ain't no good neither. We ain't the sort o' characters to presoom on our rep'tations—they're bad. If they leave the Band at the Depot we don't go, and no error there. If they take the Band we may get cast for medical unfitness. Are you medical fit, Piggy?" said Jakin, digging Lew in the ribs with force.

"Yus," said Lew with an oath. "The Doctor says your 'eart's

weak through smokin' on an empty stummick. Throw a chest an'
I'll try yer."

Jakin threw out his chest, which Lew smote with all his might.
Jakin turned very pale, gasped, crowed, screwed up his eyes and
said—"That's all right."

"You'll do," said Lew. "I've 'eard o' men dying when you 'it
'em fair on the breastbone."

"Don't bring us no nearer goin', though," said Jakin. "Do you
know where we're ordered?"

"Gawd knows, an' 'E won't split on a pal. Somewheres up to
the Front to kill Paythans—hairy big beggars that turn you inside
out if they get 'old o' you. They say their women are good-looking,
too."

"Any loot?" asked the abandoned Jakin.

"Not a bloomin' anna, they say, unless you dig up the ground
an' see what the niggers 'ave 'id. They're a poor lot." Jakin stood
upright on the branch and gazed across the plain.

"Lew," said he, "there's the Colonel coming. 'Colonel's a good
old beggar. Let's go an' talk to 'im."

Lew nearly fell out of the tree at the audacity of the suggestion.
Like Jakin he feared not God, neither regarded he Man, but there
are limits even to the audacity of a drummer-boy, and to speak
to a Colonel was—

But Jakin had slid down the trunk and doubled in the direction
of the Colonel. That officer was walking wrapped in thought and
visions of a C. B.—yes, even a K. C. B., for had he not at command one of the best Regiments of the Line—the Fore and Fit?
And he was aware of two small boys charging down upon him.
Once before it had been solemnly reported to him that "the
Drums were in a state of mutiny," Jakin and Lew being the ring-
leaders. This looked like an organized conspiracy.

The boys halted at twenty yards, walked to the regulation four
paces, and saluted together, each as well set-up as a ramrod and
little taller.

The Colonel was in a genial mood; the boys appeared very forlorn and unprotected on the desolate plain, and one of them was handsome.

"Well!" said the Colonel, recognizing them. "Are you going to pull me down in the open? I'm sure I never interfere with you, even though"—he sniffed suspiciously—"you have been smoking."

It was time to strike while the iron was hot. Their hearts beat tumultuously.

"Beg y' pardon, Sir," began Jakin. "The Reg'ment's ordered on active service, Sir?"

"So I believe," said the Colonel courteously.

"Is the Band goin', Sir?" said both together. Then, without pause, "We're goin', Sir, ain't we?"

"You!" said the Colonel, stepping back the more fully to take in the two small figures. "You! You'd die in the first march."

"No, we wouldn't, Sir. We can march with the Reg'ment anywheres—p'rade an' anywhere else," said Jakin.

"If Tom Kidd goes 'e'll shut up like a clasp-knife," said Lew. "Tom 'as very-close veins in both 'is legs, Sir."

"Very how much?"

"Very-close veins, Sir. That's why they swells after long p'rade, Sir. If 'e can go, we can go, Sir."

Again the Colonel looked at them long and intently.

"Yes, the Band is going," he said as gravely as though he had been addressing a brother officer. "Have you any parents, either of you two?"

"No, Sir," rejoicingly from Lew and Jakin. "We're both orphans, Sir. There's no one to be considered of on our account, Sir."

"You poor little sprats, and you want to go up to the Front with the Regiment, do you? Why?"

"I've wore the Queen's Uniform for two years," said Jakin. "It's very 'ard, Sir, that a man don't get no recompense for doin' of 'is dooty, Sir."

"An'—an' if I don't go, Sir," interrupted Lew, "the Bandmaster 'e says 'e'll catch an' make a bloo—a blessed musician o' me, Sir. Before I've seen any service, Sir."

The Colonel made no answer for a long time. Then he said quietly: "If you're passed by the Doctor I dare say you can go. I shouldn't smoke if I were you."

The boys saluted and disappeared. The Colonel walked home and told the story to his wife, who nearly cried over it. The Colonel was well pleased. If that was the temper of the children, what would not the men do?

Jakin and Lew entered the boys' barrack-room with great stateliness, and refused to hold any conversation with their comrades for at least ten minutes. Then, bursting with pride, Jakin drawled: "I've bin intervooin' the Colonel. Good old beggar is the Colonel. Says I to 'im, 'Colonel,' says I, 'let me go to the Front, along o' the Reg'ment.'—'To the Front you shall go,' says 'e, 'an' I only wish there was more like you among the dirty little devils that bang the bloomin' drums.' Kidd, if you throw your 'courterments at me for tellin' you the truth to your own advantage, your legs'll swell."

None the less there was a Battle-Royal in the barrack-room, for the boys were consumed with envy and hate, and neither Jakin nor Lew behaved in conciliatory wise.

"I'm goin' out to say adoo to my girl," said Lew to cap the climax. "Don't none o' you touch my kit because it's wanted for active service; me bein' specially invited to go by the Colonel."

He strolled forth and whistled in the clump of trees at the back of the Married Quarters till Cris came to him, and, the preliminary kisses being given and taken, Lew began to explain the situation.

"I'm goin' to the Front with the Reg'ment," he said valiantly.

"Piggy, you're a little liar," said Cris, but her heart misgave her, for Lew was not in the habit of lying.

"Liar yourself, Cris," said Lew, slipping an arm round her. "I'm goin'. When the Reg'ment marches out you'll see me with 'em, all galliant and gay. Give us another kiss, Cris, on the strength of it."

"If you'd on'y a-stayed at the Depot—where you ought to ha' bin—you could get as many of 'em as—as you dam please," whimpered Cris, putting up her mouth.

"It's 'ard, Cris. I grant you it's 'ard. But what's a man to do? If I'd a-stayed at the Depot, you wouldn't think anything of me."

"Like as not, but I'd 'ave you with me, Piggy. An' all the thinkin' in the world isn't like kissin'."

"An' all the kissin' in the world isn't like 'avin' a medal to wear on the front o' your coat."

"You won't get no medal."

"Oh yus, I shall though. Me an' Jakin are the only acting-drummers that'll be took along. All the rest is full men, an' we'll get our medals with them."

"They might ha' taken anybody but you, Piggy. You'll get killed —you're so venturesome. Stay with me, Piggy, darlin', down at the Depot, an' I'll love you true, for ever."

"Ain't you goin' to do that now, Cris? You said you was."

"O' course I am, but th' other's more comfortable. Wait till you've growed a bit, Piggy. You aren't no taller than me now."

"I've bin in the Army for two years an' I'm not goin' to get out of a chanst o' seein' service an' don't you try to make me do so. I'll come back, Cris, an' when I take on as a man I'll marry you— marry you when I'm a Lance."

"Promise, Piggy?"

Lew reflected on the future as arranged by Jakin a short time previously, but Cris's mouth was very near to his own.

"I promise, s'elp me, Gawd!" said he.

Cris slid an arm round his neck.

"I won't 'old you back no more, Piggy. Go away an' get your medal, an' I'll make you a new button-bag as nice as I know how," she whispered.

"Put some o' your 'air into it, Cris, an' I'll keep it in my pocket so long's I'm alive."

Then Cris wept anew, and the interview ended. Public feeling among the drummer-boys rose to fever pitch and the lives of Jakin and Lew became unenviable. Not only had they been permitted to enlist two years before the regulation boy's age—fourteen—but, by virtue, it seemed, of their extreme youth, they were allowed to go to the Front—which thing had not happened to acting-drummers within the knowledge of boy. The Band which was to accompany the Regiment had been cut down to the regulation twenty men, the surplus returning to the ranks. Jakin and Lew were attached to the Band as supernumeraries, though they would much have preferred being company buglers.

" 'Don't matter much," said Jakin after the medical inspection. "Be thankful that we're 'lowed to go at all. The Doctor 'e said that if we could stand what we took from the Bazar-Sergeant's son we'd stand pretty nigh anything."

"Which we will," said Lew, looking tenderly at the ragged and ill-made housewife that Cris had given him, with a lock of her hair worked into a sprawling "L" upon the cover.

"It was the best I could," she sobbed. "I wouldn't let Mother nor the Sergeant's tailor 'elp me. Keep it always, Piggy, an' remember I love you true."

They marched to the railway station, nine hundred and sixty strong, and every soul in cantonments turned out to see them go. The drummers gnashed their teeth at Jakin and Lew marching with the Band, the married women wept upon the platform, and the Regiment cheered its noble self black in the face.

"A nice level lot," said the Colonel to the Second-in-Command as they watched the first four companies entraining.

"Fit to do anything," said the Second-in-Command enthusiastically. "But it seems to me they're a thought too young and tender for the work in hand. It's bitter cold up at the Front now."

"They're sound enough," said the Colonel. "We must take our chance of sick casualties."

So they went northward, ever northward, past droves and droves of camels, armies of camp-followers, and legions of laden mules, the throng thickening day by day, till with a shriek the train pulled up at a hopelessly congested junction where six lines of temporary track accommodated six forty-wagon trains; where whistles blew, Babus sweated and Commissariat officers swore from dawn till far into the night amid the wind-driven chaff of the fodder-bales and the lowing of a thousand steers.

"Hurry up—you're badly wanted at the Front," was the message that greeted the Fore and Aft, and the occupants of the Red Cross carriages told the same tale.

"'Tisn't so much the bloomin' fightin'," gasped a head-bound trooper of Hussars to a knot of admiring Fore and Afts. "'Tisn't so much the bloomin' fightin', though there's enough o' that. It's the bloomin' food an' the bloomin' climate. Frost all night 'cept when it hails, and biling sun all day, and the water stinks fit to knock you down. I got my 'ead chipped like a egg; I've got pneumonia too, an' my guts is all out o' order. 'Tain't no bloomin' picnic in those parts, I can tell you."

"Wot are the niggers like?" demanded a private.

"There's some prisoners in that train yonder. Go an' look at 'em. They're the aristocracy o' the country. The common folk are a dashed sight uglier. If you want to know what they fight with, reach under my seat an' pull out the long knife that's there."

They dragged out and beheld for the first time the grim, bone-handled, triangular Afghan knife. It was almost as long as Lew.

"That's the thing to jint ye," said the trooper feebly. "It can take off a man's arm at the shoulder as easy as slicing butter. I halved the beggar that used that 'un, but there's more of his likes up above. They don't understand thrustin', but they're devils to slice."

The men strolled across the tracks to inspect the Afghan prisoners. They were unlike any "niggers" that the Fore and Aft had ever met—these huge, black-haired, scowling sons of the Beni-Israel. As the men stared the Afghans spat freely and muttered one to another with lowered eyes.

"My eyes! Wot awful swine!" said Jakin, who was in the rear of the procession. "Say, old man, how you got puckrowed, eh? *Kiswasti* you wasn't hanged for your ugly face, hey?"

The tallest of the company turned, his leg-irons clanking at the movement, and stared at the boy. "See!" he cried to his fellows in Pushto. "They send children against us. What a people, and what fools!"

"*Hya!*" said Jakin, nodding his head cheerily. "You go down-country. *Khana* get, *peenikapanee* get—live like a bloomin' Raja *ke marfik*. That's a better *bandobust* than baynit get it in your innards. Good-bye, ole man. Take care o' your beautiful figure-'ed, an' try to look *kushy*."

The men laughed and fell in for their first march when they began to realize that a soldier's life was not all beer and skittles. They were much impressed with the size and bestial ferocity of the niggers whom they had now learned to call "Paythans," and more with the exceeding discomfort of their own surroundings. Twenty old soldiers in the corps would have taught them how to make themselves moderately snug at night, but they had no old soldiers, and, as the troops on the line of march said, "they lived like pigs." They learned the heart-breaking cussedness of camp-kitchens and camels and the depravity of an E. P. tent and a wither-wrung mule. They studied animalculæ in water, and developed a few cases of dysentery in their study.

At the end of their third march they were disagreeably surprised by the arrival in their camp of a hammered iron slug which, fired from a steady rest at seven hundred yards, flicked out the brains of a private seated by the fire. This robbed them of their peace for a night, and was the beginning of a long-range fire carefully calculated to that end. In the daytime they saw nothing except an unpleasant puff of smoke from a crag above the line of march. At night there were distant spurts of flame and occasional casualties, which set the whole camp blazing into the gloom, and occasionally, into opposite tents. Then they swore vehemently and vowed that this was magnificent but not war.

Indeed it was not. The Regiment could not halt for reprisals against the sharpshooters of the country-side. Its duty was to go forward and make connection with the Scotch and Gurkha troops with which it was brigaded. The Afghans knew this, and knew too, after their first tentative shots, that they were dealing with a raw regiment. Thereafter they devoted themselves to the task of keeping the Fore and Aft on the strain. Not for anything would they have taken equal liberties with a seasoned corps—with the wicked little Gurkhas, whose delight it was to lie out in the open on a dark night and stalk their stalkers—with the terrible, big men dressed in women's clothes, who could be heard praying to their God in the night-watches, and whose peace of mind no amount of "sniping" could shake—or with those vile Sikhs, who marched so ostentatiously unprepared and who dealt out such grim reward to those who tried to profit by that unpreparedness. This white regiment was different—quite different. It slept like a hog, and, like a hog, charged in every direction when it was roused. Its sentries walked with a footfall that could be heard for a quarter of a mile; would fire at anything that moved—even a driven donkey —and when they had once fired, could be scientifically "rushed" and laid out a horror and an offence against the morning sun. Then there were camp-followers who straggled and could be cut up without fear. Their shrieks would disturb the white boys, and the loss of their services would inconvenience them sorely.

Thus, at every march, the hidden enemy became bolder and the regiment writhed and twisted under attacks it could not avenge. The crowning triumph was a sudden night-rush ending in the cutting of many tent-ropes, the collapse of the sodden canvas and a glorious knifing of the men who struggled and kicked below. It

was a great deed, neatly carried out, and it shook the already
shaken nerves of the Fore and Aft. All the courage that they had
been required to exercise up to this point was the "two o'clock in
the morning courage," and so far, they had only succeeded in
shooting their comrades and losing their sleep.

Sullen, discontented, cold, savage, sick, with their uniforms
dulled and unclean, the Fore and Aft joined their Brigade.

"I hear you had a tough time of it coming up," said the Brigadier. But when he saw the hospital-sheets his face fell.

"This is bad," said he to himself. "They're as rotten as sheep."
And aloud to the Colonel—"I'm afraid we can't spare you just yet.
We want all we have, else I should have given you ten days to
recover in."

The Colonel winced. "On my honor, Sir," he returned, "there
is not the least necessity to think of sparing us. My men have been
rather mauled and upset without a fair return. They only want
to go in somewhere where they can see what's before them."

"Can't say I think much of the Fore and Fit," said the Brigadier in confidence to his Brigade-Major. "They've lost all their
soldiering, and, by the trim of them, might have marched through
the country from the other side. A more fagged-out set of men I
never put eyes on."

"Oh, they'll improve as the work goes on. The parade gloss has
been rubbed off a little, but they'll put on field polish before
long," said the Brigade-Major. "They've been mauled, and they
quite don't understand it."

They did not. All the hitting was on one side, and it was cruelly
hard hitting with accessories that made them sick. There was also
the real sickness that laid hold of a strong man and dragged him
howling to the grave. Worst of all, their officers knew just as little
of the country as the men themselves, and looked as if they did.
The Fore and Aft were in a thoroughly unsatisfactory condition,
but they believed that all would be well if they could once get a
fair go-in at the enemy. Pot-shots up and down the valleys were

unsatisfactory, and the bayonet never seemed to get a chance. Perhaps it was as well, for a long-limbed Afghan with a knife had a reach of eight feet, and could carry away lead that would disable three Englishmen.

The Fore and Aft would like some rifle-practice at the enemy—all seven hundred rifles blazing together. That wish showed the mood of the men.

The Gurkhas walked into their camp, and in broken, barrack-room English strove to fraternize with them; offered them pipes of tobacco and stood them treat at the canteen. But the Fore and Aft, not knowing much of the nature of the Gurkhas, treated them as they would treat any other "niggers," and the little men in green trotted back to their firm friends the Highlanders, and with many grins confided to them: "That dam white regiment no dam use. Sulky—ugh! Dirty—ugh! Hya, any tot for Johnny?" Whereat the Highlanders smote the Gurkhas as to the head, and told them not to vilify a British Regiment, and the Gurkhas grinned cavernously, for the Highlanders were their elder brothers and entitled to the privileges of kinship. The common soldier who touches a Gurkha is more than likely to have his head sliced open.

Three days later the Brigadier arranged a battle according to the rules of war and the peculiarity of the Afghan temperament. The enemy were massing in inconvenient strength among the hills, and the moving of many green standards warned him that the tribes were "up" in aid of the Afghan regular troops. A Squadron and a half of Bengal Lancers represented the available Cavalry, and two screw-guns borrowed from a column thirty miles away, the Artillery at the General's disposal.

"If they stand, as I've a very strong notion that they will, I fancy we shall see an infantry fight that will be worth watching," said the Brigadier. "We'll do it in style. Each regiment shall be played into action by its Band, and we'll hold the Cavalry in reserve."

"For *all* the reserve?" somebody asked.

"For all the reserve; because we're going to crumple them up," said the Brigadier, who was an extraordinary Brigadier, and did not believe in the value of a reserve when dealing with Asiatics. Indeed, when you come to think of it, had the British Army consistently waited for reserves in all its little affairs, the boundaries of Our Empire would have stopped at Brighton beach.

That battle was to be a glorious battle.

The three regiments debouching from three separate gorges, after duly crowning the heights above, were to converge from the center, left, and right upon what we will call the Afghan army, then stationed toward the lower extremity of a flat-bottomed valley. Thus it will be seen that three sides of the valley practically belonged to the English, while the fourth was strictly Afghan property. In the event of defeat the Afghans had the rocky hills to fly to, where the fire from the guerilla tribes in aid would cover their retreat. In the event of victory these same tribes would rush down and lend their weight to the rout of the British.

The screw-guns were to shell the head of each Afghan rush that was made in close formation, and the Cavalry, held in reserve in the right valley, were to gently stimulate the break-up which would follow on the combined attack. The Brigadier, sitting upon a rock overlooking the valley, would watch the battle unrolled at his feet. The Fore and Aft would debouch from the central gorge, the Gurkhas from the left, and the Highlanders from the right, for the reason that the left flank of the enemy seemed as though it required the most hammering. It was not every day that an Afghan force would take ground in the open, and the Brigadier was resolved to make the most of it.

"If we only had a few more men," he said plaintively, "we could surround the creatures and crumple 'em up thoroughly. As it is, I'm afraid we can only cut them up as they run. It's a great pity."

The Fore and Aft had enjoyed unbroken peace for five days, and were beginning, in spite of dysentery, to recover their nerve. But they were not happy, for they did not know the work in hand, and had they known, would not have known how to do it.

Throughout those five days in which old soldiers might have taught them the craft of the game, they discussed together their misadventures in the past—how such an one was alive at dawn and dead ere the dusk, and with what shrieks and struggles such another had given up his soul under the Afghan knife. Death was a new and horrible thing to the sons of mechanics who were used to die decently of zymotic disease; and their careful conservation in barracks had done nothing to make them look upon it with less dread.

Very early in the dawn the bugles began to blow, and the Fore and Aft, filled with a misguided enthusiasm, turned out without waiting for a cup of coffee and a biscuit; and were rewarded by being kept under arms in the cold while the other regiments leisurely prepared for the fray. All the world knows that it is ill taking the breeks off a Highlander. It is much iller to try to make him stir unless he is convinced of the necessity for haste.

The Fore and Aft waited, leaning upon their rifles and listening to the protests of their empty stomachs. The Colonel did his best to remedy the default of lining as soon as it was borne in upon him that the affair would not begin at once, and so well did he succeed that the coffee was just ready when—the men moved off, their Band leading. Even then there had been a mistake in time, and the Fore and Aft came out into the valley ten minutes before the proper hour. Their Band wheeled to the right after reaching the open, and retired behind a little rocky knoll still playing while the Regiment went past.

It was not a pleasant sight that opened on the uninstructed view, for the lower end of the valley appeared to be filled by an army in position—real and actual regiments attired in red coats, and—of this there was no doubt—firing Martini-Henri bullets which cut up the ground a hundred yards in front of the leading company. Over that pock-marked ground the Regiment had to pass, and it opened the ball with a general and profound courtesy to the piping pickets; ducking in perfect time, as though it had been brazed on a rod. Being half-capable of thinking for itself, it fired a volley by the simple process of pitching its rifle into its shoulder and pulling the trigger. The bullets may have accounted for some of the watchers on the hillside, but they certainly did not affect the mass of enemy in front, while the noise of the rifles drowned any orders that might have been given.

"Good God!" said the Brigadier, sitting on the rock high above all. "That regiment has spoilt the whole show. Hurry up the others, and let the screw-guns get off."

But the screw-guns, in working round the heights, had stumbled upon a wasp's nest of a small mud fort which they incontinently shelled at eight hundred yards, to the huge discomfort of the occupants, who were unaccustomed to weapons of such devilish precision.

The Fore and Aft continued to go forward but with shortened stride. Where were the other regiments, and why did these niggers use Martinis? They took open order instinctively, lying down and firing at random, rushing a few paces forward and lying down again, according to the regulations. Once in this formation, each man felt himself desperately alone, and edged in toward his fellow for comfort's sake.

Then the crack of his neighbor's rifle at his ear led him to fire as rapidly as he could—again for the sake of the comfort of the noise. The reward was not long delayed. Five volleys plunged the files in banked smoke impenetrable to the eye, and the bullets began to take ground twenty or thirty yards in front of the firers, as the weight of the bayonet dragged down and to the right arms wearied with holding the kick of the leaping Martini. The Company Commanders peered helplessly through the smoke, the more nervous mechanically trying to fan it away with their helmets.

"High and to the left!" bawled a Captain till he was hoarse. "No good! Cease firing, and let it drift away a bit."

Three and four times the bugles shrieked the order, and when it was obeyed the Fore and Aft looked that their foe should be lying before them in mown swaths of men. A light wind drove the smoke to leeward, and showed the enemy still in position and apparently unaffected. A quarter of a ton of lead had been buried a furlong in front of them, as the ragged earth attested. That was not demoralizing to the Afghans, who have not European nerves. They were waiting for the mad riot to die down, and were firing quietly into the heart of the smoke. A private of the Fore and Aft spun up his company shrieking with agony, another was kicking the earth and gasping, and a third, ripped through the lower intestines by a jagged bullet, was calling aloud on his comrades to put him out of his pain. These were the casualties, and they were not soothing to hear or see. The smoke cleared to a dull haze.

Then the foe began to shout with a great shouting and a mass— a black mass—detached itself from the main body, and rolled over the ground at horrid speed. It was composed of, perhaps, three hundred men, who would shout and fire and slash if the rush of their fifty comrades who were determined to die carried home. The fifty were Ghazis, half-maddened with drugs and wholly mad with religious fanaticism. When they rushed the British fire ceased, and in the lull the order was given to close ranks and meet them with the bayonet.

Any one who knew the business could have told the Fore and Aft that the only way of dealing with a Ghazi rush is by volleys at long ranges; because a man who means to die, who desires to die, who will gain heaven by dying, must, in nine cases out of ten, kill a man who has a lingering prejudice in favor of life. Where they should have closed and gone forward, the Fore and Aft opened out and skirmished, and where they should have opened out and fired, they closed and waited.

A man dragged from his blankets half awake and unfed is never in a pleasant frame of mind. Nor does his happiness increase when he watches the whites of the eyes of three hundred six-foot fiends upon whose beards the foam is lying, upon whose tongues is a roar of wrath, and in whose hands are yard-long knives.

The Fore and Aft heard the Gurkha bugles bringing that regiment forward at the double, while the neighing of the Highland pipes came from the left. They strove to stay where they were, though the bayonets wavered down the line like the oars of a ragged boat. Then they felt body to body the amazing physical strength of their foes; a shriek of pain ended the rush, and the knives fell amid scenes not to be told. The men clubbed together and smote blindly—as often as not at their own fellows. Their front crumpled like paper, and the fifty Ghazis passed on; their backers, now drunk with success, fighting as madly as they.

Then the rear-ranks were bidden to close up, and the subalterns dashed into the stew—alone. For the rear-ranks had heard the clamor in front, the yells and the howls of pain, and had seen the dark stale blood that makes afraid. They were not going to stay. It was the rushing of the camps over again. Let their officers go to Hell, if they chose; they would get away from the knives.

"Come on!" shrieked the subalterns, and their men, cursing them, drew back, each closing into his neighbor and wheeling round.

Charteris and Devlin, subalterns of the last company, faced their death alone in the belief that their men would follow.

"You've killed me, you cowards," sobbed Devlin and dropped, cut from the shoulder-strap to the center of the chest, and a fresh detachment of his men retreating, always retreating, trampled him under foot as they made for the pass whence they had emerged.

> I kissed her in the kitchen, and I kissed her in the hall.
> Child'un, child'un, follow me!
> Oh Golly, said the cook, is he gwine to kiss us all?
> Halla—Halla—Halla—Hallelujah!

The Gurkhas were pouring through the left gorge and over the heights at the double to the invitation of their Regimental Quick-step. The black rocks were crowned with dark green spiders as the bugles gave tongue jubilantly:

> In the morning! In the morning by the bright light!
> When Gabriel blows his trumpet in the morning!

The Gurkha rear-companies tripped and blundered over loose stones. The front-files halted for a moment to take stock of the valley and to settle stray boot-laces. Then a happy little sigh of contentment soughed down the ranks, and it was as though the land smiled, for behold there below was the enemy, and it was to meet them that the Gurkhas had doubled so hastily. There was much enemy. There would be amusement. The little men hitched their kukris well to hand, and gaped expectantly at their officers as terriers grin ere the stone is cast for them to fetch. The Gurkhas' ground sloped downward to the valley, and they enjoyed a fair view of the proceedings. They sat upon the bowlders to watch, for their officers were not going to waste their wind in assisting to repulse a Ghazi rush more than half a mile away. Let the white men look to their own front.

"Hi! yi!" said the Subadar-Major, who was sweating profusely. "Dam fools yonder, stand close-order! This is no time for close order, it is the time for volleys. Ugh!"

Horrified, amused, and indignant, the Gurkhas beheld the retirement of the Fore and Aft with a running chorus of oaths and commentaries.

"They run! The white men run! Colonel Sahib, may we also do a little running?" murmured Runbir Thappa, the Senior Jemadar.

But the Colonel would have none of it. "Let the beggars be cut up a little," said he wrathfully. "'Serves 'em right. They'll be prodded into facing round in a minute." He looked through his field-glasses, and caught the glint of an officer's sword.

"Beating 'em with the flat—damned conscripts! How the Ghazis are walking into them!" said he.

The Fore and Aft, heading back, bore with them their officers.

The narrowness of the pass forced the mob into solid formation, and the rear-ranks delivered some sort of a wavering volley. The Ghazis drew off, for they did not know what reserve the gorge might hide. Moreover, it was never wise to chase white men too far. They returned as wolves return to cover, satisfied with the slaughter that they had done, and only stopping to slash at the wounded on the ground. A quarter of a mile had the Fore and Aft retreated, and now, jammed in the pass, was quivering with pain, shaken and demoralized with fear, while the officers, maddened beyond control, smote the men with the hilts and the flats of their swords.

"Get back! Get back, you cowards—you women! Right about face—column of companies, form—you hounds!" shouted the Colonel, and the subalterns swore aloud. But the Regiment wanted to go—to go anywhere out of the range of those merciless knives. It swayed to and fro irresolutely with shouts and outcries, while from the right the Gurkhas dropped volley after volley of cripple-stopper Snider bullets at long range into the mob of the Ghazis returning to their own troops.

The Fore and Aft Band, though protected from direct fire by the rocky knoll under which it had sat down, fled at the first rush. Jakin and Lew would have fled also, but their short legs left them fifty yards in the rear, and by the time the Band had mixed with the Regiment, they were painfully aware that they would have to close in alone and unsupported.

"Get back to that rock," gasped Jakin. "They won't see us there."

And they returned to the scattered instruments of the Band; their hearts nearly bursting their ribs.

"Here's a nice show for us," said Jakin, throwing himself full length on the ground. "A bloomin' fine show for British Infantry! Oh, the devils! They've gone an' left us alone here! Wot'll we do?"

Lew took possession of a cast-off water bottle, which naturally was full of canteen rum, and drank till he coughed again.

"Drink," said he shortly. "They'll come back in a minute or two—you see."

Jakin drank, but there was no sign of the Regiment's return. They could hear a dull clamor from the head of the valley of retreat, and saw the Ghazis slink back, quickening their pace as the Gurkhas fired at them.

"We're all that's left of the Band, an' we'll be cut up as sure as death," said Jakin.

"I'll die game, then," said Lew thickly, fumbling with his tiny drummer's sword. The drink was working on his brain as it was on Jakin's.

" 'Old on! I know something better than fightin'," said Jakin, stung by the splendor of a sudden thought due chiefly to rum. "Tip our bloomin' cowards yonder the word to come back. The Paythan beggars are well away. Come on, Lew! We won't get hurt. Take the fife an' give me the drum. The Old Step for all your bloomin' guts are worth! There's a few of our men coming back now. Stand up, ye drunken little defaulter. By your right—quick march!"

He slipped the drum-sling over his shoulder, thrust the fife into Lew's hand, and the two boys marched out of the cover of the rock into the open, making a hideous hash of the first bars of the "British Grenadiers."

As Lew had said, a few of the Fore and Aft were coming back sullenly and shamefacedly under the stimulus of blows and abuse; their red coats shone at the head of the valley, and behind them were wavering bayonets. But between this shattered line and the enemy, who with Afghan suspicion feared that the hasty retreat meant an ambush, and had not moved therefore, lay half a mile of a level ground dotted only by the wounded.

The tune settled into full swing and the boys kept shoulder to shoulder, Jakin banging the drum as one possessed. The one fife made a thin and pitiful squeaking, but the tune carried far, even to the Gurkhas.

"Come on, you dogs!" muttered Jakin to himself. "Are we to play forhever?" Lew was staring straight in front of him and marching more stiffly than ever he had done on parade.

And in bitter mockery of the distant mob, the old tune of the Old Line shrilled and rattled:—

> Some talk of Alexander,
>   And some of Hercules;
> Of Hector and Lysander,
>   And such great names as these!

There was a far-off clapping of hands from the Gurkhas, and a roar from the Highlanders in the distance, but never a shot was fired by British or Afghan. The two little red dots moved forward in the open parallel to the enemy's front.

> But of all the world's great heroes
>   There's none that can compare,
> With a tow-row-row-row-row-row,
>   To the British Grenadier!

The men of the Fore and Aft were gathering thick at the entrance into the plain. The Brigadier on the heights far above was speechless with rage. Still no movement from the enemy. The day stayed to watch the children.

Jakin halted and beat the long roll of the Assembly, while the fife squealed despairingly.

"Right about face! Hold up, Lew, you're drunk," said Jakin. They wheeled and marched back:—

> Those heroes of antiquity
>   Ne'er saw a cannon-ball,
> Nor knew the force o' powder,

"Here they come!" said Jakin. "Go on, Lew":—

> To scare their foes withal!

The Fore and Aft were pouring out of the valley. What officers had said to men in that time of shame and humiliation will never be known; for neither officers nor men speak of it now.

"They are coming anew!" shouted a priest among the Afghans. "Do not kill the boys! Take them alive, and they shall be of our faith."

But the first volley had been fired, and Lew dropped on his face. Jakin stood for a minute, spun round and collapsed, as the Fore and Aft came forward, the curses of their officers in their ears, and in their hearts the shame of open shame.

Half the men had seen the drummers die, and they made no sign. They did not even shout. They doubled out straight across the plain in open order, and they did not fire.

"This," said the Colonel of Gurkhas, softly, "is the real attack, as it should have been delivered. Come on, my children."

"Ulu-lu-lu-lu!" squealed the Gurkhas, and came down with a joyful clicking of *kukris*—those vicious Gurkha knives.

On the right there was no rush. The Highlanders, cannily commending their souls to God (for it matters as much to a dead man whether he has been shot in a Border scuffle or at Waterloo), opened out and fired according to their custom, that is to say without heat and without intervals, while the screw-guns, having disposed of the impertinent mud fort aforementioned, dropped shell after shell into the clusters round the flickering green standards on the heights.

"Charrging is an unfortunate necessity," murmured the Color-Sergeant of the right company of the Highlanders. "It makes the men sweer so, but I am thinkin' that it will come to a charrge if these black devils stand much longer. Stewarrt, man, you're firing into the eye of the sun, and he'll not take any harm for Government ammuneetion. A foot lower and a great deal slower! What are the English doing? They're very quiet there in the center. Running again?"

The English were not running. They were hacking and hewing and stabbing, for though one white man is seldom physically a match for an Afghan in a sheepskin or wadded coat, yet, through the pressure of many white men behind, and a certain thirst for revenge in his heart, he becomes capable of doing much with both ends of his rifle. The Fore and Aft held their fire till one bullet could drive through five or six men, and the front of the Afghan force gave on the volley. They then selected their men, and slew them with deep gasps and short hacking coughs, and groanings of leather belts against strained bodies, and realized for the first time that an Afghan attacked is far less formidable than an Afghan attacking; which fact old soldiers might have told them.

But they had no old soldiers in their ranks.

The Gurkhas' stall at the bazar was the noisiest, for the men were engaged—to a nasty noise as of beef being cut on the block— with the *kukri*, which they preferred to the bayonet; well knowing how the Afghan hates the half-moon blade.

As the Afghans wavered, the green standards on the mountain moved down to assist them in a last rally. This was unwise. The Lancers chafing in the right gorge had thrice dispatched their only subaltern as galloper to report on the progress of affairs. On the third occasion he returned, with a bullet-graze on his knee, swearing strange oaths in Hindustani, and saying that all things were ready. So that Squadron swung round the right of the Highlanders with a wicked whistling of wind in the pennons of its lances, and fell upon the remnant just when, according to all the rules of war, it should have waited for the foe to show more signs of wavering.

But it was a dainty charge, deftly delivered, and it ended by the Cavalry finding itself at the head of the pass by which the Afghans intended to retreat; and down the track that the lances had made streamed two companies of the Highlanders, which was never intended by the Brigadier. The new development was successful. It detached the enemy from his base as a sponge is torn from a rock, and left him ringed about with fire in that pitiless plain. And as a sponge is chased round the bath-tub by the hand of the bather, so were the Afghans chased till they broke into little detachments much more difficult to dispose of than large masses.

"See!" quoth the Brigadier. "Everything has come as I arranged. We've cut their base, and now we'll bucket 'em to pieces."

A direct hammering was all that the Brigadier had dared to hope for, considering the size of the force at his disposal; but men who stand or fall by the errors of their opponents may be forgiven for turning Chance into Design. The bucketing went forward merrily. The Afghan forces were upon the run—the run of wearied wolves who snarl and bite over their shoulders. The red lances dipped by twos and threes, and, with a shriek, uprose the lance-butt, like a spar on a stormy sea, as the trooper cantering forward cleared his point. The Lancers kept between their prey and the steep hills, for all who could were trying to escape from the valley of death. The Highlanders gave the fugitives two hundred yards' law, and then brought them down, gasping and choking ere they could reach the protection of the bowlders above. The Gurkhas followed suit; but the Fore and Aft were killing on their own account, for they had penned a mass of men between their bayonets and a wall of rock, and the flash of the rifles was lighting the wadded coats.

"We cannot hold them, Captain Sahib!" panted a Ressaidar of Lancers. "Let us try the carbine. The lance is good, but it wastes time."

They tried the carbine, and still the enemy melted away—fled up the hills by hundreds when there were only twenty bullets to stop them. On the heights the screw-guns ceased firing—they had run out of ammunition—and the Brigadier groaned, for the musketry fire could not sufficiently smash the retreat. Long before the last volleys were fired, the doolies were out in force looking for the wounded. The battle was over, and, but for want of fresh troops, the Afghans would have been wiped off the earth. As it was they counted their dead by hundreds, and nowhere were the dead thicker than in the track of the Fore and Aft.

But the Regiment did not cheer with the Highlanders, nor did they dance uncouth dances with the Gurkhas among the dead. They looked under their brows at the Colonel as they leaned upon their rifles and panted.

"Get back to camp, you. Haven't you disgraced yourself enough for one day! Go and look to the wounded. It's all you're fit for," said the Colonel. Yet for the past hour the Fore and Aft had been doing all that mortal commander could expect. They had lost heavily because they did not know how to set about their business with proper skill, but they had borne themselves gallantly, and this was their reward.

A young and sprightly Color-Sergeant, who had begun to imagine himself a hero, offered his water bottle to a Highlander, whose tongue was black with thirst. "I drink with no cowards," answered the youngster huskily, and, turning to a Gurkha, said, "Hya, Johnny! Drink water got it?" The Gurkha grinned and passed his bottle. The Fore and Aft said no word.

They went back to camp when the field of strife had been a little mopped up and made presentable, and the Brigadier, who saw himself a Knight in three months, was the only soul who was complimentary to them. The Colonel was heartbroken, and the officers were savage and sullen.

"Well," said the Brigadier, "they are young troops of course, and it was not unnatural that they should retire in disorder for a bit."

"Oh, my only Aunt Maria!" murmured a junior Staff Officer. "Retire in disorder! It was a bally run!"

"But they came again as we all know," cooed the Brigadier, the Colonel's ashy-white face before him, "and they behaved as well as could possibly be expected. Behaved beautifully, indeed. I was watching them. It's not a matter to take to heart, Colonel. As some German General said of his men, they wanted to be shooted over a little, that was all." To himself he said—"Now they're blooded I can give 'em responsible work. It's as well that they got what they did. 'Teach 'em more than a half a dozen rifle flirtations, that will—later—run alone and bite. Poor old Colonel, though."

All that afternoon the heliograph winked and flickered on the hills, striving to tell the good news to a mountain forty miles away. And in the evening there arrived, dusty, sweating, and sore, a misguided Correspondent who had gone out to assist at a trumpery village-burning, and who had read off the message from afar, cursing his luck the while.

"Let's have the details somehow—as full as ever you can, please. It's the first time I've ever been left this campaign," said the Correspondent to the Brigadier, and the Brigadier, nothing loth, told him how an Army of Communication had been crumpled up, destroyed, and all but annihilated by the craft, strategy, wisdom, and foresight of the Brigadier.

But some say, and among these be the Gurkhas who watched on the hillside, that that battle was won by Jakin and Lew, whose little bodies were borne up just in time to fit two gaps at the head of the big ditch-grave for the dead under the heights of Jagai.

1. What does Kipling gain with the three page delay in the actual start of the story?
2. Why are soldiers shot "to encourage others"?
3. Of the march to the Afghan frontier Kipling says, "All this was magnificent . . ." Does he make you feel that it was?
4. How, in its attitude toward war, does this story differ from those of our own days?
5. What do you think was Kipling's attitude toward such scenes? Was he definitely a product of his age?

*Ambrose Bierce*

# THE AFFAIR AT COULTER'S
# NOTCH

"DO YOU think, Colonel, that your brave Coulter would like to put one of his guns in here?" the general asked. He was apparently not altogether serious; it certainly did not seem a place where any artillerist, however brave, would like to put a gun. The colonel thought that possibly his division commander meant good-humoredly to intimate that in a recent conversation between them Captain Coulter's courage had been too highly extolled.

"General," he replied warmly, "Coulter would like to put a gun anywhere within reach of those people," with a motion of his hand in the direction of the enemy.

"It is the only place," said the general. He was serious, then.

The place was a depression, a "notch," in the sharp crest of a hill. It was a pass, and through it ran a turnpike, which reaching this highest point in its course by a sinuous ascent through a thin forest made a similar, though less steep, descent toward the enemy. For a mile to the left and a mile to the right, the ridge, though occupied by Federal infantry lying close behind the sharp crest and appearing as if held in place by atmospheric pressure, was inaccessible to artillery. There was no place but the bottom of the notch, and that was barely wide enough for the roadbed. From the Confederate side this point was commanded by two batteries posted on a slightly lower elevation beyond a creek, and a half-mile away. All the guns but one were masked by the trees of an orchard; that one—it seemed a bit of impudence—was on an open lawn directly in front of a rather grandiose building, the planter's dwelling. The gun was safe enough in its exposure—but only because the Federal infantry had been forbidden to fire. Coulter's Notch—it came to be called so—was not, that pleasant summer afternoon, a place where one would "like to put a gun."

Three or four dead horses lay there sprawling in the road, three or four dead men in a trim row at one side of it, and a little back, down the hill. All but one were cavalrymen belonging to the Federal advance. One was a quartermaster. The general commanding the division and the colonel commanding the brigade, with their staffs and escorts, had ridden into the notch to have a look at the enemy's guns—which had straightway obscured themselves in towering clouds of smoke. It was hardly profitable to be curious about guns which had the trick of the cuttlefish, and the season of observation had been brief. At its conclusion—a short remove backward from where it began—occurred the conversation already partly reported. "It is the only place," the general repeated thoughtfully, "to get at them."

The colonel looked at him gravely. "There is room for only one gun, General—one against twelve."

"That is true—for only one at a time," said the commander with something like, yet not altogether like, a smile. "But then, your brave Coulter—a whole battery in himself."

The tone of irony was now unmistakable. It angered the colonel, but he did not know what to say. The spirit of military subordination is not favorable to retort, nor even to deprecation.

At this moment a young officer of artillery came riding slowly up the road attended by his bugler. It was Captain Coulter. He could not have been more than twenty-three years of age. He was of medium height, but very slender and lithe, and sat his horse with something of the air of a civilian. In face he was of a type singularly unlike the men about him; thin, high-nosed, gray-eyed, with a slight blond mustache, and long, rather straggling hair of the same color. There was an apparent negligence in his attire. His cap was worn with the visor a trifle askew; his coat was buttoned only at the sword-belt, showing a considerable expanse of white shirt, tolerably clean for that stage of the campaign. But the negligence was all in his dress and bearing; in his face was a look of intense interest in his surroundings. His gray eyes, which seemed occasionally to strike right and left across the landscape, like search-lights, were for the most part fixed upon the sky beyond the Notch; until he should arrive at the summit of the road there was nothing else in that direction to see. As he came opposite his division and brigade commanders at the roadside he saluted mechanically and was about to pass on. The colonel signed to him to halt.

"Captain Coulter," he said, "the enemy has twelve pieces over there on the next ridge. If I rightly understand the general, he directs that you bring up a gun and engage them."

There was a blank silence; the general looked stolidly at a distant regiment swarming slowly up the hill through rough undergrowth, like a torn and draggled cloud of blue smoke; the captain appeared not to have observed him. Presently the captain spoke, slowly and with apparent effort:

"On the next ridge, did you say, sir? Are the guns near the house?"

"Ah, you have been over this road before. Directly at the house."

"And it is—necessary—to engage them? The order is imperative?"

His voice was husky and broken. He was visibly paler. The colonel was astonished and mortified. He stole a glance at the commander. In that set, immobile face was no sign; it was as hard as bronze. A moment later the general road away, followed by his staff and escort. The colonel, humiliated and indignant, was about to order Captain Coulter in arrest, when the latter spoke a few words in a low tone to his bugler, saluted, and rode straight forward into the Notch, where presently, at the summit of the road, his field-glass at his eyes, he showed against the sky, he and his horse, sharply defined and statuesque. The bugler had dashed down the speed and disappeared behind a wood. Presently his bugle was heard singing in the cedars, and in an incredibly short time a single gun with its caisson, each drawn by six horses and manned by its full complement of gunners, came bounding and banging up the grade in a storm of dust, unlimbered under cover, and was run forward by hand to the fatal crest among the dead horses. A gesture of the captain's arm, some strangely agile movements of the men in loading, and almost before the troops along the way had ceased to hear the rattle of the wheels, a great white cloud sprang forward down the slope, and with a deafening report the affair at Coulter's Notch had begun.

It is not intended to relate in detail the progress and incidents of that ghastly contest—a contest without vicissitudes, its alternations only different degrees of despair. Almost at the instant when Captain Coulter's gun blew its challenging cloud twelve answering clouds rolled upward from among the trees about the plantation house, a deep multiple report roared back like a broken echo, and thenceforth to the end the Federal cannoneers fought their hopeless battle in an atmosphere of living iron whose thoughts were lightnings and whose deeds were death.

Unwilling to see the efforts which he could not aid and the slaughter which he could not stay, the colonel ascended the ridge at a point a quarter of a mile to the left, whence the Notch, itself invisible, but pushing up successive masses of smoke, seemed the crater of a volcano in thundering eruption. With his glass he watched the enemy's guns, noting as he could the effects of Coulter's fire—if Coulter still lived to direct it. He saw that the Federal gunners, ignoring those of the enemy's pieces whose positions could be determined by their smoke only, gave their whole attention to the one that maintained its place in the open—the lawn in front of the house. Over and about that hardy piece the shells exploded at intervals of a few seconds. Some exploded in the house, as could be seen by thin ascensions of smoke from the breached roof. Figures of prostrate men and horses were plainly visible.

"If our fellows are doing so good work with a single gun," said the colonel to an aide who happened to be nearest, "they must be suffering like the devil from twelve. Go down and present the commander of that piece with my congratulations on the accuracy of his fire."

Turning to his adjutant-general he said, "Did you observe Coulter's damned reluctance to obey orders?"

"Yes, sir, I did."

"Well, say nothing about it, please. I don't think the general will care to make any accusations. He will probably have enough to do in explaining his own connection with this uncommon way of amusing the rear-guard of a retreating enemy."

A young officer approached from below, climbing breathless up the acclivity. Almost before he had saluted, he gasped out:

"Colonel, I am directed by Colonel Harmon to say that the enemy's guns are within easy reach of our rifles, and most of them visible from several points along the ridge."

The brigade commander looked at him without a trace of interest in his expression. "I know it," he said quietly.

The young adjutant was visibly embarrassed. "Colonel Harmon would like to have permission to silence those guns," he stammered.

"So should I," the colonel said in the same tone. "Present my compliments to Colonel Harmon and say to him that the general's orders for the infantry not to fire are still in force."

The adjutant saluted and retired. The colonel ground his heel into the earth and turned to look again at the enemy's guns.

"Colonel," said the adjutant-general, "I don't know that I ought to say anything, but there is something wrong in all this. Do you happen to know that Captain Coulter is from the South?"

"No; was he, indeed?"

"I heard that last summer the division which the general then commanded was in the vicinity of Coulter's home—camped there for weeks, and—"

"Listen!" said the colonel, interrupting with an upward gesture. "Do you hear *that?*"

"That" was the silence of the Federal gun. The staff, the order-lies, the lines of infantry behind the crest—all had "heard," and were looking curiously in the direction of the crater, whence no smoke now ascended except desultory cloudlets from the enemy's shells. Then came the blare of a bugle, a faint rattle of wheels; a minute later the sharp reports recommenced with double activity. The demolished gun had been replaced with a sound one.

"Yes," said the adjutant-general, resuming his narrative, "the general made the acquaintance of Coulter's family. There was trou-ble—I don't know the exact nature of it—something about Coul-ter's wife. She is a red-hot Secessionist, as they all are, except Coul-ter himself, but she is a good wife and high-bred lady. There was a complaint to army headquarters. The general was transferred to this division. It is odd that Coulter's battery should afterward have been assigned to it."

The colonel had risen from the rock upon which they had been sitting. His eyes were blazing with a generous indignation.

"See here, Morrison," said he, looking his gossiping staff officer straight in the face, "did you get that story from a gentleman or a liar?"

"I don't want to say how I got it, Colonel, unless it is neces-sary"—he was blushing a trifle—"but I'll stake my life upon its truth in the main."

The colonel turned toward a small knot of officers some dis-tance away. "Lieutenant Williams!" he shouted.

One of the officers detached himself from the group and coming forward saluted, saying: "Pardon me, Colonel, I thought you had been informed. Williams is dead down there by the gun. What can I do, sir?"

Lieutenant Williams was the aide who had had the pleasure of conveying to the officer in charge of the gun his brigade commander's congratulations.

"Go," said the colonel, "and direct the withdrawal of that gun instantly. No—I'll go myself."

He strode down the declivity toward the rear of the Notch at a break-neck pace, over rocks and through brambles, followed by his little retinue in tumultuous disorder. At the foot of the declivity they mounted their waiting animals and took to the road at a lively trot, round a bend and into the Notch. The spectacle which they encountered there was appalling!

Within that defile, barely broad enough for a single gun, were piled the wrecks of no fewer than four. They had noted the silencing of only the last one disabled—there had been a lack of men to replace it quickly with another. The débris lay on both sides of the road; the men had managed to keep an open way between, through which the fifth piece was now firing. The men?—they looked like demons of the pit. All were hatless, all stripped to the waist, their reeking skins black with blotches of powder and spattered with gouts of blood. They worked like madmen, with rammer and cartridge, lever and lanyard. They set their swollen shoulders and bleeding hands against the wheels at each recoil and heaved the heavy gun back to its place. There were no commands; in that awful environment of whooping shot, exploding shells, shrieking fragments of iron, and flying splinters of wood, none could have been heard. Officers, if officers there were, were indistinguishable; all worked together—each while he lasted—governed by the eye. When the gun was sponged, it was loaded; when loaded, aimed and fired. The colonel observed something new to his military experience—something horrible and unnatural: the gun was bleeding at the mouth! In temporary default of water, the man sponging had dipped his sponge into a pool of comrade's blood. In all this work there was no clashing; the duty of the instant was obvious. When one fell, another, looking a trifle cleaner, seemed to rise from the earth in the dead man's tracks, to fall in his turn.

With the ruined guns lay the ruined men—alongside the wreckage, under it and atop of it; and back down the road—a ghastly procession!—crept on hands and knees such of the wounded as were able to move. The colonel—he had compassionately sent his cavalcade to the right about—had to ride over those who were entirely dead in order not to crush those who were partly alive. Into that hell he tranquilly held his way, rode up alongside the gun, and, in the obscurity of the last discharge, tapped upon the cheek the man holding the rammer—who straightway fell, thinking himself killed. A fiend seven times damned sprang out of the smoke to take his place, but paused and gazed up at the mounted officer with an unearthly regard, his teeth flashing between his black lips, his eyes, fierce and expanded, burning like coals beneath his bloody brow. The colonel made an authoritative gesture and pointed to the rear. The fiend bowed in token of obedience. It was Captain Coulter.

Simultaneously with the colonel's arresting sign, silence fell upon the whole field of action. The procession of missiles no longer streamed into that defile of death, for the enemy also had ceased firing. His army had been gone for hours, and the commander of his rear-guard, who had held his position perilously long in hope to silence the Federal fire, at that strange moment had silenced his own. "I was not aware of the breadth of my authority," said the colonel to anybody, riding forward to the crest to see what had really happened.

An hour later his brigade was in bivouac on the enemy's ground, and its idlers were examining, with something of awe, as the faithful inspect a saint's relics, a score of straddling dead horses and three disabled guns, all spiked. The fallen men had been carried away; their torn and broken bodies would have given too great satisfaction.

Naturally, the colonel established himself and his military family in the plantation house. It was somewhat shattered, but it was better than the open air. The furniture was greatly deranged and broken. Walls and ceilings were knocked away here and there, and a lingering odor of powder smoke was everywhere. The beds, the closets of women's clothing, the cupboards were not greatly damaged. The new tenants for a night made themselves comfortable, and the virtual effacement of Coulter's battery supplied them with an interesting topic.

During supper an orderly of the escort showed himself into the dining-room and asked permission to speak to the colonel.

"What is it, Barbour?" said that officer pleasantly, having overheard the request.

"Colonel, there is something wrong in the cellar; I don't know what—somebody there. I was down there rummaging about."

"I will go down and see," said a staff officer, rising.

"So will I," the colonel said; "let the others remain. Lead on, orderly."

They took a candle from the table and descended the cellar stairs, the orderly in visible trepidation. The candle made but a feeble light, but presently, as they advanced, its narrow circle of illumination revealed a human figure seated on the ground against the black stone wall which they were skirting, its knees elevated, its head bowed sharply forward. The face, which should have been seen in profile, was invisible, for the man was bent so far forward that his long hair concealed it; and, strange to relate, the beard, of a much darker hue, fell in a great tangled mass and lay along the ground at his side. They involuntarily paused; then the colonel, taking the candle from the orderly's shaking hand, approached the man and attentively considered him. The long dark beard was the hair of a woman—dead. The dead woman clasped in her arms a dead babe. Both were clasped in the arms of the man, pressed against his breast, against his lips. There was blood in the hair of the woman; there was blood in the hair of the man. A yard away, near an irregular depression in the beaten earth which formed the cellar's floor—a fresh excavation with a convex bit of iron, having jagged edges, visible in one of the sides—lay an infant's foot. The colonel held the light as high as he could. The floor of the room above was broken through, the splinters pointing at all angles downward. "This casemate is not bomb-proof," said the colonel gravely. It did not occur to him that his summing up of the matter had any levity in it.

They stood about the group awhile in silence; the staff officer was thinking of his unfinished supper, the orderly of what might possibly be in one of the casks on the other side of the cellar. Suddenly the man whom they had thought dead raised his head and gazed tranquilly into their faces. His complexion was coal black; the cheeks were apparently tattooed in irregular sinuous lines from the eyes downward. The lips, too, were white, like those of a stage Negro. There was blood upon his forehead.

The staff officer drew back a pace, the orderly two paces.

"What are you doing here, my man?" said the colonel, unmoved.

"This house belongs to me, sir," was the reply, civilly delivered.

"To you? Ah, I see! And these?"

"My wife and child. I am Captain Coulter."

From *In the Midst of Life*, by Ambrose Bierce. Reprinted by permission of Albert & Charles Boni, Inc., Publishers, New York.

1. *What is indicated by the opening phrase "your brave Coulter"?*
2. *For the most part Bierce's diction is unadorned; how does he achieve his startling effects?*
3. *One of the greatest, if not the greatest, novels of the*

War Between the States is Stephen Crane's The Red
Badge of Courage, and yet, when he wrote that novel,
he had never seen a war. Do you feel that Bierce has
been a witness to such scenes as he describes?
4. Do you anticipate the last sentence in the story?
5. What do you believe was Bierce's attitude toward war?

## Jo Sinclair

# CHILDREN AT PLAY

IT WAS market day; and Ramon was free until three o'clock.
Until three, he could do as he liked, go where he liked; but
at three o'clock he must be here, in this same kitchen, for the
making of soup. He made beautiful soup, his father said; and
his mother said, "You are only eight, my little one, but how you
help us!"

He opened his square, wooden treasure-box. There, on the very
surface, floating on top of his three soldier buttons and the pressed
leaves, already thin as spider webs, was the letter from America.
It was a beautiful, long envelope of an orange shade; and in the
center of it was his name. It was his letter. His cousin, Manuel,
had sent it to him from America, from the large state of Ohio,
in which he lived. There it was, his name, written in black ink
upon the envelope:

SR. RAMON GOMEZ V.

His first letter; Ramon took it very carefully from the box. His
heart pounded. How good it was to be alive! To receive letters
from far countries, to be able to make beautiful soup for one's dear
mother and father, who worked.

Whistling gaily, he ran from the house. He held the letter high
in the air, like a banner. When he had come to his favorite play-

ing corner, which was close to the smells and rush and people of the marketplace, he found all his friends there.

Juan saw the letter immediately; his eyes were sharp as knives. "What have you there?" he called to Ramon; and all the others crowded close.

Ramon continued to whistle. Then he said carelessly, "It is nothing. A letter from America. My cousin, Manuel, sent it to me." His heart was almost bursting with pride and happiness. How good it was to be alive! How nice, nice to see his friends' eyes widening with curiosity and excitement.

"Manuel writes that all is well in America," Ramon said, holding the long envelope like a jewel before their eyes. "He is going to school. He has many friends. It is beginning to be warm there, and they play games in the street. The snow is gone for another season."

"Games," Elena said. "What kind of games? Like ours?"

"Ah," Ramon said, hardly able to speak for excitement, "I have here, in this letter, very careful instructions in the playing of a game. Shall we play it now?" He looked carelessly down, but he was trembling with happiness. This moment belonged only to him, and so, too, would the day be his, as he taught them the American game. He would be the leader.

"Yes, yes," they shouted. The letter had excited them, too, and they were wild to taste of its contents.

Ramon carefully took the letter from its envelope; the long, orange envelope he tucked into his open blouse, the letter he unfolded and held up for them to see. The twins, Jacinto and Jacinta, sat at his feet and stared solemnly at the letter, their eyes very big and black and round. Ramon smiled at them; they looked like two fat, little dolls, stuffed with sweet straw and sunshine and milk. He had often wished they were his brother and sister, the little dolls!

"Well," he said, reading snatches of the letter, "this game is called The Farmer in the Dell."

Isabela said, "But what is a dell, Ramon?"

"A dell is a little valley, all grassy and nice. That is what the books say."

"We have stone here," Isabela said. "How can we play then?" They were silent. Then Ramon smiled. "We must pretend," he said. "That is what a game is anyway. We will pretend that this street is full of grass and is therefore a dell. I will be the farmer. Are we ready?"

"Let us begin," the boys cried. "Be still, Isabela. Begin. Ramon, begin!"

"All right. Now, I am the farmer. I stand in the dell, alone, and all of you form a ring about me. You must all join hands. From your midst I choose a wife. We all sing . . ."

The stalls of the market were blazing with every conceivable color. In the warm sun, fruits and vegetables lay in orderly rows of concentrated sun, green and red and yellow. The fragrances, mixed in mid-air, made of the entire street a garden. There were tables of meat, red and firm and fresh blooded, and nearby were the hard, fresh-caught fish, looking almost alive. There were tables heaped high with loaves of bread, still warm; and there were the cheeses and the oils.

Between the tables and all around the stalls was the constant ebb and flow of people. Men and women buying, looking, touching to see if the product was worthy, smelling to see if the product was fresh, and sometimes actually tasting, for what is better than taste?

Today, the people seemed different. They clung, in small, compact groups to the walks, and spoke in low voices. Many of them did not even look in the direction of the foods. Their faces were tense and tight; the flesh seemed withdrawn into itself, and darkened, so that the faces appeared secretive and yet anxious at the same time. There were small, thick clumps of men, and there were women-clumps, too; and the women faces were more secretive than

the men faces, withdrawn more deeply into their own flesh and
pain and fear. The men were speaking freely, and gesticulating,
their hands fast, and sometimes a ring flashing in the sunlight. But
the women spoke in hushed voices, and sometimes an entire tight
little group of women was dead silent, just the faces turned up a
bit, and secret.

"Now that you know, let us begin," said Ramon. He was standing alone in the center of the ring of boys and girls.

He started, singing in his rather sweet, high voice: "The farmer
in the dell . . ."

Then the other voices joined his:

> "The farmer in the dell,
> Hi-o-the-merrio,
> The farmer in the dell."

"Sing, sing," Ramon commanded.

The young voices, fresh as the morning, sang gaily. The voices
of the twins were heard a little late, two tiny, frail sounds breaking with giggles.

"The farmer takes a wife," they all sang. (Ramon said, "Elena,
I pick you." The little, dark girl, her curls shaking as she tossed
her head, came to him and stood at his side. Ramon saw how she
flushed, her face warm and pink upon the brown of her skin; the
picture of her and of her blushes hung in the corner of his eyes,
and he was wild with joy and a desire to shout as loudly as he
could.)

> "The farmer takes a wife,
> Hi-o-the-merrio,
> The farmer takes a wife."

There was a burst of laughter as Elena picked as her child Pedro,
who was much taller than the farmer's wife, his game-mother.
Then Pedro picked as his dog, Isabela, and she joined the three
in the center, her blushes even warmer than Elena's, for she admired Pedro very much.

"What a wonderful game," Maria exclaimed as she danced from one foot to the other. "Let us play it all day long!"

> "The dog takes a cat,
> The dog takes a cat,"

Again the song rang out. ("I take Ricardo," Isabela said. "Ricci, Ricci," they cried, "you are the cat!" He stood in the center, grinning.)

> "Hi-o-the-merrio,
> The dog takes a cat."

Whom did Ricardo pick for his rat, but Jacinta? She toddled to his side like a little, round ball and stood very close to him, her finger in her mouth. She was frightened and happy and her eyes grew bigger and blacker every minute.

And of course for the cheese, Jacinta picked her twin, Jacinto, for they loved each other dearly, and could not bear to be apart. When they sang, "The rat takes the cheese," Jacinta trembled, and Ricardo whispered, "Pick somebody, quick."

Her finger came out of her little, round mouth with a pop and she pointed it, wet and pink and wrinkled, at Jacinto. Then there was a royal shout, and everybody laughed and laughed. Jacinto waddled over the street to stand in the center. He was not afraid at all, but grinned all over his round, red face. There, in the center, he was deserted for a moment, and he stood, very tiny and fat and pretending to be solemn, alone.

"Now," Ramon called, "let us go!"

All of them ran close to Jacinto and pulled their arms high over his head. They clapped their hands as hard as they could, while the cheese cowered and giggled.

> "The cheese stands alone,
> The cheese stands alone,
> Hi-o-the-merrio,
> The cheese stands alone!"

"Oh," gasped Maria, "how wonderful, how beautiful. Let us play it again and again."

A sound began in the air.

Faint, ever louder and stronger and deeper, the first sound began to vibrate in the ears. Hardly aware, the people still talked, yet their heads lifted slightly and cocked, before they themselves were conscious that they listened.

Faint; yet that sound grew in the memory long before the whining reality of it was born. Louder, from the skies ever louder, down, down, the vibration growing in intensity and range; until suddenly the people looked up. Suddenly, someone said: "My God, what is that?"

Then, the air was at last saturated, and the vibration and whine could reach no greater fear: then, low and graceful, the airplanes were over the marketplace.

They swooped, and were beautiful and deadly as birds of prey. They looped. As every head turned upward, with the same gesture, and every eye grew wide and blind upon the same single sight, the planes swept back and forth, up and down, until there was no sky, no sun, there were no clouds: there were only the ten planes in the world, there was no world: there were only the planes.

The children were looking and pointing. Ramon stared, thinking with excitement of the men who guided those swift, black things. He wished he could be in one of them. He held the letter very tightly in his hands, wishing suddenly that he could fly like that to America, to his cousin Manuel, in the state of Ohio. How surprised Manuel would be. Out of the sky his plane would drop, from heaven itself. Out steps Ramon. "Ah," says Ramon, carelessly, "how do you do, my dear aunt and uncle? I bring you greetings from Spain. Ah, Manuel." He would stretch, smiling at all mention of danger. . . .

Elena looked, shading her eyes. Softly, she hummed:

"Hi-o-the-merrio,
The cheese stands alone."

The ten planes created a perfect, narrow, black V, like the flight of birds who have been trained from birth for just this spectacle. For an intolerable, breathless time, for ever, the V was painted and motionless upon the sky; and all the watching people, men and women, their faces blind and flung upward, said: "Ah." It seemed one sound, from one throat, one sound of awe and terror, low, a little like a prayer of some kind: "Ah."

Then the mouths closed. The faces were turned up, sharp, the necks corded; still, voiceless and still as stone, people were turned toward that magnet in the sky.

The first bomb hit close to where Ramon was standing; it came fast, as beautiful as a live thing, then the others came, almost as fast and as unbearably, things of grace.

The silence was ended.

It was the end of a spell; now that they were released by actual pain and death, the people ran madly anywhere, anywhere so long as they moved. The throats opened so suddenly as almost to split, and the shrieks came faster than the bombs; as if a city of dumb men and women and children had been given voice miraculously. Pain was shrill and maudlin now, in male sound, and female, and the horribly frail, soprano cries of children.

The bombing went on for thirty minutes. Then, the planes were taken from the skies as suddenly as they had been put there.

Nobody knew they were gone. Nobody knew anything but his own blind terror and single pain. Madly, in horror, the people ran from the planes which were no longer there, and from the bombs which no longer fell. They would go on shrieking and moaning for a long time, not hearing or knowing their own voices.

The stalls and long tables which had been flowing with green and yellow and red, and with sun-things were smashed now. The pulped fruits and cheeses were intermingled somehow with shattered bodies, so that the two were almost the same, food, and flesh alive a short while ago. The bits of vegetables, still green, still yellow, the meat and bread, the hunks of fish, all these were hardly to be distinguished from the other fragments, the smashed flesh that had been people.

Ramon lay where he had stood and stared and wished. Ramon lay, headless; and the body that was left him was broken into orderly bits, not scattered, but each piece lying neatly where it had been broken.

The farmer's wife, Elena, lay not far from the farmer, who had been Ramon. Her left leg had been nicely snapped from her body, and it lay, whole and perfect, three or more feet away from her. She lay as if asleep, her curls spread and lovely, near Ramon.

Most of the children were there, dead, or in pain. Some of them wept bitterly, calling for their mothers. Others whimpered, dazed, their eyes staring. Many others were silent.

And the cheese, the poor, little cheese, Jacinto; he was not to be seen at all. The tiny, round baby boy had disappeared completely. His twin, Jacinta, crawled slowly upon the pavement, behind her the bloody, squat marks her hands left upon the stone. She was almost silent, her moans fragile as scent in the air. Perhaps she was looking for her brother, who had been the cheese when they had played the game.

> From *Esquire*, January, 1938. Reprinted by permission of the editor and the author.

1. Does this story have a foreign flavor?
2. Why is the story told in so simple and straightforward a manner?
3. What is the author saying? Is it propaganda?
4. What is the most effective part of the story—the singing or the bombing?
5. Is this story more moving because of the stories and pictures of wars published today; in other words, are readers' minds conditioned by recent events?

# IX. SOCIAL CONSCIOUSNESS

# IX. SOCIAL CONSCIOUSNESS

ONE of the earliest forms of the short story was didactic —the fable or parable. By putting his idea into the concrete detail of a narrative the moralist made it memorable. An ancient example of the story of social meaning is the parable of the ewe lamb by which Nathan the prophet took the conscience of King David. Such parables customarily underscored the idea by repeating it at the end as an application or a moral. In this form the fable survived, at least in juvenile literature, until almost the end of the nineteenth century.

But the very fact that the form declined from adult to juvenile literature shows increasing dissatisfaction with its obviousness. More exacting standards of art, and keener self-criticism, convinced all but the most naïve moralists that, given a valid idea and adequate expression, the reader should be able to grasp the application without having it rammed down his throat. The development of this artistic conscience can be traced, for instance, in Hawthorne, who was always preoccupied with moral ideas. In an early story like "Wakefield" he underscores and drives home the moral; in the later "Ethan Brand" he symbolizes it, but does not elaborate it in direct words. Thus the dividing line between the story of pure entertainment and the story with a purpose became more and more indistinct. In Kipling and O. Henry we are sure that some stories were meant to point a moral, and others to be merely entertaining reading, but we cannot always be certain which is which.

With the growth of the class consciousness bred by the industrialism of the later nineteenth century, the purpose of the didactic story began to take a new direction. The older fables and parables dealt with personal morals; the newer ones turned to social morals.

The theme was no longer the good or evil in a single man; it was the good or evil in a social system of which the individual was merely a type. Dickens in *Hard Times*, Mrs. Gaskell in *North and South* and *Mary Barton*, both essayed the portrayal of a social system nearly a century ago, but it was a long time before the short story made the same attempt. Rebecca Harding Davis's "Life in the Iron Mills" (1861) for many years remained the outstanding American example of the theme of social criticism. Not until the world-wide development in our own day of the battle of social and economic theories did the theme become a major one.

The besetting danger of all writing with a purpose is that the purpose may swallow everything else. Reality of character and plausibility of motive may both be sacrificed to preaching. This is not to say that the story with a purpose cannot be a work of art. It can be, and is. But its artistic success depends on which comes first, the story or the purpose. Edward Everett Hale's "The Man Without a Country" is very bad art, because the purpose came first, and the story was contrived to express it. The question of whether so terrible a punishment could have been conceived and carried out over a long period of years by a succession of normal human beings, to say nothing of whether a country capable of such implacable cruelty was worthy of any man's respect or love, never occurred to Hale. He wanted to show how frightful it would be to have no country, and he thought of nothing else. In the same way, much of what today is called proletarian literature bears about as much resemblance to real literature as *Ten Nights in a Barroom* does. The authors are not primarily concerned with telling a story; they are really making campaign speeches. They are unconsciously reverting to the worst qualities of Victorianism, merely substituting economic for moral preaching.

But if the writer sees his material first in terms of human beings acting their parts in life, he can add almost any amount of moral or social commentary by way of overtones. If he has realized his characters as sharply as a craftsman should, they themselves will keep the doctrine from running away with the story. Upton Sinclair fails as a novelist because his characters are mere pasteboard outlines cut to fit a preconceived pattern; Theodore Dreiser and John Dos Passos are equally doctrinaire, but they see their characters in the round, as people. In some chapters of *Jews Without Money* Michael Gold appears to be orating on a soapbox; in others, like the one here reprinted, his vivid memories of people and actions keep the social criticism subordinated to the human tragedy. Maltz's "Man on a Road" was inspired by the needless deaths caused by the failure of the contractors who built the Gauley Bridge power tunnel in West Virginia to provide adequate safeguards against the silica dust in which the men worked. The story might easily have been just a tract. But because his man, despite the unlikely coherence and articulateness of his letter, is brought before us as an individual, it is a minor work of art.

To put the idea in other words, art can be propaganda, but propaganda cannot be art unless the artist can give life to his figures. John Milton was not the only man in his century who sought to state theology or philosophy in poetry. Today his theology is obsolete, a stumbling block for some readers, but because he was a poet before he was a theologian his work survives while that of Du Bartas and Henry More has perished. The question to ask about any piece of "proletarian" literature is not, Is it good doctrine? but, Is it a good story? If it is a good story, it will survive whether the future brings socialism, communism, fascism, or even a return to Mr. Belloc's Middle Ages.

## Rebecca Harding Davis

# LIFE IN THE IRON MILLS

"Is this the end?
O Life, as futile, then, as frail!
What hope of answer or redress?"

A CLOUDY day: do you know what that is in a town of ironworks? The sky sank down before dawn, muddy, flat, immovable. The air is thick, clammy with the breath of crowded human beings. It stifles me. I open the window, and, looking out, can scarcely see through the rain the grocer's shop opposite, where a crowd of drunken Irishmen are puffing Lynchburg tobacco in their pipes. I can detect the scent through all the foul smells ranging loose in the air.

The idiosyncrasy of this town is smoke. It rolls sullenly in slow folds from the great chimneys of the iron-foundries, and settles down in black, slimy pools on the muddy streets. Smoke on the wharves, smoke on the dingy boats, on the yellow river,—clinging in a coating of greasy soot to the house-front, the two faded poplars, the faces of the passers-by. The long train of mules, dragging masses of pig-iron through the narrow street, have a foul vapor hanging to their reeking sides. Here, inside, is a little broken figure of an angel pointing upward from the mantel-shelf; but even its wings are covered with smoke, clotted and black. Smoke everywhere! A dirty canary chirps desolately in a cage beside me. Its dream of green fields and sunshine is a very old dream,—almost worn out, I think.

From the back-window I can see a narrow brick-yard sloping down to the riverside, strewed with rain-butts and tubs. The river, dull and tawny-colored (*la belle rivière!*), drags itself sluggishly along, tired of the heavy weight of boats and coal-barges. What wonder? When I was a child, I used to fancy a look of weary, dumb appeal upon the face of the Negro-like river slavishly bearing its burden day after day. Something of the same idle notion comes to me to-day, when from the street-window I look on the slow stream of human life creeping past, night and morning, to the great mills. Masses of men, with dull besotted faces bent to the ground, sharpened here or there by pain or cunning; skin and muscle and flesh begrimed with smoke and ashes; stooping all night over boiling caldrons of metal, laired by day in dens of drunkenness and infamy; breathing from infancy to death an air saturated with fog and grease and soot, vileness for soul and body. What do you make of a case like that, amateur psychologist? You call it an altogether serious thing to be alive: to these men it is a drunken jest, a joke,—horrible to the angels perhaps, to them commonplace enough. My fancy about the river was an idle one: it is no type of such a life. What if it be stagnant and slimy here? It knows that beyond there waits for it odorous sunlight—quaint old gardens, dusky with soft green foliage of apple-trees, and flushing crimson with roses,—air, and fields, and mountains. The future of the Welsh puddler, passing just now, is not so pleasant. To be stowed away, after his grimy work is done, in a hole in the muddy graveyard, and after that,—*not* air, nor green fields, nor curious roses.

Can you see how foggy the day is? As I stand here, idly tapping the window-pane, and looking out through the rain at the dirty back-yard and the coal-boats below, fragments of an old story float up before me,—a story of this old house into which I happened to come to-day. You may think it a tiresome story enough, as foggy as the day, sharpened by no sudden flashes of pain or pleasure—I know: only the outline of a dull life, that long since, with thousands of dull lives like its own, was vainly lived and lost: thousands of them,—massed, vile, slimy lives, like those of the torpid lizards in yonder stagnant water-butt— Lost? There is a curious point for you to settle, my friend, who study psychology in a lazy, *dilettante* way. Stop a moment. I am going to be honest. This is what I want you to do. I want you to hide your disgust, take no heed to your clean clothes, and come right down with me,—here, into the thickest of the fog and mud and foul effluvia. I want you to hear this story. There is a secret down here, in this nightmare fog, that has lain dumb for centuries: I want to make it a real thing to you. You, Egoist, or Pantheist, or Arminian, busy in making straight paths for your feet on the hills, do not see it clearly,—this terrible question which men here have gone mad and died trying to answer. I dare not put this secret into words. I told you it was dumb. These men, going by with drunken faces and brains full of unawakened power, do not ask it of Society or of God. Their lives ask it; their deaths ask it. There is no reply. I will tell you plainly that I have a great hope; and I bring it you to be tested. It is this: that this terrible dumb question is its own reply; that it is not the sentence of death we think it, but, from the very extremity of its darkness, the most solemn prophecy of which the world has known of the Hope to come. I dare make my meaning no clearer, but will only tell my story. It will, perhaps, seem to you as foul and dark as this thick vapor about us, and as pregnant with death; but if your eyes are free as mine are to look deeper, no perfume-tinted dawn will be so fair with promise of the day that shall surely come.

My story is very simple,—only what I remember of the life of one of these men,—a furnace-tender in one of Kirby & John's rolling-mills,—Hugh Wolfe. You know the mills? They took the great order for the Lower Virginia railroads there last winter; run usually with about a thousand men. I cannot tell why I choose the half-forgotten story of this Wolfe more than that of myriads of these furnace-hands. Perhaps because there is a secret underlying sympathy between that story and this day with its impure fog and thwarted sunshine,—or perhaps simply for the reason that this house is the one where the Wolfes lived. There were the father and son,—both hands, as I said, in one of Kirby & John's mills for making railroad iron,—and Deborah, their cousin, a picker in some of the cotton mills. The house was rented then to half a dozen families. The Wolfes had two of the cellar-rooms. The old man, like many of the puddlers and feeders of the mills, was Welsh,—had spent half of his life in the Cornish tin-mines. You may pick the Welsh immigrants, Cornish miners, out of the throng passing the windows, any day. They are a trifle more filthy; their muscles are not so brawny; they stoop more. When they are drunk, they neither yell, nor shout, nor stagger, but skulk along like beaten hounds. A pure, unmixed blood, I fancy: shows itself in the slight angular bodies and sharply-cut facial lines. It is nearly thirty years since the Wolfes lived here. Their lives were like those of their class: incessant labor, sleeping in kennel-like rooms, eating rank pork and molasses, drinking—God and the distillers only knew what; with an occasional night in jail, to atone for some drunken excess. Is that all of their lives?—of the portion given to them and these their duplicates swarming the streets to-day?— nothing beneath?—all? So many a political reformer will tell you,— and many a private reformer, too, who has gone among them with a heart tender with Christ's charity, and come out outraged, hardened.

One rainy night, about eleven o'clock, a crowd of half-clothed women stopped outside of the cellar-door. They were going home from the cotton-mill.

"Good-night, Deb," said one, a mulatto, steadying herself against the gas-post. She needed the post to steady her. So did more than one of them.

"Dah's a ball to Miss Potts' to-night. Ye'd best come."

"Inteet, Deb, if hur'll come, hur'll hef fun," said a shrill Welsh voice in the crowd.

Two or three dirty hands were thrust out to catch the gown of the woman, who was groping for the latch of the door.

"No."

"No? Where's Kit Small, then?"

"Begorra! on the spools. Alleys behint, though we helped her, we dud. An wid ye! Let Deb alone! It's ondacent frettin' a quiet body. Be the powers an' we'll have a night of it! there'll be lashin's o' drink,—the Vargent be blessed and praised for 't!"

They went on, the mulatto inclining for a moment to show fight, and drag the woman Wolfe off with them; but, being pacified, she staggered away.

Deborah groped her way into the cellar, and, after considerable stumbling, kindled a match, and lighted a tallow dip, that sent a yellow glimmer over the room. It was low, damp,—the earthen floor covered with a green, slimy moss,—a fetid air smothering the breath. Old Wolfe lay asleep on a heap of straw, wrapped in a torn horse-blanket. He was a pale, meek little man, with a white face and red rabbit-eyes. The woman Deborah was like him; only her face was even more ghastly, her lips bluer, her eyes more watery. She wore a faded cotton gown and a slouching bonnet. When she walked, one could see that she was deformed, almost a hunchback. She trod softly, so as not to waken him, and went through into the room beyond. There she found by the half-extinguished fire an iron saucepan filled with cold boiled potatoes, which she put upon a broken chair with a pint-cup of ale. Placing the old candlestick beside this dainty repast, she untied her bonnet, which hung limp and wet over her face, and prepared to eat her supper. It was the first food that had touched her lips since morning. There was enough of it, however: there was not always. She was hungry,—one could see that easily enough,—and not drunk, as most of her companions would have been found at this

hour. She did not drink, this woman,—her face told that, too,—
nothing stronger than ale. Perhaps the weak, flaccid wretch had
some stimulant in her pale life to keep her up,—some love or hope,
it might be, or urgent need. When that stimulant was gone, she
would take to whisky. Man cannot live by work alone. While she
was skinning the potatoes, and munching them, a noise behind her
made her stop.

"Janey!" she called, lifting the candle and peering into the darkness. "Janey, are you there?"

A heap of ragged coats was heaved up, and the face of a young
girl emerged, staring sleepily at the woman.

"Deborah," she said, at last, "I'm here the night."

"Yes, child. Hur's welcome," she said, quietly eating on.

The girl's face was haggard and sickly; her eyes were heavy with
sleep and hunger: real Milesian eyes they were, dark, delicate blue,
looking out from black shadows with a pitiful fright.

"I was alone," she said, timidly.

"Where's the father?" asked Deborah, holding out a potato,
which the girl greedily seized.

"He's beyant,—wid Haley,—in the stone house." (Did you ever
hear the word *jail* from an Irish mouth?) "I came here. Hugh
told me never to stay me-lone."

"Hugh?"

"Yes."

A vexed frown crossed her face. The girl saw it, and added
quickly,—

"I have not seen Hugh the day, Deb. The old man says his
watch lasts till the mornin'."

The woman sprang up, and hastily began to arrange some bread
and flitch in a tin pail, and to pour her own measure of ale into
a bottle. Tying on her bonnet, she blew out the candle.

"Lay ye down, Janey dear," she said, gently, covering her with
the old rags. "Hur can eat the potatoes, if hur's hungry."

"Where are ye goin', Deb? The rain's sharp."

"To the mill, with Hugh's supper."

"Let him bide till th' morn. Sit ye down."

"No, no,"—sharply pushing her off. "The boy'll starve."

She hurried from the cellar, while the child wearily coiled herself up for sleep. The rain was falling heavily, as the woman, pail in hand, emerged from the mouth of the alley, and turned down the narrow street, that stretched out, long and black, miles before her. Here and there a flicker of gas lighted an uncertain space of muddy footwalk and gutter; the long rows of houses, except an occasional lager-bier shop, were closed; now and then she met a band of mill-hands skulking to or from their work.

Not many even of the inhabitants of a manufacturing town know the vast machinery of system by which the bodies of workmen are governed, that goes on unceasingly from year to year. The hands of each mill are divided into watches that relieve each other as regularly as the sentinels of an army. By night and day the work goes on, the unsleeping engines groan and shriek, the fiery pools of metal boil and surge. Only for a day in the week, in half-courtesy to public censure, the fires are partially veiled; but as soon as the clock strikes midnight, the great furnaces break forth with renewed fury, the clamor begins with fresh, breathless vigor, the engines sob and shriek like "gods in pain."

As Deborah hurried down through the heavy rain, the noise of these thousand engines sounded through the sleep and shadow of the city like far-off thunder. The mill to which she was going lay on the river, a mile below the city-limits. It was far, and she was weak, aching from standing twelve hours at the spools. Yet it was her almost nightly walk to take this man his supper, though at every square she sat down to rest, and she knew she should receive small word of thanks.

Perhaps, if she had possessed an artist's eye, the picturesque oddity of the scene might have made her step stagger less, and the path seem shorter; but to her the mills were only "summat deilish to look at by night."

The road leading to the mills had been quarried from the solid rock, which rose abrupt and bare on one side of the cinder-covered road, while the river, sluggish and black, crept past on the other. The mills for rolling iron are simply immense tent-like roofs, covering acres of ground, open on every side. Beneath these roofs Deborah looked in on a city of fires, that burned hot and fiercely in the night. Fire in every horrible form: pits of flame waving in the wind; liquid metal-flames writhing in tortuous streams through the sand; wide caldrons filled with boiling fire, over which bent ghastly wretches stirring the strange brewing; and through all, crowds of half-clad men, looking like revengeful ghosts in the red light, hurried, throwing masses of glittering fire. It was like a street in Hell. Even Deborah muttered, as she crept through, " 'T looks like t' Devil's place!" It did,—in more ways than one.

She found the man she was looking for, at last, heaping coal on a furnace. He had not time to eat his supper; so she went behind the furnace, and waited. Only a few men were with him, and they noticed her only by a "Hyur comes t' hunchback, Wolfe."

Deborah was stupid with sleep; her back pained her sharply; and her teeth chattered with cold, with the rain that soaked her clothes and dripped from her at every step. She stood, however, patiently holding the pail, and waiting.

"Hout, woman! ye look like a drowned cat. Come near to the fire,"—said one of the men, approaching to scrape away the ashes.

She shook her head. Wolfe had forgotten her. He turned, hearing the man, and came closer.

"I did no' think; gi' me my supper, woman."

She watched him eat with a painful eagerness. With a woman's quick instinct, she saw that he was not hungry,—was eating to please her. Her pale, watery eyes began to gather a strange light.

"Is't good, Hugh? T' ale was a bit sour, I feared."

"No, good enough." He hesitated a moment. "Ye're tired, poor lass! Bide here till I go. Lay down there on that heap of ash, and go to sleep."

He threw her an old coat for a pillow, and turned to his work. The heap was the refuse of the burnt iron, and was not a hard bed; the half-smothered warmth, too, penetrated her limbs, dulling their pain and cold shiver.

Miserable enough she looked, lying there on the ashes like a limp, dirty rag,—yet not an unfitting figure to crown the scene of hopeless discomfort and veiled crime: more fitting, if one looked deeper into the heart of things,—at her thwarted woman's form, her colorless life, her waking stupor that smothered pain and hunger,—even more fit to be a type of her class. Deeper yet if one could look, was there nothing worth reading in this wet, faded thing, half-covered with ashes? no story of a soul filled with groping passionate love, heroic unselfishness, fierce jealousy? of years of weary trying to please the one human being whom she loved, to gain one look of real heart-kindness from him? If anything like this were hidden beneath the pale, bleared eyes, and dull, washed-out-looking face, no one had ever taken the trouble to read its faint signs: not the half-clothed furnace-tender, Wolfe, certainly. Yet he was kind to her: it was his nature to be kind, even to the very rats that swarmed in the cellar: kind to her in just the same way. She knew that. And it might be that very knowledge had given to her face its apathy and vacancy more than her low, torpid life. One sees that dead, vacant look steal sometimes over the rarest, finest, of women's faces,—in the very midst, it may be, of their warmest summer's day; and then one can guess at the secret of intolerable solitude that lies hid beneath the delicate laces and brilliant smile. There was no warmth, no brilliancy, no summer for this woman; so the stupor and vacancy had time to gnaw into her face perpetually. She was young, too, though no one guessed it; so the gnawing was the fiercer.

She lay quiet in the dark corner, listening, through the monotonous din and uncertain glare of the works, to the dull plash of the rain in the far distance,—shrinking back whenever the man Wolfe happened to look towards her. She knew, in spite of all his kindness, that there was that in her face and form which made him loathe the sight of her. She felt by instinct, although she could not comprehend it, the finer nature of the man, which made him among his fellow-workmen something unique, set apart. She knew, that, down under all the vileness and coarseness of his life, there was a groping passion for whatever was beautiful and pure,— that his soul sickened with disgust at her deformity, even when his words were kindest. Through this dull consciousness, which never left her, came, like a sting, the recollection of the dark blue eyes and lithe figure of the little Irish girl she had left in the cellar. The recollection struck through even her stupid intellect with a vivid glow of beauty and of grace. Little Janey, timid, help-less, clinging to Hugh as her only friend: that was the sharp thought, the bitter thought, that drove into the glazed eyes a fierce light of pain. You laugh at it? Are pain and jealousy less savage realities down here in this place I am taking you to than in your own house or in your own heart,—your heart, which they clutch sometimes? The note is the same, I fancy, be the octave high or low.

If you could go into this mill where Deborah lay, and drag out from the hearts of these men the terrible tragedy of their lives, taking it as a symptom of the disease of their class, no ghost Hor-ror would terrify you more. A reality of soul-starvation, of living death, that meets you every day under the besotted faces on the street,—I can paint nothing of this, only give you the outside out-lines of a night, a crisis in the life of one man: whatever muddy depth of soul-history lies beneath you can read according to the eyes God has given you.

Wolfe, while Deborah watched him as a spaniel its master, bent over the furnace with his iron pole, unconscious of her scrutiny, only stopping to receive orders. Physically, Nature had promised the man but little. He had already lost the strength and instinct vigor of a man, his muscles were thin, his nerves weak, his face (a meek, woman's face) haggard, yellow with consumption. In the mill he was known as one of the girl-men: "Molly Wolfe" was his *sobriquet*. He was never seen in the cockpit, did not own a terrier, drank but seldom; when he did, desperately. He fought sometimes, but was always thrashed, pommeled to a jelly. The man was game enough, when his blood was up: but he was no favorite in the mill; he had the taint of school-learning on him,— not to a dangerous extent, only a quarter or so in the free-school in fact, but enough to ruin him as a good hand in a fight.

For other reasons, too, he was not popular. Not one of themselves, they felt that, though outwardly as filthy and ash-covered; silent, with foreign thoughts and longings breaking out through his quietness in innumerable curious ways: this one, for instance. In the neighboring furnace-buildings lay great heaps of the refuse from the ore after the pig-metal is run. *Korl* we call it here: a light porous substance, of a delicate, waxen, flesh-colored tinge. Out of the blocks of this korl, Wolfe, in his off-hours from the furnace, had a habit of chipping and molding figures,—hideous, fantastic enough, but sometimes strangely beautiful: even the millmen saw that, while they jeered at him. It was a curious fancy in the man, almost a passion. The few hours for rest he spent hewing and hacking with his blunt knife, never speaking, until his watch came again,—working at one figure for months, and, when it was finished, breaking it to pieces, perhaps, in a fit of disappointment. A morbid, gloomy man, untaught, unled, left to feed his soul in grossness and crime, and hard, grinding labor.

I want you to come down and look at this Wolfe, standing there among the lowest of his kind, and see him just as he is, that you may judge him justly when you hear the story of this night. I want you to look back, as he does every day, at his birth in vice, his starved infancy; to remember the heavy years he has groped through as boy and man,—the slow, heavy years of constant, hot work. So long ago he began, that he thinks sometimes he has worked there for ages. There is no hope that it will ever end. Think that God put into this man's soul a fierce thirst for beauty,—to know it, to create it, to be—something, he knows not what,—other than he is. There are moments when a passing cloud, the sun glinting on the purple thistles, a kindly smile, a child's face, will rouse him to a passion of pain,—when his nature starts up with a mad cry of rage against God, man, whoever it is that has forced this vile, slimy life upon him. With all this groping, this mad desire, a great blind intellect stumbling through wrong, a loving poet's heart, the man was by habit only a coarse, vulgar laborer, familiar with sights and words you would blush to name. Be just: when I tell you about this night, see him as he is. Be just,—not like man's law, which seizes on one isolated fact, but like God's judging angel, whose clear, sad eye saw all the countless cankering days of this man's life, all the countless nights, when, sick with starving, his soul fainted in him, before it judged him for this night, the saddest of all.

I called this night the crisis of his life. If it was, it stole on him unawares. These great turning-days of life cast no shadow before, slip by unconsciously. Only a trifle, a little turn of the rudder, and the ship goes to heaven or hell.

Wolfe, while Deborah watched him, dug into the furnace of melting iron with his pole, dully thinking only how many rails the lump would yield. It was late,—nearly Sunday morning; another hour, and the heavy work would be done,—only the furnaces to replenish and cover for the next day. The workmen were growing more noisy, shouting, as they had to do, to be heard over the deep clamor of the mills. Suddenly they grew less boisterous,—at the far end, entirely silent. Something unusual had happened. After a moment, the silence came nearer; the men stopped their jeers and drunken choruses. Deborah, stupidly lifting up her head, saw the cause of the quiet. A group of five or six men were slowly approaching, stopping to examine each furnace as they came. Visitors often came to see the mills after night: except by growing less noisy, the men took no notice of them. The furnace where Wolfe worked was near the bounds of the works; they halted there hot and tired: a walk over one of these great foundries is no trifling task. The woman, drawing out of sight, turned over to sleep. Wolfe, seeing them stop, suddenly roused from his indifferent stupor, and watched them keenly. He knew some of them: the overseer, Clarke,—a son of Kirby, one of the mill-owners,—and a Doctor May, one of the town-physicians. The other two were strangers. Wolfe came closer. He seized eagerly every chance that brought him into contact with this mysterious class that shone down on him perpetually with the glamour of another order of being. What made the difference between them? That was the mystery of his life. He had a vague notion that perhaps to-night he could find it out. One of the strangers sat down on a pile of bricks, and beckoned young Kirby to his side.

"This *is* hot, with a vengeance. A match, please?"—lighting his cigar. "But the walk is worth the trouble. If it were not that you must have heard it so often, Kirby, I would tell you that your works look like Dante's Inferno."

Kirby laughed.

"Yes. Yonder is Farinata himself in the burning tomb,"—pointing to some figure in the shimmering shadows.

"Judging from some of the faces of your men," said the other, "they bid fair to try the reality of Dante's vision, some day."

Young Kirby looked curiously around, as if seeing the faces of his hands for the first time.

"They're bad enough, that's true. A desperate set, I fancy. Eh, Clarke?"

The overseer did not hear him. He was talking of net profits just then,—giving, in fact, a schedule of the annual business of the firm to a sharp peering little Yankee, who jotted down notes on a paper laid on the crown of his hat: a reporter for one of the city-papers, getting up a series of reviews of the leading manufactories. The other gentleman had accompanied them merely for amusement. They were silent until the notes were finished, drying their feet at the furnaces, and sheltering their faces from the intolerable heat. At last the overseer concluded with—

"I believe that is a pretty fair estimate, Captain."

"Here, some of you men!" said Kirby, "bring up those boards. We may as well sit down, gentlemen, until the rain is over. It cannot last much longer at this rate."

"Pig-metal,"—mumbled the reporter,—"um!—coal facilities,—um!—hands employed, twelve hundred,—bitumen,—um!—all right, I believe, Mr. Clarke;—sinking-fund,—what did you say was your sinking-fund?"

"Twelve hundred hands?" said the stranger, the young man who had first spoken. "Do you control their votes, Kirby?"

"Control? No." The young man smiled complacently. "But my father brought seven hundred votes to the polls for his candidate last November. No force-work, you understand,—only a speech or two, a hint to form themselves into a society, and a bit of red and blue bunting to make them a flag. The Invincible Roughs,—I believe that is their name. I forget the motto: 'Our country's hope,' I think."

There was a laugh. The young man talking to Kirby sat with an amused light in his cool gray eye, surveying critically the half-clothed figures of the puddlers, and the slow swing of their brawny muscles. He was a stranger in the city,—spending a couple of months in the borders of a Slave State, to study the institutions of the South,—a brother-in-law of Kirby's,—Mitchell. He was an amateur gymnast,—hence his anatomical eye; a patron, in a *blasé* way, of the prize-ring; a man who sucked the essence out of a science or philosophy in an indifferent, gentlemanly way; who took Kant, Novalis, Humboldt, for what they were worth in his own scales; accepting all, despising nothing, in heaven, earth, or hell, but one-idead men; with a temper yielding and brilliant as summer water, until his Self was touched, when it was ice, though brilliant still. Such men are not rare in the States.

As he knocked the ashes from his cigar, Wolfe caught with a

quick pleasure the contour of the white hand, the blood-glow of a red ring he wore. His voice, too, and that of Kirby touched him like music,—low, even, with chording cadences. About this man Mitchell hung the impalpable atmosphere belonging to the thorough-bred gentleman. Wolfe, scraping away the ashes beside him, was conscious of it, did obeisance to it with his artist sense, unconscious that he did so.

The rain did not cease. Clarke and the reporter left the mills; the others, comfortably seated near the furnace, lingered, smoking and talking in a desultory way. Greek would not have been more unintelligible to the furnace-tenders whose presence they soon forgot entirely. Kirby drew out a newspaper from his pocket and read aloud some article, which they discussed eagerly. At every sentence, Wolfe listened more and more like a dumb, hopeless animal, with a duller, more stolid look creeping over his face, glancing now and then at Mitchell, marking acutely every smallest sign of refinement, then back to himself, seeing as in a mirror his filthy body, his more stained soul.

Never! He had no words for such a thought, but he knew now, in all the sharpness of the bitter certainty, that between them there was a great gulf never to be passed. Never!

The bell of the mills rang for midnight. Sunday morning had dawned. Whatever hidden message lay in the tolling bells floated past these men unknown. Yet it was there. Veiled in the solemn music ushering the risen Saviour was a key-note to solve the darkest secrets of a world gone wrong,—even this social riddle which the brain of the grimy puddler grappled with madly to-night.

The men began to withdraw the metal from the caldrons. The mills were deserted on Sundays, except by the hands who fed the fires, and those who had no lodgings and slept usually on the ash-heaps. The three strangers sat still during the next hour, watching the men cover the furnaces, laughing now and then at some jest of Kirby's.

"Do you know," said Mitchell, "I like this view of the works better than when the glare was fiercest? These heavy shadows and the amphitheater of smothered fires are ghostly, unreal. One could fancy these red smouldering lights to be the half-shut eyes of wild beasts, and the spectral figures their victims in the den."

Kirby laughed. "You are fanciful. Come, let us get out of the den. The spectral figures, as you call them, are a little too real for me to fancy a close proximity in the darkness,—unarmed, too."

The others rose, buttoning their overcoats, and lighting cigars.

"Raining, still," said Doctor May, "and hard. Where did we leave the coach, Mitchell?"

"At the other side of the works—Kirby, what's that?"

Mitchell started back, half-frightened, as, suddenly turning a corner, the white figure of a woman faced him in the darkness,—a woman, white, of giant proportions, crouching on the ground, her arms flung out in some wild gesture of warning.

"Stop! Make that fire burn there!" cried Kirby, stopping short. The flame burst out, flashing the gaunt figure into bold relief. Mitchell drew a long breath.

"I thought it was alive," he said, going up curiously.

The others followed.

"Not marble, eh?" asked Kirby, touching it.

One of the lower overseers stopped.

"Korl, Sir."

"Who did it?"

"Can't say. Some of the hands; chipped it out in off-hours."

"Chipped to some purpose, I should say. What a flesh-tint the stuff has! Do you see, Mitchell?"

"I see."

He had stepped aside where the light fell boldest on the figure, looking at it in silence. There was not one line of beauty or grace in it: a nude woman's form, muscular, grown coarse with labor, the powerful limbs instinct with some one poignant longing. One idea: there it was in the tense, rigid muscles, the clutching hands, the wild, eager face, like that of a starving wolf. Kirby and Doctor

May walked around it, critical, curious. Mitchell stood aloof, silent. The figure touched him strangely.

"Not badly done," said Doctor May. "Where did the fellow learn that sweep of the muscles in the arm and hand? Look at them! They are groping,—do you see?—clutching: the peculiar action of a man dying of thirst."

"They have ample facilities for studying anatomy," sneered Kirby, glancing at the half-naked figures.

"Look," continued the Doctor, "at this bony wrist, and the strained sinews of the instep! A working-woman,—the very type of her class."

"God forbid!" muttered Mitchell.

"Why?" demanded May. "What does the fellow intend by the figure? I cannot catch the meaning."

"Ask him," said the other, dryly. "There he stands,"—pointing to Wolfe, who stood with a group of men, leaning on his ash-rake.

The Doctor beckoned him with the affable smile which kind-hearted men put on, when talking to these people.

"Mr. Mitchell has picked you out as the man who did this,— I'm sure I don't know why. But what did you mean by it?"

"She be hungry."

Wolfe's eyes answered Mitchell, not the Doctor.

"Oh-h! But what a mistake you have made, my fine fellow! You have given no sign of starvation to the body. It is strong,—terribly strong. It has the mad, half-despairing gesture of drowning."

Wolfe stammered, glanced appealingly at Mitchell, who saw the soul of the thing, he knew. But the cool, probing eyes were turned on himself now,—mocking, cruel, relentless.

"Not hungry for meat," the furnace-tender said at last.

"What then? Whisky?" jeered Kirby, with a coarse laugh.

Wolfe was silent a moment, thinking.

"I dunno," he said, with a bewildered look. "It mebbe. Summat to make her live, I think,—like you. Whisky ull do it, in a way."

The young man laughed again. Mitchell flashed a look of disgust somewhere,—not at Wolfe.

"May," he broke out impatiently, "are you blind? Look at that woman's face! It asks questions of God, and says, 'I have a right to know.' Good God, how hungry it is!"

They looked a moment; then May turned to the mill-owner:—

"Have you many such hands as this? What are you going to do with them? Keep them at puddling iron?"

Kirby shrugged his shoulders. Mitchell's look had irritated him.

"Ce n'est pas mon affaire. I have no fancy for nursing infant geniuses. I suppose there are some stray gleams of mind and soul among these wretches. The Lord will take care of his own; or else they can work out their own salvation. I have heard you call our American system a ladder which any man can scale. Do you doubt it? Or perhaps you want to banish all social ladders, and put us all on a flat table-land—eh, May?"

The Doctor looked vexed, puzzled. Some terrible problem lay hid in this woman's face, and troubled these men. Kirby waited for an answer, and, receiving none, went on, warming with his subject.

"I tell you, there's something wrong that no talk of 'Liberté' or 'Egalité' will do away. If I had the making of men, these men who do the lowest part of the world's work should be machines;—nothing more,—hands. It would be kindness. God help them! What are taste, reason, to creatures who must live such lives as that?" He pointed to Deborah, sleeping on the ash-heap. "So many nerves to sting them to pain. What if God had put your brain, with all its agony of touch, into your fingers and bid you work and strike with that?"

"You think you could govern the world better?" laughed the Doctor.

"I do not think at all."

"That is true philosophy. Drift with the stream, because you cannot dive deep enough to find bottom, eh?"

"Exactly," rejoined Kirby. "I do not think. I wash my hands of all social problems,—slavery, caste, white or black. My duty to my operatives has a narrow limit, the pay-hour on Saturday night. Outside of that, if they cut korl, or cut each other's throats, (the more popular amusement of the two,) I am not responsible."

The Doctor sighed,—a good honest sigh, from the depths of his stomach.

"God help us! Who is responsible?"

"Not I, I tell you," said Kirby, testily. "What has the man who pays them money to do with their soul's concerns, more than the grocer, or butcher who takes it?"

"And yet," said Mitchell's cynical voice, "look at her! How hungry she is!"

Kirby tapped his boot with his cane. No one spoke. Only the dumb face of the rough image looking into their faces with the awful question, "What shall we do to be saved?" Only Wolfe's face, with its heavy weight of brain, its weak, uncertain mouth, its desperate eyes, out of which looked the soul of his class,—only Wolfe's face turned towards Kirby's. Mitchell laughed,—a cool, musical laugh.

"Money has spoken!" he said, seating himself lightly on a stone with the air of an amused spectator at a play. "Are you answered?" —turning to Wolfe his clear, magnetic face.

Bright and deep and cold as Arctic air, the soul of the man lay tranquil beneath. He looked at the furnace-tender as he had looked at a rare mosaic in the morning; only the man was the more amusing study of the two.

"Are you answered? Why, May, look at him! 'De profundis clamavi.' Or, to quote in English, 'Hungry and thirsty, his soul faints in him.' And so Money sends back its answer into the depths through you, Kirby! Very clear the answer, too!—I think I remember reading the same words somewhere:—washing your hands in Eau de Cologne, and saying, 'I am innocent of the blood of this man. See ye to it!' "

Kirby flushed angrily.

"You quote Scripture freely."

"Do I not quote correctly? I think I remember another line, which may amend my meaning: 'Inasmuch as ye did it unto the least of these, ye did it unto me.' Deist? Bless you, man, I was raised on the milk of the Word. Now, Doctor, the pocket of the world having uttered its voice, what has the heart to say? You are a philanthropist, in a small way,—*n'est-ce pas?* Here, boy, this gentleman can show you how to cut korl better,—or your destiny. Go on, May!"

"I think a mocking devil possesses you to-night," rejoined the Doctor, seriously.

He went to Wolfe and put his hand kindly on his arm. Something of a vague idea possessed the Doctor's brain that much good was to be done here by a friendly word or two: a latent genius to be warmed into life by a waited-for sun-beam. Here it was: he had brought it. So he went on complacently:—

"Do you know, boy, you have it in you to be a great sculptor, a great man?—do you understand?" (talking down to the capacity of his hearer: it is a way people have with children, and men like Wolfe)—"to live a better, stronger life than I, or Mr. Kirby here? A man may make himself anything he chooses. God has given you stronger powers than many men,—me, for instance."

May stopped, heated, glowing with his own magnanimity. And it was magnanimous. The puddler had drunk in every word, looking through the Doctor's flurry, and generous heat, and self-approval, into his will, with those slow, absorbing eyes of his.

"Make yourself what you will. It is your right."

"I know," quietly. "Will you help me?"

Mitchell laughed again. The Doctor turned now, in a passion,—

"You know, Mitchell, I have not the means. You know, if I had it, it is in my heart to take this boy and educate him for—"

"The glory of God, and the glory of John May."

May did not speak for a moment; then, controlled, he said,—

"Why should one be raised, when myriads are left?—I have not the money, boy," to Wolfe, shortly.

"Money?" He said it over slowly, as one repeats the guessed answer to a riddle, doubtfully. "That is it? Money?"

"Yes, money,—that is it," said Mitchell, rising and drawing his furred coat about him. "You've found the cure for all the world's diseases— Come, May, find your good-humor, and come home. This damp wind chills my very bones. Come and preach your Saint-Simonian doctrines to-morrow to Kirby's hands. Let them have a clear idea of the rights of the soul, and I'll venture next week they'll strike for higher wages. That will be the end of it."

"Will you send the coach-driver to this side of the mills?" asked Kirby, turning to Wolfe.

He spoke kindly: it was his habit to do so. Deborah, seeing the puddler go, crept after him. The three men waited outside. Doctor May walked up and down, chafed. Suddenly he stopped.

"Go back, Mitchell! You say the pocket and the heart of the world speak without meaning to these people. What has its head to say? Taste, culture, refinement? Go!"

Mitchell was leaning against a brick wall. He turned his head indolently, and looked into the mills. There hung about the place a thick, unclean odor. The slightest motion of his hand marked that he perceived it, and his insufferable disgust. That was all. May said nothing, only quickened his angry tramp.

"Besides," added Mitchell, giving a corollary to this answer, "it would be of no use. I am not one of them."

"You do not mean—" said May, facing him.

"Yes, I mean just that. Reform is born of need, not pity. No vital movement of the people's has worked down, for good or evil; fermented, instead, carried up the heaving, cloggy mass. Think back through history, and you will know it. What will this lowest deep,—thieves, Magdalens, Negroes—do with the light filtered through ponderous Church creeds, Baconian theories, Goethe schemes? Some day, out of their bitter need will be thrown up their own light-bringer,—their Jean Paul, their Cromwell, their Messiah."

"Bah!" was the Doctor's inward criticism. However, in practice, he adopted the theory; for, when, night and morning, afterwards, he prayed that power might be given these degraded souls to rise, he glowed at heart, recognizing an accomplished duty.

Wolfe and the woman had stood in the shadow of the works as the coach drove off. The Doctor had held out his hand in a frank, generous way, telling him to "take care of himself, and to remember it was his right to rise." Mitchell had simply touched his hat, as to an equal, with a quiet look of thorough resignation. Kirby had thrown Deborah some money, which she found, and clutched eagerly enough. They were gone now, all of them. The man sat down on the cinder-road, looking up into the murky sky.

" 'T be late, Hugh. Wunnot hur come?"

He shook his head doggedly, and the woman crouched out of his sight against the wall. Do you remember rare moments when a sudden light flashed over yourself, your world, God? when you stood on a mountain-peak, seeing your life as it might have been, as it is? one quick instant, when custom lost its force and every-day usage? when your friend, wife, brother, stood in a new light? your soul was bared, and the grave,—a foretaste of the nakedness of the Judgment-Day? So it came before him, his life, that night. The slow tides of pain he had borne gathered themselves up and surged against his soul. His squalid daily life, the brutal coarseness eating into his brain, as the ashes into his skin: before, these things had been a dull aching into his consciousness; to-night, they were reality. He gripped the filthy red shirt that clung, stiff with soot, about him, and tore it savagely from his arm. The flesh beneath was muddy with grease and ashes,—and the heart beneath that! And the soul? God knows.

Then flashed before his vivid poetic sense the man who had left him,—the pure face, the delicate, sinewy limbs, in harmony with all he knew of beauty or truth. In his cloudy fancy he had pictured a Something like this. He had found it in this Mitchell, even when he idly scoffed at his pain: a Man all-knowing, all-seeing, crowned by Nature, reigning,—the keen glance of his eye falling like a scepter on other men. And yet his instinct taught him that he too— He! He looked at himself with sudden loathing, sick, wrung his hands with a cry, and then was silent. With all the phantoms of his heated, ignorant fancy, Wolfe had not been vague in his ambitions. They were practical, slowly built up before him out of his knowledge of what he could do. Through years he had day by day made this hope a real thing to himself,—a clear, projected figure of himself, as he might become.

Able to speak, to know what was best, to raise these men and women working at his side up with him: sometimes he forgot this defined hope in the frantic anguish to escape,—only to escape,— out of the wet, the pain, the ashes, somewhere, anywhere,—only for one moment of free air on a hill-side, to lie down and let his sick soul throb itself out in the sunshine. But to-night he panted for life. The savage strength of his nature was aroused; his cry was fierce to God for justice.

"Look at me!" he said to Deborah, with a low, bitter laugh, striking his puny chest savagely. "What am I worth, Deb? Is it my fault that I am no better? My fault? My fault?"

He stopped, stung with a sudden remorse, seeing her hunch-back shape writhing with sobs. For Deborah was crying thankless tears, according to the fashion of women.

"God forgi' me, woman! Things go harder wi' you nor me. It's a worse share."

He got up and helped her to rise; and they went doggedly down the muddy street, side by side.

"It's all wrong," he muttered, slowly,—"all wrong! I dunnot understan'. But it'll end some day."

"Come home, Hugh!" she said, coaxingly; for he had stopped, looking around bewildered.

"Home,—and back to the mill!" He went on saying this over to himself, as if he would mutter down every pain in this dull despair.

She followed him through the fog, her blue lips chattering with cold. They reached the cellar at last. Old Wolfe had been drinking since she went out, and had crept nearer the door. The girl Janey slept heavily in the corner. He went up to her, touching softly the worn white arm with his fingers. Some bitterer thought stung him, as he stood there. He wiped the drops from his forehead, and went into the room beyond, livid, trembling. A hope, trifling, perhaps, but very dear, had died just then out of the poor puddler's life, as he looked at the sleeping, innocent girl,—some plan for the future, in which she had borne a part. He gave it up that moment, then and forever. Only a trifle, perhaps, to us: his face grew a shade paler,—that was all. But, somehow, the man's soul, as God and the angels looked down on it, never was the same afterwards.

Deborah followed him into the inner room. She carried a candle, which she placed on the floor, closing the door after her. She had seen the look on his face, as he turned away: her own grew deadly. Yet, as she came up to him, her eyes glowed. He was seated on an old chest, quiet, holding his face in his hands.

"Hugh!" she said softly.

He did not speak.

"Hugh, did hur hear what the man said,—him with the clear voice? Did hur hear? Money, money,—that it wud do all?"

He pushed her away,—gently, but he was worn out; her rasping tone fretted him.

"Hugh!"

The candle flared a pale yellow light over the cobwebbed brick walls, and the woman standing there. He looked at her. She was young, in deadly earnest; her faded eyes, and wet, ragged figure caught from their frantic eagerness a power akin to beauty.

"Hugh, it is true! Money ull do it! Oh, Hugh, boy, listen till me! He said it true! It is money!"

"I know. Go back! I do not want you here."

"Hugh, it is t' last time. I'll never worrit hur again."

There were tears in her voice now, but she choked them back.

"Hear till me only to-night! If one of t' witch people wud come, them we heard of t' home, and gif hur all hur wants, what then? Say, Hugh!"

"What do you mean?"

"I mean money."

Her whisper shrilled through his brain.

"If one t' witch dwarfs wud come from t' lane moors to-night, and gif hur money, to go out,—out, I say,—out, lad, where t' sun shines, and t' heath grows, and t' ladies walk in silken gownds, and God stays all t' time,—where t' man lives that talked to us to-night,—Hugh knows,—Hugh could walk there like a king!"

He thought the woman mad, tried to check her, but she went on, fierce in her eager haste.

"If I were t' witch dwarf, if I had t' money, wud hur thank me? Wud hur take me out o' this place wid hur and Janey? I wud not come into the gran' house hur wud build, to vex hur wid t' hunch, —only at night, when t' shadows were dark, stand far off to see hur."

Mad? Yes! Are many of us mad in this way?

"Poor Deb! poor Deb!" he said, soothingly.

"It is here," she said, suddenly jerking into his hand a small roll. "I took it! I did it! Me, me!—not hur! I shall be hanged, I shall be burnt in hell, if anybody knows I took it! Out of his pocket, as he leaned against t' bricks. Hur knows?"

She thrust it into his hand, and then, her errand done, began to gather chips together to make a fire, choking down hysteric sobs.

"Has it come to this?"

That was all he said. The Welsh Wolfe blood was honest. The roll was a small green pocket-book containing one or two gold pieces, and a check for an incredible amount, as it seemed to the poor puddler. He laid it down, hiding his face again in his hands.

"Hugh, don't be angry wud me! It's only poor Deb,—hur knows?"

He took the long skinny fingers kindly in his.

"Angry? God help me, no! Let me sleep! I am tired."

He threw himself heavily down on the wooden bench, stunned with pain and weariness. She brought some old rags to cover him.

It was late on Sunday evening before he awoke. I tell God's truth, when I say he had then no thought of keeping this money. Deborah had hid it in his pocket. He found it there. She watched him eagerly, as he took it out.

"I must gif it to him," he said, reading her face.

"Hur knows," she said with a bitter sigh of disappointment. "But it is hur right to keep it."

His right! The word struck him. Doctor May had used the same. He washed himself, and went out to find this man Mitchell. His right! Why did this chance word cling to him so obstinately? Do you hear the fierce devils whisper in his ear, as he went slowly down the darkening street?

The evening came on, slow and calm. He seated himself at the end of an alley leading into one of the larger streets. His brain was clear to-night, keen, intent, mastering. It would not start back, cowardly, from any hellish temptation, but meet it face to face. Therefore the great temptation of his life came to him veiled by no sophistry, but bold, defiant, owning its own vile name, trusting to one bold blow for victory.

He did not deceive himself. Theft! That was it. At first the word sickened him; then he grappled with it. Sitting there on a broken cart-wheel, the fading day, the noisy groups, the church-bells' tolling, passed before him like a panorama, while the sharp struggle went on within. This money! He took it out, and looked at it. If he gave it back, what then? He was going to be cool about it.

People going by to church saw only a sickly mill-boy watching them quietly at the alley's mouth. They did not know that he was mad, or they would not have gone by so quietly: mad with hunger;

stretching out his hands to the world, that had given so much to them, for leave to live the life God meant him to live. His soul within him was smothered to death; he wanted so much, thought so much, and knew—nothing. There was nothing of which he was certain, except the mill and things there. Of God and heaven he had heard so little, that they were to him what fairy-land is to a child: something real, but not here; very far off. His brain, greedy, dwarfed, full of thwarted energy and unused powers, questioned these men and women going by, coldly, bitterly, that night. Was it not his right to live as they,—a pure life, a good, true-hearted life, full of beauty and kind words? He only wanted to know how to use the strength within him. His heart warmed, as he thought of it. He suffered himself to think of it longer. If he took the money?

Then he saw himself as he might be, strong, helpful, kindly. The night crept on, as this one image slowly evolved itself from the crowd of other thoughts and stood triumphant. He looked at it. As he might be! What wonder, if it blinded him to delirium,— the madness that underlies all revolution, all progress, and all fall?

You laugh at the shallow temptation? You see the error under-lying its argument so clearly,—that to him a true life was one of full development rather than self-restraint? that he was deaf to the higher tone in a cry of voluntary suffering for truth's sake than in the fullest flow of spontaneous harmony? I do not plead his cause. I only want to show you the mote in my brother's eye: then you can see clearly to take it out.

The money,—there it lay on his knee, a little blotted slip of paper, nothing in itself; used to raise him out of the pit; some-thing straight from God's hand. A thief! Well, what was it to be a thief? He met the question at last, face to face, wiping the clammy drops of sweat from his forehead. God made this money— the fresh air, too—for his children's use. He never made the dif-ference between poor and rich. The Something who looked down on him that moment through the cool gray sky had a kindly face, he knew,—loved his children alike. Oh, he knew that!

There were times when the soft floods of color in the crimson and purple flames, or the clear depth of amber in the water below the bridge, had somehow given him a glimpse of another world than this,—of an infinite depth of beauty and of quiet and rest and love. Looking up now, it became strangely real. The sun had sunk quite below the hills, but his last rays struck upward, touching the zenith. The fog had risen, and the town and river were steeped in its thick, gray damp; but overhead, the sun-touched smoke-clouds opened like a cleft ocean,—shifting, rolling seas of crimson mist, waves of billowy silver veined with blood-scarlet, inner depths unfathomable of glancing light. Wolfe's artist-eye grew drunk with color. The gates of that other world! Fading, flashing before him now! What, in that world of Beauty, Content, and Right, were the petty laws, the mine and thine, of mill-owners and mill-hands?

A consciousness of power stirred within him. He stood up. A man,—he thought, stretching out his hands,—free to work, to live, to love! Free! His right! He folded the scrap of paper in his hand. As his nervous fingers took it in, limp and blotted, so his soul took in the mean temptation, lapped it in fancied rights, in dreams of improved existences, drifting and endless as the cloud-seas of color. Clutching it, as if the tightness of his hold would strengthen his sense of possession, he went aimlessly down the street. It was his watch at the mill. He need not go, need never go again, thank God!—shaking off the thought with unspeakable loathing.

Shall I go over the history of the hours of that night, how the man wandered from one to another of his old haunts, with a half-consciousness of bidding them farewell,—lanes and alleys and back-yards where the mill-hands lodged,—noting, with a new eagerness, the filth and drunkenness, the pig-pens, the ash-heaps covered with potato-skins, the bloated, pimpled women at the doors,—with a new disgust, a new sense of sudden triumph, and, under all, a new, vague dread, unknown before, smothered down, kept under, but still there? It left him but once during the night, when, for the second time in his life, he entered a church. It was a somber Gothic pile, where the stained light lost itself in far-retreating arches; built to meet the requirements and sympathies of a far other class than Wolfe's. Yet it touched, moved him uncontrollably. The distances, the shadows, the still, marble figures, the mass of silent kneeling worshippers, the mysterious music, thrilled, lifted his soul with a wonderful pain. Wolfe forgot himself, forgot the new life he was going to live, the mean terror growing underneath. The voice of the speaker strengthened the charm; it was clear, feeling, full, strong. An old man, who had lived much, suffered much; whose brain was keenly alive, dominant; whose heart was summer-warm with charity. He taught it to-night. He held up Humanity in its grand total; showed the great world-cancer to his people. Who could show it better? He was a Christian reformer; he had studied the age thoroughly; his outlook at man had been free, world-wide, over all time. His faith stood sublime upon the Rock of Ages; his fiery zeal guided vast schemes by which the gospel was to be preached to all nations. How did he preach it to-night? In burning, light-laden words he painted the incarnate Life, Love, the universal Man: words that became reality in the lives of these people,—that lived again in beautiful words and actions, trifling, but heroic. Sin, as he defined it, was a real foe to them; their trials, temptations, were his. His words passed far over the furnace-tender's grasp, toned to suit another class of culture; they sounded in his ears a very pleasant song in an unknown tongue. He meant to cure this world-cancer with a steady eye that had never glared with hunger, and a hand that neither poverty nor strychnine-whisky had taught to shake. In this morbid, distorted heart of the Welsh puddler he had failed.

Wolfe rose at last, and turned from the church down the street. He looked up; the night had come on foggy, damp; the golden mists had vanished, and the sky lay dull and ash-colored. He wandered again aimlessly down the street, idly wondering what had

become of the cloud-sea of crimson and scarlet. The trial-day of
this man's life was over, and he had lost the victory. What followed was mere drifting circumstance,—a quicker walking over the
path,—that was all. Do you want to hear the end of it? You wish
me to make a tragic story out of it? Why, in the police-reports of
the morning paper you can find a dozen such tragedies: hints of
ship-wrecks unlike any that ever befell on the high seas; hints that
here a power was lost to heaven,—that there a soul went down
where no tide can ebb or flow. Commonplace enough the hints
are,—jocose sometimes, done up in rhyme.

Doctor May, a month after the night I have told you of, was
reading to his wife at breakfast from this fourth column of the
morning-paper: an unusual thing,—these police-reports not being,
in general, choice reading for ladies; but it was only one item he
read.

"Oh, my dear! You remember that man I told you of, that we
saw at Kirby's mill,—that was arrested for robbing Mitchell? Here
he is; just listen:—'Circuit Court, Judge Day. Hugh Wolfe, opera-
tive in Kirby & John's Loudon Mills. Charge, grand larceny. Sentence, nineteen years hard labor in penitentiary.—Scoundrel! Serves
him right! After all our kindness that night! Picking Mitchell's
pocket at the very time!"

His wife said something about the ingratitude of that kind of
people, and then they began to talk of something else.

Nineteen years! How easy that was to read! What a simple word
for Judge Day to utter! Nineteen years! Half a lifetime!

Hugh Wolfe sat on the window-ledge of his cell, looking out.
His ankles were ironed. Not usual in such cases; but he had made
two desperate efforts to escape. "Well," as Haley, the jailer, said,
"small blame to him! Nineteen years' imprisonment was not a
pleasant thing to look forward to." Haley was very good-natured
about it, though Wolfe had fought him savagely.

"When he was first caught," the jailer said afterwards, in telling
the story, "before the trial, the fellow was cut down at once,—laid

there on that pallet like a dead man, with his hands over his eyes. Never saw a man so cut down in my life. Time of the trial, too, came the queerest dodge of any customer I ever had. Would choose no lawyer. Judge gave him one, of course. Gibson it was. He tried to prove the fellow crazy; but it wouldn't go. Thing was plain as daylight: money found on him. 'Twas a hard sentence,— all the law allows; but it was for 'xample's sake. These mill-hands are gettin' onbearable. When the sentence was read, he just looked up, and said the money was his by rights, and that all the world had gone wrong. That night, after the trial, a gentleman came to see him here, name of Mitchell,—him as he stole from. Talked to him for an hour. Thought he came for curiosity, like. After he was gone, thought Wolfe was remarkable quiet, and went into his cell. Found him very low; bed all bloody. Doctor said he had been bleeding at the lungs. He was weak as a cat; yet, if ye'll b'lieve me, he tried to get a-past me and get out. I just carried him like a baby, and threw him on the pallet. Three days after, he tried it again: that time reached the wall. Lord help you! he fought like a tiger,—giv' some terrible blows. Fightin' for life, you see; for he can't live long, shut up in the stone crib down yonder. Got a death-cough now. 'T took two of us to bring him down that day; so I just put the irons on his feet. There he sits, in there. Goin' to-morrow, with a batch more of 'em. That woman, hunchback, tried with him,—you remember?—she's only got three years. 'Complice. But she's a woman, you know. He's been quiet ever since I put on irons: giv' up, I suppose. Looks white, sick-lookin'. It acts different on 'em, bein' sentenced. Most of 'em gets reckless, devilish-like. Some prays awful, and sings them vile songs of the mills, all in a breath. That woman, now, she's desper't. Been beggin' to see Hugh, as she calls him, for three days. I'm a-goin' to let her in. She don't go with him. Here she is in this next cell. I'm a-goin' now to let her in."

He let her in. Wolfe did not see her. She crept into a corner of the cell, and stood watching him. He was scratching the iron bars of the window with a piece of tin which he had picked up, with an idle, uncertain, vacant stare, just as a child or idiot would do.

"Tryin' to get out, old boy?" laughed Haley. "Them irons will need a crowbar beside your tin, before you can open 'em."

Wolfe laughed, too, in a senseless way.

"I think I'll get out," he said.

"I believe his brain's touched," said Haley, when he came out.

The puddler scraped away with the tin for half an hour. Still Deborah did not speak. At last she ventured nearer, and touched his arm.

"Blood?" she said, looking at some spots on his coat with a shudder.

He looked up at her. "Why, Deb!" he said, smiling,—such a bright, boyish smile, that it went to poor Deborah's heart directly, and she sobbed and cried out loud.

"Oh, Hugh, lad! Hugh! dunnot look at me, when it wur my fault! To think I brought hur to it! And I loved hur so! Oh, lad, I dud!"

The confession, even in this wretch, came with the woman's blush through the sharp cry.

He did not seem to hear her,—scraping away diligently at the bars with the bit of tin.

Was he going mad? She peered closely into his face. Something she saw there made her draw suddenly back,—something which Haley had not seen, that lay beneath the pinched, vacant look it had caught since the trial, or the curious gray shadow that rested on it. That gray shadow,—yes, she knew what that meant. She had often seen it creeping over women's faces for months, who died at last of slow hunger or consumption. That meant death, distant, lingering; but this— Whatever it was the woman saw, or thought she saw, used as she was to crime and misery, seemed to make her sick with a new horror. Forgetting her fear of him, she caught his shoulders, and looked keenly, steadily, into his eyes.

"Hugh!" she cried, in a desperate whisper,—"oh, boy, not that! for God's sake, not *that!*"

The vacant laugh went off his face, and he answered her in a muttered word or two that drove her away. Yet the words were kindly enough. Sitting there on his pallet, she cried silently a hopeless sort of tears, but did not speak again. The man looked up furtively at her now and then. Whatever his own trouble was, her distress vexed him with a momentary sting.

It was market-day. The narrow window of the jail looked down directly on the carts and wagons drawn up in a long line, where they had unloaded. He could see, too, and hear distinctly the clink of money as it changed hands, the busy crowd of whites and blacks shoving, pushing one another, and the chaffering and swearing at the stalls. Somehow, the sound, more than anything else had done, wakened him up,—made the whole real to him. He was done with the world and the business of it. He let the tin fall, and looked out, pressing his face close to the rusty bars. How they crowded and pushed! And he,—he should never walk that pavement again! There came Neff Sanders, one of the feeders at the mill, with a basket on his arm. Sure enough, Neff was married the other week. He whistled, hoping he would look up; but he did not. He wondered if Neff remembered he was there,—if any of the boys thought of him up here, and thought that he never was to go down that old cinder-road again. Never again! He had not quite understood it before; but now he did. Not for days or years, but never!—that was it.

How clear the light fell on that stall in front of the market! and how like a picture it was, the dark-green heaps of corn, and the crimson beets, and golden melons! There was another with game: how the light flickered on that pheasant's breast, with the purplish blood dripping over the brown feathers! He could see the red shining of the drops, it was so near. In one minute he could be down there. It was just a step. So easy, as it seemed, so natural to go! Yet it could never be—not in all the thousands of years to come—

that he should put his foot on that street again! He thought of himself with a sorrowful pity, as of some one else. There was a dog down in the market, walking after his master with such a stately, grave look!—only a dog, yet he could go backwards and forwards just as he pleased: he had good luck! Why, the very vilest cur, yelping there in the gutter, had not lived his life, had been free to act out whatever thought God had put into his brain; while he— No, he would not think of that! He tried to put the thought away, and to listen to a dispute between a countryman and a women about some meat; but it would come back. He, what had he done to bear this?

Then came the sudden picture of what might have been, and now. He knew what it was to be in the penitentiary,—how it went with men there. He knew how in these long years he should slowly die, but not until soul and body had become corrupt and rotten,—how, when he came out, if he lived to come, even the lowest of the mill-hands would jeer him,—how his hands would be weak, and his brain senseless and stupid. He believed he was almost that now. He put his hand to his head, with a puzzled, weary look. It ached, his head, with thinking. He tried to quiet himself. It was only right, perhaps; he had done wrong. But was there right or wrong for such as he? What was right? And who had ever taught him? He thrust the whole matter away. A dark, cold quiet crept through his brain. It was all wrong; but let it be! It was nothing to him more than the others. Let it be!

The door grated, as Haley opened it.

"Come, my woman! Must lock up for t' night. Come, stir yerself!"

She went up and took Hugh's hand.

"Good-night, Deb," he said, carelessly.

She had not hoped he would say more; but the tired pain on her mouth just then was bitterer than death. She took his passive hand and kissed it.

"Hur'll never see Deb again!" she ventured, her lips growing colder and more bloodless.

What did she say that for? Did he not know it? Yet he would not be impatient with poor old Deb. She had trouble of her own, as well as he.

"No, never again," he said, trying to be cheerful.

She stood just a moment, looking at him. Do you laugh at her, standing there, with her hunchback, her rags, her bleared, withered face, and the great despised love tugging at her heart?

"Come, you!" called Haley, impatiently.

She did not move.

"Hugh!" she whispered.

It was to be her last word. What was it?

"Hugh, boy, not THAT!"

He did not answer. She wrung her hands, trying to be silent, looking in his face in an agony of entreaty. He smiled again, kindly.

"It is best, Deb. I cannot bear to be hurted any more."

"Hur knows," she said, humbly.

"Tell my father good-by; and—and kiss little Janey."

She nodded, saying nothing, looking in his face again, and went out of the door. As she went, she staggered.

"Drinkin' to-day?" broke out Haley, pushing her before him. "Where the Devil did you get it? Here, in with ye!" and he shoved her into her cell, next to Wolfe's, and shut the door.

Along the wall of her cell there was a crack low down by the floor, through which she could see the light from Wolfe's. She had discovered it days before. She hurried in now, and, kneeling down by it, listened, hoping to hear some sound. Nothing but the rasping of the tin on the bars. He was at his old amusement again. Something in the noise jarred on her ear, for she shivered as she heard it. Hugh rasped away at the bars. A dull old bit of tin, not fit to cut korl with.

He looked out of the window again. People were leaving the

market now. A tall mulatto girl, following her mistress, her basket on her head, crossed the street just below, and looked up. She was laughing; but, when she caught sight of the haggard face peering out through the bars, suddenly grew grave, and hurried by. A free, firm step, a clear-cut olive face, with a scarlet turban tied on one side, dark, shining eyes, and on the head the basket poised, filled with fruit and flowers, under which the scarlet turban and bright eyes looked out half-shadowed. The picture caught his eye. It was good to see a face like that. He would try to-morrow, and cut one like it. *To-morrow!* He threw down the tin, trembling, and covered his face with his hands. When he looked up again, the daylight was gone.

Deborah, crouching near by on the other side of the wall, heard no noise. He sat on the side of the low pallet, thinking. Whatever was the mystery which the woman had seen on his face, it came out now, slowly, in the dark here, and became fixed,—a something never seen on his face before. The evening was darkening fast. The market had been over for an hour; the rumbling of the carts over the pavement grew more infrequent: he listened to each, as it passed, because he thought it was to be for the last time. For the same reason, it was, I suppose, that he strained his eyes to catch a glimpse of each passer-by, wondering who they were, what kind of homes they were going to, if they had children,—listening eagerly to every chance word in the street, as if—(God be merciful to the man! what strange fancy was this?)—as if he never should hear human voices again.

It was quite dark at last. The street was a lonely one. The last passenger, he thought, was gone. No,—there was a quick step: Joe Hill, lighting the lamps. Joe was a good old chap; never passed a fellow without some joke or other. He remembered once seeing the place where he lived with his wife. "Granny Hill," the boys called her. Bedridden she was; but so kind as Joe was to her! kept the room so clean!—and the old woman, when he was there, was laughing at "some of t' lad's foolishness." The step was far down the street; but he could see him place the ladder, run up, and light the gas. A longing seized him to be spoken to once more.

"Joe!" he called, out of the grating. "Good-by, Joe!"

The old man stopped a moment, listening uncertainly; then hurried on. The prisoner thrust his hand out of the window, and called again, louder; but Joe was too far down the street. It was a little thing; but it hurt him,—this disappointment.

"Good-by, Joe!" he called, sorrowfully enough.

"Be quiet!" said one of the jailers, passing the door, striking on it with his club.

Oh, that was the last, was it?

There was inexpressible bitterness on his face, as he lay down on the bed, taking the bit of tin, which he had rasped to a tolerable degree of sharpness, in his hand,—to play with, it may be. He bared his arms, looking intently at their corded veins and sinews. Deborah, listening in the next cell, heard a slight clicking sound, often repeated. She shut her lips tightly, that she might not scream; the cold drops of sweat broke over her, in her dumb agony.

"Hur knows best," she muttered at last, fiercely clutching the board where she lay.

If she could have seen Wolfe, there was nothing about him to frighten her. He lay quite still, his arms outstretched, looking at the pearly stream of moonlight coming into the window. I think in that one hour that came then he lived back over all the years that had gone before. I think that all the low, vile life, all his wrongs, all his starved hopes, came then, and stung him with a farewell poison that made him sick unto death. He made neither moan nor cry, only turned his worn face now and then to the pure light, that seemed so far off, as one that said, "How long, O Lord? how long?"

The hour was over at last. The moon, passing over her nightly path, slowly came nearer, and threw the light across his bed on his feet. He watched it steadily, as it crept up, inch by inch, slowly. It seemed to him to carry with it a great silence. He had been so hot and tired there always in the mills! The years had been so fierce and cruel! There was coming now quiet and coolness and sleep. His tense limbs relaxed, and settled in a calm languor. The blood ran fainter and slow from his heart. He did not think now with a savage anger of what might be and was not; he was conscious only of deep stillness creeping over him. At first he saw a sea of faces: the mill-men,—women he had known, drunken and bloated,—Janey's timid and pitiful,—poor old Deb's: then they floated together like a mist, and faded away, leaving only the clear, pearly moonlight.

Whether, as the pure light crept up the stretched-out figure, it brought with it calm and peace, who shall say? His dumb soul was alone with God in judgment. A Voice may have spoken for it from far-off Calvary, "Father, forgive them, for they know not what they do!" Who dare say? Fainter and fainter the heart rose and fell, slower and slower the moon floated from behind a cloud, until, when at last its full tide of white splendor swept over the cell, it seemed to wrap and fold into a deeper stillness the dead figure that never should move again. Silence deeper than the Night! Nothing that moved, save the black, nauseous stream of blood dripping slowly from the pallet to the floor!

There was outcry and crowd enough in the cell the next day. The coroner and his jury, the local editors, Kirby himself, and boys with their hands thrust knowingly into their pockets and heads to one side, jammed into the corners. Coming and going all day. Only one woman. She came late, and outstayed them all. A Quaker, or Friend, as they call themselves. I think this woman was known by that name in heaven. A homely body, coarsely dressed in gray and white. Deborah (for Haley had let her in) took notice of her. She watched them all—sitting on the end of the pallet, holding his head in her arms—with the ferocity of a watch-dog, if any of them touched the body. There was no meekness, or sorrow, in her face; the stuff out of which murderers are made, instead. All the time Haley and the woman were laying straight the limbs and cleaning the cell, Deborah sat still, keenly watching the Quaker's face. Of all the crowd there that day, this woman alone had not spoken to her,—only once or twice had put some cordial to her lips. After they all were gone, the woman, in the same still, gentle way, brought a vase of wood-leaves and berries, and placed it by the pallet, then opened the narrow window. The fresh air blew in, and swept the woody fragrance over the dead face. Deborah looked up with a quick wonder.

"Did hur know my boy would like it? Did hur know Hugh?"

"I know Hugh now."

The white fingers passed in a slow, pitiful way over the dead, worn face. There was a heavy shadow in the quiet eyes.

"Did hur know where they'll bury Hugh?" said Deborah in a shrill tone, catching her arm.

This had been the question hanging on her lips all day.

"In t' town-yard? Under t' mud and ash? T' lad'll smother, woman! He wur born on t' lane moor, where t' air is frick and strong. Take hur out, for God's sake, take hur out where t' air blows!"

The Quaker hesitated, but only for a moment. She put her strong arm around Deborah and led her to the window.

"Thee sees the hills, friend, over the river? Thee sees how the light lies warm there, and the winds of God blow all the day? I live there,—where the blue smoke is, by the trees. Look at me." She turned Deborah's face to her own, clear and earnest. "Thee will believe me? I will take Hugh and bury him there to-morrow."

Deborah did not doubt her. As the evening wore on, she leaned against the iron bars, looking at the hills that rose far off, through the thick sodden clouds, like a bright, unattainable calm. As she looked, a shadow of their solemn repose fell on her face: its fierce discontent faded into a pitiful, humble quiet. Slow, solemn tears gathered in her eyes: the poor weak eyes turned so hopelessly to the place where Hugh was to rest, the grave heights looking higher and brighter and more solemn than ever before. The Quaker watched her keenly. She came to her at last, and touched her arm.

"When thee comes back," she said, in a low, sorrowful tone, like one who speaks from a strong heart deeply moved with remorse or pity, "thee shall begin thy life again,—there on the hills. I came too late; but not for thee,—by God's help it may be."

Not too late. Three years after, the Quaker began her work. I end my story here. At evening-time it was light. There is no need to tire you with the long years of sunshine, and fresh air, and slow, patient Christ-love, needed to make healthy and hopeful this impure body and soul. There is a homely pine house, on one of these hills, whose windows overlook broad, wooded slopes and clover-crimsoned meadows,—niched into the very place where the light is warmest, the air freest. It is the Friends' meeting-house. Once a week they sit there, in their grave, earnest way, waiting for the Spirit of Love to speak, opening their simple hearts to receive His words. There is a woman, old, deformed, who takes a humble place among them: waiting like them: in her gray dress, her worn face, pure and meek, turned now and then to the sky. A woman much loved by these silent, restful people; more silent than they, more humble, more loving. Waiting: with her eyes turned to the hills higher and purer than these on which she lives,—dim and far off now, but to be reached some day. There may be in her heart some latent hope to meet there the love denied her here,—that she shall find him whom she lost, and that then she will not be all-unworthy. Who blames her? Something is lost in the passage of every soul from one eternity to the other,—something pure and beautiful, which might have been and was not: a hope, a talent, a love, over which the soul mourns, like Esau deprived of his birthright. What blame to the meek Quaker, if she took her lost hope to make the hills of heaven more fair?

Nothing remains to tell that the poor Welsh puddler once lived, but this figure of the mill-woman cut in korl. I have it here in a corner of my library. I keep it hid behind a curtain,—it is such a rough, ungainly thing. Yet there are about it touches, grand sweeps of outline, that show a master's hand. Sometimes,—to-night, for instance,—the curtain is accidentally drawn back, and I see the bare arm stretched out imploringly in the darkness, and an eager, wolfish face, through which the spirit of the dead korl-cutter looks out, with its thwarted life, its mighty hunger, its unfinished work. Its pale, vague lips seem to tremble with a terrible question. "Is this the End?" they say,—"nothing beyond?—no more?" Why, you tell me you have seen that look in the eyes of dumb brutes,—horses dying under the lash. I know.

The deep of the night is passing while I write. The gas-light wakens from the shadows here and there the objects which lie scattered through the room: only faintly, though: for they belong to the open sunlight. As I glance at them, they each recall some task or pleasure of the coming day. A half-molded child's head; Aphrodite; a bough of forest-leaves; music; work; homely fragments, in which lie the secrets of all eternal truth and beauty. Prophetic all! Only this dumb, woful face seems to belong to and end with the night. I turn to look at it. Has the power of its desperate need commanded the darkness away? While the room is yet steeped in heavy shadow, a cool, gray light suddenly touches its head like a blessing hand, and its groping arm points through the broken cloud to the far East, where, in the flickering, nebulous crimson, God has set the promise of the Dawn.

1. What suggestions have you for improving the conditions of such people?
2. Is this story a display of sentiment or an urge for practical reform?
3. Are the conditions among the mill people to be permanent for certain groups of mankind?
4. "Are pain and jealousy less savage realities down here in this place . . . than in your own house or in your own heart,—your heart, which they clutch sometimes?"
5. Are the strikes of today the proper solution for these conditions?

*Michael Gold*

# BLOOD MONEY

I LIKED to go on funerals with the Jewish coach drivers. What glorious summer fun. Nathan was a tall Jewish ox, with a red hard face like a chunk of rusty iron. His blustering manner had earned him many a black eye and bloody face. It was a warm bright morning. Three coaches rolled down the ramp of the livery stable, on their way to a funeral. Then appeared Nathan, cursing at his horses. I begged him to let me go along. He was grouchy, but slowed down. I scrambled up beside him on the tall seat.

Three coaches and a hearse. A poor man's funeral. We rolled through the hurly-burly East Side. The sporty young drivers joked from coach to coach. The horses jerked and skipped; Nathan cursed them.

"You she-devil," he said in Yiddish to his white horse, "steady down, or I'll kick in your belly!"

He tugged at the check-rein and cut her mouth until it bled. But she was nervous; horses have their moods.

We came to the tenement of the corpse. Many pushcarts had to be cursed out of the way. We lined the curb. There was a crowd gathered. Funerals, weddings, sewer repairs, accidents, fires and love-murders, food of the crowd.

The coffin was brought down by four pale men with black

beards. Then came the wife and children in black, meekly weeping. The family were so poor they had not the courage to weep flamboyantly.

But some of the neighbors did. It was their pleasure. They made an awful hullabaloo. It pierced one's marrow. The East Side women have a strange keening wail; it is very Gaelic. They chant the virtues of the dead sweatshop slave, and the sorrow of his family. They fling themselves about in an orgy of grief. It unpacks their hearts, but is hell on bystanders.

## 2

Then the ride across the Brooklyn Bridge, with the incredible sweep of New York below us. The river was packed tight, a street with tugboat traffic. Mammoth skyscrapers cut into the sky like a saw. The smoke of factories smeared the bright blue air. Horns boomed and wailed: Brooklyn lay low and passive in the horizon.

"A man is crazy to live in Brooklyn," said Nathan, pointing with his whip toward that side. "My God, it is dead as a cemetery; no excitement, no nothing. Look, Mikey, down there. That's the Navy Yard. That's where they keep the American warships. Sailors are a lot of Irish bums. Once I had a fight with a sailor and knocked his tooth out. He called me a Jew."

"Ain't you a Jew?" I asked timidly, as my greedy eyes drank in the panorama.

"Of course I'm a Jew," said Nathan, in his rough, iron voice, "I'm proud I'm a Jew, but no Irish bum can call me names, or call me a Jew."

"Why?" I asked.

I was very logical when I was seven years old.

"Why?" Nathan mimicked me with a sneer. "Why? You tell a kid something, and he asks why? Kids give me a headache." Nathan spat his disgust into the river. The blob of spit fell a third of a mile.

3

They put the coffin into the ground. The old Rabbi in a shiny high hat chanted a long sonorous poem in Hebrew, a prayer for dead Jews. A woman screamed; it was the dead man's wife. She tried to throw herself into the grave. Her weeping friends restrained her. The graveyard trees waved strangely. The graveyard sun was strange. The grave diggers shoveled earth into the grave. I felt lonesome and bewildered. I wanted to cry like the rest, but was ashamed because of Nathan.

Then it was over. All of us went to a restaurant at the entrance to the cemetery and ate platters of sour cream, pot cheese and black bread, the Jewish funeral food. Even the widow ate. Nathan gave me half of his portion. Then we rode home over the Bridge.

I was glad to feel the East Side again engulf our coach. I lost my vague funeral loneliness in the hurly-burly of my street. On the stoop of our tenement sat two friends, my sister Esther and Nigger's little sister Leah. In the purple and golden light of sundown they were reading a fairy-tale book and eating bread and butter. Their faces were calm and satisfied. But I made them envious.

"Nathan took me on another funeral ride," I crowed, "and I saw another man buried."

The girls were gratifyingly envious. Girls were never taken on these rides by the coach drivers. My sister Esther always wanted to go, but couldn't. She blamed me for it, and said I told the drivers not to take her. She cried now, as I teased her, and described to her how wonderful my adventure had been. She grew very jealous of my good luck. My poor dear little sister! so soon to go on that funeral ride, and not return and boast like me!

4

In that evil winter that had fallen on us my sister Esther did most of the housework while my mother was at the restaurant. The child bought groceries, she cooked, scrubbed floors, and watched our baby brother. She was my father's nurse. Once, I remember, she stood by his bedside and fondly stroking his hair, said, like some kind, beautiful woman:

"Poppa, I'm sorry you are sick. How I wish no one in the world was ever sick! But you'll be better soon; don't worry, poppa dear!"

My father clasped her to him, and kissed her eyes and mouth and hands, and called her every Yiddish name of love: his Moon, his Wealth, his Little Mother, his Rose, his Tiny Dove, his Heart of Hearts.

There was so much energy in that meager body with its long twinkling sparrow legs. There was so much affection in the great soft eyes. Esther was not driven to the housework: she herself saw its necessity, and did it with sunny cheerfulness. She wished to help my mother. She wished to help everybody; she was precociously kind.

Esther was dreamy, too; she read every book of fairy-tales, and believed in them. She was always making up new games to play, and inventing mythical characters. After she read a book she would repeat it in detail to my father, who loved any kind of story. I was a year older, but felt like a man beside Esther. When I told her the things I knew about our East Side street, she would cry, and say I was lying to her. I despised her weakness.

Why did I always fight with my sister? Why did I refuse to do the chores about the house but shifted them all to her shoulders? I remember one evening when I came in from my newspaper peddling my father asked me to go out again and find some wood for the stove. I refused and made a scene. I said Esther ought to do it. Esther was busy with a dozen other things, and said so. I called her names, and sulked. She only shrugged her shoulders at my stubbornness, and went out quietly to hunt for the stove-wood.

I was always winning these easy victories over her.

## 5

Once my little sister sat on the tenement stoop, reading the Blue Fairy Tale Book. This book was her treasure. It was a big beautiful edition with colored pictures that Harry had given her. She had copied many of those pictures with her crayons, and knew every story in the book by heart. But she loved to read them again and again, her lips moving dreamily, as if she were singing to herself. She was reading now on the stoop, while the New York sun burned out above the tenements in glorious purple, amber and rose.

Esther was in her own world. The street whirled and clashed around her, the gray old solemn Jews went by, and gabbling mommas, and pimps, pushcarts and rattling wagons. A scabby dog rummaged with its front paws in a garbage can. Three tough guys lounged nearby, and quarreled, and spat tobacco juice. The saloon was busy, the prostitutes were busy, the slum wretchedness was huge and triumphant. But Esther had escaped from it all. She was reading her book. The twilight fell on the white pages and illuminated her face.

She looked up as I approached. I can still see the flushed little face, with its Jewish cheek bones, ardent mouth, and large eyes. She looked at me and did not see me. She was lost in the land of fairies and giants, where children talked familiarly with swans and lions, and sought enchanted castles beyond the mountains of glass.

Fiend that I was, I snatched her away from that beautiful, magic land. I tore the book from her hands, and ran off with it, yelling cruel taunts. I wanted to torture her. I wanted to make her cry.

Forgive me now, Esther.

Another time I beat her until her nose bled. She had followed me into the secret fort of the Young Avengers, and had shamed me before my comrades, by saying that momma wanted me at home.

Another time I grabbed all the lovely fruit and candy Dr. Solow had brought us, and gobbled up her share as well as mine. She cried because I could be so selfish and greedy: she was never greedy.

### 6

The winter dragged on, that gloomiest of winters. My father moped and smoked about the house; my mother worked in the restaurant; I peddled papers after school; and loyal little Esther did the housework.

My aunt left our home. Dr. Solow was busy; he did not call so often to drink tea with us in the evenings.

Nothing else changed. Nothing else happened.

Until late one winter afternoon.

### 7

The world was dark. Snow smothered the city, the streets and tenements.

An Arctic midnight seemed to have usurped the day. It was strange to see so many lamps burning at noon. In school the lights were on. In the streets the stores and skyscrapers were illuminated. Along the Bowery where I peddled my papers I found the saloons blazing with gas and electricity.

The snow never stopped falling in this unnatural darkness. It was dreadful to be outdoors. One could see nothing, except queer looming shapes of horses and men plowing head-on through the snow. Toward five I was so exhausted that I decided to go home. Half my papers were unsold, but I was too frozen and blind to carry on.

When I reached home I found my mother there. The cafeteria had closed down early. My mother was exhausted by her half-mile walk from the street car. She had taken off her wet shoes, and was drying her stockings by the stove.

"Where is Esther?" she asked when I came in.

"I don't know," I said. "I haven't seen her all day."

"Herman, where is Esther?" my mother called in a louder voice.

"She has gone out to gather wood for the stove," answered my father from the bedroom.

My mother shook her head, moodily.

"Too bad," she said. "It is the devil's own weather."

The soup pot was boiling on the stove, set there by my sister Esther. There was a pot of stewing prunes, and the tea kettle. She had laid, too, the table with plates, forks and spoons for supper. The rooms were tidy; she had done the housework before leaving to forage for wood.

"Pst, the poor child, she has on such a thin jacket," said my mother. "I am sorry she went out."

I took off my own shoes and hung up my stockings to dry. I counted my money; I had earned only nineteen cents that miserable day of lead. I sat down to read a Henty tale before supper. After supper I would do my school home work. My mother hobbled with bare feet into the bedroom to look at the baby and talk to my father.

I plunged into my Henty book, and forgot everything else. It was a story of Richard Cœur de Lion. Then my mother interrupted the glorious tale. She leaned over my shoulder and asked nervously:

"So where is Esther? Hasn't she come yet?"

"No, momma."

"Pst! I am beginning to be worried. It is such a bad day! Maybe I ought to go out and find her. She may need help with the wood, my poor dove."

My mother began to draw on her stockings. Then she put on her shoes, and fussed about the kitchen before she wrapped herself in her big shawl. She had the shawl in her hand when three knocks sounded at the door. They were so violent that my mother and I both started in dread.

"Come in," said my mother, transfixed with the shawl about her.

The door was flung open. We were amazed to see a crowd of strange people in the hallway. They seemed fantastic in the gaslight, with their white faces and staring eyes. Their overcoats and hats were covered with snow. A tall, stout man with a black moustache was sobbing fiercely. The others stood stark as ghosts.

My mother held her heart.

"Quick, what has happened?" she asked.

A woman in the crowd shrieked. The crowd stirred uneasily at this, but was still mute. A little round-shouldered man with glasses stepped forward and apologized:

"Don't be excited, missus; the doctor will soon come."

"What doctor? What has happened? Tell me!" my mother demanded.

But the snow-laden people stared at her, and could not speak. Their lips were locked, as in a nightmare. They stared at us strangely. Then they parted and through their midst walked a pale man dressed in a grocer's apron. He was sweating with nervousness, and his eyes blinked. In his arms he carried the body of a little girl. She was dripping with blood. Some of it dabbled on the grocer's apron and hands.

"Esther!" my mother moaned. "Esther!"

All the ghostly people began to cry. Some turned their faces away, or covered their eyes in pain. The grocer laid Esther across a table. Her head fell back. Her eyes were shut, her face crushed and bloody.

"My darling, my flower, what have they done to you?" my mother wailed. She tried to fling herself on Esther. An old woman gently held her by the shoulder.

My mother wet a towel and wiped the blood from Esther's face. The little face was mutilated with deep wounds, as by a butcher's cleaver. My mother kissed her and kissed her again. My father came from the bedroom and howled like an animal. He fell on his knees and chafed Esther's cold hands.

My mother was walking up and down in a daze, wringing her hands.

"How did it happen? How did it happen?"

A babble of tearful voices broke out to tell her. Esther had been dragging her sled with its load of wood. She was crossing the street at our own corner, when in the blinding snow-fog an Adams Express truck hit her. She fell between the horses and the heavy wheels rolled over her body.

"My baby, my treasure!" wept my mother.

"Esther, talk to me! Open your eyes and look at poppa! Look, I have some candy for you, Esther, and a new picture book!" my father implored on his knees.

"Where is the doctor?" my mother cried frantically.

"He is coming soon. A telephone was sent him," a woman murmured in the crowd.

The truck-driver appeared. He was a burly blond young German-American in a big overcoat fastened at the neck with a safety pin. He took off his fur cap and heavy snow fell from it to the floor. He stared about him with bewildered eyes. His broad face, red and raw as beefsteak with the cold wind, was twisted grotesquely, like a baby's that wants to cry.

"Honest to God," he said, "I couldn't see her with all that snow! The first thing I knew she was under the wheels."

My father leaped up and grabbed the unfortunate driver by the throat.

"Murderer!" my father shouted.

The driver did not attempt to defend himself, but wept.

"Honest!" he sobbed, "I'm a father myself, I got two kids of my own, mister, but I couldn't see her because of all the snow, so help me Christ!"

My father was torn away from the driver's throat. Every one could see the poor driver was not to blame. People kept washing

Esther's face and talking to her. But she did not answer them. A frightened boy brought in the sled with all the wood she had gathered. The room was hot; the people packed it tightly, and groaned and talked; the gaslight flickered.

"My baby, my baby!" wailed my mother, walking up and down the room, and striking her breast. My father sat by Esther as if in a trance.

Then a young doctor in white ducks appeared. He took Esther away in his ambulance to the hospital. There she died during the night, without a word.

### 8

All the night Esther lay in her coffin on the table in the "front room." While she slept, old men hired at the synagogue sat by candlelight in our kitchen. They read Hebrew prayers until dawn. I would wake in the middle of the night, and see their huge shadows swaying on the airshaft walls. And I heard the murmur of their voices, and my father and mother groaning in sleep, and life oppressed me with its mystery and terror.

My little sister was dead. A boy does not know what the word means, but he knows the solemnity, and the horror with which it affects the grown-ups around him. I had never seen my mother so frantic.

When my little sister was put into the earth, my mother tried to fling herself into the open grave beside her. She was restrained by my father. Every one wept as the Rabbi intoned the long Hebrew prayer for the dead. I wept, too, for I was beginning to understand why people cried at funerals, though afterward they ate black bread and pot cheese at the cemetery restaurant.

During the next week my parents did *Sheva*. They sat on the floor in stockinged feet, as is prescribed, and swayed from side to side and read the Hebrew ritual. Neighbors drifted in and out, cooked our meals, took care of us.

Joy and grief were social in a tenement. The neighbors crept in, one by one, and sat with us during the *Sheva*. There were mournful groups all day in the darkened rooms.

They offered my mother the most dismal comfort. Why is there so much gloomy wisdom at the hearts of the poor?

"My sister lost a little boy in the same way," said Mrs. Lipoff, a pickle vendor's wife. "That little Morris, such a dear child, would have been seven years old now; but a street car had to kill him. Yet what can we do? It is happening every day."

"Yes," my mother mumbled.

The janitress, her fat, honest face smeared with dirt and tears, said bitterly:

"I know a Galicianer family on Columbia Street. This year they lost a girl of Esther's age. The mother saw it happen. She was standing at the window, watching the child play in the street. Then the wagon came upon the child. The mother tore her hair out for sorrow. It is a shame on America! In Russia we could not live for the pogroms, but here our children are killed!"

"Yes," my mother said.

Reb Samuel's tiny wife bowed her head, and with the corner of her apron wiped her granulated eyelids. Then in her weak, kindly voice, she said:

"Yet what can we do? The children must play somewhere."

"Yes," my mother agreed.

My mother answered only yes and no to people; she was stunned; she did not seem to feel anything. She sat on the floor, rocking herself from side to side, and pressing to her nose a handkerchief wet with vinegar. Esther was dead.

## 9

A stranger called one day during the *Sheva*. He bustled in, a swarthy powerful man, with a coarse face, lobster eyes, and short crooked legs. He looked like a gorilla, but was expensively dressed and amazingly suave. He took off his overcoat, laid it carefully over the back of a chair, and adjusted his diamond horseshoe scarfpin. Then he shook my father's hand and my mother's.

"My sincere regrets over your accident," he said with an undertaker's false, fluent pathos. "It is terrible to lose a child, especially for a mother. I am a parent myself; I know what you must feel."

He fished into his pockets and handed a business card to my father, and one to my mother. They regarded the cards dully. The stranger seemed to overpower them.

"As you will read," he went on glibly, "I am Mr. Jonas Schlessel, the well-known attorney-at-law. I am also a close friend of Mr. Baruch Goldfarb, the ward leader, who told me you were his friends, too. Eh, what a great man, a great man! Well, my friends, to come to the point, I have been studying this accident that has happened to you. I have decided you have a fine damage suit against the Adams Express. It ought to be good for a thousand dollars! I am willing to represent you, because you are friends of Mr. Goldfarb. You do not have to pay me anything now; only when I have won the case. All you have to do now is sign this paper. So let us have it signed, and then I will proceed with the case. It means a thousand dollars, my friends!"

He flashed a legal document before my father. My father sat there stupefied. He took the paper, and the fountain pen the lawyer handed him, and seemed ready to sign like an automaton.

But my mother broke into sobs. "Go away!" she said to the lawyer. "I don't want you in my house!"

Mr. Schlessel looked at her in surprise.

"What's the matter?" he asked, spreading his hands.

"I don't want your blood money!" my mother wept.

The lawyer was deeply offended.

"Blood money?" he repeated. "Why is it blood money? It is accident money! I handle hundreds such cases every year."

He tried to argue with my mother, but she became hysterical and began to abuse him. So with an outraged air, he picked up his overcoat and opened the door.

"With greenhorns I never argue," he said loftily, as he left.

My father sat there in the same stupor that had seized him when the stranger entered.

"I don't know, Katie," he said slowly. "Maybe we should take this money. God knows we need it now. I could start my shop with it. The child is gone, and nothing we do one way or the other makes any difference to our poor dove. So why—"

"Silence!" my mother said. "It is my feeling!"

My father was too bewildered and crushed by everything to answer her. He realized, too, from past experience that for some of her "feelings" my mother was ready to go to the stake. This evidently was one of the times. Esther was dead.

From *Jews Without Money*, by Michael Gold. Copyright, 1930, by Horace Liveright, Inc. Reprinted by permission of Michael Gold.

1. Do you think that the writer is a product of New York's lower East Side?
2. Why does the narrator quarrel with his sister?
3. How is the boy's romantic nature satisfied—how is it dissipated?
4. Should they have allowed Mr. Jonas Schlessel to proceed with the case?
5. What function in the composition of a short story is performed by section 6?

*Albert Maltz*

# MAN ON A ROAD

A T ABOUT four in the afternoon I crossed the bridge at Gauley, West Virginia, and turned the sharp curve leading into the tunnel under the railroad bridge. I had been over this road once before and knew what to expect—by the time I entered the tunnel I had my car down to about ten miles an hour. But even at that speed I came closer to running a man down than I ever have before. This is how it happened.

The patched, macadam road had been soaked through by an all-day rain and now it was as slick as ice. In addition, it was quite dark—a black sky and a steady, swishing rain made driving impossible without headlights. As I entered the tunnel a big cream-colored truck swung fast around the curve on the other side. The curve was so sharp that his headlights had given me no warning. The tunnel was short and narrow, just about passing space for two cars, and before I knew it he was in front of me with his big, front wheels over on my side of the road.

I jammed on my brakes. Even at ten miles an hour my car skidded, first toward the truck and then, as I wrenched on the wheel, in toward the wall. There it stalled. The truck swung around hard, scraped my fender, and passed through the tunnel about an inch away from me. I could see the tense face of the young driver with the tight bulge of tobacco in his cheek and his eyes glued on the road. I remember saying to myself that I hoped he'd swallow that tobacco and go choke himself.

I started my car and shifted into first. It was then I saw for the first time that a man was standing in front of my car about a foot away from the inside wheel. It was a shock to see him there. "For Chrissakes," I said.

My first thought was that he had walked into the tunnel after my car had stalled. I was certain he hadn't been in there before. Then I noticed that he was standing profile to me with his hand held up in the hitch-hiker's gesture. If he had walked into that tunnel, he'd be facing me—he wouldn't be standing sideways looking at the opposite wall. Obviously I had just missed knocking him down and obviously he didn't know it. He didn't even know I was there.

It made me run weak inside. I had a picture of a man lying crushed under a wheel with me standing over him knowing it was my car.

I called out to him "Hey!" He didn't answer me. I called louder. He didn't even turn his head. He stood there, fixed, his hand up in the air, his thumb jutting out. It scared me. It was like a story by Bierce where the ghost of a man pops out of the air to take up his lonely post on a dark country road.

My horn is a good, loud, raucous one and I knew that the tunnel would re-double the sound. I slapped my hand down on that little black button and pressed as hard as I could. The man was either going to jump or else prove that he was a ghost.

Well, he wasn't a ghost—but he didn't jump, either. And it wasn't because he was deaf. He heard that horn all right.

He was like a man in a deep sleep. The horn seemed to awaken him only by degrees, as though his whole consciousness had been sunk in some deep recess within himself. He turned his head slowly and looked at me. He was a big man, about thirty-five with a heavy-featured face—an ordinary face with a big, fleshy nose and a large mouth. The face didn't say much. I wouldn't have called it kind or brutal or intelligent or stupid. It was just the face of a big man, wet with rain, looking at me with eyes that seemed to have a glaze over them. Except for the eyes you see faces like that going into the pit at six in the morning or coming out of a steel mill or foundry where heavy work is done. I couldn't understand that glazed quality in his eyes. It wasn't the glassy stare of a drunken man or the wild, mad glare I saw once in the eyes of a woman in a fit of violence. I could only think of a man I once knew who had died of cancer. Over his eyes in the last days there was the same dull glaze, a far-away, absent look as though behind the blank, outward film there was a secret flow of past events on which his mind was focussed. It was this same look that I saw in the man on the road.

When at last he heard my horn, the man stepped very deliberately around the front of my car and came toward the inside door. The least I expected was that he would show surprise at an auto so dangerously close to him. But there was no emotion to him whatsoever. He walked slowly, deliberately, as though he had been expecting me and then bent his head down to see under the top of my car. "Kin yuh give me a lift, friend?" he asked me.

I saw his big, horse teeth chipped at the ends and stained brown by tobacco. His voice was high-pitched and nasal with the slurred, lilting drawl of the deep South. In West Virginia few of the town folk seem to speak that way. I judged he had been raised in the mountains.

I looked at his clothes—an old cap, a new blue work shirt, and dark trousers, all soaked through with rain. They didn't tell me much.

I must have been occupied with my thoughts about him for some time, because he asked me again. "Ahm goin' to Weston," he said. "Are you a-goin' thataway?"

As he said this, I looked into his eyes. The glaze had disappeared and now they were just ordinary eyes, brown and moist.

I didn't know what to reply. I didn't really want to take him in—the episode had unnerved me and I wanted to get away from the tunnel and from him too. But I saw him looking at me with a patient, almost humble glance. The rain was streaked on his face and he stood there asking for a ride and waiting in simple concentration for my answer. I was ashamed to tell him "no." Besides, I was curious. "Climb in," I said.

He sat down beside me, placing a brown paper package on his lap. We started out of the tunnel.

From Gauley to Weston is about a hundred miles of as difficult mountain driving as I know—a five mile climb to the top of a hill, then five miles down, and then up another. The road twists like a snake on the run and for a good deal of it there is a jagged cliff on one side and a drop of a thousand feet or more on the other. The rain and the small rocks crumbling from the mountain sides and littering up the road made it very slow going. But in the four hours or so that it took for the trip I don't think my companion spoke to me half a dozen times.

I tried often to get him to talk. It was not that he wouldn't talk, it was rather that he didn't seem to hear me—as though as soon as he had spoken, he would slip down into that deep, secret recess within himself. He sat like a man dulled by morphine. My conversation, the rattle of the old car, the steady pour of rain were all a distant buzz—the meaningless, outside world that could not quite pierce the shell in which he seemed to be living.

As soon as we had started, I asked him how long he had been in the tunnel.

"Ah don' know," he replied. "A good tahm, Ah reckon."

"What were you standing there for—to keep out of the rain?"

He didn't answer. I asked him again, speaking very loudly. He turned his head to me. "Excuse me, friend," he said, "did you say somethin'?"

"Yes," I answered. "Do you know I almost ran you over back in that tunnel?"

"No-o," he said. He spoke the word in that breathy way that is typical of mountain speech.

"Didn't you hear me yell to you?"

"No-o." He paused. "Ah reckon Ah was thinkin'."

"Ah reckon you were," I thought to myself. "What's the matter, are you hard of hearing?" I asked him.

"No-o," he said, and turned his head away, looking out front at the road.

I kept right after him. I didn't want him to go off again. I wanted somehow to get him to talk.

"Looking for work?"

"Yessuh."

He seemed to speak with an effort. It was not a difficulty of speech, it was something behind, in his mind, in his will to speak. It was as though he couldn't keep the touch between his world and mine. Yet when he did answer me, he spoke directly and coherently. I didn't know what to make of it. When he first came into the car I had been a little frightened. Now I only felt terribly curious and a little sorry.

"Do you have a trade?" I was glad to come to that question. You know a good deal about a man when you know what line of work he follows and it always leads to further conversation.

"Ah ginerally follows the mines," he said.

"Now," I thought, "we're getting somewhere."

But just then we hit a stretch of unpaved road where the mud was thick and the ruts were hard to follow. I had to stop talking and watch what I was doing. And when we came to paved road again, I had lost him.

I tried again to make him talk. It was no use. He didn't even hear me. Then, finally, his silence shamed me. He was a man lost somewhere within his own soul, only asking to be left alone. I felt wrong to keep thrusting at his privacy.

So for about four hours we drove in silence. For me those hours were almost unendurable. I have never seen such rigidity in a human being. He sat straight up in the car, his outward eye fixed on the road in front, his inward eye seeing nothing. He didn't know I was in the car, he didn't know he was in the car at all, he didn't feel the rain that kept sloshing in on him through the rent in the side curtains. He sat like a slab of moulded rock and only from his breathing could I be sure that he was alive. His breathing was heavy.

Only once in that long trip did he change his posture. That was when he was seized with a fit of coughing. It was a fierce, hacking cough that shook his big body from side to side and doubled him over like a child with the whooping cough. He was trying to cough something up—I could hear the phlegm in his chest—but he couldn't succeed. Inside him there was an ugly scraping sound as though cold metal were being rubbed on the bone of his ribs, and he kept spitting and shaking his head.

It took almost three minutes for the fit to subside. Then he turned around to me and said, "Excuse me, friend." That was all. He was quiet again.

I felt awful. There were times when I wanted to stop the car and tell him to get out. I made up a dozen good excuses for cutting the trip short. But I couldn't do it. I was consumed by a curiosity to know what was wrong with the man. I hoped that before we parted, perhaps even as he got out of the car, he would tell me what it was or say something that would give me a clue.

I thought of the cough and wondered if it were T.B. I thought of cases of sleeping sickness I had seen and of a boxer who was punch drunk. But none of these things seemed to fit. Nothing physical seemed to explain this dark, terrible silence, this intense, all-exclusive absorption within himself.

Hour after hour of rain and darkness!

Once we passed the slate dump of a mine. The rain had made the surface burst into flame and the blue and red patches flickering in a kind of witch glow on a hill of black seemed to attract my companion. He turned his head to look at it, but he didn't speak, and I said nothing.

And again the silence and rain! Occasionally a mine tipple with the cold, drear, smoke smell of the dump and the oil lamps in the broken down shacks where the miners live. Then the black road again and the shapeless bulk of the mountains.

We reached Weston at about eight o'clock. I was tired and chilled and hungry. I stopped in front of a café and turned to the man.

"Ah reckon this is hit," he said.

"Yes," I answered. I was surprised. I had not expected him to know that we had arrived. Then I tried a final plunge. "Will you have a cup of coffee with me?"

"Yes," he replied, "thank you, friend."

The "thank you" told me a lot. I knew from the way he said it that he wanted the coffee but couldn't pay for it; that he had taken my offer to be one of hospitality and was grateful. I was happy I had asked him.

We went inside. For the first time since I had come upon him in the tunnel he seemed human. He didn't talk, but he didn't slip inside himself either. He just sat down at the counter and waited for his coffee. When it came, he drank it slowly, holding the cup in both hands as though to warm them.

When he had finished, I asked him if he wouldn't like a sandwich. He turned around to me and smiled. It was a very gentle, a very patient smile. His big, lumpy face seemed to light up with it and become understanding and sweet and gentle.

The smile shook me all through. It didn't warm me—it made me feel sick inside. It was like watching a corpse begin to stir. I wanted to cry out "My God, you poor man!"

Then he spoke to me. His face retained that smile and I could see the big, horse teeth stained by tobacco.

"You've bin right nice to me, friend, an' Ah do appreciate it."

"That's all right," I mumbled.

He kept looking at me. I knew he was going to say something else and I was afraid of it.

"Would yuh do me a faveh?"

"Yes," I said.

He spoke softly. "Ah've got a letter here that Ah done writ to mah woman, but Ah can't write very good. Would you all be kind enough to write it ovah for me so it'd be proper like?"

"Yes," I said, "I'd be glad to."

"Ah kin tell you all know how to write real well," he said, and smiled.

"Yes."

He opened his blue shirt. Under his thick woolen underwear there was a sheet of paper fastened by a safety pin. He handed it to me. It was moist and warm and the damp odor of wet cloth and the slightly sour odor of his flesh clung to it.

I asked the counterman for a sheet of paper. He brought me one. This is the letter I copied. I put it down here in his own script.

My dere wife—

i am awritin this yere leta to tell you somethin i did not tell you afore i lef frum home. There is a cause to wy i am not able to get me any job at the mines. i told you hit was frum work abein slack. But this haint so.

Hit comes frum the time the mine was shut down an i worked in the tunel nere Gauley Bridge where the govinment is turnin the river inside the mounten. The mine supers say they wont hire any men war worked in thet tunel.

Hit all comes frum thet rock thet we all had to dril. Thet rock was silica and hit was most all of hit glass. The powder frum this glass has got into the lungs of all the men war worked in thet tunel thru their breathin. And this has given to all of us a sickness. The doctors writ it down for me. Hit is silicosis. Hit makes the lungs to git all scab like and then it stops the breathin.

Bein as our hom is a good peece frum town you aint heerd about Tom Prescott and Hansy MCCulloh having died two days back. But wen i heerd this i went to see the doctor.

The doctor says i hev got me thet sickness like Tom Prescott and thet is the reeson wy i am coughin sometime. My lungs is agittin scab like. There is in all ova a hondred men war have this death sickness frum the tunel. It is a turible plague becus the doctor says this wud not be so if the company had gave us masks to ware an put a right fan sistem in the tunel.

So i am agoin away becus the doctor says i will be dead in about fore months.

i figger on gettin some work maybe in other parts. i will send you all my money till i caint work no mohr.

i did not want i should be a burdin upon you all at hum. So thet is wy i hev gone away.

i think wen you doan here frum me no mohr you orter go to your grandmaws up in the mountens at Kilney Run. You kin live there an she will take keer of you an the young one.

i hope you will be well an keep the young one out of the mines. Doan let him work there.

Doan think hard on me for agoin away and doan feel bad. But wen the young one is agrowed up you tell him wat the company has done to me.

i reckon after a bit you shud try to git you anotha man. You are a young woman yit.

Your loving husband,

Jack Pitckett.

When I handed him the copy of his letter, he read it over. It took him a long time. Finally he folded it up and pinned it to his undershirt. His big, lumpy face was sweet and gentle. "Thank you, friend," he said. Then, very softly, with his head hanging a little—"Ahm feelin' bad about this a-happenin' t'me. Mah wife was a good woman." He paused. And then, as though talking to himself, so low I could hardly hear it, "Ahm feelin' right bad."

As he said this, I looked into his face. Slowly the life was going out of his eyes. It seemed to recede and go deep into the sockets like the flame of a candle going into the night. Over the eyeballs came that dull glaze. I had lost him. He sat deep within himself in his sorrowful, dark absorption.

That was all. We sat together. In me there was only mute emotion—pity and love for him, and a cold, deep hatred for what had killed him.

Presently he arose. He did not speak. Nor did I. I saw his thick, broad back in the blue work shirt as he stood by the door. Then he moved out into the darkness and rain.

1. What features of composition mark this as a contemporary short story?
2. Do you think the politeness and courtesy Jack displays is common among such men?
3. Do you find this story a bit too obvious?
4. Do you think that the man would have gone away for the last four months?
5. What idea does Maltz leave with the reader?

# X.  REPORTAGE

# X. REPORTAGE

THE term reportage has only lately been introduced into English—it still is often pronounced in the French way —to describe a type of writing which goes a step beyond ordinary journalistic reporting. Theoretically, the perfect journalist is detached, impersonal; he tells what he sees before him, and stops there. It is not part of his job to supply overtones of doctrine or philosophy, to see the episode as a manifestation of social forces or ideas. Reportage may be defined as interpretative reporting. The writer strives to penetrate below the surface of the event, and directly or indirectly to expound its meaning.

This fact at once brings up the besetting danger and weakness of the form. Some writers are so obsessed with their pet theories that everything they see becomes a symbol. They interpret the whole world in terms of one limited set of ideas. Upton Sinclair and the late G. K. Chesterton both illustrate this danger. The one is so absorbed in his socialistic doctrines, the other in his Catholicism, as to lose the capacity to look at anything objectively. They dress the fact up in doctrinal clothes without stopping to find out whether the clothes fit or not. Many of the books of literary and social criticism of America written in our own day by people like Waldo Frank, Van Wyck Brooks, Ludwig Lewisohn, and Granville Hicks illustrate the same type of wishful thinking. These authors begin with a preconceived idea, and select such facts as fit it. When such facts run out, they distort others to cram them into the pattern.

Good reportage, of course, does nothing of the sort. Its ideal is to apply the author's intellectual and artistic powers to disentangling a big idea from the mass of irrelevant detail which would otherwise obscure it. The author, still seeking to maintain the objectivity of the good reporter, focuses his camera sharply on the significant details, instead of using the broad focus which may give equal prominence to the important and the trivial. The task demands cold intellect as well as warm feelings, because success depends on the depth of the understanding which elucidates the observed facts.

But it still remains a personal form of reporting. The writer does not even claim to be objective. Another person, applying a different set of ideas to the same scene, will produce a wholly different interpretation. For instance, Mrs. Carswell's story of D. H. Lawrence's farewell dinner at the Café Royal gives the facts as she saw them and remembered them, but Middleton Murry's and Dorothy Brett's accounts of the same dinner show that although they witnessed the same events they read quite other significance into them.[1] In the same way, a fascist witnessing the congress in Santander which Dos Passos describes in "Doves in the Bullring" would have seen it in other terms, and the historian of the future will in all likelihood agree with neither. John Reed's account of the Russian Revolution comes the nearest to being an impartial document for the simple reason that Reed, despite his revolutionary sympathies, came nearest to maintaining the traditional objectivity of the reporter.

Hence good reportage is actually more difficult to write than most fiction is. Ideally, the author must observe a scene with photographic impartiality, fixing every detail in his memory. Reviewing his impressions as he sits down to write, he must ask himself what it meant in terms of ideas, or of the universals of human nature. In other words, like Wordsworth's ideal poet, he must apply creative reason to his recollections of strong emotions. It is a commonplace that the scarcity of really first-rate occasional poetry is due to the difficulty of composing in the heat of primary emotion. Exactly the same difficulty confronts the writer of re-

[1] All three accounts of the dinner are reprinted in *Men and Moments* (New York: The Cordon Company, 1938), pp. 332-42.

portage. He will usually do his best work when he is able to wait, and cool off, between the event and the record. But once in a while the fact, the emotion, and the creative impulse all function together. When that happens, reportage has a vital energy that puts it in a class by itself among the forms of expression.

*Catherine Carswell*

# AT THE CAFÉ ROYAL

T HE food was excellent, but somehow the feast did not go well. Gertler was silent and looked watchful, even contemptuous. Kot conceived a murderous dislike for Donald next to whom he was placed. Mary had nothing to say. I too was stricken with dumbness. Lawrence did his best to enliven us all with wine, bidding us to drink our fill and rejoice in a festive occasion. He set us a good example and drank level. There was no champagne. We drank claret. And never before, nor since, have I swallowed so many glasses and remained so heavily sober. With the coming of the dessert a mistake was made. What was the wine to be? asked Lawrence. Murry and Donald both said port. They had forgotten, or had not known, that port was a drink Lawrence could not well tolerate. He immediately hinted very gently that port was not his drink, but his remark was either missed or good-naturedly over-ruled. 'Port is a man's drink,' I remember either Murry or Donald announcing in solemn tones. So port it was. And Lawrence drank it with the rest of us.

It had the effect of loosening at least some of the mute tongues about the table, though none of us women were perceptibly elevated. Lawrence began to talk in Spanish (which he had learned in Mexico). Donald, who prided himself on knowing a bit of Spanish (enough to read *Don Quixote* and to reply to simple questions), endeavoured to engage in Spanish conversation with Lawrence. This, for some reason, infuriated Kot to such a degree that he looked like taking the unwary Donald's life had not Murry tactfully placed somebody between them. Kot's idea seemed to be that the Spanish language was Lawrence's special perquisite. Gertler drank, or possibly refrained from drinking, in silence, looking on, always looking on from a cold afar. Both he and Mary Cannan seem to have left early.

But not before this strange incident. It began with a speech by Kot in praise and love of Lawrence, the speech being punctuated by his deliberate smashing of a wine-glass at the close of each period. As—'Lawrence is a great man.' (Bang! down came Kot's strong fist enclosing the stem of a glass, so that its bottom came in shivering contact with the table.) 'Nobody here realises how great he is.' (Crash! another good wine-glass gone.) 'Especially no woman here or anywhere can possibly realise the greatness of Lawrence.' (Smash and tinkle!) 'Frieda does not count. Frieda is different. I understand and don't include her. But no other woman here or anywhere can understand anything about Lawrence or what kind of being he is.'

We women were silent. We felt, I think, very sympathetic to Kot. Anyhow I did. Sympathetic to his jealous, dark and overpowering affection. Even inclined to agree with what he said.

Lawrence looked pale and frightfully ill, but his eyes were starry to an extraordinary degree. It occurred to me then—and I have since had no reason to change my reading, which was revealed as by the appearance of clear writing on the wall—that the deep hold of the Last Supper on the imagination of the world is not unconnected with the mystery of Bacchus. Given a man of genius; more especially given a man whose genius runs to expression by means of symbol, his essential utterance may well be achieved only when his genius is acted upon at a crisis by the magic of the fermented grape.

Anyhow, Lawrence who, like the others present, was habitually temperate, revealed that night at the Café Royal his deepest desire to all of us simply and unforgettably. And in doing so he brought about some other revelations, as will be seen.

Without making anything approaching a speech, he caught our attention by the quiet urgency of his request. What he said, in effect, was that we were his friends here, each and all of us people he had been very fond of. He could not stay in England. He must go back to New Mexico. Would we, would any of us, go with him? He asked each of us in turn. Would we go with him? Implicit in this question was the other. Did the search, the adventure, the pilgrimage for which he stood, mean enough to us for us to give up our own way of life and our own separate struggle with the world? Though his way of life must involve also a struggle with the world, this was not—as we well knew—its main objective. Rather was it a withdrawal of one's essential being from that struggle, and a turning of what strength one had into a new channel.

Essentially the appeal was not a personal one. Though it was to his friends, it was not for his sake or the sake of friendship that he made it. It was because of something in himself which we all acknowledged. But it had never before come so near being a personal appeal. It certainly had a personal element that told of his overwhelming loneliness. It was far less 'follow me,' than 'come with me.' It was even—to my thinking at least—'come, for a time, and support me by your presence, as the undertaking is too much for me alone, yet I must not stay here with you.' I give my own reading, but I think something very like it was in the minds of all the others.

Remember we had just supped, and our glasses had been replenished with port and, as I have said, we were all normally very abstemious people.

Mary Cannan was the only one to return a flat negative to Lawrence's question. It was as plump and plain as she herself was slender and pretty. 'No,' said she hardily. 'I like you, Lawrence, but not so much as all that, and I think you are asking what no human being has a right to ask of another.'

Lawrence accepted this without cavil or offence. It was a clear, hard, honest answer.

What Gertler said, I can't remember. I rather think it was a humouring but dry affirmative, which we all understood to mean nothing. Kot and Donald both said they would go, less drily, but so that any listener guessed they were speaking from goodwill rather than from deep intention. Dorothy Brett said quietly that she would go, and I, knowing that she would, envied her. Murry promised emotionally that he would, and one felt that he wouldn't. I said yes, I would go. And I meant it, though I didn't see how on earth it could be, anyhow for a long time. Unlike Mary and Dorothy Brett I had neither money of my own nor freedom from responsibility. Dorothy Brett, who loved to serve, was always coming to a loose end. I, who did not particularly like serving, was always having fresh responsibilities put upon me by life. Mary, disappointed with her 'freedom,' had yet got used to its little self-indulgences and could not give them up. All the same, I felt that Lawrence had somehow the right to ask me to go. And I feel today equally the impossibility of my going and the wish that I had gone.

As for the supper, what I next remember is Murry going up to Lawrence and kissing him with a kind of effusiveness which afflicted me. He must have been sensible to my feeling, because he turned to me.

'Women can't understand this,' he said. 'This is an affair between men. Women can have no part or place in it.'

'Maybe,' said I. 'But anyhow it wasn't a woman who betrayed Jesus with a kiss.'

At this Murry again embraced Lawrence, who sat perfectly still and unresponsive, with a dead-white face in which the eyes alone were alive.

'I *have* betrayed you, old chap, I confess it,' continued Murry.

'In the past I *have* betrayed you. But never again. I call you all to witness, never again.'

Throughout all this Frieda remained aloof and scornful—excluded. Her innings would be later. She reminded me of King David's wife looking down in derision from an upper window. One could not but admire her.

It must have been almost immediately after the strange episode with Murry, that Lawrence, without uttering a sound, fell forward with his head on the table, was deadly sick, and became at once unconscious. The combination of the port (which when he had said he could not abide, he said truly) and the cruel loneliness which was brought home to him by the responses he had elicited from us, his friends, was too much for him.

In his sickness Lawrence was more like a child than a man. There was nothing disgusting about him. Frieda, however, remained stonily detached, while Dorothy Brett and I ministered to him as best we could—the Brett especially, who did not want me to help.

It must have been now that Mary and Gertler left us. What with the glasses broken by Kot, and Lawrence's sickness, I was sorry for the waiters who would have to clear up. But they behaved as if they had noticed nothing out of the way. Donald, as the soberest man, was handed money to pay for the wine and the damage. The bill, he tells me, struck him as wonderfully moderate.

We left in two taxi-cabs, Lawrence being still unconscious so that it was difficult getting him down in the lift. But Kot, even in liquor, was powerful. I recall that his legs seemed to fill the cab in which I was. I had been given all the hats of the party to hold, and I lost my own—a little real Russian cap of black astrakhan, which I liked better than any head covering I ever had, though I gave only three shillings for it in an antique shop, and it had a bullet hole through it.

Arrived at Hampstead the problem was how to get Lawrence up to the first floor. Kot and Murry had to carry him. But in their enthusiasm they went on with their burden, up and up, till my brother, asleep on the top story, was awakened by the trampling, stumbling sound, and ran out in alarm to the little landing. He told me afterwards that when he saw clearly before him St. John and St. Peter (or maybe St. Thomas) bearing between them the limp figure of their master, he could hardly believe he was not dreaming. However, he conducted the party downstairs again.

Next morning soon after breakfast—certainly not later than 9.30 A.M.—I was passing the open door of the Lawrences' sitting-room, when Lawrence hailed me and bade me enter. He was fresh and serene. 'Well, Catherine,' he said, 'I made a fool of myself last night. We must all of us fall at times. It does no harm so long as we first admit and then forget it.'

> From Catherine Carswell: *Savage Pilgrimage.* Copyright, 1932, by Harcourt, Brace and Company, Inc., and reprinted by permission.

1. How does Mrs. Carswell characterize the people by their actions?
2. Can you justify her pausing to describe her lost hat?
3. Do you find her symbolic references to the Last Supper irreverent, or overdone?
4. What emotional relationships are suggested in the narrative?
5. What do you think Lawrence meant by "the search, the adventure, the pilgrimage for which he stood"?

*John Reed*

# REVOLUTION

HE Congress was to meet at one o'clock, and long since the great meeting-hall had filled, but by seven there was yet no sign of the presidium. . . . The Bolshevik and Left Social Revolutionary factions were in session in their own rooms. All the livelong afternoon Lenin and Trotsky had fought against compromise. A considerable part of the Bolsheviki were in favour of giving way so far as to create a joint all-Socialist government. "We can't hold on!" they cried. "Too much is against us. We haven't got the men. We will be isolated, and the whole thing will fall." So Kameniev, Riazanov and others.

But Lenin, with Trotsky beside him, stood firm as a rock. "Let the compromisers accept our programme and they can come in! We won't give way an inch. If there are comrades here who haven't the courage and the will to dare what we dare, let them leave with the rest of the cowards and conciliators! Backed by the workers and soldiers we shall go on."

At five minutes past seven came word from the left Socialist Revolutionaries to say that they would remain in the Military Revolutionary Committee.

"See!" said Lenin. "They are following!"

A little later, as we sat at the press table in the big hall, an Anarchist who was writing for the bourgeois papers proposed to me that we should go and find out what had become of the presidium. There was nobody in the *Tsay-ee-kah* office, nor in the bureau of the Petrograd Soviet. From room to room we wandered, through vast Smolny. Nobody seemed to have the slightest idea where to find the governing body of the Congress. As we went my companion described his ancient revolutionary activities, his long and pleasant exile in France. . . . As for the Bolsheviki, he confided to me that they were common, rude, ignorant persons, without aesthetic sensibilities. He was a real specimen of the Russian *intelligentsia*. . . . So he came at last to Room 17, office of the Military Revolutionary Committee, and stood there in the midst of all the furious coming and going. The door opened, and out shot a squat, flat-faced man in a uniform without insignia, who seemed to be smiling—which smile, after a minute, one saw to be the fixed grin of extreme fatigue. It was Krylenko.

My friend, who was a dapper, civilized-looking young man, gave a cry of pleasure and stepped forward.

"Nicolai Vasilievitch!" he said, holding out his hand. "Don't you remember me, comrade? We were in prison together."

Krylenko made an effort and concentrated his mind and sight. "Why, yes," he answered finally, looking the other up and down with an expression of great friendliness. "You are S——. *Zdra'-stvuitye!*" They kissed. "What are you doing in all this?" He waved his arm around.

"Oh, I'm just looking on. . . . You seem very successful."

"Yes," replied Krylenko, with a sort of doggedness. "The proletarian Revolution is a great success." He laughed. "Perhaps—perhaps, however, we'll meet in prison again!"

When we got out into the corridor again my friend went on with his explanations. "You see, I'm a follower of Kropotkin. To us the Revolution is a great failure; it has not aroused the patriotism of the masses. Of course that only proves that the people are not ready for Revolution. . . ."

It was just 8:40 when a thundering wave of cheers announced the entrance of the presidium, with Lenin—great Lenin—among them. A short, stocky figure, with a big head set down in his shoulders, bald and bulging. Little eyes, a snubbish nose, wide, generous mouth, and heavy chin; clean-shaven now, but already beginning to bristle with the well-known beard of his past and future. Dressed in shabby clothes, his trousers much too long for him. Unimpressive, to be the idol of a mob, loved and revered as perhaps few leaders in history have been. A strange popular leader—a leader purely by virtue of intellect; colourless, humourless, uncompromising and detached, without picturesque idiosyncrasies—but with the power of explaining profound ideas in simple terms, of analysing a concrete situation. And combined with shrewdness, the greatest intellectual audacity.

Kameniev was reading the report of the actions of the Military Revolutionary Committee; abolition of capital punishment in the Army, restoration of the free right of propaganda, release of officers and soldiers arrested for political crimes, orders to arrest Kerensky and confiscation of food supplies in private store-houses. . . . Tremendous applause.

Again the representative of the Bund. The uncompromising attitude of the Bolsheviki would mean the crushing of the Revolution; therefore the Bund delegates must refuse any longer to sit in the Congress. Cries from the audience, "We thought you walked out last night! How many more times are you going to walk out?"

Then the representative of the Mensheviki Internationalists. Shouts, "What! You here still?" The speaker explained that only part of the Mensheviki Internationalists left the Congress; the rest were going to stay—

"We consider it dangerous and perhaps even mortal for the Revolution to transfer the power to the Soviets"—Interruptions— "but we feel it our duty to remain in the Congress and vote against the transfer here!"

Other speakers followed, apparently without any order. A delegate of the coal-miners of the Don Basin called upon the Congress to take measures against Kaledin, who might cut off coal and food from the capital. Several soldiers just arrived from the Front brought the enthusiastic greetings of their regiments. . . . Now Lenin, gripping the edge of the reading stand, letting his little winking eyes travel over the crowd as he stood there waiting, apparently oblivious to the long-rolling ovation, which lasted several minutes. When it finished, he said simply, "We shall now proceed to construct the Socialist order!" Again that overwhelming human roar.

"The first thing is the adoption of practical measures to realise peace. . . . We shall offer peace to the people of all the belligerent countries upon the basis of the Soviet terms—no annexations, no indemnities, and the right of self-determination of peoples. At the same times, according to our promise, we shall publish and repudiate the secret treaties. . . . The question of War and Peace is so clear that I think that I may, without preamble, read the project of a Proclamation to the Peoples of All the Belligerent Countries. . . ."

His great mouth, seeming to smile, opened wide as he spoke; his voice was hoarse—not unpleasantly so, but as if it had hardened that way after years and years of speaking—and went on monotonously, with the effect of being able to go on forever. . . . For emphasis he bent forward slightly. No gestures. And before him, a thousand simple faces looking up in intent adoration.

John Reed: *Ten Days That Shook the World* (N. Y., Boni & Liveright, 1919). Reprinted by permission of International Publishers.

1. *The marks of omission are in the original. Why?*
2. *What is Reed's attitude towards the Revolutionary leaders?*

3. What does he suggest as the reason for the failure of the Mensheviki, or Moderates?
4. How does he suggest the atmosphere of breathless expectation?
5. How much description of Lenin is given? Do you visualize him?

## John Dos Passos

# DOVES IN THE BULLRING

I T WAS a hot Sunday morning in July. Members of the Socialist Party had come from all over northern Spain for the big meeting in Santander. They had come with their red gold-lettered trade-union banners, with their wives and children and lunches in baskets and leather canteens of wine. They had come in special trains and in busses and in mule carts and on bicycles and on foot. The bullring held about ten thousand; every seat was taken, agreeable mildly intelligent-looking people mostly, mechanics, small storekeepers and farmers, shoemakers, tailors, clerks, school teachers, bookkeepers, a few doctors and lawyers; for this part of the world a quiet characterless crowd, but a big crowd.

The proceedings began by the singing of the *Internationale* by a bunch of school children in white dresses with red bows. They sang it very nicely. It passed the time while we waited for the speakers to arrive. The more important dignitaries seemed to be late. Then when the speakers filed onto the stand set up in the broiling sun in the center of the bullring, everybody sang the *Internationale* again, standing, red bunting waved.

Somebody may have gotten the idea that it would be effective to send up two white pigeons with red ribbons round their necks, but (maybe it was the heat or that the ribbons were tied too tight or that the pigeons were sick) the pigeons couldn't seem to fly, they fluttered groggily over the heads of the crowd, and crashed against the wall of the bullring. One of them managed to rise over the roof of the stands and disappeared into the sizzling sunny sky, but the other fell back into the crowd. People tried to coax it to fly, to give it a starting toss into the air but it was too weak. It finally came to rest in the middle of the bullring, right in front of the speaker's stand. It stayed there all through the speaking, a very sick-looking pigeon indeed. I kept expecting it to flop over dead, but it just stood there teetering, with its head drooping.

The first speakers were local leaders, working men or trade-union officials. They spoke simply and definitely. The fight at home, as all over the world, was between socialism and fascism, the kind of order the workers and producers wanted and the kind of order the exploiting class wanted. The Socialist Party had no choice but to go ahead and install socialism right away (cheers) . . . through a dictatorship if need be (more cheers). When the deputy to the Cortes spoke he was a little vaguer, he talked more about world conditions and the course of history and economic trends, but in the end he could think of no other way of finishing his speech than by promising socialism (wild cheers). But when the Socialist Minister spoke (cheers, cries of *Vivan los hombres honrados*, Hurray for honest men) things became very vague indeed. It was very hot by this time, the Socialist Minister was a stout man with a neat academic beard. Neither the stunning heat nor his obvious sweating under the black broadcloth suit introduced a single tremor into his long carefully modulated sentences. He used the classical form of address, subjunctives and future subjunctives and future conditional subjunctives and conditional subjunctive futures. He brought in history and literature, philosophy and the fine arts as if he was speaking to his students at the university, and he ended with a throaty oratorical period that quite took the audience's breath away. The gist of it was that the Socialist Party was the party of discipline and order and that the best thing sincere

Socialists could do was stay at home and pay their dues and leave talk about attaining a socialist state in the interest of the workers to their betters, their political leaders who had the interest of all humanity at heart and understood the need for law and order and were honest men besides. The interests of all humanity demanded confidence and discipline from the Socialist Party.

When the speaking stopped, the sick pigeon was still teetering in the center of the bullring. With as much discipline, but perhaps with less confidence than they'd had that morning, the members of the Socialist Party grouped themselves for the parade through the center of town. Everybody was telling everybody else that the watchword was order.

By that time it was afternoon and very hot indeed. The Socialist Party members with their banners and their children and their lunch baskets marched without music through the center of the town to the beach, mild, straggling, well-mannered and a little embarrassed. All the cafés were full. The people sitting at the café tables were telling examples of the type of Spaniard who's hated in Mexico. A gachupin, pear-shaped men with gimlet eyes and predatory lines on their faces, jerkwater importers and exporters, small brokers, loan sharks, commission merchants, pawnbrokers, men who know how to make two duros grow where one had grown before, men who'd discovered the great principle that it's not work that makes money. They'd never been much before, mostly they'd had to scrape up their livings in America; at home the hierarchy, the bishops, the duchesses, the grandees and the Bourbons had high-hatted them off the map, but now the feudal paraphernalia was gone, the gachupinos were on top of the world. They sat silent at their tables looking at the embarrassed socialists straggling by. There are a great many socialists; it took them a long time to pass with their banners and their children and their red ribbons and their lunch baskets. The silent hatred of the people at the café tables was embarrassing to them. They filed on by as innocent as a flock of sheep in the wolf country.

From John Dos Passos: *In All Countries*. Copyright, 1934, by Harcourt, Brace and Company, Inc., and reprinted by permission of the publishers.

1. Whereabouts in Spain is Santander, and what part did it play in the civil war of 1936-8?
2. What is the Internationale?
3. Had Dos Passos any hope that the Spanish Socialists would succeed?
4. What symbolism does he read into the pigeons?
5. Does his narrative suggest any reasons for the success of the fascist revolution under Franco?

# NOTES ON CONTRIBUTORS

### The Town-Ho's Story

HERMAN MELVILLE (1819-1891), greatest and most uneven of American romancers, compressed his significant literary career into the years 1846-1851. His four best books, *Typee* (1846), *Omoo* (1847), *White Jacket* (1850), and *Moby Dick* (1851), are all set against the backgrounds of his own adventures as whaler, man-of-warsman, beachcomber, and prisoner among the cannibals. The sterility of his later years, for which sentimental biographers seek explanations in psychology and sociology, probably means only that his creative imagination had to be fired by personal experience. He had emptied all he had into the magnificent chaos of *Moby Dick*.

### The Man Who Would Be King and The Drums of the Fore and Aft

RUDYARD KIPLING (1865-1936) was born in Bombay, India, educated in England, and returned to India as a journalist during the years 1882-1889. His popular reputation still rests largely on the stories he wrote in his early twenties in *Plain Tales from the Hills*, *Soldiers Three*, *Under the Deodars*, and other volumes. His true stature as an artist may be measured in such later tales as "They," "An Habitation Enforced," "Friendly Brook," "The Tree of Justice," and "The Church That Was at Antioch." He is the greatest, and least understood, of British short story writers.

### The Price of the Head

JOHN RUSSELL (1885-　　) was born in Davenport, Iowa. In his earlier years he traveled widely, as explorer and special correspondent, especially in South America, the South Seas, and the East Indies. The Samoans made him an honorary chief, with the title "Toleafoa Tusitala"; more recently, Hollywood has made him editor and technical adviser. He has written some 600 short stories, some of which are collected in *The Red Mark* (1919), *Where the Pavement Ends* (1921), *In Dark Places* (1922), and *Far-Wandering Men* (1928).

### The Black Cat and The Purloined Letter

Every so often a critic comes along to prove that EDGAR ALLAN POE (1809-1849) was really a very bad writer. Rufus Griswold proved it in the 1850s; Yvor Winters and Aldous Huxley have proved it in the 1930s. And somehow his best stories and poems go right on living in spite of the critics.

### The Yellow Wallpaper

CHARLOTTE PERKINS GILMAN (1860-1935), great-granddaughter of Lyman Beecher, inherited the family eloquence and crusading temper. From 1890 onward she wrote and lectured on ethics, economics, and sociology, and was active for labor and women's rights. Though she wrote some good stories and poems, most of her work is more propaganda than literature. In 1935, finding herself condemned to lingering illness, she killed herself. *The Living of Charlotte Perkins Gilman* (1935) is her autobiography.

### Clay-Shuttered Doors

HELEN ROSE HULL graduated from the University of Chicago in 1912, and since 1916 has been a member of the English Department at Columbia University. In 1931 she received a Guggenheim Fellowship for creative writing. Her novels include *The Islanders* (1927), *The Asking Price* (1930), *Morning Shows the Day* (1934), and *Uncommon People* (1936).

### The Company of the Marjolaine

JOHN BUCHAN (1875-    ) was born in Scotland and educated at Glasgow University and Brasenose College, Oxford. In addition to a full career as publisher and government official, he is the author of more than a score of popular novels and of a number of excellent histories and biographies. In 1935 he was raised to the peerage as Baron Tweedsmuir, and was appointed Governor-General of Canada.

### A Lodging for the Night

ROBERT LOUIS STEVENSON (1850-1894) is too well known to need introduction. "A Lodging for the Night," based on intensive study of the life and poetry of François Villon (1431-1484?), was his first published story. It appeared in *Temple Bar* magazine, October, 1877.

*Adam Helmer's Run*

WALTER DUMAUX EDMONDS (1903-    ) was born at Boonville, New York, where he still lives, and graduated from Harvard in 1926. As a novelist he has devoted himself to the history of central New York State. His chief works are *Rome Haul* (1929), *The Big Barn* (1930), *Erie Water* (1933), and *Drums Along the Mohawk* (1936).

*Jim Baker's Blue-Jay Yarn*

Of MARK TWAIN (Samuel Langhorne Clemens, 1835-1910) is it enough to say that after the years of misinterpretation which followed the publication of Van Wyck Brooks's *The Ordeal of Mark Twain* (1921), he is now restored to his rightful place as the greatest American humorist, a man who of his free choice practiced humor as a fine art.

*A Keeper of Tradition*

DON MARQUIS (1878-1937) holds high place among modern humorists for his skill in conceiving and developing fantastic situations. Though he was a good poet and the author of some excellent serious stories, he is best known as the creator of archy the literary cockroach, mehitabel the *toujours gai* alley cat, and Clem Hawley the Old Soak, whose adventures and comments originally appeared in Marquis's column in the New York *Sun*.

*You Were Perfectly Fine*

DOROTHY ROTHSCHILD PARKER (1893-    ), unlike Don Marquis, is a humorist whose work has always a strong dash of vermouth or angostura. In addition to editorial and critical work on *Vogue*, *Vanity Fair*, and *The New Yorker*, Miss Parker has published several volumes of satiric verse, of which the best are *Enough Rope* (1926) and *Sunset Gun* (1928), and two collections of short stories, *Laments for the Living* (1930) and *After Such Pleasures* (1933).

*The Red-Headed League*

SIR ARTHUR CONAN DOYLE (1859-1930) began writing to fill the hours of enforced leisure while he tried, without much success, to establish himself in medical practice. Though he himself preferred his novels, such as *Micah Clarke* (1888) and *The White Company*

(1890), his reputation rests almost wholly on Sherlock Holmes. The great detective made his first bow in *A Study in Scarlet* (1887), and was continued in *The Sign of Four* (1890), *The Adventures of Sherlock Holmes* (1892), *Memoirs of Sherlock Holmes* (1894), *The Hound of the Baskervilles* (1902), and *The Return of Sherlock Holmes* (1905).

### The Entertaining Episode of the Article in Question

DOROTHY LEIGH SAYERS (1893-    ), born and reared in Oxford, graduated from Somerville College in 1915 with honors in medieval history. *Whose Body?* (1923) initiated a series of a dozen mystery stories which represent the highest sustained level of modern detective fiction. Her detective, Lord Peter Wimsey, the prototype of Philo Vance, is everything that Vance would be were Vance human.

### The Country Doctor

RAY STANNARD BAKER (1885-    ) was engaged from 1892 to 1915 in newspaper and magazine journalism, and is now the official biographer of Woodrow Wilson. The half-dozen volumes of essays and sketches which he has published under the pen-name of David Grayson began with *Adventures in Contentment* (1907) and *Adventures in Friendship* (1910).

### The Trap

MERIDEL LESUEUR (1900-    ) was born in Iowa, and now lives in St. Paul, Minnesota. Her short stories have appeared in numerous magazines, and have been reprinted in several anthologies and year-books.

### The Maysville Minstrel

RING LARDNER (1885-1933) was born in Niles, Michigan, gained his first newspaper experience on the South Bend *Times*, and then became a sports writer in Chicago. He won national attention in 1915 with his collection of baseball stories, *You Know Me, Al*. Most of his later work is included in *How to Write Short Stories* (1924), *Round Up* (1929), and *First and Last* (1934). Though popularly reputed a humorist, his best stories, like "Haircut," "The Love Nest," and "The Maysville Minstrel," are really bitter satires on human smugness, stupidity, and cruelty.

The Furnished Room

WILLIAM SYDNEY PORTER (1862-1910) was born in Greensboro, North Carolina, and went to Texas in 1882. He wrote extensively, mostly humorous journalism, during the earlier 1890s; his first stories over his pseudonym of O. Henry were written in the Columbus, Ohio, penitentiary between 1898 and 1901, while he was serving a Federal sentence on the charge of embezzling funds from an Austin bank.

The Pig

BEN HECHT (1894-      ), newspaperman, novelist, and dramatist, was born in New York City and educated in Racine, Wisconsin. *1001 Afternoons in Chicago* was written while he was on the staff of the *Daily News*, 1914-23. *Erik Dorn* (1921) is the best-known of his novels, and *The Front Page* (1928) of his plays.

Pennsylvania Station

WILLIAM FAULKNER (1897-      ), who has recently changed the spelling of his name to Falkner, is a native of Mississippi. During the World War he served with the British Royal Air Force. Besides short stories he is the author of *The Sound and the Fury* (1929), *As I Lay Dying* (1930), *Sanctuary* (1931), *Pylon* (1935), and *The Unvanquished* (1938).

The Affair at Coulter's Notch

AMBROSE BIERCE (1842-1914?) was the son of a poor farmer in Meigs County, Ohio. After the Civil War service which supplied the material for his best stories, he practiced journalism in San Francisco until 1872, when he went to London. Four years later he returned to San Francisco, where he spent most of the rest of his active life. Late in 1913 he disappeared in Mexico, where he is supposed to have been shot by Pancho Villa's troops. His best stories are collected in *In the Midst of Life* (originally called *Tales of Soldiers and Civilians*, 1891) and *Can Such Things Be?* (1893).

Children at Play

JO SINCLAIR (1912-      ) was born in Brooklyn, New York, and now lives in Cleveland. "Children at Play" was his second published story.

Life in the Iron Mills

REBECCA BLISS HARDING (1831-1910), who married L. Clarke Davis in 1863 and was the mother of the novelists Richard Harding Davis and Charles Belmont Davis, began early to write fiction. She first attracted notice when Lowell published "Life in the Iron Mills" in the *Atlantic Monthly*, April, 1861. "None of her later works . . . fulfilled the promise of her first *Atlantic* stories. With achieved reputation she allowed herself to drift into the prevailing fictional conventions and sentimentality." (*DAB*)

Blood Money

MICHAEL GOLD (1894-    ) was born and reared in New York City, on the East Side. He has worked on a dozen different newspapers in various cities, has been on the editorial staffs of *The Liberator*, *The New Masses*, and *The Daily Worker*, and has produced plays. His chief books are *120 Million* (1929), *Jews Without Money* (1930), and *Change the World!* (1936).

Man on a Road

ALBERT MALTZ (1908-    ), dramatist and teacher, has had three plays produced in New York: *Merry-Go-Round* (1932), *Peace on Earth* (1934), and *Black Pit* (1935). His only volume of stories to date is *The Way Things Are and Other Stories* (1938).

At the Café Royal

CATHERINE ROXBURGH MACFARLANE CARSWELL (1879-    ) is a Scottish journalist, novelist, and biographer. Her works include *Open the Door* (novel, 1920), *The Life of Robert Burns* (1930), *Savage Pilgrimage* (1932), and *The Tranquil Heart, The Life of Giovanni Boccaccio* (1937).

Revolution

JOHN REED (1887-1920), poet, journalist, and revolutionist, was the son of wealthy parents in Portland, Oregon. After graduating from Harvard in 1910 he took up journalism in New York, where Lincoln Steffens and Ida Tarbell gave him his first bias towards the political Left. In 1913 he joined the staff of *The Masses*. Later he acted as special correspondent in Mexico and Europe, and in 1917 was in Moscow during the October Revolution. After standing trial in New York as a Communist agitator, he returned to Moscow, where typhus transmitted by the impartial Russian lice killed him.

*Doves in the Bullring*

JOHN DOS PASSOS (1896-    ) was born in Chicago, and graduated from Harvard in 1916. Before the United States entered the World War he served with the American Ambulance, and after April, 1917, transferred to the U. S. Infantry. His revulsion against the war produced his first novel, *Three Soldiers* (1921). His other novels are *Manhattan Transfer* (1925), *The 42d Parallel* (1930), *1919* (1931), and *The Big Money* (1936). In 1937 the three last named were republished in a single volume entitled *U. S. A.*